CW00871224

Dedicated to D, J, M, O and S

Obedient Heretics

Mennonite identities in Lutheran Hamburg and Altona during the confessional age

MICHAEL D. DRIEDGER

Ashgate

Aldershot • Burlington USA • Singapore • Sydney

Published by
Ashgate Publishing Limited
Gower House
Croft Road
Aldershot
Hants GU11 3HR
England

Ashgate Publishing Company
131 Main Street
Burlington, VT 05401-5600 USA

Ashgate website: http://www.ashgate.com

British Library Cataloguing-in-Publication Data

Driedger, Michael D.
Obedient heretics: Mennonite identities in Lutheran Hamburg and Altona during the confessional age. – (St Andrews studies in Reformation history)
1. Mennonites – Germany – Hamburg – History – 16th century
2. Mennonites – Germany – Hamburg – History – 17th century
3. Group identity – Germany – Hamburg
I. Title
289.7'43515

Library of Congress Cataloging-in-Publication Data

Driedger, Michael D.
Obedient heretics : Mennonite identities in Lutheran Hamburg and Altona during the confessional age / Michael D. Driedger.
p. cm. – (St Andrews studies in Reformation history)
Includes bibliographical references and index.
1. Mennonites – Germany – Hamburg – History – 17th century. 2. Hamburg-Altona (Hamburg, Germany – Church history. I. Title. II. Series.

BX8119.G3 D75 2001
289.7'43515–dc21 2001022824

ISBN 0 7546 0292 3

This book is printed on acid free paper

Typeset in Sabon by J.L. & G.A. Wheatley Design, Aldershot

Printed and bound by Athenaeum Press, Ltd.,
Gateshead, Tyne & Wear.

Contents

St Andrews Studies in Reformation History

The Shaping of a Community: The Rise and Reformation of the English Parish c. *1400–1560*
Beat Kümin

Seminary or University? The Genevan Academy and Reformed Higher Education, 1560–1620
Karin Maag

Marian Protestantism: Six Studies
Andrew Pettegree

Protestant History and Identity in Sixteenth-Century Europe
(2 volumes) edited by Bruce Gordon

Antifraternalism and Anticlericalism in the German Reformation: Johann Eberlin von Günzburg and the Campaign against the Friars
Geoffrey Dipple

Reformations Old and New: Essays on the Socio-Economic Impact of Religious Change c. *1470–1630*
edited by Beat Kümin

Piety and the People: Religious Printing in French, 1511–1551
Francis M. Higman

The Reformation in Eastern and Central Europe
edited by Karin Maag

John Foxe and the English Reformation
edited by David Loades

The Reformation and the Book
Jean-François Gilmont, edited and translated by Karin Maag

The Magnificent Ride: The First Reformation in Hussite Bohemia
Thomas A. Fudge

Kepler's Tübingen: Stimulus to a Theological Mathematics
Charlotte Methuen

'Practical Divinity': The Works and Life of Revd Richard Greenham
Kenneth L. Parker and Eric J. Carlson

Belief and Practice in Reformation England: A Tribute to Patrick Collinson by his Students
edited by Susan Wabuda and Caroline Litzenberger

Frontiers of the Reformation: Dissidence and Orthodoxy in Sixteenth-Century Europe
Auke Jelsma

The Jacobean Kirk, 1567–1625: Sovereignty, Polity and Liturgy
Alan R. MacDonald

John Knox and the British Reformations
edited by Roger A. Mason

The Education of a Christian Society: Humanism and the Reformation in Britain and the Netherlands
edited by N. Scott Amos, Andrew Pettegree and Henk van Nierop

Tudor Histories of the English Reformations, 1530–83
Thomas Betteridge

Poor Relief and Protestantism: The Evolution of Social Welfare in Sixteenth-Century Emden
Timothy G. Fehler

Radical Reformation Studies: Essays presented to James M. Stayer
edited by Werner O. Packull and Geoffrey L. Dipple

Clerical Marriage and the English Reformation: Precedent Policy and Practice
Helen L. Parish

Penitence in the Age of Reformations
edited by Katharine Jackson Lualdi and Anne T. Thayer

The Faith and Fortunes of France's Huguenots, 1600–85
Philip Benedict

Christianity and Community in the West: Essays for John Bossy
edited by Simon Ditchfield

Reformation, Politics and Polemics: The Growth of Protestantism in East Anglian Market Towns, 1500–1610
John Craig

The Sixteenth-Century French Religious Book
edited by Andrew Pettegree, Paul Nelles and Philip Conner

Music as Propaganda in the German Reformation
Rebecca Wagner Oettinger

John Foxe and his World
edited by Christopher Highley and John N. King

Confessional Identity in East-Central Europe
edited by Maria Crciun, Ovidiu Ghitta and Graeme Murdock

The Bible in the Renaissance:
Essays on Biblical Commentary and Translation
in the Fifteenth and Sixteenth Centuries
edited by Richard Griffiths

Preface and Acknowledgements

I have been working on this study on and off since 1991, when I began the research in Hamburg for a dissertation which has now grown into a book. My original intention was to study early Anabaptism in northern German territories, but I had to abandon this plan when I learned that too few documents had survived the destruction of war. Hans-Jürgen Goertz suggested the current project. He pointed me to a large and underutilized archival collection at the State Archives in Hamburg, which was well suited to addressing debates about confessional affiliation and social order after the Reformation.

I have included no map with this book. In addition to any standard map of Europe, readers can turn to the *Mennonite Historical Atlas* (2nd edn, Winnipeg, 1996), by William Schroeder and Helmut Huebert, which includes a map of the region around Oldesloe in Holstein and another of Mennonite sites in Altona. Since the 1930s Altona has been a district in the western part of Hamburg, within walking distance of the downtown core. Before the twentieth century it was a distinct political entity separated from Hamburg by that city's fortress walls. In the period discussed in this study, Altona was under the jurisdiction first of the Schauenburg counts and later of the Danish monarchy.

Names in the early modern period were seldom standardized. For example, the family name Plus also appears in sources as Plüß or Plußen, while other common Mennonite names, Roosen and Goverts, also appear as Rosen, Roose, Rooze, Rose, Govers and Gouers. For the sake of simplicity and consistency I have always tried to use the version that appears most frequently in both the secondary literature and the primary documents. This has sometimes required an arbitrary decision.

The Dutch custom of using patronymics also calls for comment. Instead of listing a patronymic in last position (as was often done among Dutch speakers in Hamburg), I have always (again for the sake of consistency and to make clear which name is the family name) used the following order: given name, patronymic, family name. Thus, I refer to Ernst Pieters Goverts instead of Ernst Goverts Pieters. In northern German territories the patronymic was formed by adding an 's' (or sometimes 'ß') to the father's given name, while in Dutch territories the suffix 'sz' was most common. The added 's' or 'sz' usually indicated descent – for example, Ernst, the son of Pieter Goverts.

Over the years I have received funding from a number of agencies: the German Academic Exchange Service (DAAD), the Ontario Government

(Ontario Graduate Scholarship), the Social Sciences and Humanities Research Council of Canada, the School of Graduate Studies and Research at Queen's University at Kingston, the Johanna and Fritz Buch Gedächtnis-Stiftung of Hamburg, the Institut für Europäische Geschichte (Abteilung abendländische Religionsgeschichte) in Mainz and the Institute for Research in the Humanities at the University of Wisconsin-Madison. My thanks go to all of these institutions.

My thanks also go to a large number of librarians and archivists. They include staff members of the Staatsarchiv, Staatsbibliothek, Bibliothek des Vereins für Hamburgische Geschichte, Bibliothek des Museums für Hamburgische Geschichte and the Bibliothek der Genealogischen Gesellschaft in Hamburg; the Landesarchiv in Schleswig; the Stadtarchiv in Friedrichstadt; the Mennonitische Forschungsstelle in Weierhof; the Hauptstaatsarchiv in Düsseldorf; the Gemeentearchief and Universiteitsbibliotheek (especially the Mennozaal) in Amsterdam; the Mennonite Historical Library in Goshen, Indiana; the Mennonite Library and Archives in North Newton, Kansas; and the library of Conrad Grebel College at the University of Waterloo in Ontario.

The present book is one of two I am publishing on the subject of Mennonites in Hamburg and Altona. The other, appearing in German, is shorter and covers a 500-year period. It is available through the Mennonitischer Geschichtsverein in Germany.

Elements of Chapter 5 appeared in the *Mennonitische Geschichtsblätter* in 1995, and the part of Chapter 6 about Hans Plus appeared in an earlier version in an edited volume entitled *Aussenseiter zwischen Mittelalter und Neuzeit*, published by Brill in Leiden in 1997. I should like to thank the publishers of both articles for kind permission to reuse material in this book.

I have many other debts of gratitude. Franklin Kopitzsch, Anke Martens, Ed Pries, James Pritchard, Joe Springer, Sem Sutter and Viktor Zacharov made me aware of valuable information and sources. Sara Driedger read the entire text carefully and made numerous helpful suggestions. I should also like to thank the many people who offered me places to stay while I was researching. Special thanks for their generosity in this regard go to the Kraas family in Aumühle and the Foth family in Hamburg.

I have been fortunate to have two excellent mentors: James Stayer at Queen's University, and Hans-Jürgen Goertz at the Institut für Sozial- und Wirtschaftsgeschichte of the Universität Hamburg. Many of the ideas presented here were formed in the aftermath of conversations and seminars with both. While I have benefited from their advice and direction, I take full responsibility for the ideas presented in this study.

Last but certainly not least I have my family and many friends in North America and Europe to thank for advice and non-confessional distractions.

Abbreviations

StAHbg	Staatsarchiv Hamburg
StAHbg/MG	Staatsarchiv Hamburg, Bestand: Mennonitengemeinde

Introduction

In 1601 Count Ernst von Schauenburg granted privileges to a group of Mennonites in Altona. In the course of the seventeenth century, more and more families moved to Altona and to the nearby port city of Hamburg. These early immigrants, most from the Netherlands, and their descendants formed the core of the local Mennonite community until the nineteenth century, when the congregation lost its predominantly Dutch character. Like the majority of northern Germans, they were Protestants. But, unlike their Lutheran neighbours, they practised adult baptism administered after a public confession of the believer's faith, held dissenting views about oaths and the use of arms, organized their community on a congregational rather than a parish basis, often strove to lead simple lives following the example of Christ, and maintained strong connections with other Mennonites in the Netherlands. And like all other non-Lutherans in Hamburg and Altona, they were excluded from active participation in local governance. In short, in an era when politics and religion were closely intertwined, they were marginal members of a society which was dominated by Lutherans.

Mennonites, who today are found around the world, are the best known subgroup of Anabaptists. 'Anabaptism', literally meaning the practice of rebaptism, has taken on a generally neutral connotation in scholarly English in recent decades and simply refers to those people who are in the continental European tradition of adult-baptizing Protestants. The situation is more complicated in German, in which a distinction is made between *Täufer* ('baptists', the term used by scholars who are generally more knowledgeable about and sympathetic towards the Anabaptist past) and *Wiedertäufer* ('rebaptists', still a common term today, occasionally used with innocent intentions). The reason that the distinction between baptism and rebaptism is important in German is that during the early modern era the act of rebaptism was a heresy and a crime in many European jurisdictions: the rejection of child baptism in favour of adult baptism implied the rejection of established ecclesiastical (and secular) authority in favour of free choice. Labels such as *Wiedertäuferei* ('rebaptism') put an emphasis on the act of rebaptism of adults who, it was assumed, were baptized for the first time as infants. The Anabaptists avoided such labels, preferring to call themselves *Mennoniten*, *Taufgesinnten* (German) or *Doopsgezinden* (Dutch), the last two terms translating roughly as 'the baptism-minded'. Almost all Anabaptists after the middle of the sixteenth century were baptized only once and in adulthood, and we would therefore be mistaken to put too much emphasis on the idea of rebaptism when interpreting their history.

In recent decades, the great majority of research on European Anabaptist groups has been concentrated on the first half of the sixteenth century. But the focus in Reformation studies more generally has been widening to include the long-term consequences of early sixteenth-century socio-religious change. A major purpose of this book is to show how important it is to expand the scope of Radical Reformation studies to include 'the confessional age'. Used in this sense, 'confession' means 'religious tradition' or 'church community' in a large sense. For example, Catholicism, Lutheranism and Calvinism were the three most established confessions in early modern Germany. Although scholars are not in agreement about issues of periodization,[1] it is enough to say that the confessional age lasted roughly from 1550 to 1750 and was a period during which competing religious traditions had a heightened significance in European public life. This study looks most closely on the second half of the seventeenth century.

There are three main reasons why it is valuable to examine Mennonite history in Hamburg and Altona during the confessional age. The first concerns Anabaptist history. Starting by the middle of the sixteenth century, there was a major shift occurring in the character of European Anabaptism: diverse religious movements were consolidating themselves in sets of institutionalized congregations.[2] This shift often goes unacknowledged in the historiography, but it was part of a major trend in the development of Christian and Jewish life after the upheaval of the Reformation era. My study looks at some of the seventeenth- and early eighteenth-century implications of an increasingly institutionalized Anabaptist way of life. The second reason concerns the history of Hamburg and Altona. Although Mennonites amounted to only a small proportion of the total population in and around Hamburg,[3] they and other minority groups had a

1 For works that raise questions about the traditional chronological limitations of the 'confessional age', see Etienne François, *Die unsichtbare Grenze: Protestanten und Katholiken in Augsburg 1648–1806*, trans. Angelika Steiner-Wendt (Sigmaringen, 1991); and Joel F. Harrington and Helmut Walser Smith, 'Confessionalization, Community, and State-Building in Germany, 1555–1870', *Journal of Modern History*, 69 (1997), pp. 77–101.

2 See James M. Stayer, 'The Passing of the Radical Moment in the Radical Reformation', *Mennonite Quarterly Review*, 71 (1997), pp. 147–52.

3 For numbers, see Ch. 1. Also see Joachim Whaley, *Religious Toleration and Social Change in Hamburg 1529–1819* (Cambridge, 1985). Whaley examines the relationships between Hamburg's Lutheran rulers and the Calvinist, Catholic and Jewish minorities who lived within its walls. He explains the 'tolerant' policies of Hamburg's magistrates as a result of economic and political interests, not enlightened philosophies. Although tolerated in Hamburg for much the same economic reasons as Calvinists and Jews, the Mennonite community in Hamburg and Altona receives little attention in Whaley's study. This is not for lack of source material.

disproportionately large role in economic affairs (see Ch. 1). Furthermore, the presence of non-believers in Hamburg upset the city's guardians of Lutheran orthodoxy, who from time to time complained loudly to secular officials and all others who would listen. Because of this campaigning, minority groups like Calvinists, Catholics, Jews and Mennonites played a role in the official Lutheran imagination that far outweighed their numbers. The third and most important reason concerns European history generally. Mennonite interactions with local Lutheran rulers and neighbours shed light on major developments of interest to more than just specialists in Anabaptist culture or northern German urban history. For example, any reader interested in the history of minority groups or recent debates about 'confessionalism' and 'confessionalization' will find ample points of connection in the chapters that follow. One of the general goals of this book is to show that studies of Anabaptist communities belong within and contribute to the mainstream of historiographical discussions.

The oxymoron 'obedient heretics' in the book's title is a conflation of the two most common stereotypes or public portrayals of Mennonites used by non-Mennonites in the early modern period. These stereotypes can be illustrated by an example. On 8 May 1672, Emperor Leopold I (1658–1705) sent an anti-Anabaptist mandate to Hamburg's Senate.[4] In the letter, he indicated that he had received word that there were 300 to 400 Anabaptists in Hamburg illegally; he demanded they be expelled immediately, if the city wanted to avoid legal sanctions. Since the high Middle Ages, a common way in which clerical and secular officials had conceived of and dealt with heretics was as 'enemies of Christ' – and, by extension, enemies of the rulers sanctioned by Christ.[5] This is certainly the image most people in positions of authority held of Anabaptists in the generations immediately after the time of their origins in the early Reformation. It was because he shared this interpretation of Anabaptism that the Emperor complained to Hamburg's government. The mandate came as a surprise to the Senate of Hamburg. In early June 1672, Hamburg's officials 'had let the most notable Anabaptists be questioned'

---

4 This correspondence between Hamburg and the Emperor is found at StAHbg, Senat, Cl. VII Lit. Hf Nr. 4 Vol. 1a (15)–(18); and StAHbg, Reichshofrat, 298. Also see Robert Dollinger, *Geschichte der Mennoniten in Schleswig-Holstein, Hamburg und Lübeck* (Neumünster, 1930), p. 142.

5 For a provocative study of this theme, see R. I. Moore, *The Formation of a Persecuting Society: Power and Deviance in Western Europe, 950–1250* (Oxford and Cambridge, Mass., 1987). Also see John S. Oyer, *Lutheran Reformers against the Anabaptists: Luther, Melanchthon and Menius and the Anabaptists of Central Germany* (The Hague, 1964); and the essays in Silvana Seidel Menchi (ed.), *Ketzerverfolgung im 16. und frühen 17. Jahrhundert* (Wiesbaden, 1992).

concerning this matter.[6] The Senate reported its findings to the Emperor on 22 June. Contrary to the Emperor's assertion, the people in question living in Hamburg were Mennonites, not Anabaptists as defined in Imperial laws from the sixteenth century. Furthermore, the Senate claimed that, in addition to contributing to the economic prosperity of the region and the Empire as a whole, the Mennonites lived peacefully, separately and obediently. They even prayed in their church services for the well-being of rulers. The status quo, the Senate argued, was far more preferable than the Emperor's radical demand of expulsion. The Emperor did not press the matter any further and there were no expulsions. Although this is the only major example of the Emperor being personally interested in Mennonites in Hamburg and Altona, his attitudes are typical of those held by early modern opponents of 'sectarianism' and 'heresy'. The response of Hamburg's magistrates in 1672 reflected a more positive attitude among some rulers towards Mennonites, which was spreading (albeit slowly) by the early seventeenth century.

The tension evident in the competing views was not merely a product of the political rhetoric of non-Mennonites. There were important strands in Mennonite society that each side – Empire and city – could point to when making its case in 1672. Although the Mennonites of course did not think of themselves as heretics, and although many of their leaders wanted to emphasize that they held orthodox Protestant beliefs about God, Mennonites were religious nonconformists. They refused to accept many of the central rituals and institutions of their Protestant and Catholic neighbours, the key among these being child baptism; this left them open to the charge of heresy. Maintaining their distinct character had great social and political consequences. Although seldom under threat themselves by the early seventeenth century, Mennonites in northern Germany and the Netherlands were sensitive to the charge of heresy, which still helped incite waves of repression in some southern German and Swiss territories into the eighteenth century.[7] Mennonites were also very aware that because of their beliefs they were granted fewer social and political rights than their neighbours, even in territories where rulers never considered repression to be a serious option. Balanced against their group-defining religious nonconformity was an equally important and group-defining

---

6 StAHbg, Senat, Cl.VII Lit. Hf Nr. 4 Vol. 1a (18): 'haben die vornembste denselben [wiederteuffer] darvber alhie befragen lassen'.

7 For examples of repression in Switzerland, see Mark Furner, 'The Repression and Survival of Anabaptism in the Emmental, 1659–1743' (Ph.D. diss., Clare College, University of Cambridge, 1998); and Hanspeter Jecker, *Ketzer, Rebellen, Heilige: Das Basler Täufertum von 1580–1700* (Liestal, 1998). Also see A. van Gulik, 'Uit de geschiedenis van de overkomst der vervolgde Zwitzers in 1710 en 1711', *Doopsgezinde Bijdragen*, 48 (1908), pp. 85–105, and 49 (1909), pp. 127–55.

political conformity. In reaction against extreme charges first levelled against their forebears in the early Reformation, Mennonites insisted that they were obedient followers of Christ as well as obedient subjects of secular rulers. In most publicly advertised Mennonite self-definitions in the early modern era (and even beyond), these two poles of identity were inseparable. Although the balancing act between distinctiveness and conformity could cause difficulties, the Mennonites' political conformity often made it easier for them to avoid renewed persecution and thus maintain their brand of religious nonconformity.

It should be clear from these examples that the theme of identity is central to my study. Because the literature on the subject is vast, it is impossible to review it adequately in an introduction such as this. For the purposes of this study it is enough to define terms in a basic way and say a little about 'Mennonite identity' and group identity in general.

An older style of thinking about Mennonite identity is evident in the work of such mid-twentieth-century scholars as Robert Friedmann,[8] who felt that aspects of early sixteenth-century Anabaptism embodied the timeless, true and pure expression of Anabaptism: all later forms which differed from this supposedly pure, original form were bastardized and corrupted. For example, Friedmann considered the Zonist variant of seventeenth-century Mennonitism to be purer than the Lamist variant. In other words, he interpreted Anabaptist diversity as a problem to be lamented rather than a historical fact to be understood. This older approach is ill-suited for historians, because, at least implicitly, it denies the importance of historical development by insisting in a partisan way on the unchanging core character of a group.

My own guiding assumption is that it was (and is) normal for groups to change. Each new generation of group members faced possibilities and limitations unique to their time and place, and they developed interpretations of their group's significance which often make sense only as a response to these changing and now largely forgotten circumstances. Although some aspects of Mennonite belief and ideology remained fairly stable over many generations, it is fair to say that as groups changed, so

---

[8] Robert Friedmann, *Mennonite Piety through the Centuries: Its Genius and its Literature* (Goshen, Ind., 1949). In the book's introduction (p. xiv), Friedmann and his colleague Harold Bender call for 'the re-quickening of modern Mennonitism in the spirit of its sixteenth century Anabaptist fathers'. Friedmann's book, which includes a chapter about Hamburg and Altona, has had a great deal of influence on Mennonite scholars. One example is Ernst W. Schepansky, 'Mennoniten in Hamburg und Altona zur Zeit des Merkantilismus', *Mennonitische Geschichtsblätter*, 38, new ser. 32 (1980), pp. 54–73; also published in *Hamburger Jahrbuch für Wirtschafts- und Gesellschaftspolitik*, 24 (1979), pp. 219–34. Friedmann's views have, however, also been critiqued; see Theron F. Schlabach, 'Mennonites and Pietism in America, 1740–1880: Some Thoughts on the Friedmann Thesis', *Mennonite Quarterly Review*, 57 (1983), pp. 222–40.

did group identities. There is nothing in the very nature of past interpretations of identity which make earlier ones truer than later ones.

These assumptions have implications for my understanding of 'collective identity'.[9] By the term, I do not mean what or who groups of people 'really' were, but rather the standards that opinion leaders used to define who they or others were. These were standards against which individuals could model their own lives or using which they could demand changes in others' lives. And these standards were always subject to elaboration, modification, objection or even neglect.[10]

For the purposes of analysis, I make a distinction between two types of action related to confessional identity. First, there was the articulation of official standards, programmes and intentions. The people involved were usually men in leading public positions like preachers and lawyers, and could be non-Mennonite or Mennonite, friend or foe. One of the key figures who contributed over several decades to the definition and advertisement of a brand of Mennonite identity in seventeenth-century Hamburg and Altona was the businessman and lay preacher Geeritt Roosen (1612–1711). While my work is not a biography of Roosen, it does rely a great deal on sources that he played a major role in creating. These sources include congregational protocols, a congregational membership book, confessions of faith, sermons, pamphlets, chronicles, letters, court documents, inquisition reports, law books and commercial documents. Secondly, while it is important to examine official aspects of identity, this is not enough, for it tells us only how opinion leaders felt that rank-and-file believers should have acted on a day-to-day basis, not how they actually behaved. That is why I also examine in some detail the behaviour of individual believers with regard to such central Mennonite issues as non-resistance, oath-swearing and marriage in the community of faith. The distinction between official standards and lived experience becomes a more and more important theme of the book as the chapters progress.

---

9 The evidence I provide is best suited for an analysis of officially stated standards of collective behaviour and the ways in which individual congregational members responded to these standards. This approach is not the same as a discussion of 'the self', individuality or personal identity. I do not consider this latter problem-set to be a major subject of my work. My subject has a mainly historical and sociological focus. The latter problem-set, while it certainly does have an historical dimension, is concerned more with psychological and philosophical issues.

10 My views have been shaped by Peter L. Berger and Thomas Luckmann's classic work, *The Social Construction of Reality* (Garden City, NY, 1967). 'Reality', write the authors (p. 116), 'is socially defined'. They then qualify this statement with the further observation that 'the definitions are always *embodied*, that is, concrete individuals and groups of individuals serve as definers of reality. . . . [I]t is essential to keep pushing questions about the historically available conceptualizations of reality from the abstract "What?" to the sociologically concrete "Says who?"'

Chapter 1 provides historical context for the study. While Chapters 2 through 4 focus primarily on officially stated programmes, Chapters 5 through 7 focus on the often complex relationship between programmes and practice. The Appendices provide background data for Chapters 1, 5 and 7. The central argument of the book, suggested throughout but discussed most fully in the Conclusion, is that group identity was strongest and clearest amid public controversies.[11]

[11] Although Leo Driedger (to whom I am not related) makes a similar argument in *Mennonite Identity in Conflict* (Lewiston and Queenston, 1988) about the dynamic, contingent and contested nature of group identity, his work is focused almost entirely on twentieth-century North American Mennonites and takes a very schematic sociological perspective. These two features make our books very different.

CHAPTER ONE

Confessional Migration: The Dispersion of Anabaptists to Northern Germany

Expulsion and refuge are among the major themes of early modern European history. For example, 1492 is famous not only in connection with Christopher Columbus but also as the date of the expulsion of Jews from Spanish territory. The ecclesiastical and political divisions resulting from the Reformation also led to waves of expulsion. Catholics were forced from Protestant territories, and Protestants were forced from Catholic territories. The situation was especially acute in the territories of the Holy Roman Empire and the Netherlands, where political and ecclesiastical authority was very fragmented and confessional animosities were high. Anabaptists, like early modern Jews, led much more precarious legal existences than most minorities, for they had few co-religionists in positions of political authority anywhere in Europe. Even if these believers did not have to flee their homelands to practise their unique religious rites in peace, they did have to live in host societies that nurtured intolerant attitudes towards their nonconformity.

It is Protestant migration from the Netherlands to northern German territories like Hamburg that is most significant for this study.[1] In an instructive book and set of articles, in which he develops the category 'confessional migration', the German historian Heinz Schilling has written about waves of Protestant migration from the Netherlands during a century-long period starting in the 1530s and 1540s.[2] It is useful to describe

---

1 The theme of migration is central to Anabaptist history into the twentieth century. For a discussion of the topic as it concerns North American Mennonite history, see Calvin Redekop, *Mennonite Society* (Baltimore, 1989) and Royden Loewen, *Family, Church, and Market: A Mennonite Community in the Old and New Worlds, 1850–1930* (Urbana, 1993).

2 Heinz Schilling: *Niederländische Exulanten im 16. Jahrhundert: Ihre Stellung im Sozialgefüge und im religiösen Leben deutscher und englischer Städte* (Gütersloh, 1972); id., 'Innovation through Migration: The Settlements of Calvinist Netherlanders in Sixteenth- and Seventeenth-Century Central and Western Europe', *Histoire sociale – Social History* (Ottawa), 16 (1983), pp. 7–33; id., 'Die niederländischen Exulanten des 16. Jahrhunderts: Ein Beitrag zum Typus der frühneuzeitlichen Konfessionsmigration', *Geschichte in Wissenschaft und Unterricht*, 43 (1992), pp. 67–78; and id., 'Confessional Migration as a Distinct Type of Old European Longdistance Migration' in Simonetta Cavaciocchi (ed.), *Le migrazioni in Europa* (Florence, 1994), pp. 175–89. Another text which emphasizes the importance of migration in the development of European Mennonite life is Wolfgang Froese (ed.), *Sie kamen als Fremde: Ihre Stellung im Sozialgefüge und im religiösen Leben deutscher und englischer Städte* (Krefeld, 1995).

this migration as confessional in character for at least two reasons: persecution, one of the key factors leading to exile, was targeted by governments against particular religious groups; and the experience and memory of exile often contributed to the cohesion of religious groups, shaping most aspects of their collective lives for several generations. Schilling's analysis, while concentrated on Calvanists, does apply well to Anabaptists, for their collective religious, political, social and economic lives were also shaped decisively by experiences of persecution, expulsion and relocation. In many regards, this chapter is an elaboration on Schilling's concept of confessional migration.

The rise of a Mennonite brand of Anabaptism in the sixteenth century

The reasons for Anabaptist persecution and exile were rooted in mainstream Christian attitudes towards baptism and social order. During the early sixteenth century, reform-oriented Christians attacked clerical privileges, the mass, the veneration of saints and the traditional sacramental system, and in so doing they also attacked cornerstones of medieval social, political and religious organization. Few reformers, however, were interested in questioning the practice of child baptism. Child baptism was a ceremony regulated by custom and law in medieval Christian communities, and it remained the practice of an overwhelming majority of Christians after the Reformation. Even the majority of Protestants, who like the Anabaptists were opposed to the old sacramental order and the authority of the Pope, continued to baptize children. In so doing, parents were professing publicly that they would raise their children as orthodox believers and obedient subjects in the parish community. In other words, baptism as a child marked an individual's entry into not merely the religious but also the socio-political community. The campaigns of the early Anabaptists to reconstitute the Christian community based on the ideals of a believers' church challenged the very foundations of this established social, political and religious order. If an individual could choose as an adult whether to join the community of believers, was it not then also possible to choose whether to join the political community? Before the late eighteenth century, governments usually interpreted religious nonconformity of the type advocated by Anabaptist reformers as a form of political nonconformity. In 1529 *Wiedertäuferei* (rebaptism) was declared a capital offence in Imperial territories. For most of the sixteenth century, the great majority of Protestant and Catholic governments looked upon Anabaptists not simply as nonconformists but also as heretics and criminals.

The propaganda that Anabaptism was socially disruptive was reinforced in the popular imagination by two main sets of events: the Peasants' War of 1524–26 and the short-lived Anabaptist regime in Münster, Westphalia, in the mid-1530s. In southern German-speaking territories, the Anabaptist groups known as the Swiss Brethren and the Hutterites arose amid and in the aftermath of the Peasants' War.[3] Adult baptism in northern Germany and the Netherlands began somewhat later, in the early 1530s, with the missionary activity of Melchior Hoffman. The Mennonite tradition grew from the foundations that Hoffman had helped to establish.[4] The namesake of the Mennonites, the former Catholic priest Menno Simons, began championing the Anabaptist cause around 1536, shortly after the bloody end to a siege of the Anabaptist-controlled city of Münster.[5] In early 1534 an Anabaptist party had won civic elections there. Hundreds of Anabaptists or Anabaptist sympathizers from the surrounding countryside and as far away as the Netherlands travelled to the Westphalian city, which they thought was the New Jerusalem where believers could gather in safety to await the coming End Times. In February 1534, Catholic and Protestant rulers in the region decided to combine their military strength against the Anabaptists. The regional overlords felt it was their duty to defeat the unlawful Anabaptist city, but the attack on the city also provided an opportunity to limit traditional civic freedoms and increase princely authority. The rhetoric and violence used by both sides increased as the siege progressed. To complicate matters, a small number of Dutch sympathizers of Münster's Anabaptist regime protested in a series of dramatic actions in the Low Countries.[6] Some of these actions were non-violent: in 1534 prophets displaying unsheathed swords in the streets of Amsterdam warned of God's impending judgement over the ungodly;[7] and in 1535 twelve naked men and women ran along Amsterdam's streets,

---

3 See James M. Stayer, *The German Peasants' War and Anabaptist Community of Goods* (Montreal and Kingston, 1991); and Werner O. Packull, *Hutterite Beginnings: Communitarian Experiments during the Reformation* (Baltimore and London, 1995).

4 On Hoffman, see Klaus Deppermann, *Melchior Hoffman: Social Unrest and Apocalyptic Visions in the Age of Reformation*, trans. Malcolm Wren, ed. Benjamin Drewery (Edinburgh, 1987).

5 The most recent monographs on the subject are Ralf Klötzer, *Die Täuferherrschaft zu Münster: Stadtreformation und Welterneuerung* (Münster, 1992); and Sigrun Haude, *In the Shadow of Savage Wolves: Anabaptist Muenster and the German Reformation during the 1530s* (Leiden, 2000).

6 For general background, see work by A.F. Mellink: 'Das münsterische Täufertum und die Niederlande', *Jahrbuch für Westfälische Kirchengeschichte*, 78 (1985), pp. 13–18; *Amsterdam en de Wederdopers in de zestiende Eeuw* (Nijmegen, 1978); 'Das niederländisch-westfälische Täufertum im sechzehten Jahrhundert', in Hans-Jürgen Goertz (ed.), *Umstrittenes Täufertum* (Göttingen, 1975), pp. 206–22; and 'The Mutual Relations between the Münster Anabaptists and the Netherlands', *Archiv für Reformationsgeschichte*, 50 (1959), pp. 16–33.

7 A.F. Mellink (ed.), *Documenta Anabaptistica Neerlandica: Amsterdam (1531–1536)* (Leiden, 1985), p. 28.

'saying that they had been sent from God to communicate the naked truth to the godless'.[8] Other actions had a decidedly violent character: in 1535 armed Anabaptist militants captured a cloister in Friesland;[9] and a small group of Anabaptists even stormed Amsterdam's city hall.[10] The siege of Münster finally ended tragically. In the middle of 1535 the besieging forces broke the city's defences and Münster's Anabaptist Reformation came to an abrupt end. The city was reconverted to Catholicism, and the city's Anabaptist leaders were executed in a public and gruesome fashion. The episode remains today a mythic part of Münster's history and the history of Anabaptism.

Because early modern propagandists throughout Europe used the episode of Anabaptist rule as a key example of fanaticism and crime, Münster marked a serious setback for the Anabaptist cause in northern Europe. Yet despite this setback, several northern European Anabaptist groups remained active after 1535. Each tried to rally support from among the scattered Münsterite remnant. One was a small faction loyal to Jan van Batenburg, whose members resorted to terrorism to exact revenge against the ungodly. Few post-Münsterite Anabaptists shared the Batenburgers' extreme stance. Another group following the spiritualist leader David Joris was more successful in attracting adherents immediately after the fall of Anabaptist Münster. But Joris's pre-eminence lasted for only a few brief years. By the 1540s the most successful Anabaptist leader was Menno Simons.[11]

For generations after the sixteenth century, Mennonite apologists tried to emphasize that Menno Simons and his followers had no connection whatever with the Münsterite regime,[12] while confessional opponents favoured interpretations which portrayed the Mennonites as heretics in the Münsterite mould. Both views are exaggerations. While it is true that Simons himself accepted adult baptism only after the defeat of the Münsterite regime, it is impossible to draw an absolute distinction between the two streams of Anabaptism. Both groups arose out of the same general tradition of northern German and Dutch Anabaptism, and many of Simons's followers had been supporters of the Münsterite regime before its violent end. From 1530 to about 1533, Anabaptists in these regions had looked to Melchior Hoffman as a leader. Besides propagating an enthusiastic but still largely nonviolent form of apocalypticism, Hoffman

[8] Ibid., p. 110.

[9] See James M. Stayer, 'Oldeklooster and Menno', *Sixteenth Century Journal*, 9 (1978), pp. 52–5.

[10] Mellink (ed.), *Documenta Anabaptistica Neerlandica*, p. 128.

[11] See Klaus Deppermann, *Melchior Hoffman*, ch. 9, §4; and Gary K. Waite, *David Joris and Dutch Anabaptism, 1524–1543* (Waterloo, Ont., 1990).

[12] For examples, see Ch. 4.

believed in the doctrine of the celestial flesh: Christ, although born through Mary, was untainted by human weakness. While followers of Simons had dampened the apocalyptic enthusiasm so typical of early Dutch Anabaptists, they continued to believe in the doctrine of the celestial flesh throughout the sixteenth century.[13] It is probably because the Mennonites shared these kinds of close connections in personnel and theology with their Melchiorite forebears that Simons reacted so strongly against other aspects of the Mechiorite–Münsterite legacy. He wanted to rescue the Anabaptist cause from what he felt was the criminal and unbiblical character it had acquired under Münsterite leadership.[14] In reaction against the violence associated with Münsterite Anabaptism, he and his followers struggled to form communities of self-disciplined Christians 'without spot or wrinkle' (Eph. 5: 27), dedicated to the preservation of God's Word and free from the corruption of the established clergy.[15] This was an important intermediate step in the process that James Stayer has called 'the passing of the radical moment in the Radical Reformation'.[16]

Burdened by the stigma of the Münsterite regime, Mennonites sought refuge from persecution. Anabaptist migration from the Netherlands was never steady, but there were high points. One phase of voluntary and forced migration was naturally enough during the 1530s, when Anabaptism was a new movement growing in prominence and infamy in the shadow of the Münsterite regime. During this early, pre-Mennonite period, Anabaptists were a large percentage of the then small Protestant population in the Netherlands, especially the northern provinces, the historic heartland of northern Anabaptism. Conditions changed by the 1550s to limit (but not eliminate) intolerance against Anabaptists in the northern Netherlands. First, events at Münster, which had been among the major justifications for the persecution, became less of an immediate memory. Furthermore, the much less socially radical Mennonites became the dominant Anabaptist faction. The way in which the small Mennonite community behaved bore little resemblance to the exaggerated image prevalent in polemical literature. Mennonites even helped finance the Dutch campaigns against the Spanish Habsburgs.

The focal point of persecution against Anabaptists after the mid-1550s was the southern Netherlands. There was a small Anabaptist population in the provinces of Flanders and Brabant, but towards the middle of the

---

13 By the mid-seventeenth century, almost all Mennonites had abandoned the doctrine of the celestial flesh.

14 See Stayer, 'Oldeklooster and Menno'.

15 See Hans-Jürgen Goertz, 'Der fremde Menno Simons: Antiklerikale Argumentation im Werk eines melchioritischen Täufers', in Irwin Horst (ed.), *The Dutch Dissenters: A Critical Companion to their History and Ideas* (Leiden, 1986), pp. 160–76.

16 Stayer, 'The Passing of the Radical Moment'.

century, when Calvinism began spreading, it amounted to only a minority of the Protestant population. At that time, the Netherlands was under the control of the Spanish line of the Habsburg Empire. Under the Habsburg monarch Philip II (1556–98), Spain intensified measures to limit local liberties and combat Protestant heresy in the Netherlands. Popular dissatisfaction mounted. In 1566 there were widespread outbursts of public protest and iconoclasm, organized largely by the Calvinist opponents of the Catholic monarchy. To bring the situation under control, Philip II sent a highly effective military commander, the Duke of Alva, to the Netherlands. Alva set up a military dictatorship and used ruthless measures to combat heresy and dissent. At the same time, Calvinist rebels based in the northern Netherlands organized a guerrilla campaign against the Spanish. The Dutch War of Independence, which began in the 1560s, resulted in the provinces of the northern Netherlands declaring their independence from Spain.

The conflict was important in Mennonite history not only because of the support which Mennonites gave to Protestant rebels. It also marked the high point of executions of Protestants in the Netherlands, which was the hot spot of heresy executions in sixteenth-century Europe. The great majority of those executed were Anabaptists.[17] The early years of suffering were memorialized by later generations of Protestant martyrologists. The Mennonites too developed their own rich martyrological tradition, the most famous product of which is *Het Bloedigh Tooneel* (The Bloody Theatre, more commonly known in English as the Martyrs' Mirror), first published in 1660.[18] Another reason for the importance of southern Netherlandish conflict is that it sparked new waves of Protestant migration. From the 1560s until the end of the century, the largest proportion of refugees who fled war, persecution and economic instability in the Spanish Netherlands were Calvinists, but Anabaptists also sought a better life in new territories.[19] Many fled to the newly formed republic of the United Provinces in the northern Netherlands. A small number made their way to England or to German territories, including the territories near Hamburg.

---

17 See William Monter, 'Heresy Executions in Reformation Europe, 1520–1565', in Ole Peter Grell and Bob Scribner (eds), *Tolerance and Intolerance in the European Reformation* (Cambridge, 1996), pp. 48–64.

18 See Brad S. Gregory, *Salvation at Stake: Christian Martyrdom in Early Modern Europe* (Cambridge, Mass., and London, 1999). For more background on the *Martyrs' Mirror*, see Ch. 3 of the present study.

19 For references to the appropriate literature, see Heinz Schilling's essays on confessional migration, as well as O.S. Knottnerus, '"Gijlieden/ die aen alle wateren zaeyt": doperse immigranten in het Nordduitsche kustgebied (1500–1700)', *Doopsgezinde Bijdragen*, new ser. 20 (1994), pp. 11–60; and Susanne Woelk, 'Menno Simons in Oldersum und Oldesloe: "Häuptlingsreformation" und Glaubensflüchtlinge im 16. Jahrhundert', *Mennonitische Geschichtsblätter*, 53 (1996), pp. 11–33.

Most of northern Germany had been officially converted to Lutheranism by the 1530s. Lutheran governments in the sixteenth century, like the one in Hamburg, were among those that strongly opposed what they thought was the heretical sect of *Wiedertäufer*. However, no single government controlled the northern German countryside. The reason Anabaptists could find sanctuary in the countryside of Holstein to the east of Hamburg is that a small number of local Lutheran noblemen were willing to tolerate their presence. Among these noblemen was Bartholomäus von Ahlefeldt (d. *c.* 1568), the Lutheran lord of a small landholding called Fresenburg, located near Oldesloe (now Bad Oldesloe), about halfway between Hamburg and Lübeck.[20] This is where Menno Simons had found refuge from about the late 1540s or early 1550s until his death in 1561,[21] and before he arrived a number of Anabaptist families had probably already established themselves there in a small village called Wüstenfelde. Because of a lack of sources, it is not clear why Ahlefeldt decided to tolerate Simons and his followers. Ahlefeldt certainly did not share the widespread opinion that Anabaptists were criminals, and we can speculate that he may even have had religious sympathies for the men and women he protected on his lands. However, he never accepted their faith. A very likely explanation for his decision is that he hoped to gain an economic advantage by bringing hard-working and self-disciplining refugees to his lands from the economically prosperous and more technologically advanced regions of the Netherlands. Whatever the reasons for his protection, Ahlefeldt required his new subjects to pay a yearly tax of 1 Reichstaler per household.[22]

The havens provided in places like Fresenburg did not shelter believers from internal controversies. Diversity was a part of Anabaptist life from the very beginning in the early Reformation, and little changed after the forces of institutionalization took hold by the end of the sixteenth century. Later generations created new alliances and broke apart into new factions amid occasional disputes. As a result, several new northern European Anabaptist groups developed in the last half of the sixteenth century. One

---

[20] For a map of this region, see William Schroeder and Helmut Huebert, *Mennonite Historical Atlas* (2nd edn, Winnipeg, 1996), pp. 3 and 8.

[21] For a narrative of Menno Simons's activities in Holstein, see Harold Bender's 'Brief Biography', in *The Complete Writings of Menno Simons, c. 1496–1561*, ed. J.C. Wenger (Scottdale, Pa., 1956), pp. 21–8. Also see Marja Keyser, 'The Fresenburg Press: An Historical Investigation Pertaining to Menno Simons' Printing Office in Holstein, Germany, 1554–1555', in Irwin Horst (ed.), *The Dutch Dissenters: A Critical Companion to their History and Ideas* (Leiden, 1986), pp. 179–86.

[22] On Fresenburg, see G. Roosen, *Unschuld und Gegen-Bericht der Evangelischen Tauffgesinneten Christen* (Ratzeburg, 1702), pp. 97–104; and Ernst F. Goverts, 'Das adelige Gut Fresenburg und die Mennoniten', *Zeitschrift der Zentralstelle für Niedersächsiche Familiengeschichte (Sitz Hamburg)*, 7 (1925), pp. 41–55, 69–86 and 97–103.

group was led by Menno Simons, Dirk Philips and Leonard Bouwens.[23] This group, the only group properly called Mennonites, parted ways in the 1550s with two other groups, which became known as the Waterlanders and the High Germans. The ostensible issue about which they disagreed was how strictly leaders should apply religious discipline to maintain a pure, visible church of believers. The Mennonites took a hardline position on congregational discipline. Other disputes soon followed. In order to escape the violence and instability resulting from Spanish anti-Protestant campaigns in Flanders and Brabant in the 1560s and 1570s, Flemish Mennonite refugees settled with coreligionists in places like Friesland in the northern Netherlands. In the 1560s disagreements between the Flemish visitors and Frisian Mennonite hosts about how to coordinate congregational government led to a division which spread to other regions. A distinction developed in Mennonite circles between Flemish and Frisian factions. With time the names 'Flemish' and 'Frisian', like 'Waterlander' and 'High German', became factional designations more than indications of regional origin.[24] Each group broke into further factions.[25]

The Anabaptists who eventually settled in Hamburg and Altona were largely Flemish Mennonites. They were 'Flemish' in two senses. First, many were born in or were descended from refugees from Flanders. Northern German Mennonite family names like Goverts, Noë and van der Smissen were all of southern Netherlandish origin. Furthermore, in factional terms the largest, but not the only, Mennonite group in early modern Hamburg and Altona considered itself part of the Flemish Mennonite faction in the Netherlands. Despite the ethnic origins of many of its members, it retained few connections with Flanders and Brabant after the early seventeenth century. Rather, its main ties to the Netherlands were to Flemish Mennonite congregations in the United Provinces, not the Spanish Netherlands, which after the forced re-Catholicization at end of the sixteenth century was no longer a significant centre of Anabaptist life.

---

23 See Jacobus ten Doornkaat Koolman, *Dirk Philips: Friend and Colleague of Menno Simons, 1504–1568*, trans. William E. Keeney, ed. C. Arnold Snyder (Kitchener, Ont., 1998). The literature on Menno Simons is too extensive to cite here.

24 A good reference for more details about these divisions is George Huntston Williams, *The Radical Reformation* (3rd edn, Kirksville, Mo., 1992), ch. 19. For longer general works on northern European Anabaptist history, see S. Blaupot ten Cate, *Geschiedenis der Doopsgezinden in Holland, Zeeland, Utrecht, en Gelderland* (Amsterdam, 1847); A. Brons, *Ursprung, Entwicklung und Schicksale der altevangelischen Taufgesinnten oder Mennoniten*, ed. E.M. ten Cate (3rd edn, Amsterdam, 1912); W.J. Kühler, *Geschiedenis van de Doopsgezinden in Nederland (1600–1735)* (Haarlem, 1940); and C. Arnold Snyder, *Anabaptist History and Theology: An Introduction* (Kitchener, Ont., 1995).

25 For more details on some later schisms, see W.I. van Douwen, 'De afscheiding van de Huiskoopers of Oude Vlamingen (1587) en die van de Janjacobsgezinden (1599)', *Doopsgezinde Bijdragen*, 52 (1912), pp. 49–75.

Mennonites in Hamburg and Altona

In 1597 Rinsken Quins, a Mennonite refugee from the Spanish Netherlands, opened a small store in Hamburg to help raise money to support her children after her husband had died.[26] She was almost certainly not the first Mennonite in Hamburg, but records and evidence about earlier Mennonites in the city are especially sketchy.[27] In some regards it might seem surprising that Mennonites lived in Hamburg in the late sixteenth and early seventeenth centuries. In 1529 the Hanseatic port became a Lutheran stronghold and remained so into the eighteenth century. In the 1603 constitutional recess, the first article began: 'Because unity in religion is also the true bond of freedom and trust in political affairs; therefore, in this city and its associated churches and congregations the true, pure religion . . . will be held to firmly and, by the grace of Almighty God, will be propagated for posterity.'[28] This meant that only Lutherans were allowed to worship publicly, vote or hold political offices. A fundamental presupposition shared in many parts of Christian Europe in the sixteenth and seventeenth centuries was that the political community should be united by adherence to one common form of religion. This conviction, which lay at the heart of the 1603 constitutional recess, was also expressed decades earlier in a mandate against Anabaptists and Sacramentarians published in 1535 by the league of Wendish cities (Hamburg, as well as Lübeck, Lüneburg, Rostock, Stralsund and Wismar).[29] Hamburg's government reissued the mandate several times, even as late as the middle of the seventeenth century.[30] Many of Hamburg's Lutheran clergymen in the

---

26 See [Geeritt Roosen], 'Geeritt Roosen und seine Geschichte der Kriegsereignisse seiner Zeit', transcription and introduction by Paul Piper, *Germania*, 1 (1899), pp. 367–8. A copy of this difficult-to-find journal article is found at StAHbg.

27 For a summary of older research, see B.C. Roosen, *Geschichte der Mennoniten-Gemeinde zu Hamburg und Altona* (2 parts, Hamburg, 1886–87), part 1, pp. 6–8.

28 [Johann Klefeker], *Sammlung der Hamburgischen Gesetze und Verfassungen*, 12 vols (Hamburg 1765–73), viii, p. 430: 'Anfenglich dewile de Einigheit in der Religion ock de rechte Band des Fredes und Vertruwens is in politischen Handelen; Also schall in düsser Stadt und dartho gehörigen Kercken und Gemeine de wahre reine Religion . . . festiglich beholden, und dorch deß Allmechtigen Gottes Gnaden up de leve Posteritet propagiret und gebracht werden . . . '.

29 Despite the obvious coincidence, this mandate probably had little to do with a campaign against the Anabaptist regime at Münster. A more likely reason for its original publication is concern about the government of Jürgen Wullenwever in Lübeck between 1533 and 1535. Wullenwever had reformist (although probably not Anabaptist) plans and policies which angered many of his enemies. Before they had him executed in 1537, Wullenwever's enemies had accused him of *Wiedertäuferei* and other crimes.

30 An original copy of the 1555 mandate is found at StAHbg, Senat, Cl. VII Lit. Hf Nr. 4 Vol. 1a, (1). Also see StAHbg, Handschriftensammlung, 130, (5); StAHbg, Handschriftensammlung, 138, pp. 312–24 and 326–43; StAHbg, Handschriftensammlung,

sixteenth and seventeenth centuries also wrote long treatises and preached severe sermons against Anabaptists and other non-Lutheran minorities. If Lutheran clergymen had had their way, all non-Lutherans would have been barred from entering the city's fortress walls.

Hamburg's government of lawyers, merchants and religious leaders was rarely united on the issue of how to treat confessional minorities. Members of the Senate (*Senat*, also called the *Rat*), the city's main governing institution, were in favour of combating the abstract threat posed by Anabaptists (*Wiedertäufer*), but they took few concrete steps to discourage Mennonite settlement. It seems that the Senate preferred to treat the Mennonites as ethnic Netherlanders rather than a confessional minority. For example, in 1605 and 1639 it arranged temporary agreements known as *Fremdenkontrakten* (contracts with foreigners) with Dutch immigrant families. Most of those families included in the contracts were Calvinists, but some were Mennonites.[31] By the seventeenth century, Mennonites could claim their rights to settle inside Hamburg's walls by paying on an individual basis to become *Einwohner* (residents), a legal category which brought with it fewer rights and responsibilities than citizenship but still allowed a person the legal right to live in the city. According to the terms of Hamburg's constitution non-Lutherans could not accept public office, participate in political decision-making nor worship openly in the city. But in legal practice after the middle of the seventeenth century, and with these limitations of rights in mind, members of non-Lutheran Christian communities could nonetheless become citizens. Towards the end of the seventeenth century, more and more Mennonites who met the residency and financial requirements of citizenship were choosing to become citizens. Although Mennonite citizens had limited political and religious rights, they did at least have full economic rights in the important trading port.

In normal circumstances, Hamburg's Mennonites left the city's walled boundaries and travelled a short distance to Altona in Danish territory whenever they wanted to worship. However, they did occasionally hold private religious services inside Hamburg's walls during times of war and plague, when city gates were closed and they could not travel. Because this practice was illegal or at least of questionable legal status in the minds of most magistrates, seventeenth-century Mennonites tried to cover up their activity. As a result, evidence of Mennonite religious activity in Hamburg is scarce at best. Only in the eighteenth century, when their place in Hamburg's society had become more secure, did Mennonites dare raise the issue of private worship in Hamburg with the city's Senate. In an

396, pp. 649–60; StAHbg, Handschriftensammlung, 1968, pp. 1711–18; and J.F. Blank (ed.), *Sammlung der . . . Gesetze und Verfassungen*, 6 vols (Hamburg, 1763–74), i, pp. 152–4.

31 Roosen, *Geschichte der Mennoniten-Gemeinde*, part 1, pp. 8–14.

undated letter from the early eighteenth century to officials in Hamburg, they requested that an order to end all Mennonite worship services in the city be repealed.[32] Because of continuing pressure from the city's clergymen, Hamburg's magistrates in the eighteenth century were still not in favour of allowing non-believers to practise their faith in the city, even though their relations with the Mennonite minority were generally polite. In their letter of response, the congregation's representatives noted precedents for Mennonites worshipping inside Hamburg's walls. In previous years of misfortune (1675, 1679, 1686 and 1700) services had been held with little disturbance to the Lutheran community, the letter's authors claimed.[33] It is unclear exactly how this issue was resolved, if at all. Although Mennonites were not seriously persecuted in Hamburg in the seventeenth and early eighteenth centuries, they were not accepted as equals either. It took until the nineteenth century before they received the legal right to worship in Hamburg.[34]

Economic considerations were a main reason why the Mennonites were able to establish themselves in the Lutheran stronghold. Hamburg's secular rulers tolerated non-Lutherans because trade with regions like the Netherlands and the Iberian Peninsula was crucial to the city's economic well-being.[35] Much of this trade was organized by recent non-Lutheran immigrants, whether Calvinist, Jewish or Mennonite. Another factor which heightened the interest of Hamburg's magistrates in keeping minority businessmen in the city was competition with Altona.

Like most of the rest of Schleswig and Holstein, Altona was a Lutheran territory. In the sixteenth century it was little more than a small Elbian fishing community a few kilometres west of Hamburg's walls. A transformation began when the local lord, Count Ernst von Schauenburg (d. 1622), invited non-Lutheran businessmen and craftsmen to settle in Altona. The reason for the invitation was that the Count hoped to attract economic activity away from Hamburg. The first Mennonite to arrange a special privilege with the Count was François Noë. In the early seventeenth century, he and his Mennonite associates operated as the Count's business agents. Together with a pair of Mennonite brothers, Cornelius and Hans

32 The Mennonites were probably responding to a 1716 order by Hamburg's Senate that Mennonite worship services in the city be stopped. See StAHbg/MG, 9.

33 The letter is dated 27 January 1712 and was signed by Jan Geerling, Jacob Becker, Ernst Peters Goverts, Jan de Lanoy, Reindert Jansen and Jan Beets; see StAHbg, Ministerium, IIIA1k, pp. 679–80. An undated draft of this letter is located at StAHbg, Mennonitengemeinde, 8, 'Wy cunne niet nalaate . . . '. Dollinger, *Geschichte der Mennoniten*, p. 144, mentions that Mennonites had also been worshipping in Hamburg in 1711.

34 For a survey of the treatment of Calvinists, Catholics and Jews in Hamburg, see Whaley, *Religious Toleration and Social Change*.

35 See Ernst Baasch, *Holländische Wirtschaftsgeschichte* (Jena, 1927), pp. 300–302.

Simons and Walrave and Hilger Hilgers, Noë supplied the Count with velvet, lace trimmings, wine, fur and salmon, among other luxury goods, many of these acquired in Russia or southern Germany.[36] According to Berend Carl Roosen,[37] a nineteenth-century Mennonite pastor and amateur historian, the Count's privilege allowed Noë and his Mennonite associates to set up a special economic zone in one district of Altona. This district became known as the *Freiheit* (freedom). The Mennonites who lived here were required to pay a yearly tax of 1 Reichstaler per household, a condition similar to that expected of Mennonites on the noble landholding of Fresenburg during the late sixteenth century and early seventeenth century. This tax was higher than that paid by Lutheran residents of Altona. In exchange for the higher tax rate, Mennonites obtained the right to work and trade free from guild rules and restrictions. This was an enormous advantage, for guilds tried to protect the economic security of their members by excluding newcomers like the Mennonites. After 1601 Mennonites could establish their enterprises under favourable conditions near the major port of Hamburg.

The privilege of 1601 granted Noë and his Mennonite associates more favourable economic rights than they were allowed in Hamburg, but it still did not allow them to worship publicly. According to B.C. Roosen, it was only in 1622, when a new Schauenburg count came to power, that Mennonites were granted more religious rights.[38] The privileges granted in 1601 were renewed each time a new Schauenburg count came to office. This happened only twice (1622 and 1635). When the last male heir to the Schauenburg line died in 1640, Christian IV (1588–1648) of Denmark inherited sovereignty over Altona. He too renewed the Mennonites' privilege in 1641, as did each of his successors to the Danish throne. Several copies of the 1641 document have survived in the archives.[39] The document is especially noteworthy for the way it characterizes Mennonites. It indicates that Christian IV pledged to protect 'all members, relatives, merchants and artisans belonging to the so-called Mennonites of Altona'.[40] He also

36 Richard Ehrenberg, 'Gewerbefreiheit und Zunftzwang in Ottensen und Altona 1543 bis 1640', p. 25, independently paginated chapter in Richard Ehrenberg, *Altona unter Schauenburgischer Herrschaft* (Altona, 1893).

37 See B.C. Roosen, *Geschichte unseres Hauses* (n.p., 1905), pp. 25–6. To the best of my knowledge, a copy of the original privilege of 1601 has not survived.

38 Roosen, *Geschichte der Mennoniten-Gemeinde*, part 1, pp. 11 and 37.

39 To find copies of the 1641 privilege, see StAHbg/MG, 1; Landesarchiv Schleswig, Abt. 65.1/Nr. 1729a; and Landesarchiv Schleswig, Abt. 11/Nr. 237 (1641). Also see L.H. Schmid, *Versuch einer historischen Beschreibung der an der Elbe belegenen Stadt Altona* (Hamburg, 1975 [1747]), pp. 208–9; E.H. Wichmann, *Geschichte Altona's* (2nd edn, Altona, 1896), pp. 58–9; and Roosen, *Geschichte der Mennoniten-Gemeinde*, part 1, pp. 37–8.

40 Roosen, *Geschichte der Mennoniten-Gemeinde*, part 1, pp. 37–8: 'die sämtliche angehörige und Mittverwandte[,] Kauff- und Handwerksleute der genandten Ministen zu Altenah'.

gave them their old economic and religious privileges. From Christian IV's perspective, the Mennonites were as much an economic community as they were a religious one.

There were some important conditions to the privileges. Neither Christian IV nor any of his successors granted the Mennonites enduring rights. When Altona became a part of Christian IV's empire, the local Mennonites had to pledge their loyalty to him. The 1641 document records that their representatives expressed their wishes for his regime's 'joyful stability and longevity' (*glückseliges stabiliment und beharlichkeit*).[41] It was only following this pledge of fealty that Christian IV renewed the privileges originally granted by the Schauenburg counts. The privileges could also be revoked or renewed according to the will of each successive ruler. Given these conditions, it was important for the Mennonites to remain loyal to their Danish rulers. The post-Münsterite ethic of non-resistance did not prohibit this pragmatic kind of loyalty towards secular rulers. In fact, loyalty towards tolerant rulers had been as much a part of the Mennonite ethic and public life in the northern Netherlands and Holstein since the middle of the sixteenth century as had been the refusal to bear arms or swear solemn oaths (see Chs 4–6). In the 1570s in the Netherlands during the war with Spain, William of Orange had begun officially tolerating the Mennonite minority, which in turn helped to finance his war efforts. Furthermore, Mennonites in Holstein, including Menno Simons, had been depending on noble protection since at least the middle of the sixteenth century.

In addition to expectations of fealty, there were other conditions. The Mennonites were not allowed to seek Lutheran converts. The relevant passage reads: 'they [the Mennonites] are required to keep their distance from all others, cause no offence, and never dare try to convert members of our [Lutheran] religion to their fold . . . '.[42] These prohibitions were not serious limitations on Mennonite freedom. First, the requirement of acting peacefully and obediently corresponded closely to the early Mennonite goal of creating a community 'without spot or wrinkle'. Secondly, it was quite normal for groups like the Mennonites to keep to themselves. By the early seventeenth century, Mennonite communities throughout northern Europe were composed almost entirely of people who had been born into the community of faith. In Altona these families were of Netherlandish heritage and continued to speak Dutch as their mother tongue. In other words, the Mennonites were a separate ethno-confessional community

---

41 Ibid.

42 Ibid.: 'Hergegen aber müßen und sollen sie [die Mennoniten] sich gegen männiglich schiedlich verhalten, durchauß ein unärgerlich Leben führenn und niemandt so unserer Religion, an sich zu ziehen oder zu locken sich unterstehen . . . '.

whose members often kept to themselves without being told to do so.[43] Finally, Christian IV's expectations were reasonable because they were based on reciprocity: the Mennonites would refrain from proselytizing or otherwise disrupting the life of Altona's Lutheran majority, while Christian IV and his officials would protect and represent his Mennonite subjects. This kind of mutual forbearance was one important and successful way of dealing with confessional diversity in an age when religious difference was a common excuse for political violence and even war.

The Mennonites were not the only non-Lutherans to be granted privileges by Altona's Schauenburg counts and Danish monarchs. Calvinist, Catholic and Jewish minorities were treated similarly. Although no member of these officially tolerated minority groups could hold political office in Altona, they could conduct their religious rites and earn a living without fear of official persecution. Thus the Mennonites in Altona lived in a multi-confessional and economically dynamic environment. Altona was one of several such settlements established around the turn of the seventeenth century. In Schleswig and Holstein these included Glückstadt, Friedrichstadt and Wandsbek.[44] A combination of two factors made Altona special. First, it was situated on the boundary with one of northern Europe's most active ports, Hamburg. And secondly, it was also located on the shores of the Elbe River, which made it more attractive to merchants. By the middle of the seventeenth century, Mennonites who migrated from the Netherlands or the Holstein countryside could choose to be subjects of Altona's lord or to be citizens of Hamburg. Because they could move easily between jurisdictions, it was possible to live in Hamburg, where they enjoyed no rights of worship, and travel regularly to Altona to listen to sermons, take communion, and meet with other family and congregation members. Or they could live in Altona and travel to Hamburg to do business. The congregation, although headquartered in Altona, straddled political boundaries.[45]

In the seventeenth century, the population of Hamburg and Altona rose sharply. Hamburg's population had grown from 36,000 in 1600 to 75,000 in 1662, plateauing at 70,000 for the rest of the century after the plague year of 1664.[46] Altona grew just as quickly. In 1650 its population

---

43 There were significant exceptions to the trend of separateness. These exceptions became more and more pronounced with time. See Ch. 7 for details.

44 On Friedrichstadt, see Sem Sutter, 'Friedrichstadt an der Eider: An Early Experience in Religious Toleration, 1621–1727' (Ph.D. diss., University of Chicago, 1982).

45 This point is also emphasized in Schepansky, 'Mennoniten in Hamburg und Altona zur Zeit des Merkantilismus'.

46 See Hans-Dieter Loose, 'Das Zeitalter der Bürgerunruhen und der grossen europäischen Kriege 1618–1712', in Hans-Dieter Loose (ed.), *Hamburg: Geschichte der Stadt und ihrer Bewohner*, 2 vols (Hamburg, 1982), i, pp. 265–6.

was around 3,000 inhabitants, but by 1710 that number had increased to about 12,000.[47] While the dramatic increase was due in large measure to the influx of people from surrounding regions and more distant lands (mainly the Netherlands) who were seeking employment and refuge, Mennonite immigration played only a small role in the overall trend. By the middle of the seventeenth century (around 1655 or 1656) the Flemish congregation included approximately 200 baptized members;[48] by 1676 the number had risen to about 250.[49]

Favourable economic and political conditions in Hamburg and Altona, as well as persecution in the Netherlands, provide only a partial explanation for the growth of the Mennonite community. An added reason was that conditions deteriorated on the landholding of Fresenburg, the main site of Mennonite life in the Holstein countryside. Although Hamburg was never attacked during the Thirty Years War (1618–48), several of the war's campaigns were fought in the regions around Hamburg and Altona. In 1627 armies destroyed Fresenburg.[50] The Mennonites there were forced to flee to places like Altona. They were refugees at least twice over, once from the Netherlands and another time from the territory of the Ahlefeldt family. After the Thirty Years War there were still a few scattered families in the Holstein countryside. Nonetheless, the focus of Mennonite life had shifted to the urban centres of Hamburg and Altona, as well as Glückstadt and Friedrichstadt. In an otherwise hostile world, these towns and cities were relatively safe havens in which strangers could begin to establish themselves religiously and economically.

The transfer of economic practices from the Netherlands

Mennonite economic activity in Hamburg and Altona was shaped strongly by connections throughout the religious diaspora, especially in the Low

47 Franklin Kopitzsch, 'Altona – ein Zentrum der Aufklärung am Rande des dänischen Gesamtstaats', in Klaus Bohnen and Sven Aage Jørgensen (eds), *Der dänische Gesamtstaat* (Tübingen, 1992), p. 93.

48 This number is based on a count of the names at the beginning of the congregational membership book: StAHbg/MG, 147, vol. 1, pp. 2–37. In the early 1650s, a breakaway faction known as the Dompelaars (see Ch. 2) took the original membership book with them. Unlike all later sections of the membership book, in which men and women are recorded on the same page, the first pages of the book are divided by sex: pages 2 to 18 only men, and pages 19 to 37 only women. All indications suggest that around 1655 or 1656 (the dates of the first recorded deaths and baptisms), leaders began a new list of church members to replace the missing one.

49 Ibid., p. 87: 'om deese tyt [May 1676] heeft de gemeente geweest circa 250 ledematen'.

50 Documents that would have given us a clearer idea of early Anabaptist life in Holstein were also destroyed. See Roosen, *Unschuld und Gegen-Bericht*, pp. 97–104.

Countries. The textile industry provides several good examples. Flanders and Brabant had been major centres of fifteenth- and sixteenth-century textile manufacturing and distribution,[51] and Altona's early administrators were anxious to attract industrialists and workers from those regions to their territory with the hope that immigrants would contribute to the economic prosperity of the territory. In 1637 Altona's Schauenburg Count granted the Mennonite Peter de Voss special privileges to operate his textile manufacturing business in Altona free from existing guild obligations on the condition that de Voss encourage other industrialists in his trade and from his home region in the Low Countries to settle in Altona. At the same time as this privilege was established, the Count also issued a related decree in which the acceptance of foreign business procedures was explicitly acknowledged: 'just as such statutes [regulating the new textile industries] have been maintained in Brabant, the Netherlands and other areas, so shall these be observed and maintained in this our County'.[52] Although Altona's governing administrators did not want to allow the uncontrolled influx of foreign workers and the demise of the guild system,[53] they were nonetheless willing to accept many of the rules of business according to which their Netherlandish guest-workers operated. Many leading Mennonite entrepreneurs in the textile industry took advantage of favourable regulations like the privileges of 1601 or 1637. Among these men were leather tanners, manufacturers of finer products like silks and socks, and blue-dyers.[54]

In the early modern period, Mennonites in Hamburg and Altona earned a living by practising a variety of trades and professions. Because of the scarcity of reliable records,[55] it is difficult to speculate about the exact numbers or even the relative proportions of Mennonites who were craftsmen as opposed to merchants and industrialists. It is especially difficult to find reliable information about the economic lives of poorer

---

51 See Myron P. Gutmann, *Toward the Modern Economy: Early Industry in Europe 1500–1800* (Philadelphia, 1988), pp. 15–47.

52 Cited from Ehrenberg, 'Gewerbefreiheit und Zunftzwang', p. 38: '". . . daß gleich wie es in Braband, Niederland und anderen Orten solcher Statuten halber gehalten wird, es auch in dieser unserer Graffschaft observieret und gehalten werden soll."'

53 Ibid., p. 40.

54 There are two surviving examples from the seventeenth century of Mennonite businessmen's balance books. The first, probably belonging to Hans Simons, dates from the 1620s (StAHbg/MG, 225), and the second, belonging to Jan Harmens, dates from the late seventeenth century (StAHbg/MG, 229).

55 Mennonite leaders kept no systematic or detailed notes about the economic activities of congregational members. Because the Altona archives (now kept in Hamburg's Staatsarchiv) were being reorganized in the years when I was doing my research, I was not able to make thorough use of Danish tax records or other documents that might have helped to provide more details.

and less powerful men and women. In the Flemish congregation's membership book, the first surviving volume of which was begun in the 1650s, there are, however, occasional references to the livelihoods of some of the more transient congregational members. For the last fifty years of the seventeenth century there are relevant records for sixteen individuals. The majority (seven) of these were sailors, while four were shoemakers, two were textile workers, one was a servant, another was a knife maker and yet another was a tailor.[56] From a variety of other scattered sources, we know that local Mennonites also worked as bakers, brewers, doctors, millers, smiths and sugar refiners.[57]

Sea-borne shipping and other related activities, so far mentioned only in passing, deserve special attention. Many men worked as sailors, while a few were even ships' captains. However, by far the wealthiest, most influential and easiest to follow in sources were the men who worked as brokers, insurance agents, merchants and shipowners.[58] Many shipowners transported cargoes across Europe. Over the course of several generations, a few Mennonite families established the very largest of Hamburg's early modern shipping firms. In 1798, for example, there were 276 sea-going merchant ships registered to owners in Hamburg. Of these, fifty (or 18%) were owned by three Mennonite firms: Berend Roosen Erben, Salomon Roosen Sal. Sohn and Hinrich Theunis de Jager. The percentage of shipping activity in the hands of Mennonite firms is staggering, especially when we remember how tiny the Mennonite population of Hamburg was (1% or less). In that same year (1798) the firm Berend Roosen Erben alone owned twenty-five large seagoing vessels.[59] At no point in the eighteenth century did any single Hamburg firm own more.

---

56 StAHbg/MG, 147, vol. 1, pp. 49, 54, 57, 58, 60, 73, 81, 84, 89, 98, 104, 108, 110, 119, 121 and 136–7.

57 For further notes on Mennonite economic activity, see Dollinger, *Geschichte der Mennoniten*, pp. 156–8.

58 Rich and as of yet largely unexplored sources for Mennonite economic activity are records from Imperial Cameral Court cases. See especially StAHbg, Reichskammergericht, E15, F11, J2, J3, J18 and M28, all of which involved Abraham Stockman, his associates and heirs (among them the early seventeenth-century preacher Hinrich Sicks); B1b and V9, which involved members of the de Vlieger family; S37, in which François Noë had a small role; S84, which included a statement by Peter Goverts's widow; S172, in which the eighteenth-century businessman Berend Roosen was involved. In the eighteenth century probably the most lively case surrounding a Mennonite was the dispute over Ernst Pieters Goverts's estate. See StAHbg, Reichskammergericht, R25; StAHbg, Familienarchive, Goverts, 44; and Landesarchiv Schleswig, Reichskammergericht, 72. Also see R38 for a further Imperial Cameral Court case of interest. Finally, see Ch. 6 for a detailed analysis on yet another Imperial Cameral Court trial involving a Mennonite.

59 The statistics are taken from Walter Kresse, *Materialien zur Entwicklungsgeschichte der Hamburger Handelsflotte 1765–1823* (Hamburg, 1966). For more on Berend Roosen, see Erich von Lehe, *Schipp op Scharhörn: Strandung eines hamburgischen Schiffes im Jahre 1755* (n.p., 1967).

The foundations for the merchant empires of the eighteenth century were laid in the seventeenth century. Involvement in the lucrative whale fishery was a major path to economic prominence for a significant number of Mennonite families. While Mennonites were very active and important in the history of whaling based out of Hamburg, their early role has been exaggerated a little by historians. A yearly list of whaling departures from the city's port exists from 1669 until the middle of the nineteenth century, when the industry disappeared. In his history of the industry in Germany, the early twentieth-century historian Ludwig Brinner claimed that the majority (22 of 37) of whaling departures from Hamburg in 1669 were organized by Mennonite shipowners.[60] This is almost certainly incorrect. The number of Mennonites active that year as ship directors should be more accurately placed at thirteen, or about one-third of all whaling ships.[61] While not a majority, this was nonetheless a significant minority. Only in 1689 did Mennonites first organize more than half of Hamburg's whaling fleet, which they continued to dominate through most of the 1690s, led then by the well-established de Vlieger family. From 1669 until the beginning of the 1690s, Carel de Vlieger Senior was the single most active of all ship organizers, whether Mennonite or not. He sent out sometimes as many as nine ships in a whaling season. Other local Mennonites who sent whaling ships out from Hamburg's port during the later seventeenth century belonged to the Beets, Goverts, de Jager, Kipping, Koen, Kramer, van Laar, Münster, Pender, Peters, de Ruyscher, Schoemacher, van der Smissen and Stockman families. Members of the Flemish Mennonite congregation continued to work in the whaling industry throughout the eighteenth century. Again, the Mennonites' role as whalers is especially significant when we remember that a group that formed less than 1 per cent of Hamburg's population had a major stake in somewhere between a third and a half of a major profitable industry in the seventeenth century.

There are several explanations for the importance of Mennonites in Hamburg's merchant shipping and whaling fleets. Generally, their marginal social position in Lutheran society played a role in their growing wealth. Mennonites were almost never permitted to hold political offices in the early modern period, unless they chose to convert to Lutheranism. However, there were fewer barriers to their full participation in economic life in Altona, where they had official economic privileges, and Hamburg, where they had none. Isolated from political life, Mennonites had little

---

60 Ludwig Brinner, *Die deutsche Grönlandfahrt* (Berlin, 1913), p. 150. Brinner mistakenly counted the Baker family as Mennonites; see Ch. 5 for a discussion of this issue.

61 These include C. de Vlieger and H. Penner (Pender) (7 ships), P.J. Schomaker (3), L. Koen and company (2) and P. Goverts (1). The names and numbers of ships are based on Wanda Oesau, *Hamburgs Grönlandfahrt auf Walfischfang und Robbenschlag vom 17.-19. Jahrhundert* (Glückstadt and Hamburg, [1955]), p. 281.

choice, therefore, but to focus their energies on their families, their church life and their places of work. In the process, they achieved a significance in the economy of early modern Hamburg and Altona which was disproportionately high compared with their small numbers. Their specific role in the whaling industry was owed to experience gained in long-distance sea-borne trade. Mennonite captains, crew members and ship directors were quite familiar with operations in the northern waters.[62] They had been involved in trade with Archangel since the first half of the seventeenth century, and whalers and Archangel traders sailed along the same route. Furthermore, their connections with the Netherlands were important. Whaling was well established in the Netherlands in the earlier part of the seventeenth century, and the pioneer of whaling in Hamburg was a Dutchman (although probably not a Mennonite), Johann Been, in the 1640s. Many Mennonites had close familial and business ties with the Netherlands, so, compared with the native Lutheran residents of Hamburg, they would have had relatively easy access to the necessary training. Mennonite newcomers to the business thus had an advantage getting started, for they could acquire the necessary know-how from relatives and friends they met at home, in the church or through contacts in the larger Dutch-speaking business community.

An example of the huge financial benefits that whaling could bring and the way these in turn shaped the collective lives of Mennonites is provided by the record whaling seasons of the early 1670s. The Dutch were the most active of northern Europe's so-called Greenland fishers in the seventeenth century. However, war between England and Holland in the years 1672–4 prevented their safe passage to the rich fishing grounds near the Spitsbergen Islands in the Arctic Ocean. During this period few Dutch ships went to sea, and, therefore, German whalers faced little competition. Hamburg's whalers reaped the rich rewards. Thus, the early and mid-1670s, when the Mennonite congregation's new church was being built in Altona, was probably the single most successful period on record for Hamburg's whalers. Mennonite families who profited from these record catches donated a small but significant portion of their earnings towards the construction of the new church.[63]

---

62 This fishery was erroneously associated in the popular imagination with Greenland and is often referred to as the Greenland fishery, but in the second half of the seventeenth century was concentrated around the open waters off the Spitsbergen Islands in the Arctic Ocean.

63 On the size of the catches in this period, see Wanda Oesau, *Schleswig-Holsteins Grönlandfahrt auf Walfischfang und Robbenschlag vom 17. bis 19. Jahrhundert* (Glückstadt, 1937), p. 35; and Joachim Münzing, *Jagd auf den Wal: Schleswig-Holsteins und Hamburgs Grönlandfahrt* (Heide, 1978), pp. 29–30. For records of the cost of church construction, see StAHbg/MG, 86, vol. 1, 'sloet Reeckening wat het nieuwe preeckhuys te bouwen gekost

The transfer of religious practices from the Netherlands

The completion of a new church building in Altona was an important benchmark in the institutional history of the Flemish congregation. On 14 March 1675 Ocke Pieters preached the first sermon in the new building on the site of the old one on Altona's street called Grosse Freiheit. This building was the congregation's meeting place until it was burned down in the Great Fire of Altona in 1713.[64] Up until 1675 the congregation had met in a simple meeting house, which was becoming too small for the growing group. Another indication of the congregation's growth is the establishment in 1678 of a Mennonite cemetery in Altona. In the first part of the seventeenth century, all Mennonites had buried their dead in Lutheran or Calvinist cemeteries in and around Hamburg and Altona. The new church and cemetery were symbols of the growing wealth, confidence and autonomy of a group that had made northern Germany its home already for several generations.

Even after the congregation began establishing itself more securely in Hamburg and Altona, flux and migration remained characteristics of the Mennonite population. At any one time in the later seventeenth century there seems to have been around 250 adult members registered in the congregation (see above), but over a forty- to fifty-year period during the last half of the seventeenth century, there were about 1,000 men and women who kept at least a semi-official connection with the Flemish congregation and were therefore entered in its membership book.[65] Almost 200 of these individuals were certainly not born in Altona or Hamburg.[66] A common point of origin for these individuals was the Netherlands, but many others came from the northern European Mennonite diaspora, which stretched from East Frisia (Emden, for example) to the eastern shores of the Baltic Sea (Danzig/Gdańsk was a major Mennonite centre there). A small number of Anabaptist refugees even arrived from the Palatinate in 1671 and the

---

heeft 1674'. Those who contributed the funds necessary to build the church included Hans Hermans; Hans, Geeritt and Coert Roosen; Herman, Paul, Elisabeth and Hans Goverts; Dina and Hendrik Stockmann; Lucas Koenen; Hendrik de Jaeger; Carel and Salomon de Vlieger; and Anthony Jacobs. These men and women were among the most well-to-do members of the congregation. Poems commemorating the completion of the new church are found at StAHbg/MG, 126.

64 The church was rebuilt only a few short years after it was destroyed by fire, and this new building served as the congregation's meeting house until the early twentieth century. For a map of eighteenth-century Altona which shows the church, see Schroeder and Huebert, *Mennonite Historical Atlas*, p. 10.

65 StAHbg/MG, 147, vol. 1.

66 See Roosen, *Geschichte der Mennoniten-Gemeinde*, part 1, pp. 59–60. People born to members in Hamburg and Altona often left for other communities for professional, religious or familial reasons. These migrations have not been quantified.

1690s. Preachers sometimes kept notes in the congregation's membership book about the fate of some of the people who participated in the congregation's life. Thus, we know that some Mennonites based in Hamburg or Altona died as far away as France,[67] London,[68] the Iberian Peninsula,[69] and even the Dutch East Indies,[70] while ten members moved to Pennsylvania in 1700.[71] Although Mennonite mobility was great in the seventeenth century, the Flemish congregation in Altona, like all Anabaptist congregations, was interested in regulating this movement to insure that only people baptized as adults were among its members. It did this by requesting a transfer document (*aenwys* or *attestie*) from Mennonites new to the congregation who were already members of another congregation.

As the number of people attending the Flemish congregation increased, the operations of congregational government became more regular. Officially membership was voluntary, but it was largely a ritualized voluntarism. Mennonite parents usually expected their children to be baptized when they were in their teens or early twenties. All baptized men not subject to church discipline had the right at special gatherings to approve new preachers and to vote on contentious issues presented to them by the congregation's governing board, which until the nineteenth century was usually called the congregational council (*collegie*). The members of the congregational council included all deacons and preachers. Until the twentieth century, deacons were almost always men. The only exceptions were Rinsken Quins[72] (d. 1626) and Maeyken Goverts[73] (d. 1672), who served as deaconesses in an era when the institutional and patriarchal structures of congregational life had not yet been firmly entrenched. Deacons were responsible for the care of the poor, widowed and orphaned. The men who held this honorary office were almost invariably well-to-do businessmen.[74] In the seventeenth century, deacons remained in office until they died, resigned or, only very occasionally, were expelled for immoral behaviour. In the seventeenth century, a preacher or teacher (*dienaar im woort*) also served for life. In the seventeenth-century Netherlands, this office was sometimes filled by trained professionals. However, in Hamburg and Altona, at least until the

67 StAHbg/MG, 147, vol. 1, p. 127.

68 Ibid., pp. 111, 127 and 128.

69 Ibid., p. 73.

70 Ibid., pp. 117, 121 and 143.

71 Ibid., pp. 92, 93, 100, 101, 113, 122, 130, 151, 161. Also see Roosen, *Geschichte der Mennoniten-Gemeinde*, part 1, p. 63.

72 [Geeritt Roosen], 'Geeritt Roosen und seine Geschichte der Kriegsereignisse seiner Zeit', p. 369.

73 StAHbg/MG, 147, vol. 1, p. 19. For more background, see Snyder, *Anabaptist History and Theology*, ch. 18, 'Equality in the Community of Saints'.

74 For a list of deacons in the later seventeenth century, see App. 2.

early eighteenth century, it was an office usually occupied by laymen like the merchant Geeritt Roosen (1612–1711), the skilled craftsman Willem Wynantz (1630–58), or the doctor Warner Jansen Colombier (d. 1664).[75] These lay preachers had to be ordained if they were to lead marriage ceremonies or administer the sacraments of communion and baptism. Once ordained they were called elders (*oudsten*). By the late seventeenth century there were usually several preachers serving the congregation at any one time.

Travel and migration were also important for the Flemish congregation's ecclesiastical life in the last half of the seventeenth century. Preachers from Altona were involved in pastoral duties in other Mennonite congregations. Geeritt Roosen was the most active in this regard, making trips to the Netherlands in 1660, 1665, 1670 and 1675 and once going to visit Mennonite settlements around Danzig (Gdańsk) in 1676.[76] Preachers used these trips to maintain a sense of shared religious and cultural identity, while also substituting for colleagues in the congregations they visited. In addition to sending its preachers to help other Mennonite congregations, the Altona-based congregation itself relied on preachers from other Mennonite communities for temporary as well as permanent service. Nineteen of the twenty-four preachers who served the Hamburg–Altona congregation on a full-time basis in the seventeenth century came from the Netherlands, Prussia, Lübeck or Friedrichstadt. Furthermore, between 1660 and the beginning of the eighteenth century, thirty-three visiting preachers from the Netherlands and Friedrichstadt spent time in Altona.[77] These visiting elders were usually the ones who ordained new elders by laying hands on the candidate, normally a man who had already had several years of preaching experience.

So far, almost all of what has been written above concerns the Flemish congregation, which was only one of several Mennonite groups in seventeenth-century Hamburg and Altona. Although the Flemish congregation was by far the largest and the one from which almost all surviving documentary evidence originated, it was not the only group of Mennonites in Hamburg and Altona. One of the consequences of Anabaptist migration was that factional differences were transferred from the Netherlands to northern Germany. Until the latter part of the seventeenth century, there was, in addition to the main Flemish congregation, another small Flemish group in Hamburg and Altona known as 'House Buyers' (*Huiskooper*). Also known as Thomas Bintgen People,

---

[75] For a list of preachers in the later seventeenth century, see App. 1.

[76] See StAHbg/MG, 246b, a single sheet outlining Geeritt Roosen's travels; and ibid., Geeritt Roosen's preaching diary.

[77] StAHbg/MG, 261c, 'leeraaren van doopsgesinde of Mennonitische gemeenten, die als buitenleeraaren hier geweest zyn en gedient hebben'.

this group, which was led by Jan de Buyser,[78] remained separate from its larger Flemish neighbour congregation. Furthermore, a small group of Old Frisians (also known as Pieter Jansz Twisck People) held meetings in and around Altona in the mid-seventeenth century under the leadership of Jan de Marné. Little is known about these House Buyer and Old Frisian congregations, but both were probably socially and religiously more conservative than their neighbours in the larger Flemish congregation. By the end of the seventeenth century the small congregations had disappeared. Their leaders died and many of the remaining members, hardly a large number of people, joined the Flemish congregation. Not all groups, not even the new congregation of Dompelaars (see Ch. 2), were able to adapt as effectively as the Flemish to new circumstances. Of local Mennonite factions, the Flemish benefited the most from the confessional migrations begun in the sixteenth century.

Conclusion

Anabaptist life was shaped decisively by the experience of persecution, exile and refuge. By the beginning of the seventeenth century the intensity of persecution and exile had diminished, but intolerance and migration remained crucial features shaping Mennonite life in and around Hamburg. Mennonites were not only a group of religious nonconformists; they were also an ethnic minority in Lutheran northern Germany. Religious traditions, ecclesiastical exchanges, collective memories of persecution, familial ties, language and international business activity all helped to preserve the Netherlandish character of the Flemish congregation in Hamburg and Altona – the inheritor-congregation of Menno Simons's congregation at Fresenburg in Holstein – throughout the early modern period.

---

[78] De Buyser was the author of several texts. See the *Mennonite Bibliography, 1631–1961*, 2 vols (Scottdale, Pa. and Kitchener, Ont., 1977) for details.

CHAPTER TWO

The Short-lived Ceremonialism of the Dompelaars

In 1648 a major schism began in the Flemish Mennonite congregation in Altona. A new group emerged. The Dompelaars, as the new group became known popularly (in Dutch *dompelen* means to immerse or dunk), quickly developed a character very different from the congregation they left. Today the history of the Dompelaars has been largely forgotten. Unlike the Flemish, whose successor congregation still meets in Hamburg, the Dompelaars disappeared within a century of the schism. Before it disappeared, this new group underwent an important transformation. While its first generation of leaders placed a premium on the proper celebration of the sacraments, the last Dompelaars were spiritualist Protestants who had little concern for the proper form of sacramental ceremonies.

The origins and early years of the schism

It is difficult to reconstruct in any great detail how the schism began. What we can determine from later records indicates that in 1648 seventeen[1] members of the Altona-based Flemish congregation made known their conviction that adult baptism should be a baptism by immersion. This was a departure from the common method of baptism in the congregation, which was by sprinkling. Two further issues were involved. The supporters of immersion also argued that communion should be celebrated (1) in the evening with unleavened bread, (2) after the washing of feet.

To ease the difficult task of accounting for the origins of the schism, one possibility would be simply to repeat the speculations of Altona's late eighteenth-century church historian Johann Adrian Bolten.[2] His proposals included: English Baptist influence brought to Altona via Colchester; influences from Poland and Prussia, presumably from Socinians; influences from Dutch Collegiants; and ideas taken from Jacob Mehrning's *Heilige Tauff-Historia* (History of Holy Baptism), a book published shortly before

1 The number of participants is based on a later report by Jodocus Edzardi Glanäus, *Geistliches Bad-Tuch den Newen Widertäufferschen Täuchern* (Hamburg, 1651), p. 106.

2 J.A. Bolten, *Historische Kirchen-Nachrichten von der Stadt Altona*, 2 vols (Altona, 1790–91), i, pp. 311–12.

the controversy began.[3] Baptists, Socinians and Collegiants did practise adult baptism by immersion, and there were occasional contacts between these groups and some groups of Mennonites, particularly in the Netherlands. Collegiants, for example, traced their origins to a schism within the Dutch Calvinist community in the early seventeenth century. Unlike most Calvinists, they placed little value on doctrines like predestination, preferring instead to emphasize the importance of a Christian lifestyle. The name Collegiant referred to the group's basic institution. Their *collegen* (lectures) were a freer form of religious service in which all members were encouraged to participate instead of deferring to the authority of a preacher. Because few requirements besides voluntary baptism were placed on members, Collegiant ranks even included Protestants from non-Calvinist churches. In 1646, for example, officials in Amsterdam had conducted an investigation of the recently organized local Collegiant group and had concluded that its nearly one hundred members constituted a 'gathering of Mennonites' (*verzameling van Mennisten*).[4] Although it is impossible to confirm Jacob Mehrning's religious affiliation, he too was an advocate of adult baptism by immersion, which he considered the only scriptural form of the sacrament. In his long history of baptism, he included the Mennonites among those Christians who had continued to practise Christ's baptismal ordinance faithfully, even though it brought them suffering at the hands of others.

Despite these superficial similarities, none of Bolten's suggestions is especially convincing. The most credible concerns Jacob Mehrning. The original source of the suggestion that his work inspired immersionist ideas among Altona's Mennonites was the Lutheran polemicist Jodocus Edzardi Glanäus,[5] whom Mehrning had attacked in his *Tauff-Historia*. By the 1660s Dompelaar publicists were in fact citing Mehrning's work, but there is no evidence that the *Tauff-Historia* was read by Mennonites in Altona before then, or that they had any personal contact with Mehrning. We know very little about Mehrning, except that he claimed to be from Holstein. It is unlikely that he was a Mennonite, for he referred to them

3 Jacob Mehrning, *S. Baptismi Historia: Das ist/ Heilige Tauff-Historia* (Dortmund, 1646–7).

4 Quoted from H.W. Meihuizen, *Galenus Abrahamsz 1622–1706: Strijder voor een onbeperkte verdraagzaamheid en verdediger van het Doperse Spiritualisme* (Haarlem, 1954), p. 47. For general background on the Collegiants, see J.C. van Slee, *De Rijnsburger Collegianten* (Utrecht, 1980 [1895]); and three recent works by Andrew Fix: 'Mennonites and Rationalism in the Seventeenth Century', in Alastair Hamilton, Sjouke Voolstra and Piet Visser (eds), *From Martyr to Muppy (Mennonite Urban Professionals)* (Amsterdam, 1994), pp. 159–74; *Prophecy and Reason: The Dutch Collegiants in the Early Enlightenment* (Princeton, 1991); and 'Mennonites and Collegiants in Holland, 1630–1700', *Mennonite Quarterly Review*, 64 (1990), pp. 160–77.

5 Glanäus, *Geistliches Bad-Tuch*.

only as like-minded Christians, not coreligionists. However, because of a total lack of evidence that might raise Bolten's suggestions above the level of mere speculation, the most we can say is that there were a number of groups active in northern Europe around the time of the schism whose members practised immersionist adult baptism.

The few relevant Mennonite primary sources that do survive from the period before the schism indicate that the issues at stake in 1648 had been festering for some time. The evidence of rising tensions about baptism are letters from the 1620s and 1630s from Hamburg that survive in archives in Amsterdam. They were the local contribution to interregional discussions aimed at uniting fractious Anabaptist groups (see Ch. 3). The oldest of the surviving letters, which is unsigned, dates from 1628.[6] It was probably a response to an earlier Dutch request for local German opinions about issues of faith, which the Dutch hoped to use in their search for a consensus among Mennonites. The representatives of the northern German congregation emphasized four points, which they considered cornerstones of their faith: secular rulers were like fathers who corrected the wrongs of disobedient sons; husbands were lords over their wives; foot-washing was a sign of Christian humility; and adult baptism should be practised by sprinkling rather than immersion. The authors' views on baptism are particularly noteworthy. According to the authors, the water of baptism did not wash a sinner of his or her sins. That was what Christ's blood had accomplished.[7] Baptism was a sign that the sinner accepted God, and, since 'John the Baptist had baptized not in but with water',[8] sprinkling was the appropriate method to indicate acceptance of faith in Christ.

Concern about this issue continued in the following years. In a further series of letters from 1631 and 1632, congregational leaders from Altona asked colleagues in Amsterdam for advice on a number of questions. These included how to respond to a controversy about baptism in Friedrichstadt involving a faction called the Klas Wolters People, about which little is known.[9] The men who signed these documents included the preachers Hinrich Sicks and Jan Barchman, as well as the deacons Hans Amoury and Paul Roosen. Unlike the unsigned letter of 1628, the letters from 1631 and 1632 do not give substantial evidence about the beliefs of their

---

6 Universiteitsbibliotheek Amsterdam, Handschriften, XXVII, 567.

7 This enunciation of the doctrine of satisfaction is also found in the *Olijftaxcken* (see the section in it on holy baptism).

8 Universiteitsbibliotheek Amsterdam, Handschriften, XXVII, 567, fol. 3^{v}: 'dat Johannes niet int mar mit water gedoopt heeft . . .'.

9 The letters are found at Universiteitsbibliotheek Amsterdam, Handschriften, XXVII, 578 (28 June 1631); and Gemeentearchief Amsterdam, PA 1120, 1023 (three letters dated 1 February 1631, 1632 and 1 February 1632). The letter which concerns baptismal innovations is the last of these.

authors. For this we need to rely on later sources. The best example concerns the preacher Jan Barchman. In 1634 Uco Walles led a faction of Flemish Mennonites who parted company with fellow congregational members in the northern Netherlands. Among the practices of the Ucowallists was baptism by immersion and foot-washing before communion. Jan Barchman published a text against the immersionist faction of Ucowallists in 1639.[10] If any precedents are necessary to account for the rise of the immersionist faction in Altona, an Ucowallist source is perhaps more likely than the suggestions made by Bolten. Nonetheless, as of yet, evidence of a direct connection between Dutch Ucowallists and the new faction in Altona has not been found. Be this as it may, what can be concluded from the letters written before the schism is that long before 1648 Mennonite leaders were articulating theological views which ruled out baptism by immersion. They were also aware of opposition.

It is particularly difficult to say much of substance about the nature of this opposition before 1648, or about the earliest phases of the schism in 1648 and 1649. One of the few valuable observations from contemporaries involved directly in the affair was made by Geeritt Roosen in the 1650s. Roosen stated that the preachers Jan Borchers and Jacob Beerens were the immediate source of the schismatic ideas about baptism.[11] Borchers and Beerens remain mysterious figures. By contrast, we know a great deal about Geeritt Roosen, who was the most prolific record-keeper among Mennonites in Hamburg and Altona during the last half of the seventeenth century. Roosen was the son-in-law of Hans Amoury and the son of Paul Roosen, the two Flemish deacons who had been involved in correspondence with Dutch colleagues about doctrinal matters in the 1630s. He also became a deacon in the Flemish congregation in 1649, filling a position left empty when his father died. The Roosen family owned the house in Altona on the street Große Freiheit where Flemish congregants met regularly to worship. Access to that property quickly became an issue between supporters and opponents of immersionist adult baptism. February 1649 marked an escalation of differences, for it was then that Paul Roosen's heirs, including Geeritt Roosen, asserted their rights as owners to exclude unwanted groups from the property.[12] This move amounted to the forced expulsion of the immersionists from the congregation.

There were some attempts to repair the division.[13] The earliest of these was organized by Dutch Mennonites. In 1649 a group of congregational

---

10 I[ohann] B[archmann], *Drye brieven tegen de gene die den vrede verstooren* (Amsterdam, 1639). I have not had an opportunity to examine this text.

11 See Roosen's notes in the opening, unnumbered pages of StAHbg/MG, 147, vol. 1.

12 Ibid., p. 1.

13 Bolten, *Historische Kirchen-Nachrichten*, i, p. 313, claimed that early negotiations between the two Mennonite factions were so tense that police forces ('ein militairisches

representatives from the Netherlands arrived in Altona. The group consisted of important leaders like Tobias Govertsz van den Wyngaard and Tielemann Tielen from Amsterdam, Isaac Jansz Snep from Haarlem and Pieter Jansz Moyer from Leiden. All four were representatives at the Haarlem Synod. The Synod had been arranged in 1649 by Dutch Mennonites who supported the strategy of using confessions of faith to reunite the divided Anabaptist fold (see Ch. 3). During the Synod's last session,[14] delegates addressed the problems surrounding baptism in Hamburg and Altona. They stated their conviction that baptism was important for what it symbolized and its validity did not depend on the amount of water used to administer it. They also decided to organize a visitation of the Altona congregation. Little is known about the events or discussions in which the visiting Dutch preachers were involved upon their arrival in Altona and Hamburg. They had probably hoped for a resolution similar to that was reached between Flemish, Frisian, and High German factions in 1639 in Amsterdam. However, their mediating efforts failed, which is not surprising given the at least implicitly anti-immersionist position of the delegates at the Haarlem Synod.

In the years following the failed mediation attempt, the immersionist faction received attention from Jodocus Edzardi Glanäus, a Lutheran clergymen in Hamburg. Long before the immersionist schism, Glanäus was already an experienced anti-Mennonite propagandist. In 1636 he had published *Nothwehr für die Kindertauffe* (Defence of Child Baptism), in which he repeated the charges of the sixteenth-century Lutheran historian Johann Sleidan that Mennonites were the spiritual children of Thomas Müntzer and the Anabaptist regime of Münster.[15] In 1651 Glanäus preached two sermons in his parish of St Michaelis against the immersionists. He published them the same year in a little book entitled *Geistliches Bad-Tuch den Newen Widertäufferschen Täuchern* (Spiritual Towel for the New Anabaptist Dippers). According to Glanäus, the new sect made two mistakes: it treated the unimportant matters of external ceremonies far too seriously and neglected the essentials of faith and public order.[16] Glanäus wrote that he did not care a great deal about the practices of this small, new sect of Anabaptists, but he felt compelled to speak and

---

Friedestiften') had to be brought in to keep the two sides apart. He gives no source for this statement, and I have been unable to confirm it. If the information is reliable, it is not possible to say with certainty when the 'peacekeeping' effort was made.

14 *Handelinge/ Der Ver-eenigde Vlaemse, en Duytse Doops-gesinde Gemeynten* (Vlissingen, 1666), minutes from 29 June 1649.

15 Jodocus Edzardi Glanäus, *Nothwehr für die Kindertaufe welche die Wiedertauffer den Kindern wehren* (Hamburg, 1636 and 1637). Also see Johann Müller, *Anabaptismus. Das ist: Wiedertauffer Irrthumb* (Hamburg, 1645).

16 Glanäus, *Geistliches Bad-Tuch*, pp. 3–5.

write against them because they were offending public decency by their open displays of fanaticism during river-side baptisms. He even claimed that members of the new group were actively seeking converts from among their Lutheran, Calvinist and Catholic neighbours.[17] This aggressiveness was evidence of the 'Münsterite spirit', and its propagators would not rest until they had achieved their goals of disrupting Christian life; it was also evidence of the spirit of 'the Roman Antichrist', who burdened others' consciences with concern for unimportant ceremonies.[18] Glanäus also included a defence of the Lutheran practice of baptism by sprinkling or dousing. According to the biblical record, John the Baptist had not immersed Christ in the Jordan but had poured water over him. Even if members of the early church baptized by immersion, this was not reason enough for contemporary Christians to abandon their time-tested customs of child baptism by sprinkling. After all, the Greek word for baptism had a range of meanings, including immersion, washing, dousing and sprinkling.[19] The immersionists were creating controversy where none was necessary.

Five years later, in 1656, rumours of immersionist-incited disorder were still circulating in the region. In Altona, a Danish official was ordered to investigate reports that the new group was holding suspicious evening meetings and acting contrary to God's word. The official associated these traits with the heretical sect of the Davidjorists, referring to the reputed followers of the early sixteenth-century spiritualist Anabaptist. By contrast, he found nothing ominous about the immersionists. They lived peacefully, holding communion twice a year and practising their baptisms away from public view. What is more, among their ranks were several families of manufacturers (which was important given the Danish crown's interest in making Altona into an economic strong point). The official assured the king that there was no reason to worry about separatist Mennonites, whom he also called *Immergenten* (immersionists).[20] The Danish government official's evaluation of the immersionists was diametrically opposed to that of Hamburg's clergyman.

1656 is an important year in the history of the schism also for other reasons. In a document dated 11 January of that year and recorded on the first page of the church's membership book, the Roosen family restated its intention of controlling the church building on the street Große Freiheit.[21]

---

17 Ibid., p. 106.

18 Ibid., p. 107.

19 Ibid., pp. 14–17.

20 Landesarchiv Schleswig, Abt. 65.1/Nr. 1643, letter dated 10 September 1656.

21 StAHbg/MG, 147, vol. 1, p. 1. A High German transcription of this document is found in Roosen, *Geschichte der Mennoniten-Gemeinde*, part 1, pp. 41–2. For a map of Roosen family landholdings in Altona in the seventeenth and eighteenth centuries, see G. Arthur Roosen, 'Die Familie Roosen und ihre Anverwandten' (Caracas, 1952), p. 19.

Sometime before 1656 the immersionists had taken the congregation's membership book with them. Geeritt Roosen began a new one, probably around 1656. The first thirty-seven pages of the book have the character of a mass census of members, about 200 in total, with baptized males listed first, followed by the women.[22] The first deaths recorded in the book date from 1655 and 1656. By this time the schism between the immersionists and their former church colleagues was well beyond repair. As far as evidence allows a glimpse of their activities, the new group gathered in a meeting house on the Reichenstraße and held baptisms by immersion in a pond in Barmbek, a district to the north-east of Hamburg, not far outside the city's walls.[23] Altona's Flemish congregation had become two congregations.

Negotiations between the Flemish and the Dompelaars in the 1660s

In the 1660s, after the schism was well established, the two factions continued to interact, albeit very tentatively. The sources produced in these exchanges give the first clear evidence of the immersionists' beliefs, as stated by their own representatives.

A key figure in the Flemish interactions with the immersionists was Bastiaan van Weenigem, an ordained preacher from Rotterdam who paid a pastoral visit to Altona in July 1663. On 6 July he ordained Geeritt Roosen as an elder with the authority to conduct all religious ceremonies. Soon thereafter, on 11 July, the visiting elder baptized a group of seven young Mennonite adults.[24] The sermon that van Weenigem delivered at this service provoked a response from one of the immersionists' newest leaders, Samuel Stockman the Elder. Stockman had been the Flemish deacon responsible for keeping the church's accounts in Altona, but he had resigned from these responsibilities in late 1659.[25] He remained a deacon until May 1661, when he gave up this position to join the immersionists. His resignation and defection did not, however, prevent him from attending sermons in his old congregational meeting house, like the one delivered

---

This is a privately produced typescript. Copies can be found at Staatsarchiv Hamburg, as well as the libraries of the Museum für Hamburgische Geschichte and the Genealogische Gesellschaft, Sitz Hamburg.

22 Throughout the rest of the membership book, members (regardless of sex) are entered in the order in which they were baptized or transferred their membership to the congregation.

23 Bolten, *Historische Kirchen-Nachrichten*, i, p. 315. For a map of eighteenth-century Altona, see Schroeder and Huebert, *Mennonite Historical Atlas*, p. 10; the old Dompelaar meeting house on the Reichenstrasse is not noted on the map.

24 StAHbg/MG, 147, vol. 1, pp. 55–6.

25 Ibid., p. 3; and StAHbg/MG, 59, vol. 1. Geeritt Roosen began keeping the congregation's financial records in December 1659.

by van Weenigem in 1663. Stockman rejected what van Weenigem told the congregation about baptism, and he expressed his concerns in a letter delivered to the Dutch visitor in Hamburg on 14 July.[26]

The delivery of this letter marked the beginning of a long exchange of letters and texts between van Weenigem and the immersionists. Van Weenigem made his first written contribution on 18 October 1663, after his return to Rotterdam. His response to Stockman's defence of immersion baptism was reminiscent of the Hamburg Lutheran preacher Jodocus Edzardi Glanäus's attack on the immersionists from the previous decade. Van Weenigem used the philological argument that the Greek word for baptism had several meanings, including to immerse and simply to make wet. No single meaning was authoritative, and, therefore, no particular kind of ceremony was required to make the baptism legitimate. In 1665 van Weenigem arranged for these and several other related letters to be published in two separate volumes.[27]

In 1666, when the immersionists did not respond to these little booklets, he published a long, three-part book entitled *De maniere van Doop, Voetwasschinge en Avontmael soo by de Dompelaers tot Hamborg gebruyckt wert* (The Manner of Baptism, Foot-washing and Communion as Practised by Hamburg's Dompelaars). With van Weenigem's text the name often applied to Collegiants in the Netherlands, 'Dompelaar', came into regular usage when referring to the immersionists, who called themselves *gedoopte Christenen* (Baptized Christians). The text was both a further attack on immersionist practices and a call for reunification. Van Weenigem's positions are summarized well in a section called 'De Middelen, tot vrede en eendracht' (Ways to Peace and Unity).[28] He maintained 'that Christ's example must be followed strictly in matters of the moral duties of godliness . . . but not in all external things'.[29] Baptism, foot-washing and communion were symbolic ceremonies during which members of the church made their faith public. The form of these Christian practices was not as important as the intent which motivated them. Because they were not essential for a believer's salvation, the practices themselves were not worthy subjects of dispute and division. Therefore, baptism by sprinkling, the ceremony used in Flemish Mennonite gatherings in Altona, was sufficient.[30] Van Weenigem ended his reflections on peace and unity

---

26 Roosen had been ordained by Bastiaan van Weenigem only a week before, on 6 July.

27 See *Twee Brieven, Een van de Dienaren, der Gemeente tot Hamborch, die haer selven de gedoopte Christenen noemen* (Amsterdam, 1665); and *Seven Brieven, Tot vervolg van twee Brieven* (Rotterdam, 1665).

28 Van Weenigem, *De maniere van Doop, Voetwasschinge en Avontmael* (Rotterdam, 1666), part 3.

29 Ibid., part 3, p. 105: 'Dat Christus exempel strictelijcke moet werden naegevolght in de zede-plichten der Godtsaligheyt. . . . Maer niet in alle uyterlijcke dingen.'

30 Ibid., pp. 102–11.

by proposing three steps intended to help the two sides move towards a solution to the problems dividing them. First, the Dompelaars should admit that both sprinkling and immersion were correct forms of baptism. Secondly, those who had been baptized by sprinkling did not have to be rebaptized by immersion as long as they met moral requirements for church membership. Finally, returning members should agree to live peacefully according to the standards of the Flemish congregation.[31]

Bastiaan van Weenigem's proposals were designed to achieve a resolution to the conflict on the Flemish congregation's terms and were thus guaranteed to be received with suspicion by the Dompelaars. As the immersionist spokesman Jan Arents outlined in 1667 in a response to van Weenigem's book, the Dompelaars understood the dispute to centre around the lawful and biblical nature of baptism. Baptism, the Lord's Supper and foot-washing were acts of obedience to Christ, not merely symbolic celebrations. Van Weenigem had acknowledged that baptism by immersion was one scriptural form of baptism but not the only true and proper form of the ceremony. In so doing, he was not attacking the immersionists so much as Christ and his biblical ordinances.[32] This held also for the Dompelaars' practice of holding communion in the evening with unleavened bread after the participants' feet had been washed. The correct, obedient practice of these ceremonies was important because Christ 'leads us to spiritual things, which are signified and received through the tangible'.[33] Responding to van Weenigem's offers of peace, Jan Arents also declared the Baptized Christians' readiness to work towards unity. And they too offered to tolerate the practice of baptismal sprinkling if the Flemish congregation would also tolerate their form of baptism. In contrast to assertions made by van Weenigem, Arents complained that the immersionists had been forced out of the congregation against their will; they had not instigated the division.[34]

A Dutch translation of Arents's 1667 text, together with an appendix by Antoony de Grijs, appeared in 1668. De Grijs's contribution included little of the conciliatory tone of Arents's text. He declared that to interpret sprinkling to be a legitimate form of baptism would be like transforming Satan into an angel of light.[35] Addressing van Weenigem, he wrote that 'power or truth does not consist of loud bellowing or many words; rather,

---

31 Ibid., pp. 147–9.

32 Jan Arents, *Eindelijke Verklaeringe Der gedoopten Christenen* (n.p., 1667), pp. 18–53.

33 Ibid., pp. 121–2: 'sondern er erfordert di Tauffe und das Fusswaschen/ di wir mit augen sehen/ und durch dise sichtbare dinge leitet er uns zu den geistlichen/ welche durch di sichtbaren bezeichnet und empfangen werden'.

34 Ibid., pp. 161–2.

35 Antoony de Grijs, 'Appendix', in Arents, *Eindelijcke Verklaringe der gedoopte Christenen*, pp. 207–8.

it is but three things about which we are disputing, namely, baptism, foot-washing and communion'.[36] This brand of strict ceremonialism was exactly what concerned Flemish leaders in the 1660s.

It is hardly surprising that representatives for the two sides could find no solution. While they both declared their readiness to end the schism, neither was willing to compromise on any fundamental point. The exchange of letters and books continued with little in the way of new ideas or serious proposals. Samuel Stockman sent Bastiaan van Weenigem another letter late in 1668, which, together with Jan Arents's book, were Bastiaan's target in the 1669 book *Antidotum Ofte Tegengift, Op een Brief, geschreven uyt Hamborgh* (Antidote to a Letter from Hamburg). The exchange of texts did not last much longer than this,[37] but the division between the immersionists and the sprinklers remained.

The Dompelaar shift from ceremonialism to spiritualism

The 1670s marked an important period of transition for the Dompelaar congregation in several regards. In November 1670 the Danish crown granted the Dompelaar church privileges similar to those possessed by other non-Lutheran groups in Altona.[38] As with other such privileges, theirs required that they refrain from causing a public disturbance or attempting to convert Lutherans. About two decades after their initial separation from the Flemish, the Dompelaars now had official status as defined by at least one of the jurisdictions along the Elbe.

Not too long after gaining official recognition, the Dompelaars were undergoing other fundamental changes. With the passage of time, the first generation of believers was beginning to disappear. Because congregational records are not extant,[39] it is difficult to say a great deal about the character of the Dompelaar rank and file. However, we do know from fragmentary evidence (some of it discussed below and in Ch. 7) that the congregation was losing members.

---

36 Ibid., p. 213: 'Bastiaen, de kracht oft de Waerheyt bestaet niet in starck geroep, oft in veelen woorden: 't zijn maer drie saeken, naementlijck, Doop, Voetwasschingh en Nachtmael . . .'.

37 The *Antidotum* itself became a target of attack, this time from the Netherlands; see Davidz Willem Redoch, *Antidoti Weenigani Vanitas, Of Ydelheydt Van Bastiaans van Weenigem Laatste uyt-gegevene Tracktaatje* (Haarlem, 1672–73). I have not had an opportunity to examine this text.

38 Bolten, *Historische Kirchen-Nachrichten*, i, pp. 315–16 and 318–20. The privileges were renewed by successive Danish monarchs in 1699, 1732 and 1747.

39 In the late eighteenth century, Bolten wrote: 'Von einem Protocolle der ehemaligen Gemeine der Dompelaers sind keine Spuren zu finden' (*Historische Kirchen-Nachrichten*, i, p. 326).

Sources allow us to learn a little more about the changing character of its leadership. It might seem curious, especially given the injunction in Altona against proselytizing, that Jacob Taube and Christian Hoburg, a pair of Lutheran separatists, led the Dompelaars for a short period in the first half of the 1670s. It is unlikely that either had any well-established institutional ties to Altona. This, combined with the difficulties of policing a small group of quiet nonconformists in the confessionally diverse enclave of Altona and the short duration of two preachers' service with the Dompelaars, meant that the group did not receive too much negative scrutiny for having Lutherans in its midst.

The most prominent of these Lutheran preachers was Christian Hoburg, who led the Dompelaars from 1674 until his death in October 1675.[40] According to his son and biographer, Philipp Hoburg, the immersionists had begun reading Hoburg's work in the early 1670s, before his arrival in Altona.[41] Although nominally a Lutheran, Hoburg held views about the fallen state of the institutional church and about the need for simple and unmediated faith which made him unpopular with mainstream Lutheran officials in northern Germany. For example, in the later stages of the Thirty Years War he was writing against wars justified by church leaders. His efforts earned him the attention of Johann Müller, a preacher and polemicist in Hamburg. In 1645, the same year that Müller published *Anabaptismus. Das ist: Wiedertauffer Irrthumb*, he penned an attack on Hoburg. This kind of negative publicity was among the reasons why Hoburg lived an itinerant life. Jacob Taube, who had led the immersionists for a short time around 1673 and early 1674, rejoined the Lutheran church in Altona around the time of Hoburg's arrival.[42] When the Dompelaars learned of Hoburg's presence in or around Hamburg, they pleaded with him to join them as a preacher. He agreed.[43]

---

40 For a recent biography, see Hans-Jürgen Schrader, 'Hoburg, Christian' in Olaf Klose, Eva Rudolf and Ute Hayessen (eds), *Schleswig-Holsteinisches Biographisches Lexikon* (Neumünster, 1979), v, pp. 133–7. Also see Martin Brecht, 'Die deutschen Spiritualisten des 17. Jahrhunderts', in Martin Brecht (ed.), *Geschichte des Pietismus* (Göttingen, 1993), i, pp. 223–8; and Martin Fischer-Hübner, *Geistchristentum in der lutherischen Kirche Lauenburgs 1626–1711* (Ratzeburg, [1925]).

41 Philipp Hoburg, *Lebens-Lauff Des seligen Christian Hoburgs* (n.p., 1698), p. 21.

42 Bolten, *Historische Kirchen-Nachrichten*, i, pp. 329–31. According to Bolten's notes, Taube preached and printed a sermon in 1675 in which he stated his regret about his time among the Dompelaars. Its title is *Hertzens-grund Jac. Tauben, darinn er . . . absaget allen irrigen Lehren, deren man ihn, wegen . . . seiner Conversation mit unterschiedlichen irrenden Secten, verdächtig gehalten . . .* (Glückstadt, 1675). I have not been able to find a copy of this text.

43 It was during Hoburg's time among the Dompelaars that he completed his anti-war text *Vaterlandes Praeservatif*, in which he wrote about war as God's punishment for His people's disobedience and sin. The text of *Vaterlandes Praeservatif* is bound together with other texts in Hoburg's volume *Drey geistreiche Tractätlein* (Hamburg and Frankfurt, 1677).

What is remarkable about the arrangement is its terms. Philipp Hoburg, in his biography of his father, wrote that 'they [Hoburg and the Dompelaars] set each other free on the issue of ceremonies . . . because he had never fought with anyone over externals but rather taught pure faith in Christ which is active in love'.[44] Altona's late eighteenth-century church historian Johann Adrian Bolten interpreted this phrase to mean that Christian Hoburg – who, as a Lutheran, was no Anabaptist, let alone an immersionist – had adopted immersionist practices. The quotation is ambiguous.[45] On the one hand, it could mean that Hoburg, although a Lutheran, was so indifferent to ceremonies that he was willing to conduct Anabaptist ones. There is, however, no way of confirming this possibility. It is just as likely – perhaps more so – that the Dompelaars in no way required Hoburg to accept their formerly uncompromising position on the immersionist baptism of adults. They simply wanted, and needed, spiritual guidance, and the dissident Lutheran Hoburg was tolerant enough to provide it.

There are some indications that the Dompelaars still had an active leader after Hoburg died in 1675. For example, in 1676 Claes Boudt, a member of the Flemish congregation, was married in the rival Dompelaar church by an unidentified preacher.[46] Nonetheless, most other indications are that Hoburg's death left the small congregation with a leadership vacuum and a diminishing membership base. Since the former Flemish deacon Samuel Stockman had converted to the immersionists in 1661 (probably the last conversion of a local Flemish Mennonite to the new group), there had been occasional defections of Dompelaars back to the Flemish congregation (see Ch. 7). In the same period the Flemish congregation was gathering rather than losing institutional strength. For example, in 1675, when the new Flemish church building was completed in Altona, the Flemish could boast the services of four preachers (Romke Gosling, Ocke Pieters, Geeritt Roosen and Jacob Symons de Vlieger). By contrast, the Dompelaars lacked strong, consistent leadership for most of the rest of the seventeenth century.

The only documented Dompelaar leader after Hoburg was Jacob Denner (1659–1746).[47] Denner, the son of one of the Dompelaars' first deacons, Balthasar Denner, did not take over from Hoburg immediately after his

44 Philipp Hoburg, *Lebens-Lauff*, p. 22: 'Ihre Ceremonien angehend/ hat er ihren dieselbe/ und sie ihme darinnen frey gelassen/ und sich niemals daran verbunden/ denn er niemahls mit jemand um die Zeichen gestritten/ sondern wie vor erwehnet den reinen Glauben an Christum/ so durch Liebe thätig ist/ gelehret . . .'.

45 See Bolten, *Historische Kirchen-Nachrichten*, i, pp. 316–17.

46 StAHbg/MG, 147, vol. 1, p. 84. See Ch. 4 for more on the Boudt family.

47 For biographical details on Denner, see Jacob Denner, *Christliche und erbauliche Betrachtungen: Über die Sonn-und Festtags-Evangelien des ganzen Jahres* (Philadelphia, 1860), pp. 14–16. Also see Bolten, *Historische Kirchen-Nachrichten*, i, pp. 337–40.

death in 1675. As a young man he travelled extensively to Spain, Portugal, Italy and northern Russia as a secretary on merchant ships. After this apprenticeship, he was chosen as the congregation's new preacher in September 1684. After this appointment, he stayed in Altona for a few years, but soon moved on, again leaving the group without a capable leader. By 1687 he was preaching in Lübeck.

Although he had little formal theological training, Denner developed a reputation as an effective, charismatic preacher. His skills and the weakness of the Altona congregation of his birth did not escape the attention of the Dompelaars' local Mennonite rivals. Flemish leaders tried to capitalize on the situation. In January 1691 Geeritt Roosen acted as secretary during a meeting of the Flemish congregational council.[48] The issue before the preachers was whether to invite Jacob Denner to give sermons before congregants. There was even talk of reunification with the Dompelaars, or at least the possibility of full and permanent membership being granted to Denner as an individual. Most of what Roosen wrote, however, was a reiteration of old arguments. Citing John 1: 33, Roosen wanted to prove once again that the Apostles had not been baptized by immersion but by the outpouring over them of the Holy Spirit, just as John the Baptist had done symbolically with water in the Jordan. The proposal of the Flemish preachers was that, if their Dompelaar colleagues disagreed with this position, they should search for better evidence from the Bible alone. Evidence from chronicles and other human explanations should not be relied upon when seeking to strengthen contrary claims about apostolic baptism.

Neither Denner nor any other Dompelaar spokesman seems to have responded to the renewed arguments of the Flemish, or the evidence has not survived. The discussions about matters of faith did, however, continue among Flemish leaders. In a manuscript dated 22 February 1691 entitled 'Schriftuerlycke Gemoets t'Samenspracke' (Scriptural Spiritual Conversations),[49] Roosen applied the principle of using the Bible alone as the foundation for matters of faith. The 'Gemoets t'Samenspracke' was a long manuscript, a catechism consisting of 148 questions and answers intended for an audience of young Christians about to accept baptism and membership in the congregation. Considering its timing, Roosen's text may very well have been intended to be a reference work in negotiations with Denner or the Dompelaars more generally, a text which was meant

[48] StAHbg/MG, 246b, '. . . oft men Jacob denner by ons niet soude connen en mogen dienen laeten . . .', 10 January 1691.

[49] StAHbg/MG, 246b, 'Schriftuerlycke Gemoets t'Samenspracke gestelt In vraegen en antwoorden voor de aencomende ionckheyt om te comen tot een Hysame oefeninge van Het christelicke en salichmackende geloove, ende de kennisse der waerheyt, die tot der godtsalicheyt leyet, tot hoope des Eeuwigen Leevens', 22 February 1691.

to clarify the beliefs he and his colleagues felt were essential for membership in the Christian community.

There is no evidence of Denner ever having preached in Altona in the 1690s. By 1694 he had moved once more, this time from Lübeck to Friedrichstadt, where he was employed as a preacher in the united Flemish–High German Mennonite congregation. He left again in 1698 and relocated to Danzig, where he took up another preaching position with the Flemish–High German congregation there. This stay was also short-lived. He was soon back in Altona.

In May 1701 the Flemish congregational council renewed its invitation to Jacob Denner.[50] Members agreed to invite him to act as a visiting preacher, providing he abided by a number of conditions: he would have to limit his preaching to the Flemish congregation alone (that is, he would not preach to the Dompelaars); he would avoid raising controversial subjects in public; and he would refrain from administering baptism. Unlike the notes Geeritt Roosen had taken a decade earlier, the decision in 1701 does not seem to have been accompanied by the detailed theological arguments against baptism by immersion, at least not in writing.[51] And again in contrast to 1691, Denner accepted the invitation, preaching several times in 1701 as a guest.

Altona had become Denner's main base by the beginning of the eighteenth century and was to remain so for the rest of his long life. However, he remained only briefly in the position of visiting preacher, beginning to work again as preacher to the Dompelaars. And although the number of Dompelaar congregants was certainly very small and the condition of the group's meeting house on Altona's Reichenstraße was deteriorating badly, Denner nonetheless gained quite a reputation as a popular preacher. In his sermons he recommended an active, humble and tolerant Christian life,[52] emphasized repentance and inward conversion as necessary experiences for a follower of Christ,[53] and decried theological disputation as an unproductive and even destructive habit.[54]

The same skills that had led Flemish leaders twice to seek his services also led to confrontations with Hamburg's magistrates and clergymen. In the years following his time in the Flemish church, his preaching activities began to attract the scrutiny of Hamburg's clerical authorities. Between

50 StAHbg/MG, 6, vol. 1, p. 13.

51 The notes were kept by a secretary other than Geeritt Roosen. Roosen remained a member of the congregational council, but due to his age he no longer kept notes for the church.

52 See, for example, his pronouncements on Jews, Turks, heathens and heretics in *Christliche und erbauliche Betrachtungen*, pp. 336, 688–9, 748, 842 and 837.

53 See the many index references ibid., pp. 1222 and 1224.

54 See the many index references ibid., pp. 1226. Also see the Conclusion to the present study.

February 1706 and August 1709, officials in the *Ministerium* (the city's Lutheran administrative body) petitioned Hamburg's Senate again and again to forbid Hamburg's Lutherans from attending Denner's services in Altona. The complaints of one Lutheran preacher are particularly noteworthy, for the tone is mild compared with an earlier generation of anti-Anabaptist polemicists represented by men like Jodocus Edzardi Glanäus. The preacher, Daniel Severin Schultze, praised Denner for his theology, which Schultze felt was admirably close to Lutheran teachings. However, Schultze also repeated the common charges that Anabaptists refused to baptize children, swear oaths or acknowledge the authority of the magistracy. He also complained that 'Denner flatters his congregants and does not denounce their sinful lives.'[55] Lutheran complaints and actions against Denner were ultimately unsuccessful, despite occasional Senate injunctions and despite the threat of church discipline (the ban from communion and confession) being imposed on offenders.[56] Denner even received a glowing eulogy in 1746 in the newspaper *Hamburgischer Correspondent*.[57]

In some regards, the Dompelaar congregation experienced a renaissance under Denner's leadership in the eighteenth century. His preaching attracted enough visitors that he was able to arrange for the construction of a new meeting house in Altona. In April 1708 he received the necessary approval from the Danish crown to build a new church on the street Große Freiheit.[58] According to Johann Adrian Bolten, the Flemish Mennonite congregation member Ernst Pieters Goverts contributed much of the money required to finance the construction.[59] The Goverts connection suggests that the differences between the Flemish and Dompelaar congregations had diminished, at least at some level, for Goverts was a wealthy, important,

55 Daniel Severin Schultzen, *Wolgemeinte Warnung für der gemeinschaft des Gottesdientes der Mennonisten* (Hamburg, 1706), pp. 108–12; the quotation is from p. 110: 'Denner smeichelt den seinigen/ straffet nie ihr sündlich leben.'

56 This paragraph is based on research recorded by Dollinger, *Geschichte der Mennoniten*, p. 147. Also see StAHbg, Ministerium, II 5, pp. 57, 88 and 142.

57 The eulogy, from the no. 58 (1746) of the newspaper, is reprinted in Denner, *Christliche und erbauliche Betrachtungen*, p. 11: 'Im Monat Februar verstarb zu Altona der exemplarische Lehrer der Mennonitischen Gemeine, Herr Jacob Denner, im 87sten Jahre seines Alters. Ueberhaupt hat sich derselbe bei allen Glaubensverwandten den Namen eines ehrlichen und redlichen Mannes erworben, und eben hierinnen hat er die Ausübung seiner Pflichten gesuchet. Seine Predigten, die er in Druck gegeben, haben wegen ihrer redlichen Absicht, und erbaulichen Ausführung vieles Lob erhalten.'

58 For transcriptions of the document approving the new building, see Bolten, *Historische Kirchen-Nachrichten*, i, pp. 318–20; Schmid, *Versuch einer historischen Beschreibung*, pp. 210–11; and StAHbg, Handschriftensammlung, 1501. For the location of the new church, see Schroeder and Huebert, *Mennonite Historical Atlas*, p. 10.

59 Bolten, *Historische Kirchen-Nachrichten*, i, pp. 319–21.

well-connected man in the Flemish congregation. In 1705 he had married Ida de Lanoy, the daughter of the Altona Flemish elder Jan de Lanoy. His support for Denner's church did not weaken his status in the Flemish congregation, for in 1711 he became a deacon.[60] When Ernst Pieters Goverts died in 1728, his estate owed creditors a massive amount of money. A bitter dispute lasted several years in the courts.[61] Because Denner's church belonged among the capital reserves of Goverts's estate, one of his creditors, Countess Benedikte Margarethe Reventlow, the wife of Altona's early eighteenth-century administrator Christian Detlev Reventlow, took control of the property. She allowed Denner to continue to use the premises on one condition: his son Balthasar (1685–1749),[62] an accomplished portrait painter, would have to paint her a portrait per year. The arrangement lasted until the Countess's death in the early 1730s, when Denner was able to raise enough money through a regular collection from listeners to reassert control over the church.[63]

The financial support Denner received from men like Goverts and other congregants throughout the early eighteenth century is an indication of his popularity as a preacher. Although there are no surviving records which might indicate how many attended his sermons, an eighteenth-century report suggests that he attracted a very diverse group of listeners to the new building on the Große Freiheit.[64] Among these people were members of all Protestant churches – Lutheran, Calvinist and Mennonite. Catholics also attended occasionally. Denner even attracted listeners of significant social status, like the Duke of Schleswig-Holstein-Gottorp, Adolf Friedrich (1710–71). From 1727 until 1750 – in other words, during the time he would have visited Denner's sermons – Adolf Friedrich served as the bishop of Lübeck, and after Denner's death he reigned as king of Sweden (1751–71).

---

60 StAHbg/MG, 147, vol. 1, p. 161. Goverts was not a deacon before 1711, as is suggested by Bolten.

61 See StAHbg, Reichskammergericht, R25; and Landesarchiv Schleswig, Reichskammergericht, 72.

62 See Hans Konrad Röthel, *Bürgerliche Kultur und Bildnismalerei in Hamburg während der ersten Hälfte des 18. Jahrhunderts* (Hamburg, 1938); and William Schroeder, *Balthasar Denner, 1685–1749: Portrait Artist* (Winnipeg, 1994).

63 Bolten, *Historische Kirchen-Nachrichten*, i, pp. 320–21.

64 Ibid., pp. 338–9: 'Sein Auditorium bestand in seiner Kirche aus einem vermischten Haufen von Mennoniten, Lutheranern, Reformierten, und selbst einigen pieusen Katholiken, solchen nämlich, welche die Mystik liebeten, weil er an den Vätern und Mystikern der römischen Kirche großen Geschmack fand. Selbst Separatisten und einzelne Quäker frequentirten seine Kirche, welche (vielleicht auch mit aus diesem Grunde) die Quäkerkirche gescholten ward. . . . Auch hatte er manchen Besuch vom hohen und niedrigen Adel beydes des herzöglich-holsteinischen und des königlich-dänischen Hofes; insbesondere beehrte der verstorbene König von Schweden, Adolf Fridrich, als gottorp-eutinischer Prinz, seine Predigten mit seiner öftern Gegenwart.'

Despite these signs of strength, the Dompelaars were in decline as a congregation. Particularly remarkable is Denner's attitude towards the sacraments. Probably the last person he baptized by immersion, according to Bolten, was the non-Mennonite Johann Jacob Flügge, sometime around the turn of the century.[65] And most probably the last person he baptized by any means (in this case sprinkling) was his daughter Agnetha. Furthermore, he rarely if ever celebrated communion publicly.[66] The very ceremonies that had once been essential to his predecessors were not so essential for him. Compared with the strict ceremonialism of the first immersionists, the Dompelaars of the eighteenth century were a congregation of spiritualists who were much more flexible about the proper practice of adult baptism.[67] In retrospect, it is clear that the short period in the 1670s during which the Lutheran spiritualist and separatist Christian Hoburg led the congregation was the beginning of a major shift in theological emphasis for the Dompelaars.

More important than theology for the long-term survival of the Dompelaar congregation was the character of the group's membership. While Denner seems to have attracted many casual listeners, the congregation itself probably had few active members in the eighteenth century. In fact, the core of the Dompelaar congregation consisted only of Denner's own family. In 1747, not long after Denner's death the previous year, the new Danish monarch reconfirmed the Dompelaars' privileges. What the new king was unaware of was that the congregation had effectively ceased to exist. The new church built in 1708 remained in the hands of the Denner family, but the family allowed a series of freethinking Lutherans and Moravian Brethren to use it.[68] This marked the end of Dompelaar history in Hamburg and Altona.[69]

---

65 I have been able to find out very little about Flügge; see Roosen, *Geschichte der Mennoniten-Gemeinde*, part 1, p. 68, who says Flügge was originally a Lutheran and was baptized in 1701, later becoming an important figure in political tensions between Hamburg and Altona.

66 Bolten, *Historische Kirchen-Nachrichten*, i, pp. 317–18 and 339.

67 For examples from his sermons, see Denner, *Christliche und erbauliche Betrachtungen*, pp. 58–9 and 1145.

68 Bolten, *Historische Kirchen-Nachrichten*, i, pp. 321–5 and 341–8.

69 An interesting footnote to the Dompelaars' history is that, at about the same time as Jacob Denner's congregation was starting to decline, another group known as Dompelaars was growing rapidly in Krefeld in the Rhineland. On the Krefeld Dompelaars, see Peter Kriedte, 'Taufgesinnte, Dompelaars, Erweckte: Die mennonitische Gemeinde und der Aufstieg des proto-industriellen Kapitalismus in Krefeld im 17. und 18. Jahrhundert', in Rudolf Vierhaus (ed.), *Frühe Neuzeit – Frühe Moderne? Forschungen zur Vielschichtigkeit von Übergangsprozessen* (Göttingen, 1992), pp. 260–64. Although the two groups of Dompelaars in Altona and Krefeld shared a name and some common beliefs, there was probably no direct connection between them, for the Dompelaars under Denner were distancing themselves from adult baptism by immersion at a time when Krefeld's Dompelaars were just beginning to practise it in the 1710s.

Conclusion

The Dompelaar congregation's later history fits in poorly with the prevailing character of the confessional age. Jacob Denner's spiritualistic form of religious practice had elements which might seem out of step with his time. In an age when social and political rights depended on religious affiliation, Denner tried to maintain a church whose doors were open to all, regardless of affiliation. In other words, he tried to run a modern free church before its time.

By contrast, the early history of the Dompelaars is more characteristic of the confessional age. The origins of this immersionist faction, as well as the early Flemish reactions against it, provide further evidence of the lively exchange of people and ideas between the Netherlands and northern Germany that was typical of the sixteenth and seventeenth centuries. In addition to people, resources and know-how, religious ideas were also transferred throughout the Mennonite diaspora. As noted in Chapter 1, this could result in the spread of old factional differences to northern Germany. But it could also encourage new confessional conflicts.

The Dompelaar schism was symptomatic of a problem arising from the Mennonites' congregational form of organization. In daily practice, a congregation was usually administered by a small group of men. However, the authority of leaders could be challenged at any time by the congregants they served. Because there was no central Mennonite institution which could act as a final arbiter in disputes over governance or belief, congregational schisms were not uncommon. In fact, the 1648 schism over baptismal practice was not the only such dispute facing Flemish Mennonite leaders in the later seventeenth century. The next chapter looks at another.

CHAPTER THREE

The Confessionalist Strategy of Flemish Leaders

The congregation of Flemish Mennonites was by far the largest and most historically significant in Hamburg and Altona. At the same time that the Dompelaars were losing members, the Flemish were building a strong set of institutions and growing in size. There were also strong differences in the two groups' respective religious characters. Whereas Dompelaar identity was based upon an originally strict but later weakening brand of ceremonialism, official Flemish identity was based fairly consistently throughout the seventeenth century and beyond on standards codified in confessions of faith.

The Flemish reliance on confessions of faith was hardly unique, and historians have already written much about the topic as it concerns other early modern Christian groups. One of these historians, R. Po-chia Hsia, has suggested the term 'confessionalism'[1] to help think about this historical trend. He writes: 'By "confessionalism," I mean the formation of religious ideologies and institutions in Lutheranism, Calvinism, and Catholicism. The concept denotes the articulation of belief systems (in "confessional texts"), the recruitment and character of various professional clerical bodies, the constitution and operations of church institutions, and systems of rituals.'[2] Hsia's definition is influenced greatly by the work of Ernst Walter Zeeden, who wrote of 'the intellectual and organizational entrenchment' of competing Christian groups after the Reformation into 'halfway stable churches in terms of dogma, constitution and a religious-moral way of life'.[3] Hsia, Zeeden and other historians of confessionalism are interested in the comparative study of post-Reformation religious life.

---

1 Terminology is sometimes a problem in this field of study. To refer to essentially the same set of issues and developments, some historians (including Ernst Walter Zeeden) prefer the terms 'confession-building' (*Konfessionsbildung*) or 'confessionalization' (*Konfessionalisierung*). In current historiographical literature, 'confessionalization' often has a generally more specialized set of meanings, which I discuss in Ch. 4.

2 R. Po-chia Hsia, *Social Discipline in the Reformation: Central Europe, 1550–1750* (London and New York, 1989), pp. 4–5.

3 Ernst Walter Zeeden, *Die Entstehung der Konfessionen: Grundlagen und Formen der Konfessionsbildung im Zeitalter der Glaubenskämpfe* (Munich and Vienna, 1965), pp. 9–10: 'Unter Konfessionsbildung sei also verstanden: die geistige und organisatorische Verfestigung der seit der Glaubensspaltung auseinanderstrebenden christlichen Bekenntisse zu einem halbwegs stabilen Kirchentum nach Dogma, Verfassung und religiös-sittlicher Lebensform.'

One result of comparative research in recent decades has been to suggest that there were important structural similarities between Lutheran, Calvinist and Catholic institutional cultures. However, a reasonable version of the model in no way denies that there were important and deep-seated cultural differences distinguishing members of Protestant and Catholic groups from one another. It simply emphasizes that the various mainstream Christian groups used similar means – for example, confessions of faith, church histories, laws, visitations, the threat of church discipline, the formation of interregional alliances, and so on – to compete with and distinguish themselves from one another.

Historians interested in early modern European confessionalism have seldom paid much attention to Anabaptists, who were never a large percentage of Europe's overall population. Most have simply assumed that 'Anabaptist confessionalism' is a contradiction. Preconceptions about Anabaptists falling outside the paradigm of confessionalism are perhaps justified if we turn our attention to areas like Switzerland, where unrelenting persecution forced Anabaptists to lead an underground existence until the beginning of the eighteenth century. Nonetheless, it would be a mistake to consider, as some historians have,[4] that all Anabaptists by definition did not conform to the broader pattern of socio-historical development outlined in the paradigm. The Flemish congregation of Hamburg and Altona, which belonged to one of the largest and most established of Mennonite groups in northern Europe, provides good examples of the socio-historical trends highlighted by the paradigm of confessionalism.

'The intellectual and organizational entrenchment'[5] of Mennonite life began by the middle of the sixteenth century and took on a clear character towards the very end of the sixteenth century and the beginning of the seventeenth century. At this time Mennonites took advantage of unprecedented degrees of governmental toleration to establish and consolidate shared institutions and doctrines that could in turn form the basis of a domesticated kind of religious nonconformity acceptable to accommodating rulers.[6] Confessions of faith were a central tool in this process. The typical seventeenth-century Mennonite confession of faith[7] began with a statement about the nature of God, which was intended to demonstrate their orthodox trinitarianism to any reader who might consider labelling them heretics. Most of the rest of the text outlined the biblical basis for Mennonite beliefs about the central role of adult baptism

4 See, for example, Heinz Schilling's statement, quoted in Ch. 4, that Anabaptists belonged to 'the nonconfessionally organized denominations'.

5 Zeeden, quoted above.

6 For more on religious principles and political conformity, see Chs. 4, 5 and 6.

7 Here I am referring specifically to the texts included in the *Algemeene Belydennissen* (Amsterdam, 1665), the history of which is discussed below.

in Christian life, the necessity of shunning stubborn sinners, the refusal to swear solemn oaths, the commitment to a non-resistant faith, the necessity of obedience which believers owed to secular authorities and the character of the Final Judgement. The adoption of this (in large part) religiously distinctive yet politically conformist kind of statement of faith marked an important stage in a long transformation towards ever more established church communities. Mennonites were aspiring to belong to the socio-political mainstream while still preserving their unique character. Compared with the very first Anabaptists, newer generations had reached a truce with the societies in which they lived by the seventeenth century. Flemish Mennonites in Hamburg and Altona during the seventeenth century are a good example of confessional Anabaptism.

A Dutch schism over the confessionalist strategy

Background about Dutch Mennonite history is necessary to understand the development of Mennonite confessionalism in Hamburg and Altona. Like other mainstream Protestant and Catholic confessional documents, seventeenth-century Dutch Mennonite confessions of faith were frequently the collective statements resulting from negotiations between groups of religious leaders. The need for such negotiations was made particularly urgent by a quickly increasing number of sixteenth-century schisms among Anabaptists (see Ch. 1). The negotiation of confessions of faith became the preferred strategy of a new generation of Mennonite leaders who wanted to mend old divisions and avoid new ones. For convenience, I call this the 'confessionalist strategy' and the men who advocated it 'confessionalists'. Over a 200-year period starting around the beginning of the seventeenth century, Dutch Mennonites published nineteen separate confessions of faith, plus two major collections in which several of these individual texts were released again. In most cases, each of these texts was reprinted several times, so that altogether there were over 100 printings before the end of the eighteenth century. Most volumes were published in the first two-thirds of the seventeenth century.[8]

The reason for this large output is that the confessionalist strategy was at least initially quite successful. The first successful round of negotiations resulted in the *Concept van Keulen* (Concept of Cologne) (1591), an agreement between High German and moderate Frisian factions. In the 1620s and 1630s leaders were especially busy trying to arrange further

[8] These data are taken from Dirk Visser, 'A Checklist of Dutch Mennonite Confessions of Faith to 1800', *Documenta Anabaptistica Neerlandica*, bulletins 6 and 7 (1974–75). Geeritt Roosen's confessions of faith are not included in Visser's list.

agreements. A local reunification between Flemish and Frisians in Harlingen in 1626 led to mixed results. On the one hand, a dissatisfied remnant of the Frisian faction broke off contacts with their former brothers and sisters; on the other hand, despite the setback, leaders in Amsterdam and Dordrecht were encouraged to make larger-scale attempts to put an end to long-standing divisions throughout the Netherlands. The results were a series of confessions of faith: the *Olijftacxken* (Little Olive Branch) (1626), the Jan Cents Confession (1630), and the Dordrecht Confession (sometimes called the Adriaan Cornelisz Confession) (1632). A high point of these negotiations was reached in Amsterdam in 1639 when the Church *bij het Lam* (by the Lamb), one of the biggest and best-established of several Anabaptist congregations in the city, became the place of worship of a newly united congregation which included members of Flemish, Frisian and High German groups.[9]

Despite these triumphs, not all northern European Anabaptist leaders were equally committed to the confessionalist strategy as a means of resolving divisions and disagreements.[10] In September 1647, Waterlander Anabaptist leaders presented Flemish Mennonites with a proposal for unification.[11] Although Waterlanders did have their own confessions of faith, their proposal expressed a reserved attitude towards the role of confessions of faith in regulating collective life: 'We understand that all propositions in confessions of faith do not bind every individual. Rather, one must look to God's word and may accept confessions of faith only in so far as they are in agreement with the Bible.'[12] The Waterlander concern was that confessions like the *Olijftacxken* had taken on an unwarranted authority of their own. Flemish leaders met several times in 1649 to consider the Waterlander proposal. The most significant of these meetings took place at a synod in June in Haarlem. On the first day of the Haarlem

---

9 For more on Mennonite confessions of faith, see N. van der Zijpp, *De belijdenisgeschriften der Nederlandse Doopsgezinden* (Haarlem, 1954); Hans-Jürgen Goertz, 'Zwischen Zwietracht und Eintracht: Zur Zweideutigkeit täuferischer und mennonitischer Bekenntnisse', *Mennonitische Geschichtsblätter*, 43–4 (1986–7), pp. 16–46; and Karl P. Koop, 'Early Seventeenth Century Mennonite Confessions of Faith: The Development of an Anabaptist Tradition' (Ph.D. diss., Toronto School of Theology, University of St Michael's College, 1999).

10 Major sources for the narrative in this section are Meihuizen, *Galenus Abrahamsz*, and J. Wuite, 'De scheuring tusschen het Lam en de Zon', *Doopsgezinde Bijdragen*, 40 (1900), pp. 1–37. For general information on Abrahamsz in English, see Leszek Kolakowski, 'Dutch Seventeenth-Century Anticonfessional Ideas and Rational Religion', trans. and intro. James Satterwhite, *Mennonite Quarterly Review*, 64 (1990), pp. 259–97 and 385–416.

11 On the Waterlanders, see Ch. 1.

12 Quoted in Kühler, *Geschiedenis van de Doopsgezinden in Nederland*, pp. 202–3: 'Wij verstaan dat alle stellingen van geloofsbelijdenissen zoodanig zijn, dat men daaraan elkander niet behoort te binden, maar dat men alleen op Gods Woord moet zien en de confessies slechts zoover mag aannemen als zij met den Bijbel overeenstemmen.'

Synod, delegates listened as the *Olijftacxken*, the Jan Cents Confession and the Dordrecht Confession were read aloud. By consensus they acknowledged the three confessions of faith 'to be the nearest means to govern the congregations in peace . . . although everything remains subject to God's word'.[13] Unification with the Waterlanders could only proceed on the same basis – that is, confessions of faith – already used successfully in the past to reconcile differences between Flemish, Frisian and High German factions in Amsterdam in 1639. Although both sides acknowledged the ultimate authority of the Bible, the Flemish placed greater emphasis on the authority of confessions of faith. The response of Flemish leaders amounted to a rejection of the Waterlander proposal. These failed negotiations in the late 1640s revealed the disputed character of the Mennonites' confessionalist strategy. Similar disputes later reached a climax in the Netherlands in the 1660s.

A key player in the disputes of the 1660s was a young medical doctor and preacher in Amsterdam's Church *bij het Lam* named Galenus Abrahamsz de Haan. Soon after being instated as a preacher in 1648, Abrahamsz had supported the confessionalist position of the Flemish agreed to in Haarlem in 1649. After the Haarlem Synod, Abrahamsz's attitude towards confessions of faith took a fateful turn. In 1650 he became a participant in Collegiant meetings in Amsterdam, which had been founded in 1646 by Adam Boreel and Daniel de Breen. Abrahamsz was not the only member of his congregation who developed such contacts. Jarig Jelles and Pieter Balling, both close associates of the famous philosopher Baruch Spinoza, as well as the deacon Cornelis Jansz Moorman and the preacher Frans Beuns were also members of the Church *bij het Lam* and the Amsterdam Collegiant meetings. Confessionalists were highly suspicious of Mennonites who participated in such circles, for Collegiants were opposed to all group-defining statements of faith. To the committed confessionalists, the Collegiants' irenical inclusiveness seemed based on a disregard for traditional standards. Mennonites, it was claimed, who participated in such gatherings were helping to undermine the doctrinal and sacramental foundations of congregational unity and leadership. Abrahamsz was viewed as a traitor to the cause he had once championed at the Haarlem Synod.

Over the next several years the rift between factions in the Church *bij het Lam* became ever more public. In early 1657 the simmering controversy took on a new character. That is when, in answer to critics, Galenus

[13] The Synod's proceedings were published nearly two decades later under the title *Handelinge/ Der Ver-eenigde Vlaemse, en Duytse Doops-gesinde Gemeynten, Gehouden Tot Haerlem, Ao. 1649 in Junio* (Vlissingen, 1666). For the quotation, see the summary of 26 June 1649: '. . . het naeste middle te zijn/ om de Gemeynten in vreden te regeeren/ datmen blijve by het inhouden deser drie Belijdenissen/ doch alles greserveert den woorde Gods'.

Abrahamsz and David Spruyt presented their fellow congregational leaders with a manuscript outlining their position and convictions concerning matters of faith and congregational government.

The manuscript consisted of nineteen articles. The authors stated that the first apostolic congregation had received its authority directly from God. However, through carelessness and neglect this church had fallen irreparably (article 10). Thus, those holding church offices did not have the same authority as the Apostles of old, and the ceremonies and practices (preaching, baptism, communion, church discipline, ordination of elders by laying on of hands, and the selection of preachers) common in the present-day Mennonite community were not of the same value as those of the first church (article 17). Thus, neither the Flemish Mennonites nor any other group was the remnant of the true apostolic church. Abrahamsz and Spruyt called on their peers not to demand absolute conformity in doctrinal or ceremonial matters but rather to remain true to the examples found in the New Testament (article 18). In other words, peace and unity among Mennonites were not best achieved through the use of confessional statements but rather through common adherence to the Bible, which was a sufficient standard for those who wished to live godly lives. Finally, they emphasized that they were not rejecting practices like baptism and communion; they were only asking that their peers follow Christ's ways (article 19). In 1657 Abrahamsz was clearly advocating a position he had rejected in 1649.

Abrahamsz and Spruyt had circulated their manuscript among colleagues with the understanding that it was not to be published. This understanding was broken in 1659. The first printing portrayed the articles unfavourably. Spruyt and Abrahamsz felt betrayed and compelled to respond. Later in 1659 they published *Nader verklaringe Van de XIX. Artikelen* (Further Explanation of the Nineteen Articles),[14] which included not only the articles themselves but also a lengthy defence of the authors' intentions.

Formulated in the course of interactions with spiritualist Collegiants, the programme of Galenus Abrahamsz and David Spruyt was in large part a reaction against the confessionalist strategy of their church colleagues in Amsterdam. And, seen from another perspective, the confessionalists came increasingly to define themselves in contrast to the Galenists. The more the two sides became aware of differences, the more aggressive became their respective convictions and public positions.

From 18 to 23 June 1660, Leiden was the site of a synod of pro-confession, anti-Galenist Mennonites. The meeting at Leiden marked yet

---

14 G. Abrahamsz and D. Spruyt, *Nader verklaringe Van de XIX. Artikelen* (Amsterdam, 1659).

a further escalation of the controversy, for there Amsterdam's confessionalist leaders gathered together like-minded colleagues from throughout the Netherlands to help strengthen their cause. The chairman of the meetings in Leiden was the Dordrecht elder Thieleman Jansz van Braght, and the secretary was the Rotterdam elder Bastiaan van Weenigem. Van Braght had been one of the delegates to the Haarlem Synod in 1649, and both men were committed confessionalists. The forty-two delegates discussed several questions, central among which concerned the formulation of a single new, authoritative confession of faith. Six men – Tobias Govertsz and Bartel Louwer from Amsterdam's Church *bij het Lam*, Pieter Markusz, Isaac Jansz Snep and Boudewijn Doom from Haarlem, and Mees Jansz – were assigned the task of formulating this document. In addition to the Concept of Cologne (1591), their models were to be the three confessions – the *Olijftacxken* (1626), the Jan Cents Confession (1630), and the Dordrecht Confession (1632) – approved at the Haarlem Synod of 1649. The plan was to present this new confession to another gathering, held at a time and place to be determined later. Delegates to the Leiden Synod also agreed that Galenus Abrahamsz and David Spruyt were examples of unorthodox preachers who denied the principles a person in their position should be expected to uphold. A group of four deputies of the synod – Pieter Markusz, Hendrick Gijsbrechtsz, Bastiaan van Weenigem and Thieleman Jansz van Braght – was organized to confront the two Amsterdam preachers. Given the animosities that had been building over the last several years between the pro-Collegiant and pro-confession factions, it is hardly surprising that Abrahamsz and Spruyt refused to acknowledge either the decisions reached at the synod or the authority of the synod's emissaries. In fact, synods and the like were the work of the Antichrist, or so Spruyt proclaimed from the pulpit soon after the Leiden delegates had spoken with him. The conflict had reached a stalemate.

Following the Leiden Synod, the confessionalists continued to exert pressure on their opponents. This included the release of the martyrology *Het Bloedigh Tooneel* (The Bloody Theatre, or Martyrs' Mirror) about one month after delegates had gathered at Leiden. The editor of the long, two-part martyrology was the Synod's chairman, Thieleman Jansz van Braght. He had of course begun the project well in advance of the meeting at Leiden. His introductory comments were completed in the middle of 1659. Van Braght divided the main body of his text into two parts: the first surveyed the practice of adult baptism and persecutions against the faithful from the first through the fifteenth centuries; the second, the larger part of the text, did the same for the period since 1500. A major part of his motivation in publishing the *Bloedigh Tooneel* was to warn faithful Mennonites that all was not well in the true church. Compared with the martyrs of old, he claimed, Mennonites of the mid-seventeenth century were less aware of the dangers threatening their souls. Instead of living in obedience to God, they had succumbed to worldly pleasures and distractions. They should return to living according to Christ's example and the example of their suffering Anabaptist ancestors.[15]

In addition to this ethical purpose, van Braght's project in the *Bloedigh Tooneel* was also motivated by politics. The volume expressed clearly and forcefully the confessionalist attitudes delegates had supported not only in Leiden but also a decade earlier at the Haarlem Synod. In the book's introduction, van Braght included the text of the Apostles' Creed, to which he also added the same three confessions of faith approved in Haarlem in 1649 and again in Leiden just before the book's publication.[16] In the 'Introduction' he explained that, while the Apostles' Creed should be a sufficient doctrinal foundation for the Christian church, attacks upon the Creed by ill-intentioned people made it necessary for Christ's followers to clarify the proper interpretation of the principles of faith. The three Mennonite confessions might seem in superficial ways to be different, but, as was the case with the whole tradition of Christian faith since the time of the first persecutions, all orthodox confessions elaborated on the same unchanging beliefs. In short, Mennonite confessions of faith were simply restatements of the faith of the first Christians. One of the main points of the *Bloedigh Tooneel* was to show that not only was there a continuity of doctrine over the centuries, but also that this doctrine had been passed from one faithful believer to another since the time of Christ. The Mennonites were the contemporary manifestation of Christ's church, which had survived underground for many generations before the Reformation and which was maintained through the personal succession of preachers.[17] This doctrine of personal succession was the reason why ordination through the laying on of hands was so important in Mennonite congregations.

The doctrine of the church was the main issue that divided the pro-Collegiant and pro-confession factions in the late 1650s and early 1660s. On this issue contemporaries would have recognized that the *Bloedigh Tooneel* was an anti-Galenist text. This is not a new observation,[18] but the

---

15 Thieleman van Braght, *The Bloody Theater or Martyrs Mirror of the Defenseless Christians*, trans. Joseph F. Sohm (8th edn, Scottdale, Pa., 1968), pp. 8–11. For a thorough treatment of the Anabaptist martyr tradition in comparative perspective, see Gregory, *Salvation at Stake*.

16 Van Braght, *The Bloody Theater or Martyrs Mirror*, pp. 27–44.

17 Ibid., pp. 16–19, 21–4 and 26–7.

18 See Meihuizen, *Galenus Abrahamsz*, p. 70; and C.B. Hylkema, *Reformateurs: Geschiedkundige Studiën over de Godesdienstige Bewegingen uit de nadagen onzer Gouden Eeuw* (2 parts, Haarlem, 1900 and 1902), part 1, p. 135, n. 162.

unmistakable contrast between Abrahamsz's *XIX. Artikelen* and van Braght's martyrology has been forgotten in recent English-language historiography. After the early 1650s, Abrahamsz believed that the apostolic church had disappeared long ago, and, at least until the mid-1660s, he also believed that contacts with other moderate spiritualist Christians like the Collegiants were worth encouraging. Van Braght believed that the Mennonites were responsible for keeping alive beliefs and a way of life begun by Christ himself and that Christ's true (Mennonite) church needed to be protected against innovating and perverting influences like Collegiantism.

Internecine Mennonite power struggles continued to escalate in intensity through the early 1660s in Amsterdam. As they had been since the 1640s, the actions of leading members of the Church *bij het Lam* were at the centre of attention. Among other disputes, the supporters and opponents of Galenus Abrahamsz's pro-Collegiant faction struggled for control over the selection of preachers and access to the treasury. Each side also exchanged polemics from the pulpit. The boisterous exchanges quickly became a public spectacle in Amsterdam, attracting Calvinists, Catholics and Lutherans to services in the Church *bij het Lam*. Playing on the Mennonites' professed peacefulness, a contemporary wit coined the name 'War of the Lambs' (*Lammerenkrijgh*) to describe developments.[19]

In 1663 the stakes in the dispute grew still higher. With the help of a Calvinist associate, some of Abrahamsz's opponents arranged to have him put on trial in The Hague. The charge was that he held Socinian views, such as the rejection of the doctrine of the satisfaction, that is, the belief that Christ's sacrifice on the cross had atoned for the sins of humanity. Because Dutch secular authorities had outlawed the antitrinitarianism of the Socinians in September 1653,[20] the charges were serious; the Collegiant sympathizers were being labelled as heretic-criminals. Confessionalists had tested this tactic already in the 1650s, but until 1663 they had not dared to try to give legal weight to their accusations. And when they did try to silence Abrahamsz using the authority of the Dutch state, they failed. He was acquitted in September 1663. Although a failure, their attempt illustrates the acrimony that had built up between the pro-Collegiant and pro-confession factions.

The conflict developed into an open schism. In January 1664 Amsterdam's mayors intervened in the Mennonites' on-going dispute. They demanded that all Mennonites refrain from preaching controversial sermons and directed them to arrange for new administrators to oversee

---

19 See the anonymous pamphlet *Lammerenkrijgh, anders Mennonisten Kerckentwist* (n.p., 1663).

20 See W.J. Kühler, *Het Socinianisme in Nederland* (Leeuwarden, 1980 [1912]), p. 142.

the congregation's finances. Two supporters of Abrahamsz were elected to oversee the accounts, which upset the confessionalists. In the following months communion became an equally central issue. Members of the confessionalist faction refused to celebrate the Lord's Supper with their opponents, and, unable to gain control of the Church *bij het Lam*, they decided to establish their own separate congregation. On 22 June 1664 they held their first separate service in an Amsterdam warehouse. The preacher at this gathering was Haarlem's elder Isaac Jansz Snep, a familiar name to Altona and Hamburg's Flemish Mennonite leaders.

After the schism, confessionalist leaders did not relinquish their claims to regain control of Galenus Abrahamsz's congregation. In September 1664 the confessionalists bought a building called *de Zon* (the Sun), which they intended to use as a temporary meeting house. But their efforts to return to the Church *bij het Lam* were for naught. The schism became permanent. The group that stayed in the Church *bij het Lam* became known as 'Lamists', while those who refused communion with Abrahamsz became known as 'Zonists'.

Despite the setbacks they had suffered, the new Zonist congregation in Amsterdam did not abandon its hopes for general Mennonite unity facilitated by clear principles outlined in confessional statements. Their efforts even led to some degree of success. After meetings between allied congregations in September and October 1664, confessionalists issued a policy statement entitled *Oprecht Verbondt van Eenigheydt* (Sincere Alliance of Unity). The *Verbondt* was based on the draft resolutions from the Leiden Synod, and its main article stated that all who subscribed to the document would use five confessions of faith as the foundations of congregational life and belief. In addition to the four approved at the Leiden Synod, these confessions also included the Jaques Outerman Confession (1626).[21] The *Verbondt* and the texts of five confessions of faith were published in 1665 in Amsterdam under the title *Algemeene Belydennissen Der Vereenighde Vlaemsche, Vriesche, en Hooghduytsche Doopgesinde Gemeynte Gods* (Common Confessions of Faith of the United Flemish, Frisian and High German Mennonite Congregation of God). In 1674 the *Oprecht Verbondt van Eenigheydt* became the model for the constitution (the *Vreedens Concept* or Peace Treaty) of a new umbrella organization of confessionalist Mennonite congregations throughout northern Europe. The new organization, known as the Zonist Society, was an amalgamation of confessionalist Flemish Mennonites and some of the more confessionally oriented Waterlander congregations. In the first

21 The other confessions of faith were the Concept of Cologne, the *Olijftacxken*, the Jan Cents Confession and the Dordrecht Confession. The hope, expressed at Leiden in 1660, of composing one confession of faith based on already accepted ones was never realized.

article the authors stated that unification was to be based on two sets of confessions of faith, chief among which were the documents in the *Algemeene Belydennissen*.[22] Preachers on both sides were to hold to the articles of faith as outlined in these confessional documents. If there were disagreements about doctrine, the two sides were to look to the Bible or simply agree to disagree. Furthermore, new preachers and deacons would be required to conform to these principles before they could begin their duties. The second article declared that only baptized members would be allowed to take communion in congregations adhering to the *Vreedens Concept*. The third and fourth articles outlawed all relations with the Collegiants and denied rank-and-file members the right to speak freely during congregational meetings. The final article concerned visiting preachers, who were expected, like all regular preachers, to have signed the *Vreedens Concept*.[23] Thus, at regular meetings held throughout the late seventeenth and eighteenth century, representatives were able to discuss, debate and regulate Mennonite life in member congregations according to a common set of norms.

Not all Waterlander congregations in the Netherlands joined the Zonist Society. At about the same time that Amsterdam's Zonist congregation was busy forming the Zonist Society, Amsterdam's Lamists were also gathering allies together into a competing bloc. Many of these allies were Waterlander congregations. In 1668 Abrahamsz's Church *bij het Lam* united with the Amsterdam Waterlander Church *bij de Toren*. Several years later, between 1674 and 1675, Flemish congregations mainly from southern Holland which were loyal to the Church *bij het Lam* formed an alliance with a number of further Waterlander congregations. The congregations, which sent representatives to the yearly meetings resulting from this accord, were known collectively as the South Holland or Lamist Society.

With time, the acrimony that had led to the schism diminished. Nonetheless, the two institutional blocs remained cornerstones of northern European Mennonite life until the early nineteenth century, when they

---

22 The other confessions of faith belonged to the Waterlanders' tradition. Although some Waterlander representatives had expressed concern in 1647 that Flemish confessions of faith like the *Olijftacxken* had begun to replace the Bible, there was also a long-standing confessional tradition among Waterlanders. Hans de Ries had spearheaded efforts towards inter-Mennonite unification around the beginning of the seventeenth century using confessions of faith as peace treaties, a strategy which Flemish leaders later made their own. See C.J. Dyck, 'The First Waterlandian Confession of Faith', *Mennonite Quarterly Review*, **36** (1962), pp. 5–13; and id., 'The Middelburg Confession of Hans de Ries', ibid., pp. 147–54.

23 For a printed copy of the *Vreedens Concept*, see *Grondt-steen Van Vreede en Verdraegsaemheyt, Tot Opbouwinge van den Tempel Christi Onder de Doops-Gesinde* (Amsterdam, 1674).

were replaced by one single umbrella organization. It is ironic that the root of the schism which led to the creation of the Zonist and Lamist societies was disagreement over the strategy of using confessions of faith to repair or avoid schisms.

The integration of Mennonites in Hamburg and Altona into Dutch Zonist networks

A major reason for both the reliance of Flemish Mennonites in Hamburg and Altona on confessions of faith and their strength compared with the Dompelaars was the congregation's integration into Dutch Mennonite networks. The local Flemish congregation regularly sent representatives to meetings of the Zonist Society throughout most of the eighteenth century. In retrospect, it seems clear that they should have joined the Society when it was formed in 1674.[24] The great majority of official activity pointed in this direction. As early as the 1620s and 1630s leaders from Hamburg and Altona had become involved in the Dutch Mennonite process of writing confessions of faith as part of an attempt to end schisms. Later, in the period of the Dompelaar and Zonist schisms, the connections between Dutch Mennonite confessionalists and the congregation in Hamburg and Altona became even more striking. In 1649, during the early stages of the dispute over baptism in Altona, Tobias Govertsz and Tielemann Tielen from Amsterdam and Isaac Jansz Snep from Haarlem were among those who tried to mediate between the immersionist and Flemish factions. Boudewijn Doom from Haarlem had served as a preacher in Altona in the aftermath of the baptismal controversy. In 1660 Mees Jansz assisted Altona's Flemish leaders. In 1662 Jan Sievers from Emden conducted baptisms in Altona as a guest elder. Twice (1661 and 1663) Bastiaan van Weenigem, the anti-Dompelaar publicist (see Ch. 2) and a distant relative of the local preacher Geeritt Roosen through marriage,[25] served the Altona congregation as a visiting elder; on 6 July 1663 he also ordained Geeritt Roosen. All these men were active in the Netherlands as proponents of the confessionalist cause. They had either attended the synods of Haarlem (1649) or Leiden (1660) or signed the confessionalist manifesto, the *Oprecht Verbondt van Eenigheydt* (1664). Most were involved in more than one of these key developments. By contrast, until the later 1670s, no outspoken representative of the pro-Collegiant Galenist faction had

---

24 A handwritten copy of the *Vreedens Concept* is on file in the records of the Hamburg–Altona congregation: StAHbg/MG, 2.

25 See StAHbg, Genealogische Sammlungen, Roosen, 'Notitie of Geslachtregister opgesteld door Gerrit Roosen A° 1683', p. 11.

comparable ties to Hamburg-Altona. Altona's Flemish Mennonite congregation, or at least its leadership, was clearly in the confessionalist camp. The confessionalist orientation of local Flemish Mennonites was also reinforced in the regular devotions of believers. Since at least 1652 congregation members had been using the Jaques Outerman and *Olijftacxken* confessions of faith in their services.[26] Yet despite all these clear markers of group affiliation, the congregation did not join the Zonist Society officially until 1706.

Before, during and after the so-called War of the Lambs, Mennonite leaders in Hamburg and Altona were clearly on the side of Dutch confessionalists. Nonetheless, the Flemish in Hamburg and Altona were preoccupied in this period with local leadership issues. These included conflicts in the 1660s, a visit by Galenus Abrahamsz to Altona in 1678 and uncertainty over the future of congregational leadership around the beginning of the eighteenth century. By following these decades of local leadership disputes, we get a better sense of just how complex the institutionalization of collective identity and the formation of alliances in the Mennonite diaspora was.

1659 and 1660 were years of turmoil for Mennonites in Germany and the Netherlands. That is when the anticonfessionalist manifesto of Galenus Abrahamsz and David Spruyt was published and when the confessionalists met in Leiden in an unsuccessful attempt to marginalize the pro-Collegiant faction. It is also when the Flemish deacon Samuel Isaacs Stockman converted to the Dompelaars. Added to these negative developments were the missionary campaigns of English Quakers.

In a first wave of missionary activity on the European continent, the Quakers John Stubbs and William Caton had been active in the Netherlands as early as 1653. They were soon followed by others. The first missionaries in Amsterdam arrived around 1655 and established contacts with Galenus Abrahamsz and his Collegiant friends. Initially, relations between the two groups were friendly. After all, there were several points of affinity between them. Collegiants, Quakers and some Mennonites favoured spiritualistic kinds of religious commitment, which led them to question a brand of faith oriented around confessional statements. Despite this affinity, differences arose towards the end of the 1650s over the Quakers' teachings about the Inner Light. The Quakers' conviction that they possessed direct inspiration from God conflicted with views of Collegiants and Mennonites like Abrahamsz who felt that Christianity's purity had been lost after its early, apostolic era. By the early 1660s a pamphlet war had begun between members of the two groups.[27]

---

26 See Visser, 'A Checklist of Dutch Mennonite Confessions of Faith', II.J (*Korte Belydenisse des Gheloofs*), nos. 67–9.

27 See Fix, *Prophecy and Reason*, pp. 150–56, 193–205 and 211–13.

While there was ultimately a falling out between most Mennonites and Quakers, the missionaries from England did manage to convince a few Mennonites to convert. The first Quaker missionaries reached German-speaking territories by the late 1650s and early 1660s. There is only a little surviving evidence of the visits to Hamburg.[28] In fact, most of the available sources concern fallout from the visits. Among this evidence is an entry in the membership book of Altona's Flemish Mennonite congregation, recorded by Geeritt Roosen: 'On 30 November 1659 he [the Mennonite preacher Baerent Roelifs] resigned, stopped preaching, joined the English Quakers, and spoke scornfully against baptism, communion and preaching, so that there was great sadness in the congregation and later outside it.'[29] Baerent Roelifs's entire family[30] – his wife Eeyken, his two sons Cornelis and Jan, and his two daughters Grietgen and Neeltgen – as well as three other congregation members[31] converted along with him. The family's decision must have been made only shortly before Roelifs's public announcement, for the youngest daughter Neeltgen had been baptized in the congregation on 25 March 1659.

Several months after the Roelifs family's defection,[32] three Quakers were taken into custody in Hamburg: Cornelis Roelifs, Heinrich Deen and Peter Heinrichs, the last two a father and son pair.[33] Despite their petitions to

28 The twentieth-century Quaker historian William Hull suspects that the Quaker William Ames made three missionary trips to Hamburg (1656, late 1658 and mid-1661); see Hull, *The Rise of Quakerism in Amsterdam* ([Swarthmore, Pa.], 1938), pp. 57–9 and 69. The course of Ames's travels is, however, far from clear. Writing in the mid-nineteenth century, B.C. Roosen ('Die Mennoniten und Quäker', *Mennonitische Blätter*, 1 (1854), p. 43) suspected that Ames had visited Hamburg in 1659 (not 1658), after having spent time in the Palatinate. This suggestion is supported by the timing of Mennonite conversions to Quakerism in Altona.

29 StAHbg/MG, 147, vol. 1, p. 2: 'A^{o} 1659 den 30 November heeft hy synen dienst opgeseyt het predicken staen laeten/ de engelse quaeckers by geuallen doop, auontmael en predicken tegen gesprocken/ met versmadinge soo dat daer ouer grote droefheyt in de gemente & later buyten de gemente onstaen is . . .'. Baerent Roelifs, originally a Calvinist, had joined a Mennonite congregation in Alkmaar before arriving in Altona in 1650. See S. Blaupot ten Cate, *Geschiedenis der Doopsgezinden*, i, p. 194.

30 StAHbg/MG, 147, vol. 1, pp. 16, 31, 35, 39 and 45.

31 Ibid., pp. 43, 44 and 45. Two of these converts were the husband and wife Thomas and Lucia Major, an English couple from Sussex who had married in the Reformed church in Glückstadt before being baptized into the Altona Flemish Mennonite congregation in 1658.

32 Based on reports from John Higgins to Quakers in Amsterdam, Roelifs, Deen and Heinrichs may have been imprisoned as early as March 1660. See Hull, *The Rise of Quakerism*, pp. 194–5.

33 Heinrichs and Deen may have been from a Mennonite background. Hull (ibid., pp. 68–9) says that the two were converted in Glückstadt, just west of Altona along the Elbe. While this may indeed have been the case, they may also have had family connections with the Frisian Mennonites in Hamburg and Altona. In 1675, for example, Grietgen Deen transferred her membership to the Flemish congregation; see StAHbg/MG, 147, vol. 1, p. 84. In 1661 P.H. (probably Peter Heinrichs) Deen wrote a book published in Amsterdam denouncing

magistrates,[34] they were treated as heretics and criminals. On 24 June 1660[35] Hamburg's civil authorities released a mandate in which they declared that the sect commonly known as the Quakers led Christians away from the path of salvation towards divine punishment. The sect's members' subversive schemes and poisonous teachings were a threat to God's word, legitimate government and good Christian order. The city's inhabitants were commanded to be on their guard and report such gang members to the authorities. Under no circumstances were these sectarians to be afforded shelter or protection, and any person found to be in collusion with the Quakers would be subject to severe but unspecified punishments. As was threatened in the mandate, the three prisoners were eventually expelled from Hamburg. They left for the Netherlands. Their departure marked the end of the first and most public phase of early modern Quaker missionary activity in the region.[36]

Developments connected with Quaker missionary campaigns were a serious setback to the Mennonite community in a number of ways. Roelifs's defection left the Flemish Mennonite congregation with a much-weakened preaching staff, for he was the congregation's main elder. The youngest preacher at the time, Willem Wynantz, had died at age 28 in December 1658; his colleague Joost van Steen had been placed under the ban between 1656 and 1657 for committing adultery;[37] and Hilbrandt Harmens from Campen had just joined the congregation as a junior preacher in October 1659. Except for Joost van Steen, whose moral authority had been put into question, there were thus no elders remaining who were ordained and therefore could administer sacraments. A temporary solution to the shortage of preachers was to elect Warner Jansen Colombier, a doctor,

---

the preacher of the Frisian Mennonites in Hamburg and Altona. The text, of which I have been unable to find a copy, was entitled *Ontdeckinge eens Predigers tot Hamburg, genaemt Jan de Marne*.

34 See 'Eine Schrifft an die Obrigkeit/ Richters/ und Regirers/ insonderheit an Bürgermeister und Rath der Stadt Hamburg durch Hinrich Dehn/ Cornelius Roeloffs/ Peter Hinrichs/ in Hamborg auff dem Bohm/ im Jahr 1660'. I have been unable to find a copy of this document. A reference to it is found in the appendix to *Quäcker Grewel* (Hamburg, 1661).

35 *Sammlung der . . . Gesetze und Verfassungen*, ed. J.F. Blank, 6 vols (Hamburg, 1763–74), i, pp. 172–4.

36 Roger Longworth organized small Quaker meetings for believers in Hamburg and Friedrichstadt beginning in 1682. According to Hull, Longworth and William Penn helped to convince several Mennonite families from Hamburg to move to Germantown, Pennsylvania in 1700. See Hull, *The Rise of Quakerism*, p. 69. For details about the migration of Mennonite families from Hamburg to Germantown, see William I. Hull, *William Penn and the Dutch Quaker Migration to Pennsylvania* ([Swarthmore, Pa.], 1935), p. 410; Roosen, *Geschichte der Mennoniten-Gemeinde*, part 1, p. 63; and StAHbg/MG, 203, vol. 2 (Pennsylvanien).

37 Joost van Steen served in Altona between 1652 and 1656. See StAHbg/MG, 147, vol. 1, pp. 2, 32, 40 and 44.

and Geeritt Roosen, then a deacon and merchant, as preachers on 8 April 1660. But neither Colombier, Roosen nor Harmens was an ordained elder.

To help cope with the unpleasant political and ecclesiastical circumstances, Altona's Flemish leaders turned again, as they had done in 1649 during the rising crisis over baptism, to Mennonites in the Netherlands for assistance. In April 1660 a fully ordained Dutch Mennonite preacher named Mees Jansz arrived in Altona. Jansz, as the only qualified elder present, performed a series of baptisms. Both he[38] and Roosen[39] also preached sermons (Roosen's first as a new preacher) against heterodox Mennonites and groups like the Quakers – but neither man mentioned the Quakers by name, preferring instead to use somewhat more vague references.[40]

Roosen was much more explicit in a text printed in Amsterdam later in 1660 – *Schriftelick Bericht Over eenige aenmercklijcke puncten de Engelschen Die Quaeckers genoemt worden* (Written Remarks about Some Notable Claims of the English, who are Called Quakers). As he explained in the pamphlet's introduction, preaching against the Quakers before his congregation in Altona had struck such a chord with the majority of congregants that some had asked for printed versions of his thoughts. *Schriftelick Bericht* was the result. If the pamphlet was based on sermons given in the congregation, texts of those sermons have not survived. In the pamphlet Roosen did not shy away from naming the itinerant preacher William Ames as the source of confusion and disorder in the congregation, and he attacked the Quakers on four subjects: God's word in the Bible, baptism, communion and church offices. After detailed refutations of the Quakers' positions on each of these subjects, he ended by granting that some groups – perhaps referring to the immersionists or the Frisian Mennonites – did indeed interpret church ordinances and ceremonies too rigidly. The proper response, however, was for the faithful to strengthen 'correct procedures' (*het rechte gebruyck*), for outward ceremonies practised properly were meant to reinforce the believer's spirit (*gemoedt*). In itself, there was nothing wrong with the Quakers' desire to live by the Holy Spirit, but their failing was the attempt to do this beyond the

38 StAHbg/MG, 248, vol. 4, 'getrocken uyt een doop predicatie van meyß Jansen matt 28v18 oft markus 16v16'. The manuscript is undated and written in Geeritt Roosen's hand. Mees Jansz also preached in Altona in spring 1674. The justification for the 1660 dating of the sermon is that Jansz administered baptism in Altona only once – in 1660. See B.C. Roosen's notes in StAHbg/MG, 261c, 'leeraaren van doopsgesinde of Mennonitische gemeenten, die als buitenleeraaren hier geweest zyn en gedient hebben'.

39 StAHbg/MG, 248, vol. 4, 'predicatie wt Micha 6v8'. See especially fols [9]^r–[18]^v, which amount to a long defence of the written word in the Bible.

40 Ibid., fol. [14]^r: 'die haer douen verklaeren datse Christus in haer hebben & dat die het spreeckt wat wt oft door haer voort compt . . .'.

boundaries of a recognized church organization. Roosen thought it unlikely that the Quakers' teachings would prove as powerful as those of a reformer like Menno Simons, whose successors had been willing to suffer persecution to preserve the truth of their faith. Roosen was particularly disturbed by the Quaker missionary's interest in proselytizing among Mennonites. If Ames wanted to show his love for all people, as he claimed, then he should spend more time among the Reformed, Catholics, Lutherans and, above all, the Jews. All these groups were more sinful than the Mennonites. The text ended with an anonymous defence of textual authority[41] and a satirical poem by 'J.V.V'.[42]

Roosen published his *Schriftelick Bericht* in Amsterdam in 1660. On 1 May of that year Roosen, Jansz and two other Dutch colleagues – Jan Jansen from Alkmaar and Walch Paulsen from Zaandam – left for the Low Countries. Roosen's two-month trip included stops in Emden, Huisduinen and Alkmaar, where he acted as a guest preacher.[43] He also stayed a while in Amsterdam, where he arranged the printing of his anti-Quaker pamphlet and a collection of sermons by his recently deceased colleague Willem Wynantz.[44] On 2 July he returned to his home in Hamburg.[45]

The disputes with the Quakers marked Geeritt Roosen's first open, public contributions as preacher to the interregional project of codifying Mennonite standards of belief and practice. His activities are especially significant for two reasons. First, they took place in the midst of far-reaching disputes among Mennonites in Amsterdam about the nature of the church. Second, Roosen was later to become the most influential leader in the local Mennonite community, as well as an author of confessional documents. His allegiance to the Dutch confessionalist cause is a major reason why his congregation eventually developed institutional ties with the Dutch Zonists.[46]

---

41 'Aenhangsel door een ander', in G[eeritt] Roose[n] *et al.*, *Schriftelick bericht over eenige aenmercklijcke puncten der Engelschen die Quaeckers genoemt worden* (Amsterdam, 1660), pp. 34–8.

42 'Antidotum. Tegen het vergift der Geestdryvers. Tot verdedigingh van 't beschreven woord Godts', ibid., pp. 38–40. 'J.V.V'. refers to the Dutch poet-polemicist Joost van den Vondel, who at one time had been a deacon in Amsterdam's Waterlander congregation before converting to Roman Catholicism in 1641. For background to the poem, which was published originally in 1626, see Sjouke Voolstra, 'The Path to Conversion: The Controversy between Hans de Ries and Nittert Obbes', in Walter Klaassen (ed.), *Anabaptism Revisited* (Scottdale, Pa. and Waterloo, Ont., 1992), pp. 98–114.

43 See Berend Carl Roosen, *Gerhard Roosen* (Hamburg, 1854), p. 22.

44 Willem Wynantz, *LVIII Stichtelycke Predicatien* (Amsterdam, 1660).

45 Although Roosen was in the Netherlands at the time of the Leiden Synod, there is no evidence that he visited Leiden.

46 The claim in Hylkema, *Reformateurs*, part 1, p. 87, that Geeritt Roosen was a Galenist sympathizer is incorrect.

An important step along the way to an alliance with the confessionalists was a grant of land Roosen made to his congregation in January 1669. It was a tool with which to try to discourage future divisions like the ones that had plagued Dutch and German Mennonites in recent years. The property involved was a farm northwest of Hamburg near Uetersen. Roosen valued it at 10,000 marks *lübsch*, a very significant sum. He declared himself to be the administrator of the land for as long as he lived. Rent from it was to be used either as a fund for lay preachers' households or for emergencies occasioned by war or persecution. He also left careful instructions for administering the land after his death. These included the following passage:

> Because misunderstandings over beliefs, congregational government or temporal questions can sometimes unfortunately arise through the influence of strange opinions or stubbornness, so that divisions or schisms and difficult disputes about congregational finances result; it is therefore my desire (because I have with God's grace based our congregation's government and teachings on God's word, following our printed confessions, particularly those included in the *Verbondt van Eenigheydt*, a book published four to five years ago) that, if such strange interpretations of beliefs arise which are contrary to the confessions and order in the congregation, and schisms result, my donation will not go to those who oppose the confessions but will remain with those who continue to abide by the teachings and order in the congregation as conceived of in the confessions which we hold to today.[47]

With this donation of land, Roosen was not only trying to discourage future schisms. He was also taking the first step towards formalizing the personal ties he had developed with Zonists in the Netherlands.

One thing about this donation is worth highlighting. Roosen, not the congregational council collectively, controlled the terms of the land grant. The Flemish congregation had of course been in the confessionalist sphere of influence for some time already. Nonetheless, it was through Roosen's

[47] StAHbg/MG, 59, vol. 1, 11 January 1669: 'maer die wyle het leyder door bevindinge . . . somtyts can gebeuren/ dat eenige mißverstanden door vrembde gevoelen/ oft harde hoofden/ in de gementen voorvallen tsy in oft ouer geloofs poinckten/ gemeente Regiering/ oft tytlycke questien/ datter deelingen oft scheuringen wt volgen, en dan swaere commerlycke dispuyten ouer die gemeenten middelen comen soo is die weegen myn begeeren hiermeede (die wyle ick door godts genade onse gemeenten Regieringe end leere in godts woort gegront . . . achternvolgens onse gedruckte confessien insonderheyt begreegen int verbont van eenicheyt synde een boeck soo voor 4 a 5 Jaeren gedruckt) dat soo soodanige vremde verstanden in geloofs poinckten teegen die gedachte confessien en Regeringe der gemeente opstanden/ en scheuringen wt mochten volgen dat alsdan deese myne leegaet niet sal mogen comen aen soodanige cant/ die die confessien comen aftegaen maer verblyuen by die geene die daer continueeren en blyuen by die leere en gemeenten Regeeringe volgens voor gedachte conffessien en als von uns tegenwoordich beleest wort . . .'.

personal authority that ties with the Dutch Zonists were being strengthened in the aftermath of the Amsterdam schism, Quaker missionary activity and renewed squabbles with the immersionists. The donation of land indicated the extent to which Roosen was attempting to exert his influence over beliefs and congregational government in the interests of the confessionalist cause.

In the years following Roosen's grant of land, the confessionalist allegiances of leaders in Hamburg and Altona did not wane. In 1672 they helped silence an anticonfessionalist, pro-Galenist leader in the northern German port settlement of Friedrichstadt.[48] Why they declined to join the Zonists a short time later when the Zonist Society formed in 1674 is not clear. One possibility is that the congregation was then preoccupied with local affairs, as it had been in previous years. The 1670s saw such important developments as the building of the Flemish congregation's new church on the site of the old building (completed 1675), and the establishment of the congregation's first official cemetery (completed 1678), located only a short distance from the church in Altona.[49] Another possibility is that the vocal support of leaders for the confessionalist cause was not shared by all congregants, and this possible lack of agreement may have given leaders pause.

The best evidence that congregants held diverging attitudes towards the Zonist–Lamist schism is a visit by Galenus Abrahamsz to Altona in 1678. Abrahamsz arrived in the region on 6 May of that year, apparently without much prior notice. He immediately visited Ocke Pieters, since 1676 a fully ordained elder like Roosen and Abrahamsz, to ask for the privilege of preaching in the new church in Altona. Much discussion followed among the congregation's members. On 8 May local leaders decided to send a delegation consisting of Pieters, Roosen and the deacon Hans Harmens to question Abrahamsz and recommend whether or not his request should be granted. Roosen acted as secretary.[50] After the three men reported the results of the interview to their colleagues, the congregation's leaders decided to allow Abrahamsz to appear before congregants, but with restrictions. In his notes Roosen outlined the concerns he and others had raised in the process of making their decision.

For one thing, the members of the delegation were understandably reluctant to give the enemy of their friends access to the pulpit. Seriously listening to the views of the most prominent Lamist might upset Zonists

---

[48] See Dollinger, *Geschichte der Mennoniten*, pp. 27–30; and Stadtarchiv Friedrichstadt, Mennonitengemeinde, 0.07.

[49] For more background on the building of the Flemish church, see Ch. 1. For locations of the church and cemetery, see Schroeder and Huebert, *Mennonite Historical Atlas*, p. 10.

[50] See StAHbg/MG, 3.

in the Netherlands and lead to the collapse of old alliances which the community relied on as a source of pastoral assistance.[51] The more immediate concern, however, was local unity. Roosen made it clear that there was the potential for disruptions over the issue of Abrahamsz's appearance, for members were deeply divided in their attitudes towards the controversial Dutch churchman.[52] Despite long-standing connections with the Zonists in the Netherlands, apparently not all of the rank-and-file members shared Geeritt Roosen's anti-Galenist enthusiasm. Some members were unsettled by rumours that Abrahamsz deviated from true Mennonite teachings and they did not want him to be allowed to give sermons. But others were either curious to hear the much discussed preacher or had already attended his talks elsewhere and had been impressed. In the end, permission was granted.

The issue of unity within the Flemish congregation was closely connected with the existence of competing Anabaptist congregations in Hamburg and Altona. Concern about the larger local implications of Abrahamsz's visit was probably decisive for the ultimate decision to allow him to preach. If leaders decided to forbid Abrahamsz the privilege of preaching before members, he might, they feared, seek contacts with the Dompelaars. If he spoke before their immersionist rivals, he might attract Flemish members to the Dompelaars' gatherings.[53] This would have been a direct threat to Flemish unity, at least from the point of view of leaders like Roosen. It was thus the wisest policy to let Abrahamsz speak – assuming first of all that his theology was not blatantly objectionable and that he was willing to avoid controversial subjects.

The purpose of the interview of 8 May was to test the orthodoxy of Abrahamsz's beliefs and teachings. Roosen, Pieters and Harmens raised four issues with him. The first concerned baptism. The members of the delegation wanted to know if Abrahamsz denied that baptism with water was an ordinance of Christ, or whether spiritual baptism was enough. He answered that baptism with water was necessary for all faithful followers of Christ's commandments. He elaborated on his answer by distinguishing himself from the Socinians, who he said claimed that a person could be a Christian without first being baptized. Before becoming members in his congregation, he explained, people were taught the fundamentals of Christian faith and were only then baptized. On the second, related issue of participation in communion, Abrahamsz said that communicants had

51 Ibid., fol. [1]^{r}: 'en ter ander syden waß men beducht dat het in hollant sommige dienaeren en gemeenten die ons altyt gunstich en geneegen waeren geweest bedroeven en van ons afkeerich maecken soude'.

52 Ibid.: '. . . soo waeren wy dienaeren over de eene cant bevreest voor unlust onder de gemeente . . .'.

53 Ibid: 'dat hy dan licht by onse afgeschydene vrinden soude gaen . . .'.

to be baptized; only the most infrequent exceptions had been made in his church in the past. Roosen, Pieters and Harmens continued by asking him what he believed about the nature of God. He gave an orthodox answer: Christ was God's son who existed in eternity before his birth to Mary.

The final issue concerned the status of Mennonite confessions of faith, the very issue that had been at the centre of controversy several decades earlier in the Netherlands. The delegation members told Abrahamsz that there were rumours that he considered confessions of faith to be a mish-mash of articles which should not have any authority in the lives of Christians. They found this view unacceptable, for, like Menno Simons, they considered confessions of faith to be clear expressions of their common, unifying beliefs. They did add a qualification: unlike the House Buyers or Pieter Jansz Twisck People – two of the competing local Mennonite groups – they always used the Bible as the foundation for their articles of faith. Abrahamsz admitted that he had spoken out in the past against people who had demanded adherence to confessions at the expense of the Bible. However, this did not mean he was against confessions of faith. Roosen wrote that 'he [Abrahamsz] considers Mennonite confessions in general, among all texts and propositions conceived by people, to be closest to Holy Scripture'.[54] Abrahamsz's answers reassured his interrogators.

But Geeritt Roosen and his companions had probably wanted to be reassured. After all, they had not pressed Abrahamsz very hard, especially on the issue of confessions of faith. In 1669 Roosen had declared that the *Oprecht Verbondt van Eenigheydt* was the measure of orthodoxy and a point of reference during disputes about matters of faith, but a decade later he did not insist that Abrahamsz declare his support for the partisan Zonist document and the confessional statements approved in it. Abrahamsz's general assurances about his attitudes towards confessions were enough. The inquisitors also did not ask who in particular Abrahamsz thought had diminished the importance of the Bible in favour of confessional statements. If they had asked, they would certainly have heard the names of many of their old Zonist friends – including Tieleman Tielen van Sittert, Tobias Govertsz van den Wijngaard, Bastiaan van Weenigem, Mees Jansz and Isaac Jansz Snep – with whom Abrahamsz had fought in the early 1660s. Whether or not they had planned the outcome of the discussion, the delegation's members had succeeded in avoiding differences

---

[54] Ibid., fol. [2]^r: 'dat hy de confessien der doopsgesinde int algemen onder alle menschelycke schriften opstellingen/ de naeste aen de H schrifture achten te syn'. After the Zonist–Lamist schism, Galenus Abrahamsz developed a slightly more conservative attitude towards confessions of faith; see Kolakowski, 'Dutch Seventeenth-Century Anticonfessional Ideas and Rational Religion'.

which in past years had seemed so fundamental that they had been the ostensible causes of a schism in Amsterdam. After he declared himself to be 'an enemy of all unrest and division',[55] Abrahamsz took to the pulpit in Altona five times during Easter commemorations in 1678. His visit went so well that he was welcomed back to the Flemish congregation in Altona in 1681.

Abrahamsz's visits to Altona were a sign of a general pattern of normalizing relationships between the Zonists and Lamists. The acrimony of the 1660s was fading into the distant past. Throughout most of the 1680s and 1690s, the Zonist–Lamist divide played little significant role in the congregational life of the local Mennonites. However, the basic division remained an institutional fact, as did the informal alliance that had emerged in the course of the schism. Hamburg and Altona continued to be within the Zonist sphere of influence throughout the seventeenth century, even though the alliance depended in large part on the active role of leaders like Geeritt Roosen and not on a institutionalized relationship. When that relationship was finally codified at the very beginning of the eighteenth century, decision-making was no longer driven by events in the Netherlands so much as by local developments and concerns. Among these were polemical battles between Lutherans and Mennonites in Hamburg (see Ch. 4). Another was concern about the congregation's future leadership and regulation.

Geeritt Roosen had been a key leader in the congregation since the middle of the seventeenth century, and it was upon his personal authority and initiative that the congregation had relied more and more towards the end of the century. However, although still quite fit and active into his nineties, Roosen, who was born in 1612, was obviously approaching the end of his unusually long life. When he died, the congregation would lose one of its main links to ecclesiastical allies in Dutch Zonist congregations. Even during times of factional peace in the Mennonite world, these ties were crucial for the regular functioning of religious life, for without a dependable supply of preachers from the Netherlands the congregation was threatened with ecclesiastical isolation and a loss of spiritual direction. For a period in the 1690s, the elderly Roosen was the congregation's only ordained preacher qualified to administer the sacraments of communion and baptism. During this period, several visiting preachers from the Netherlands provided assistance in Altona. One of these preachers, Riewart Dircks, was appointed a permanent member of the preaching staff in 1697, but he was soon forced out of the congregation in an episode that was to play an important role in the regulation and standardization of congregational government (see Ch. 4). In July 1699 another visitor, the

[55] StAHbg/MG, 3, fol. [2]^{v}: 'want hy van all onruste en twisten een vyant waß'.

Dutch Zonist elder Dirck Symons Moriaan, laid hands on Jan de Lanoy, Pieter Verhelle and Jacob Cornelis van Campen. This act of ordination meant the Flemish congregation now had four elders. This was a major step away from reliance on the personal leadership of Roosen.

Another major step took place in the next decade in response to tensions among congregants. The exact reason for these tensions is difficult to discover from available sources. In a letter addressed to Geeritt Roosen, Jan de Lanoy and the rest of the preaching staff, the anonymous author decried the moral state of many of his co-religionists. The congregation was a 'fallen Zion'[56] and had been so for several years, wrote the letter's author. He called upon preachers to work to restore outer order as well as the morality of individuals by holding firm to 'the example of the first apostolic church and the ordinances of Paul in his letters to Timothy and Titus'.[57] At the bottom of the letter's second side the author expressed the worry that the old Geeritt Roosen, who had contributed so much over the years to good order in the congregation, would go to his grave in sadness caused by the moral degeneracy of congregants and the laxness of preachers. At its 5 December 1703 meeting Roosen threatened to quit the congregational council. Following the proposal raised by Jan de Lanoy and Pieter Verhelle, council members resolved 'that preachers shall work in general and in particular towards that which can bring about peace and unity as well as the happiness of the father [Geeritt Roosen]'.[58] Roosen, already well into his nineties, had been considering retirement for some time. As early as the 9 September 1703 council meeting, his colleagues had thanked him for his many years of service and asked him to remain a council member.[59] Despite his second thoughts later that year, he remained active as a congregational leader. His reservations of 1703 might suggest that the undated letter was written around this time.

---

[56] Mennonite Archives, Bethel College, SA.I.93, third side; I have used a photocopy found at the Mennonite Historical Library, Goshen College. The letter is incorrectly labelled with a title added by an archivist in the 1970s: 'A Significant Dutch Letter by Gerrit Roosen about Conditions in the Altona-Mennonite Church around 1675'. The letter was not by Roosen but was addressed to Roosen and others. Although undated, it was also certainly written much later than the archivist's title suggests. There would have been no point in naming both Roosen and de Lanoy before 1699, when de Lanoy was ordained; from then on he was the most senior elder after Roosen. The date 1675 was probably chosen for no other reason than because it was in the middle of the preaching career of the incorrectly attributed author, Geeritt Roosen.

[57] Ibid.: ''t voorbeeld, van de eerste Apostolise Kerck, en de Ordonantie van Paulus in syne Brieven aen Timotheus en Titus geschreeven . . .'.

[58] StAHbg/MG, 6, vol. 1, p. 21: 'en dat dienaren soo int algemeen als Particulier, sulle Tragten soo veel haar mogelyck is, t:geene tot vreede en eendragt, en tot vergenouging van vader can dienen bytebrengen'.

[59] Ibid., p. 18.

Some leaders and congregational members continued to be dissatisfied with the status quo. In 1705 two Dutch mediators, Pieter Beets and Harmen Reynskes, travelled to Altona to help negotiate an end to continuing conflicts among congregants. On 12 September, the mediators distributed a congregational ordinance designed to eliminate the source of problems.[60] The ordinance declared the *Oprecht Verbondt van Eenigheydt* to be a cornerstone of future decisions about ecclesiastical and theological matters. It also built on a congregational ordinance that Geeritt Roosen had written in response to the controversy over Riewart Dircks's alleged antitrinitarianism (see Ch. 4). An important addition to the 1705 agreement was the demand that preachers carefully prepare their sermons so as not to encourage members to visit other church's services (articles 4 and 5), a provision perhaps occasioned by the popularity of the sermons of the Dompelaar Jacob Denner. Together with twenty-three preachers, deacons and prominent members of the congregation, Beets and Reynskes signed the agreement on 20 September 1705, after it was presented before the congregation's members.[61]

The two mediators were both deputies of the Zonist Society. Since the beginning of the Society's existence in 1674, Geeritt Roosen's congregation had been within its sphere of influence, but it had not been an official member. That changed in 1706. In that year the congregational council sent a letter to Amsterdam requesting admittance into the organization. The request was granted. Altona's Flemish Mennonites first appeared in the membership rolls of the Society's May 1707 annual meeting.

Of course, admittance into the Society and the ordination of several new elders did not eliminate disputes within the congregation.[62] But these developments were nonetheless very significant, for they meant that congregational governance was significantly more standardized and regulated than it had been previously. The congregation in Hamburg and Altona was becoming less and less dependent on the leadership of strong-willed individuals like Geeritt Roosen to lead them through times of dispute. They were now officially part of an interregional decision-making body that coordinated the interests and oversaw the internal affairs of a large

60 StAHbg/MG, 5.

61 The ordinance of 1705 served as the cornerstone of the congregation's constitution throughout the eighteenth century. In 1771 it was used as the model for a new ordinance. See StAHbg/MG, 6, vol. 1, pp. 266–8.

62 Examples include disputes over the theological and administrative positions of Jacob Cornelis van Campen. See Geeritt Roosen's 1707 manuscript, 'oover Jacob Corneelsen syn stiel van Preedickinge', StAHbg/MG, 248, vol. 4. More documentation can probably be founded in the as of yet only partially catalogued resources of the Mennonite Library and Archives in North Newton, Kansas. My thanks go to John Thiesen for making me aware of these sources.

number of Mennonite congregations throughout the Netherlands and Germany.

Conclusion

Although it joined the Zonist Society relatively late, the congregation in Hamburg and Altona was one of the key centres of Mennonite confessionalist activity into the early nineteenth century. For example, its leaders in the later eighteenth century had strong ties to Cornelis Ris, one of the last enthusiastic early modern Dutch Mennonite proponents of clear confessional statements. In 1776, leaders of the congregation in Hamburg and Altona published a German translation of Ris's *De Geloofsleere Der Waare Mennoniten of Doopsgezinden* (The Faith of the True Mennonites or Baptism-Minded People) (1766), which they entrenched as their official confession of faith in 1803.[63] By this time, however, Dutch Mennonite confessionalism was on the wane.

The golden age of Dutch and northern German Mennonite confessionalism was the seventeenth century. Like other confessional churches, Mennonites developed a system of routines and practices which solidified their unique way of life. First and perhaps most obviously, there was the unique ritual of adult baptism, the cornerstone of the Mennonites' congregationally organized believers' church. Passions about the practice of adult baptism could lead to schisms, as was the case in Hamburg and Altona in the middle of the seventeenth century, but the majority of Mennonites in northern Germany and the Netherlands upheld sprinkling as the proper form of the ritual. Secondly, lay preachers and deacons played a key role in the maintenance of an active local and interregional confessional life. While Dutch Mennonite communities were already beginning to professionalize their pastorate in the seventeenth century, their northern German colleagues held for the most part onto the tradition of lay ministry until the later eighteenth century.[64] Nonetheless, lay preachers fulfilled roles similar to the clergy in other confessional churches. They preached, administered the sacraments, married young believers, guarded against heterodox and heretical ideas, disciplined stubborn sinners, and negotiated on behalf of their congregants. Some, like Geeritt Roosen, were especially active, committing personal resources of land and money to the maintenance of church institutions and orthodoxy. Preachers were

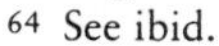

63 For more background, see Michael Driedger, 'Gerrit Karsdorp (1729–1811): Mennonitenprediger und Förderer der Aufklärung in Hamburg. Die Bibliothek eines Hamburger Kaufmanns', *Mennonitische Geschichtsblätter*, 56 (1999), pp. 35–53.

64 See ibid.

also responsible for nurturing connections between congregations separated in some cases by great distances. Traditions of ecclesiastical mutual aid emerged; preachers from one congregation would travel as needed to others to assist colleagues there. Thirdly, an interconnected set of institutions and administrative bodies emerged to help coordinate local congregational life and relations between congregations. In Hamburg and Altona there were the congregational ordinances of the late seventeenth and early eighteenth century, but the process of institutionalization and routinization of congregational life had begun much earlier than that. Dutch Mennonites provided models to their northern German colleagues for institutional order, and after years of informal but close relations with Dutch confessionalists leaders in Hamburg and Altona eventually joined the Zonist Society, which they remained a member of throughout the rest of the eighteenth century. Finally, the centrepiece of Mennonite confessionalism was the codifying of clear beliefs in confessions of faith. Leaders collected key texts in the *Oprecht Verbondt van Eenigheydt*, and using these as a model, northern German Mennonites like Geeritt Roosen composed further confessional statements for local believers.

While the development of an interregional Mennonite confessional community was a part of a major trend in the history of early modern European Christianity, it was not a trend reflected with equal strength in all quarters of the northern European Anabaptist tradition. One of the best examples of anticonfessionalism is the history of the Dompelaar congregation. Although, unlike their Flemish Mennonite neighbour, its leaders never showed much enthusiasm for confessions of faith, they did show early signs of developing a strong institutional tradition built around a strict interpretation of ritual practice. This, however, was not to be. The congregation disbanded after about a century of activity. This very small group lacked ideological cohesion, material resources and ecclesiastical support networks of the kind that helped the Flemish Mennonites in Hamburg and Altona maintain a strong sense of institutional identity in urban Lutheran Germany.

The much larger and significant community of Dutch Lamists, too, provides a contrast with the Zonist brand of Mennonite institutional culture. However, while Lamist leaders were originally against the codification of Mennonite beliefs in confessions of faith and nurtured a more spiritualistic understanding of Christian community, their congregations established their own unique brand of Mennonite institutional tradition, which, by the later seventeenth century, even included a few moderate confessions of faith. In other words, the Lamists are an example of 'the intellectual and organizational entrenchment' (Zeeden) of Mennonite life, despite their downplaying of the binding nature of confessional statements. There was not merely one but rather several brands of Mennonite confessionalism.

CHAPTER FOUR

Mennonite Confessionalization and Beyond: Polemics and the Articulation of a Conformist Ideology

Mennonites and the historiography of confessionalization

The previous two chapters have concentrated on relations between various groups of Mennonites. This concentration provides only part of the picture necessary to understand the significance of public definitions of Mennonite identities. In the early modern era, when public rights depended almost everywhere on religious affiliation, faith and belief were politically charged. This was as true of the Mennonites, who seldom held political office and certainly held no high-ranking government positions, as of mainstream Protestants and Catholics, from whose ranks came Europe's most powerful men and women. The paradigm of confessionalization,[1] which is now receiving a great deal of attention from

---

[1] The literature in the field is far too extensive to summarize in a footnote. Some important reviews of this extensive literature include (earliest to most recent): Peter Thaddäus Lang, 'Konfessionsbildung als Forschungsfeld', *Historisches Jahrbuch*, 100 (1980), pp. 479–93; Hsia, *Social Discipline in the Reformation*; Harm Klueting, *Das konfessionelle Zeitalter 1525–1648* (Stuttgart, 1989); Heinz Schilling, '"Konfessionsbildung" und "Konfessionalisierung"', *Geschichte in Wissenschaft und Unterricht*, 42 (1991), pp. 447–63 and 779–94; Heinrich Richard Schmidt, *Konfessionalisierung im 16. Jahrhundert* (Munich, 1992); Heinz Schilling, 'Die Konfessionalisierung von Kirche, Staat und Gesellschaft – Profil, Leistung, Defizite und Perspektiven eines geschichtswissenschaftlichen Paradigmas', in Wolfgang Reinhard and Heinz Schilling (eds), *Die katholische Konfessionalisierung* (Münster, 1995), pp. 1–49; Harrington and Smith, 'Confessionalization, Community, and State-Building'; Wolfgang Reinhard, 'Sozialdisziplinierung – Konfessionalisierung – Modernisierung: Ein historiographischer Diskurs', in Nada Boskovska Leimgruber (ed.), *Die frühe Neuzeit in der Geschichtswissenschaft: Forschungstendenzen und Forschungserträge* (Paderborn, 1997), pp. 39–55; Anton Schindling, 'Konfessionalisierung und Grenzen von Konfessionalisierbarkeit', in Anton Schindling and Walter Ziegler (eds), *Die Territorien des Reichs im Zeitalter der Reformation und Konfessionalisierung: Land und Konfession 1500–1650*, 7 vols (Münster, 1989–97), vii, pp. 9–44; Heinrich Richard Schmidt, 'Sozialdisziplinierung? Ein Plädoyer für das Ende des Etatismus in der Konfessionalisierungsforschung', *Historische Zeitschrift*, 265 (1997), pp. 639–82; and Andreas Holzem, 'Die Konfessionsgesellschaft: Christenleben zwischen staatlichem Bekenntniszwang und religiöser Heilshoffnung', *Zeitschrift für Kirchengeschichte*, 110 (1999), pp. 53–85.

historians and even sociologists,[2] focuses attention on this interconnectedness of politics and religion in Europe in the generations after the Reformation. Because its meaning is a matter of dispute among historians, 'confessionalization' requires some explanation.

In the most common definition, confessionalization is a recent elaboration on the concept of confessionalism (see Ch. 3). Its two main advocates are the German historians Heinz Schilling and Wolfgang Reinhard. The innovation that Schilling and Reinhard have brought to debates is the following: they argue that there was a close connection between the formation of distinct Catholic, Lutheran and Calvinist confessional cultures, on the one hand, and state-building and modernization in the sixteenth and seventeenth centuries, on the other. Their claim is that after the Reformation, rulers and state bureaucracies (especially in German-speaking Europe) used the institutions of the territorial church to transform society fundamentally and at all levels,[3] and this growing cooperation between church and state encouraged the emergence of modernity.

To emphasize their point that secular rulers and clergymen cooperated to establish and maintain new forms of order in society, both Schilling and Reinhard have linked the older concept of confessionalism with Gerhard Oestreich's concept of 'social discipline'.[4] In the 1960s Oestreich coined the phrase as an alternative to the traditional concept of 'absolutism'. Traditional research on absolutism in Oestreich's day was largely about the political measures taken by individual rulers at the highest levels of territorial governments. It was almost exclusively a narrow kind of political and institutional history. Reacting against this view, Oestreich pointed to the importance of a much more fundamental social, psychological and moral reordering of public and private life in 'the age of absolutism'. He argued that the reordering of social norms in the seventeenth and eighteenth centuries was initiated by lawgivers, educators and official opinion-makers

---

2 For example, see two essays by Philip S. Gorski: 'The Protestant Ethic Revisited: Disciplinary Revolution and State Formation in Holland and Prussia', *American Journal of Sociology*, 99 (1993), pp. 265–316; and 'Historicizing the Secularization Debate: Church, State, and Society in Late Medieval and Early Modern Europe (ca. 1300 to 1700)', *American Sociological Review*, 65 (2000), pp. 138–67.

3 See, for example, Heinz Schilling, *Die Stadt in der Frühen Neuzeit* (Munich, 1993), p. 99: 'Die "Konfessionalisierung" gilt auch stadt- und bürgergeschichtlich als "gesellschaftsgeschichtlicher Fundamentalvorgang" . . ., der das öffentliche und private Leben in den Städten tief umpflügte.'

4 Gerhard Oestreich, 'The Structure of the Absolute State', in Brigitta Oestreich and H.G. Königsberger (eds), *Neostoicism and the Early Modern State*, trans. David McLintock (Cambridge, 1982), pp. 258–73. Also see Winfried Schulze, 'Gerhard Oestreichs Begriff "Sozialdisziplinierung in der Frühen Neuzeit"', *Zeitschrift für Historische Forschung*, 14 (1987), pp. 265–302.

working for the central government at all levels, from courts to villages. By issuing decrees or otherwise setting new standards for morals and behaviour, governments shaped public attitudes in ways which made subjects more governable. It was to this coordinated standardizing activity that governments owed their growing authority, which was effective first among governmental agents in armies and bureaucracies and later among the population generally. Understood in this way, social discipline has a greater socio-historical component than the old concept of absolutism. Reinhard and Schilling modified Oestreich's model by identifying church discipline and other uses of official religion as early, post-Reformation forms of social discipline conducted for the ultimate benefit of the modernizing and centralizing state. Using religion, rulers and their allied church leaders forced or educated subjects to behave in ordered and routine ways.

There are two main advantages to the paradigm of confessionalization. First and foremost, it is intended as a step towards a comparative history of the linkages between religion, society, politics, economics and culture. Developments in Catholic and Protestant territories are of equal interest. Scholars try to avoid the most parochial and partisan aspects of old-fashioned church histories, while still focusing on the central importance of religion in historical change. Secondly, the paradigm has provided a large framework in which more specialized scholars can orient their local research. This common point of reference has made it easier for otherwise isolated specialists to communicate their work to a larger audience.

Despite its advantages, there is growing unease among scholars about the paradigm. Subjects of concern include: the assumption by some advocates that the complex details of local history conform to the grand generalizations of the paradigm; a dominant structural-functionalist focus on institutions, combined sometimes with an apparent lack of interest in actual lived experience and belief at the local level; the often unconfirmed assumption that the programmes and intentions of rulers were transformed into reality; and the 'whiggishness' of the paradigm's focus on the rise of modernity.

The main focus here, however, is on another weak point in the paradigm: the portrayal of the history of religious minorities. The standard definition of confessionalization has implications for the way we think about religious minorities. Members of only three Christian traditions had access to leading governmental offices in early modern central Europe. This arrangement was entrenched legally in the Peace of Westphalia of 1648. Article VII.2 of the Peace Treaty reads: '. . . but, besides the religions named above [that is, Catholic, Lutheran and Calvinist], no other shall be accepted or tolerated in the Holy Roman Empire'.[5] In a way, the legacy of 1648 lives

[5] Quoted from *Documents of the Christian Church*, ed. Henry Bettenson (New York, 1947), p. 307.

on in the historiography of confessionalization, for the groups which were denied official rights in the Holy Roman Empire are also the ones that are defined as victims of confessionalization or are simply ignored by historians today. R. Po-chia Hsia expresses the conventional attitude among historians of confessionalization when he writes: 'Not everyone was included in the process of confessionalization. But the outsiders – Jews, Anabaptists, freethinkers, and spiritualists – were nonetheless affected by the confessionalization of early modern Europe.'[6]

In at least one important regard, Hsia's conclusion is useful. The categorization of Anabaptists as the 'Other' has a long tradition. For example, Joannes Schröter, a Jesuit, wrote in 1691: 'O dear people, you hate the Jews as enemies of Christ and so should you hate their offspring, the Mennonites.'[7] Schröter hoped to stir up popular indignation against non-Catholic minorities. Similarly, orthodox Lutheran clergymen in central Europe campaigned from the pulpit and in official political circles to have all non-Lutherans expelled from their regions. Their position, summarized in the following prayer found at the beginning of a polemical pamphlet from 1702, was that non-Lutherans presented a looming danger to the spiritual and social order: 'Keep us by your Word, o Lord, and deflect the murderous intentions of the Quakers, Jews and Turks, who desire to dethrone your Son, Jesus Christ. Also defend us against all gangs, sects and scandals. Hear our prayers, dear Lord God!'[8] In another part of the same text the author made it clear that Anabaptists were amongst these abominable 'gangs, sects and scandals'. Clergymen in official churches demonized groups like the Mennonites as enemies of Christ in order to strengthen their own group's sense of identity. Studying how representatives of majorities treated minorities can reveal a great deal about historical mentalities and dominant ideologies. In this sense, it is fruitful to think of Mennonites and other minorities as victims of confessionalization.

Stopping here would, however, be ill-advised and unsatisfactory. The reason is that well-established minority groups like Jewish and Mennonite communities were not merely passive victims or objects of the actions of mainstream churchmen; they too took steps to maintain order in their communities and preserve their unique religious identities. Social order and religious affiliation were intimately connected features of their collective lives. This was also true of minority communities of Calvinists, Catholics and Lutherans living in territories controlled by confessional

6 Hsia, *Social Discipline in the Reformation*, p. 168.

7 Joannes Schröter, *Stammbuch Der Mennistischen Ketzerey Sambt dero Gespanschafften Lehr und Sitten* (Neyß, 1691), p. 24.

8 The quotation is from the title-page of *Erschröckliche Brüderschafft der Alten und Neuen Wiedertäuffer/ Quäcker/ Schwärmer und Frey-Geister/ mit Denen Heil- und Gottlosen Juden*, found in *Anabaptisticum et Enthusiasticum Pantheon* (n.p., 1701–2).

opponents. In all these cases, alliances between church and state, so much the focus of the standard presentation of confessionalization, can only be part of the picture linking religious identity and the emergence of social order. This old and standard presentation, based partly on secularized preconceptions inherited from the bygone age of religious partisanship, is a major impediment stopping historians of confessionalization from looking seriously at minority groups like the Mennonites.

Even some staunch defenders of the confessionalization paradigm recognize the need to look at groups other than merely those granted rights under the terms of the Peace of Westphalia. For example, Heinz Schilling has acknowledged that it is time to expand research on confessionalization to include Jews and Anabaptists. Concerning Anabaptists he writes: 'As for Christian dissent, it needs to be examined whether at least some of the nonconfessionally organized denominations such as the Anabaptists displayed patterns of development which are comparable to the confessionalization of the major churches.'[9] But then, before going on to recommend the work of Hans-Jürgen Goertz (see below) as a model for research in this area, Schilling adds a qualification: 'An essential difference [between mainstream Christian confessions and Anabaptists], which forbids the direct application of the confessionalization paradigm [to Anabaptists], lies naturally in their fundamental distance from the state and official society.'[10]

Despite its generally welcome message, there are at least two flawed assumptions in Schilling's passage. Both need to be addressed in order to avoid fundamental misunderstandings of the character of post-Reformation Anabaptism. The first is the idea that Anabaptist groups were among 'the nonconfessionally organized denominations'. With regard to the majority of Mennonites, Chapter 3 provides an antidote to this statement. The second flawed assumption is the idea of the Anabaptists' 'fundamental distance from the state and official society'. This claim is based on a simplistic and static conception of Anabaptist history. Rather than keeping their distance, many of the very earliest Anabaptist reformers had begun their reforming careers trying to transform government and society on a Christian model.[11] This kind of radical goal quickly failed. After the early

---

[9] Schilling, 'Die Konfessionalisierung von Kirche, Staat und Gesellschaft', p. 21: 'Was den christlichen Dissens anbelangt, so wäre zu prüfen, ob nicht zumindest einige der nicht konfessionskirchlich verfaßten Denominationen, etwa die Täufer, eine der Konfessionalisierung der Großkirchen vergleichbare Formierung erfuhren.'

[10] Ibid.: 'Ein grundlegender Unterschied, der die direkte Anwendung des Konfessionalisierungsparadigmas verbietet, liegt natürlich in der prinzipiellen Distanz zu Staat und offizieller Gesellschaft.'

[11] Gottfried Seebaß makes this point in response to Schilling's claims. See Schilling, 'Die Konfessionalisierung von Kirche, Staat und Gesellschaft', pp. 47–8.

1530s it was no longer realistic, because, in territories where persecution remained intense, Anabaptist groups were forced to live underground existences, usually in remote rural areas away from organized police forces. These dissenting groups rejected official society, just as its leaders rejected them. This remained true of many Swiss territories into the eighteenth century.[12] The best-known example of the Anabaptist rejection of official society, the Schleitheim Articles of 1527,[13] comes from the Swiss and southern German context. In this text, rulers and official society were portrayed as belonging to the kingdom of the Antichrist from which believers were to separate themselves. While there is some provisional evidence that branches of the Mennonite tradition in northern Europe accepted aspects of the Schleitheim tradition in the years after Menno Simons's death,[14] this tradition never became dominant in northern European Mennonite circles in the seventeenth and eighteenth centuries. True, almost everywhere, Mennonites were religious nonconformists. But with few exceptions in the early modern period they were also political conformists who were treated by governments with increasing tolerance in many northern European jurisdictions, both urban and rural. They acted as trading agents for princes, participated as litigants in court cases, paid taxes, received local legal privileges, prayed for the safety and well-being of secular rulers, and even held public office in places where this was allowed by territorial authorities.

The issue of office-holding is important, because it can serve as a test of attitudes towards the Schleitheim tradition of voluntary separation from the sinful world. In Friedrichstadt, a small Danish-controlled mercantilist town on the North Sea coast established around the beginning of the seventeenth century, there were several Mennonite congregations with which Mennonites in Altona and Hamburg had close ecclesiastical and familial ties. Among Friedrichstadt's Mennonites there was no consensus either for or against the holding of public office.[15] On the one hand, leaders of some factions strongly opposed believers holding public office, for with

---

12 See Jecker, *Ketzer, Rebellen, Heilige*, pp. 610–11.

13 The Articles have been reprinted many times. See, for example, *Confessions and Catechisms of the Reformation*, ed. Mark A. Noll (Grand Rapids, Mich., 1991), pp. 50–58. For historical background, see C. Arnold Snyder, *The Life and Thought of Michael Sattler* (Scottdale, Pa., and Kitchener, Ont., 1984).

14 See James M. Stayer, *Anabaptists and the Sword* (Lawrence, Kans., 1972), pp. 324–8. For a more recent statement of his views about Anabaptist radicalism after the first generation of the Reformation, see id., 'The Passing of the Radical Moment'.

15 See three texts by Sem Sutter: 'Friedrichstadt an der Eider: An Early Experience in Religious Toleration, 1621–1727', pp. 30–37 and 99–107; 'Die Anfänge der Mennonitengemeinde in Friedrichstadt 1621–1650', *Mennonitische Geschichtsblätter*, 37, new ser. 32 (1980), pp. 42–53; and 'Friedrichstadt: An Early German Example of Mennonite Magistrates', *Mennonite Quarterly Review*, 53 (1979), pp. 299–305.

it came the responsibility to swear oaths and stand in judgement over others, which for some were beyond the pale of proper Christian activity. On the other hand, members of other factions regularly accepted leading roles as civic councilmen, although they often avoided judicial responsibilities that came with the position. For their part, Flemish Mennonites in seventeenth-century Altona and Hamburg expressed no principled, religious objections to office-holding. They also did not ask their Lutheran rulers in Hamburg and Altona for equal access to public offices. Mennonite leaders simply accepted the legal fact that they were forbidden by their governors from participating actively in political decision-making. The important point here, which applies equally well to the Waterlander, Zonist and Lamist traditions of Dutch Anabaptism, is that most early modern Mennonites considered themselves a part of (not apart from) the established political order. They accepted most of its legal norms and even accepted their subordinate position in it.

How did Mennonites, descendants of early Anabaptist radical reformers, become political conformists? Hans-Jürgen Goertz has provided a recent account of this transformation, which he has intended as a contribution to the historiography of confessionalization and social discipline.[16] The earliest Anabaptists were lay women and men (some of whom were even former monks and priests) who wanted to institute an ethically pure form of a believers' church. To achieve their goal, they agitated against a socially and politically entrenched clerical establishment they felt was corrupt, as well as practising strict personal and collective discipline. The intensity of anticlerical agitation quickly diminished after the first years of Reformation upheaval (by the late 1530s), and as this happened self-discipline took on a greater significance in Anabaptist communities. This is the stage of historical development at which Mennonite communities emerged as distinct groups. Mennonites were motivated by the pressures of survival in hostile circumstances but also by their religious constitution to live morally upright lives 'without spot or wrinkle'. Energies which had once been directed outward towards the reformation of society in general were now directed inward to the community of believers in particular. Although it was not intended as such, the Mennonites' community discipline amounted to a form of self-directed and pre-emptive social discipline which promoted the interests of rulers (the obedience of subjects and the maintenance of social order, for example) without requiring their direct action.

---

16 Hans-Jürgen Goertz, 'Kleruskritik, Kirchenzucht und Sozialdisziplinierung in den täuferischen Bewegungen der Frühen Neuzeit', in Heinz Schilling (ed.), *Kirchenzucht und Sozialdisziplinierung im frühneuzeitlichen Europa* (Berlin, 1994), pp. 183–98; and id., 'Zucht und Ordnung in nonkonformistischer Manier', *Antiklerikalismus und Reformation: Sozialgeschichtliche Untersuchungen* (Göttingen, 1995), pp. 103–14.

This kind of interpretation – that is, a picture of social and political order emerging without the initiative of rulers – has several implications for debates about the confessionalization paradigm. These are discussed in the conclusion to this chapter. First, however, a case study is in order. While Goertz has provided a general framework for thinking about Mennonite discipline and obedience in terms of the confessionalization paradigm, a detailed micro-study remains to be done on the subject. The value of such a study is to reveal the mechanisms which encouraged and sustained Mennonite self-regulation and, perhaps by extension, self-regulation in other confessional groups.

Theological polemics and political turmoil in Hamburg during the 1690s

In Hamburg during the 1690s, the processes of Lutheran identity formation served to weaken more than strengthen the established political order. In other words, this example does not confirm the conventional expectations about the process of confessionalization. The problems that surfaced at the end of the seventeenth century were made possible by institutional arrangements that went back much further. In 1593, because of concerns about possible repetitions of mid-sixteenth-century inter-Lutheran theological controversies, Hamburg's Senate abolished the office of the *Superintendent*, which since 1529 had been the highest authority in theological and ecclesiastical matters. It was replaced with the office of *Senior*, which was filled by one of the four (and after 1686, five) parish head pastors (*Hauptpastoren*). The move in no way diminished the central place of Lutheranism in the city's life. However, the *Senior*, acting as a spokesman for the Ministry (*Ministerium*, the representative body of the Lutheran clergy in the city), had less authority than the *Superintendent* had had. After the abolition of the office of *Superintendent*, the Senate claimed final authority in both religious and political affairs, although its claims were disputed occasionally by the Ministry. The most dramatic of these disputes took place in the 1690s. Troubles began first within the ranks of the Ministry. Some pastors capitalized on the ineffectiveness of the Senate to assert its dual authority over church and state, which proved a crucial factor in a series of events which led the city into turmoil.[17]

17 For more details on the structure of civic government, as well as the political turmoil of the 1690s, see Whaley, *Religious Toleration and Social Change*. Whaley's main source for details about the political turmoil of the 1690s is Hermann Rückleben, *Die Niederwerfung der hamburgischen Ratsgewalt: Kirchliche Bewegungen und bürgerliche Unruhen im ausgehenden 17. Jahrhundert* (Hamburg, 1970). Unless otherwise noted, I too have used Rückleben as the source for the information about Hamburg's urban politics in the 1690s. For analysis which helps to put events in Hamburg into a broader context, see three works

A major issue of dispute among pastors at the end of the seventeenth century was the spread of the Lutheran reform movement known as Pietism. Among other characteristics, reformers put more emphasis than many of their colleagues on lay participation and education. The Lutheran church in the course of the sixteenth and seventeenth centuries had become a church like most others – controlled by a clerical elite. Most reformers were certainly not revolutionaries; they were members of this elite. They simply wanted believers to participate more actively in religious life than had been the norm in the official Lutheran church. To realize this goal, they organized official Bible-study meetings for the laity, which supplemented regular church services. At first the activity of these pastors sympathetic to reform caused no problems. Private Bible-study meetings were even en vogue in Hamburg around 1688. This situation changed around 1689. In addition to preacher-led meetings, some church members were organizing their own private religious meetings. This was the spark of controversy.

Ministry members did not agree about whether the existence of Bible-reading conventicles was appropriate in a strictly Lutheran city. The disagreements were increased around the beginning of 1689 when a letter by a brewer named Hinrich Grevers came to the attention of the Ministry.[18] Grevers echoed early Reformation themes of anticlericalism and lay Christianity. He attacked church leaders for what he considered to be their disregard for Bible-oriented Christianity, and he demanded a return to the practices of the apostolic church. Samuel Schultz, head pastor of the St Petri parish and *Senior* of the Ministry, used his pulpit to charge Grevers with heresy. *Senior* Schultz took an especially active role against private religious meetings. Under his guidance and that of his supporters, names of other private conventicle leaders and participants were gathered and inquisitions were started at the end of January 1689. Opponents like Schultz charged that such gatherings were heretical cells and also violated article 1 of Hamburg's 1603 constitutional recess (see Ch. 1). In response to the charges, the Senate banned all private conventicles on 15 February 1689. This step greatly weakened the cause of reformist pastors. It also marked the beginning of a series of events which drew the city's secular rulers ever deeper into a quagmire of internecine Lutheran battles.

Battles in the Lutheran church were not limited to Hamburg. In fact, they were spreading at this time throughout Lutheran territories in

by Christopher R. Friedrichs: 'German Town Revolts and the Seventeenth-Century Crisis', *Renaissance and Modern Studies*, 26 (1982), pp. 27–51; *The Early Modern City, 1450–1750* (London and New York, 1995), chs. 10–12; and *Urban Politics in Early Modern Europe* (London, 2000).

[18] A transcription of the letter is found in Rückleben, *Die Niederwerfung der hamburgischen Ratsgewalt*, pp. 378–9.

German-speaking Europe, and they consisted of heated polemical exchanges between those for and those against reform. The ostensible issue was the character – even the existence – of Pietism. Conservatives argued that the new Pietist movement shared more in common with seditious heretics like the Anabaptists than it did with good, orthodox Lutherans. They attacked reformers publicly in long, detailed theological tracts, calling on them to end their dangerous ways which threatened the integrity of God's truth. In effect, these orthodox polemicists wanted to end the semi-official campaign of reform within the Lutheran church. The use of polemics, which were intended to protect God's truth by pressuring opponents to concede defeat and be silent, was a common instrument of public discipline in the early modern era. Clergymen learned the rules and techniques of polemics during their university training. In university settings, polemical contests were moderated and a conclusion was programmed into the staged event. Because literary polemics outside the monitored setting of university halls lacked any effective kind of referee, they regularly grew out of control. Martin Gierl, who has examined the Lutheran publicists' battles about Pietism, counts several dozen sets of polemical exchanges in German territories over the course of the 1690s, each involving multiple texts on both sides. Needless to say, reformers used a number of rhetorical strategies to counter their attackers' arguments. These included denying their association with any radical groups and even denying the very existence of a category of people known as Pietists.[19]

Subjects of polemical exchange throughout Lutheran Germany included the existence of Bible-reading groups, as well as the nature of the End Times and the validity of lay prophecy. One further important set of exchanges early on during these Lutheran publicists' campaigns was focused on Hamburg and concerned an oath of orthodoxy required of Hamburg's Ministry members. On 14 March 1690 *Senior* Schultz tabled a document before the Ministry. Part of the text read:

> So that we may rid ourselves of all suspicion, it is our resolve to continue loyally all church ceremonies which we have inherited from our blessed forebears and have until now maintained, and, on the other hand, zealously to prevent any innovation, whatever it may be

[19] See Martin Gierl, *Pietismus und Aufklärung: Theologische Polemik und die Kommunikationsreform der Wissenschaft am Ende des 17. Jahrhunderts* (Göttingen, 1997). Gierl's main thesis is that the traditional rules of polemical exchange themselves became a central issue of controversy in the heated debates about the nature of Pietism. Dissatisfaction among Lutheran publicists with these rules, and the culture and institutions that supported them, helped force the creation of a public sphere which provided fruitful soil for the spread of the Enlightenment in Lutheran Germany. On the topic of polemical culture and its reform, also see Hans-Joachim Müller, 'Irenik, eine Kommunikationsform: Das Colloquium Charitativum in Thorn 1645' (doctoral diss., Universität Göttingen, 2000).

> called, even if it has the appearance of achieving improvements in Christendom, so long as our church does not make other arrangements. And this in order to promote and maintain ecclesiastical peace.[20]

The stated intention was to help re-establish a semblance of unity among Lutheran representatives. The basis of the unity, however, was to be a conservative faith without any hint whatever of reform-oriented Lutheranism. All members of the Ministry were asked to sign the document to indicate their agreement. The reform-oriented head pastors refused to sign. The dispute led not only to polemical exchanges but also to a political tug-of-war, for some pastors protested to the Senate against the actions of the Ministry's leaders. When the Senate declared in early April 1690 that it disapproved of the Ministry's steps for enforcing clerical unity, old issues of jurisdiction, which had been resolved temporarily at the end of the sixteenth century by the abolition of the office of *Superintendent*, were ignited anew. In the following months the Senate and Ministry battled over which institution had the right to make binding decisions in ecclesio-political affairs. By July, the Senate had become especially sensitive to Ministry actions. It even confiscated a newly printed set of Ministry documents on the grounds that the documents contained ideas contrary to the constitution of the city. And at the same time, pastors were not only publishing polemics but also using their pulpits to attack one another publicly. Despite repeated efforts, the Senate was unable to bring an end to the pastors' public campaigns against one another.

Battle lines were becoming increasingly entrenched. While they did not have the Senate's full and unwavering support, reformers in Hamburg tended to get a sympathetic hearing from Senators, who saw their jurisdiction impinged upon by overzealous, orthodox clergymen. To strengthen their position in the city amid the growing controversies of the 1690s, orthodox members in the Ministry, who controlled that institution, sought allies from among the ranks of guild leaders and other citizens.

Guild leaders had some important leverage to exercise against the Senate. In 1689 the Empire had gone to war with France over the French invasion of the Palatinate. The Emperor required funds, and to collect these he demanded more taxes from his clients, including Hamburg. In order to gather the needed money, Hamburg's Senate had to get the approval of the Citizenry (*Bürgerschaft*), the representative body of enfranchised

---

20 Quoted from Rückleben, *Die Niederwerfung der hamburgischen Ratsgewalt*, p. 380: 'Damit wir uns auch ferner alles frembden Verdachts entledigen, ist unsre beständige Meynung, alle Kirchenceremonien, wie wir sie von unsern gottseligen Vorfahren überkommen und bisher im Gange erhalten, getreulich fortzupflantzen, und dagegen alle Neuerung, sie habe Name wie sie wolle, ob sie gleich das Ansehen gewinne der Verbesserung der Christentums, so lange unsere Kirche nicht ein anders veranlasset, eifferigst zu verhütten. Also den Kirchenfrieden zu befördern und zu erhalten.'

commoners. However, 'governmental tax requests from 1687 until April 1690 . . . were always reduced by the citizens by 33%'.[21] Encouraged by anti-Pietist preachers, some factions of citizens became progressively bolder in their opposition to Senate tax requests and even developed republican justifications for a revolt against the established constitutional order.

Contributing to the radicalization of anti-Senate politics was another religious controversy, this time centred on the person of Johann Heinrich Horb, the reformist head pastor of the St Nikolai parish since 1685.[22] Horb had prepared an edition of an anonymously published text entitled *Die Klugheit der Gerechten/ Die Kinder nach den wahren Gründen des Christenthums/ von der Welt zu dem Herrn zu erziehen* (The Wisdom of the Righteous in Raising Children away from the World and to the Lord, according to the True Principles of Christianity),[23] which he distributed to children during celebrations to usher in the New Year 1693. He was interested in the *Klugheit* because its author taught that education should awaken the heart of the learner rather than merely train the mind. What he did not know was that the text's author, Pierre Poiret, was a nonconformist par excellence, the very kind of person against whom Hamburg's clergymen were careful to protect their parishioners. The Lutheran head pastor simply ignored those parts of the text which were obviously unorthodox from a Lutheran point of view.

While Horb seems not to have been concerned with the identity of the text's author, others were, and word of Horb's actions spread among the members of the Ministry. New polemics and pulpit battles ensued. To put pressure on Horb to resign, his opponents in the Ministry banned him from confession and communion. But while the Ministry did succeed in excluding Horb from its meetings, it did not have the legal authority to stop him from preaching or exerting influence in his own parish. To achieve this objective and force the Senate to concede to its authority in ecclesiastical affairs, the Ministry made effective use of its guild contacts in some parishes. Because the Citizenry elected representatives by parish districts, an energetic and charismatic group of parish preachers could make a significant difference in the course of civic politics. An example of the explosive type of message parishioners heard during these days was one preached on 12 May 1693. Citing Luke 6: 22–6, Johann Friedrich Mayer,

---

21 Rückleben, *Die Niederwerfung der hamburgischen Ratsgewalt*, p. 36: 'Sie [obrigkeitliche Steuerwünsche] wurden von den Bürgern in den Jahren 1687 bis April 1690 . . . stets um 33% gekürzt.'

22 For a general biography, see Friedrich Sander, *Der Pastor Johann Heinrich Horb* (Hamburg, 1995).

23 See Marjolaine Chevallier, *Pierre Poiret* (Baden-Baden, 1985). Poiret's text appeared originally in French in 1690 and went through many translations and editions, including Horb's.

one of the chief opponents of the Pietists and head pastor of the St Jacobi parish, declared: 'Blessed are the militants who have to fight against heretics and fanatics.'[24] The 'heretics and fanatics' included Horb. He was eventually forced to leave the city in disgrace.

The belligerent rhetoric helped to inspire anti-Senate agitators in the Citizenry. Horb denied all charges of heresy and publicly condemned all forms of doctrinal error.[25] This defence satisfied the Senate. It turned back calls to dismiss Horb, for to do so would have been to concede final authority in ecclesiastical affairs to the Ministry. On 22 May 1693 the Senate published a mandate in which 'preachers were forbidden under threat of punishment "to judge the government, whether openly or secretly, or otherwise to make it hated among citizens"'.[26] The Senate succeeded only in achieving the opposite of its intentions. The day after the mandate was passed a large group of preachers walked out in the middle of a funeral service Horb was conducting. At the instigation of *Senior* Schultz this kind of public and humiliating avoidance of Horb became an official policy of the Ministry. The controversies had become so public that even children were playing games in which they pretended to be supporters of either Johann Heinrich Horb or Johann Friedrich Mayer.[27] The weakening Senate was also sensitive to a growing threat of mass violence. On 9 June 1693 it had published another mandate threatening to punish severely all those who upset peace and order. Like many of its other mandates from these years, this one had little effect.

Orthodox Lutheran forces in Hamburg were moving closer and closer to open rebellion in late 1693. One important point in these developments was the Citizenry meetings of September 1693. The Senate urgently needed extra funds to pay for ever-pressing wartime expenses. Among other costs these included almost a year's pay owed to the civic militia. The only way it could get the money was to have the Citizenry approve new taxes. On 14 September the Citizenry was gathered at the city hall. According to an anonymous eyewitness, the gathering was the biggest in memory. The majority of the people attending the meeting were supporters of the anti-Horb faction, and they refused to allow representatives to approve any taxes until Horb had been expelled from the city.[28] Violence broke out

---

24 Rückleben, *Die Niederwerfung der hamburgischen Ratsgewalt*, p. 151: '"Selig sind die Unfriedfertigen, die streiten müssen wider die Ketzer und Schwärmer".'

25 Ibid., p. 382.

26 Ibid., p. 149: '. . . ein Dekret, das den Predigern bei Strafe verbot, "die Obrigkeit, es sey öffentlich oder heimlich zu richten oder sonst bey der Bürgerschaft verhaßt zu machen"'.

27 Ibid., p. 193.

28 See Johannes Geffcken, 'Hamburgische Zustände am Ende des 17ten Jahrhunderts, aus gleichzeitigen Aufzeichnungen mitgetheilt', *Zeitschrift des Vereins für Hamburgische Geschichte*, 3 (1851), pp. 597–635, at p. 610. Also see Rückleben, *Die Niederwerfung der hamburgischen Ratsgewalt*, pp. 179–80.

several times among the hundreds of people that were gathered there. There were even physical attacks on several parish officials who were suspected of sympathizing with Horb and who had supported the Senate's policies on religious matters. The eyewitness wrote: 'in the last hundred years there has never been such violence; some people even reached for their knives'.[29] Several days after the 14 September meeting, Mayer was heard to say that 'he would rather be with his mob from St Jacobi than travel to heaven with the fat Horbianers'.[30]

The anti-Horb agitation of preachers like Mayer and Schultz was having serious consequences for the Senate. In late November 1693 mob politics became a still more immediate concern. Groups of citizens who were pressing for Horb's expulsion were stopping *Oberalten* members from leaving the city hall under threat of violence. Faced with these siege tactics, the Senate finally gave in to the Ministry and Citizenry's demand regarding Horb. Once he was told that serious civil unrest was likely unless he resigned, Horb volunteered his resignation. Lutheran preachers were setting the political agenda. Politics and religion were becoming ever more entangled.

Another high point of violence in Hamburg was the Citizenry meeting of 18 January 1694. The Senate had called the meeting to try again to arrange for much needed taxes. The representatives of St Jacobi rejected the request. The meeting degenerated into a confrontation between representatives from the St Michaelis parish (sympathetic to the reformers and the Senate) and the St Jacobi parish (a conservative, anti-Pietist stronghold). The next day the factional violence was repeated, claiming a number of lives. The opposing groups were arming their members in preparation for a confrontation. Small skirmishes lasted for a few more days, during which time civil war was a real possibility. But it did not come to that.

A consequence of the violent disputes starting in 1693 was that the guilds had grown into a political force which was much better organized than before and was able to take action independent of clerical leadership. Many guild leaders did in fact begin to assert their own authority with increasing confidence in the latter part of the 1690s. By the end of 1694, the Imperial resident in Hamburg, Count Christian von Eck, was reporting that some of the guilds had even established their own judicial system beyond the influence of the Senate. And by the beginning of 1698 the

---

29 Geffcken, 'Hamburgische Zustände am Ende des 17ten Jahrhunderts', p. 610: 'In Summa in 100 Jahren ist solche Gewalt nicht geuebet, einige haben die Messer hervorgesuchet.'

30 Quoted in Rückleben, *Die Niederwerfung der hamburgischen Ratsgewalt*, p. 182: '"er wollte lieber mit seinen Jacobitern Pöbel seyen, als mit den fetten Horbianern gen Himmel fahren".'

Citizenry was claiming absolute sovereignty, relegating the Senate to a minor constitutional role. A self-appointed ideologue for the Citizenry, August Wynand, had even taken it upon himself to attack the historical foundations of Senate authority, claiming that it had usurped power illegitimately from community representatives in the high Middle Ages. This kind of theoretical justification for sovereignty of the Citizenry gave already bold leaders added confidence. Citizenry and Senate meetings of August 1699 marked the low point of Senate authority. Unable to assert themselves in any way, Senate members resigned and handed over power to the Citizenry's representatives on 18 August 1699. The capitulation began a nine-year period during which the Citizenry held *de facto* power. The Senate continued to exist as an institution, but only men who were approved by the Citizenry could occupy government positions at any level. This situation remained in force until 1708, when Imperial soldiers occupied Hamburg to help enforce order in the city while an Imperial commission began its work. The commission's four years of activity resulted in the Constitutional Recess of 1712, in which sovereignty was declared to be the shared property of the Senate and Citizenry in cooperation with one another.[31] The Recess marked the effective end of the political chaos that had begun with the Pietist controversy more than two decades earlier.

A Mennonite family converts to Lutheranism

Because of an untimely conversion of a Mennonite family to Lutheranism, Mennonite leaders quickly became entangled in the polemics being exchanged by Lutheran preachers. While the Pietist controversy was growing in seriousness in Hamburg, the issue of baptism was occupying Mennonites in Hamburg and Altona. At the beginning of 1691, the council of the local Flemish Mennonite congregation had discussed the possibility of inviting the immersionist Jacob Denner to be a visiting preacher (see Ch. 2). Perhaps it was only a coincidence, but at around the same time Juditha Boudt, originally from the Dompelaar congregation, began attending sermons in the St Michaelis parish church where Johann Winckler, a reform-oriented Lutheran, was the head pastor. Juditha Boudt eventually convinced her husband, Claes, nominally a member of the Flemish Mennonite congregation, to join her from time to time. The couple had apparently had misgivings about the Mennonite practice of adult baptism. Their visits became ever more frequent, and eventually they made their presence known to Winckler through a third party. They were

[31] See Gerd Augner, *Die kaiserliche Kommission der Jahre 1708–1712: Hamburgs Beziehung zu Kaiser und Reich zu Anfang des 18. Jahrhunderts* (Hamburg, 1983).

considering conversion but had reservations. Winckler responded by preparing a sermon on the text of Mark 10: 14: 'Let the little children come to me.' On 23 June 1691 he preached it, talking about the error of heretics like Thomas Müntzer, Quakers, Socinians and Mennonites, as well as about the necessity of child baptism. After Winckler's sermon, Claes and Juditha presented themselves to the Lutheran head pastor and asked to join his church. Before a large audience on 29 or 30 July 1691, St Michaelis's archdeacon Hieronymus Pasman baptized the Boudts' four children: Maria Elisabeth (10), Anna Sophia (6), Susanna Gertrud (3) and Philip Nicolaus (9 months).[32]

Claes Boudt was a complex character. In the Flemish Mennonite congregation's membership book, Geeritt Roosen described him as 'confused' (*loshoofdich*).[33] Boudt had certainly not been satisfied with congregational life for some time before his conversion to Lutheranism in 1691. In November 1676 he was married to Juditha in the Dompelaar congregation; she was the daughter of Jacob Borchers, perhaps the same person or a member of the same family as Jan Borchers, the man Roosen had named as one of the instigators of the disagreements over immersion baptism in the 1640s. After the marriage, Boudt remained a member of the Flemish congregation for a short time, but within a few years he left it, letting it be known through his brother Dirick that he did not want to be a member of any kind of church. It is unclear how long he remained estranged from the Mennonite congregation, but Roosen noted that in 1690, around the same time Boudt began visiting sermons at St Michaelis, he had reappeared briefly with his wife at congregational services. Although the Boudt family's conversion was a horrible embarrassment for the Mennonites, Roosen was not altogether disappointed that Boudt had left for good.

Claes Boudt's brother Dirick was also seeking religious fulfilment beyond the bounds of the Mennonite congregation. Around mid-year 1676 two spiritualist activists named Antoinette Bourignon and Pierre Poiret (the latter who would gain notoriety after 1693 among Lutherans because of Johann Heinrich Horb's republication of *Klugheit der Gerechten*) had arrived in Hamburg, where they lived in hiding into the

32 Sources for this narrative are: StAHbg/MG, 1a (handwritten notes about local Mennonite history, probably recorded in the mid-eighteenth century by the Lutheran Barthold Nicolaus Krohn), which includes the names of the Boudt's children; StAHbg/MG, 147, vol. 1, pp. 82, 84 and 138; and two texts by Johann Winckler – *Gründlicher Beweiß der Kinder-Tauffe aus Marc. X.v.14.* (Hamburg, 1691); and *Vertheidigung Seines Gründlichen Beweises Der Kinder-Tauffe Gegen Die Einwürffe Etlicher Holländischen Wider-Täuffer* (Hamburg, 1696).

33 StAHbg/MG, 147, vol. 1, p. 138: 'A° 1691 den 29 July [Claes Boudt] met de vrou luyters geworden en daer 4 kinder byde laten doopen tot een glorie voor de luyterse maer met geen droefhyt by ons om dat hy een loshoofdich man was . . .'.

following year.[34] Bourignon was a leader of a small group of scattered but committed followers. She rejected the teachings and practices of all official churches in favour of a spirit-inspired godly life of self-denial. Poiret, a Reformed preacher but free spirit nonetheless, was inclined towards Bourignon's brand of mysticism. Either directly or through intermediaries, at least two members of Altona's Flemish Mennonite congregation came in contact with Bourignon. One was the merchant Claes Flores, who left his wife in 1679 and committed himself to the ascetic demands of life on the northern German island Nordstrand, where Bourignon and associates had established a commune. He died there in 1680.[35] The second was Dirick Boudt, who joined the commune in 1676, around the time of Bourignon and Poiret's visit to Hamburg. He was absent from Altona for two to three years before returning to the Flemish congregation. Later, in 1686, he married the Dompelaar Sara Coopman.[36] Dissatisfaction with established congregational life ran in the Boudt family.

For the Lutheran Johann Winckler, the voluntary conversion of an entire Mennonite family seemed to have been arranged by God – and this act of divine intervention could hardly have come at a better time. The 1689 inquisitions of conventicle leaders had uncovered a link between the private Bible meetings and Winckler's household, for Eberhard Zeller, one of the leaders of the unsanctioned conventicles, happened to be the private tutor to Winckler's sons.[37] In the context of the conservative-led inquisitions this revelation was not merely an embarrassment but also threatened to spell an end to Winckler's own more official brand of conventicle meetings. In fact, around the time of the inquisition's activities, Winckler began to take a more negative view of unsanctioned religious gatherings.[38] Even before the inquisition's revelations, he had begun to preach sermons against Quakerism, but he now used attacks on the English spiritualists as a way of emphasizing to his parish audiences the great distance between proper Lutheran Christianity and nonconformist heresy.[39] In the minds of Hamburg's clerics and their listeners, Mennonitism and Quakerism were part of the same species of heresy. Given these circumstances, the baptism

---

[34] For notes on Bourignon and her circle, see Cornelia W. Roldanus, *Zeventiende-Eeuwsche Geestesbloei* (Amsterdam, 1938), esp. pp. 152–160. Also see Rudolf Mohr, 'Bourignon, Antoinette', *Schleswig-Holsteinisches biographisches Lexikon* (Neumünster, 1979), v, pp. 48–50; and Ernst Feddersen, *Kirchengeschichte Schleswig-Holsteins*, 2 vols (Kiel, 1938), ii, 325–36.

[35] StAHbg/MG, 147, vol. 1, p. 9. Claes Flores had been on trading missions with Geeritt Roosen's brother Herman in the 1650s; see StAHbg/MG, 242, pp. 27–8.

[36] StAHbg/MG, 147, vol. 1, p. 82.

[37] Rückleben, *Die Niederwerfung der hamburgischen Ratsgewalt*, p. 99.

[38] Ibid., p. 100.

[39] Ibid., pp. 90 and 105.

of the Boudt children was a welcome opportunity for Winckler to demonstrate his orthodoxy publicly. Contrary to the charges of men like Johann Friedrich Mayer, Winckler portrayed himself not as an ally of heretics but as their uncompromising opponent whose words were confirmed by his actions. Because of the success of his 23 June 1691 sermon, Winckler decided to have it published. That same year the sermon appeared in print under the title *Gründlicher Beweiß der Kinder-Tauffe aus Marc. X.v.14.* (Thorough Proof of Child Baptism from Mark 10: 14).[40]

The first recorded Mennonite responses made in public to the conversion came in the form of a pair of sermons delivered by Geeritt Roosen in Altona on 14 and 21 February 1692.[41] Both were about baptism. In the first Roosen told his listeners that the simple and true form of baptism was conducted in the name of the Father, Son and Holy Spirit. Without faith it was impossible to obey God, and children were not capable of faith. However, on the strength of Christ's personal sacrifice on the cross, small children could enter the Kingdom of Heaven if they died early. In other words, despite evidence from Acts 2: 39 and Mark 10: 14 cited by mistaken preachers, child baptism was not scriptural. Roman Catholics, for example, conducted child baptism not according to God's authority but the authority of church councils. In the second sermon Roosen continued his attack on child baptism, but he also addressed baptismal disputes among supporters of adult baptism such as the Dompelaars, and he repeated earlier defences of baptism by sprinkling.

The rhetoric of obedience and orthodoxy

As the internecine Lutheran battles grew in intensity throughout the 1690s, Johann Winckler turned again to a strategy he had used at the time of the Boudt family conversion – that is, the strategy of aggressively attacking religious nonconformists when his own orthodoxy came under scrutiny. At the same time that the anti-Pietist Johann Friedrich Mayer was inciting his parishioners to oppose heresy openly in a sermon on Luke 6: 22–6, Winckler was also preaching on themes from the same verses, but with a different emphasis. On 25 April, 2 May, 9 May and 16 May 1693 he told his parishioners about 'the unjustly Quakerized good Lutheran'.[42] He was referring to himself and Horb. The sermons had three major themes: the heresy of Quakerism itself; the innocence of those unjustly charged with

40 A copy of this rare text can be found at the university library in Göttingen. Winckler's preface is dated 18 August 1691.

41 Both are found among the sermons in StAHbg/MG, 248, vol. 2.

42 Johann Winckler, *Der unrechtmäßig verquakerte gute Lutheraner* (Hamburg, 1693) (four parts in three pamphlets: 1, 2/3 and 4).

it; and the impropriety of the accusers. Winckler declared that, despite Horb's obvious mistake in the affair with the *Klugheit*, he was a man of sincere belief and orthodoxy, which he had proven with his words and actions since the beginning of 1693. Winckler's portrayal of Quakerism was in no way so forgiving. Its adherents were heretics because they were against holy baptism, the Trinity, the doctrine of justification, the preaching office and civil government, among other things. Baptism was necessary to achieve salvation, and Quaker denunciations of baptism thus threatened the eternal lives of those enthralled by their errors. They also 'speak of the Father, Son and Holy Spirit but in a way which could satisfy Arians'.[43] They thought rebirth and a good life were enough to earn God's reward, but they neglected faith and were therefore again in error. They also neglected to show proper respect for social superiors. For example, they would not remove their hats or use the appropriate titles of honour when meeting important people, and they refused to swear oaths or participate in war. Rather than advocating rebellion, as Mayer had done, Winckler stressed an orthodox Christian's duty to obey secular rulers.

Just as conservative Lutheran attacks on their reformist colleagues sparked Winckler's impassioned assertion of his innocence and his attacks on nonconformists, so did Winckler's anti-Mennonite polemics from 1691 spark public responses from the Mennonite side. In the last half of 1693 an anonymous Dutch Mennonite published a pamphlet entitled *Grondig Bewijs tegen den Kinder-doop uit Marc 10,14* (Thorough Proof against Child Baptism from Mark 10: 14).[44] It was a response to Johann Winckler's 1691 pamphlet of a similar title. In addition to a confession of faith divided into ten chapters, the text consisted of a long defence of adult baptism and the historical legacy of Mennonitism. The main part of the text ended with a discussion of claims made by anti-Mennonite propagandists that Anabaptists were the offspring of Thomas Müntzer and the fanatics from Münster. The author's answer was that Menno Simons and not Thomas Müntzer was the forefather of the Mennonites, and, what was more, Christ was the true authority for all Christian Mennonites. The anonymous author continued:

> Supposing that we did originate with the Münsterites or Thomas Müntzer who rebelled in Germany, which we did not, . . . he [Winckler] ought not to consider this an objection against us; rather, he should hold us dear, recognizing that we were no longer like those godless ones. Regarding our behaviour, all faithful magistrates, teachers, citizens and peasants may stand as witnesses.[45]

---

43 Ibid., part 2/3, p. 20: 'Also reden sie zwar von Vater/ Sohn und H. Geist/ aber also daß auch wohl die Arrianer damit könten zufrieden seyn.'

44 A copy of this text is found in the library of the Mennonite church in Hamburg.

45 *Grondig Bewijs*, pp. 156–7: 'En genomen wy waren uyt die van Munster, of Thomas Munzer die in Duytsland opstonde/ gelijk wy niet en zijn/ . . . zoo en behoorde hy [den Autheur (Winckler)] ons dat noch niet tot bezwaaring op te dringen/ maar veel meer ons lief

The author went on to state that Mennonites practised apostolic baptism, it was true, but they did not participate in robbery, murder, polygamy, rebellion, and the like. They were good Christians and good subjects who rejected the heresy and sedition of Münster as much as did their Lutheran neighbours.

This kind of rhetoric of obedience was engrained deeply in the self-understanding of at least one local Mennonite leader, Geeritt Roosen. By the middle of the 1690s, when guild leaders and conservative Lutheran pastors had become bolder in their opposition to Senate authority, Roosen submitted a proposal for the improvement of the common tile oven to the Potters' Guild: *Nutzbahrer und Gründlicher Unterricht Von dem jetzo gewöhnlichen Brauch and Art Der Unrahtsahmen Kachel-Ofen* (Useful and Fundamental Lesson about the Current Custom and Type of Inadvisable Tile Oven). Printed in 1695 at the Senate's press, the pamphlet was addressed to Roosen's 'much honoured and loved fellow citizens'.[46] Roosen complained that tile ovens were becoming little more than cumbersome and inefficient pieces of household decoration. They were no longer built to provide heat. The consequence was that unnecessary amounts of fuel wood were being burnt to produce enough warmth during the cold and windy northern German winters. In the text he described and provided detailed drawings for a better alternative, which he explained he had presented to guild masters on 26 February 1695. He received no reply, which was hardly surprising given the political situation of previous months. One of the striking features of the pamphlet is that Roosen presented himself not as a Mennonite but simply as a loyal citizen of Hamburg who was acting only out of his concern for the city's best interest. He even pledged his services to the Senate, if he could be of further help.[47] Although Roosen did assert his obedience to Hamburg's secular rulers, he did not do so in explicit response to Lutheran charges of heresy and sedition, nor did he make an explicit link between Mennonite identity and obedience. Only because we know the broader circumstances – that Roosen was a Mennonite leader and that Senate–guild relations in Hamburg were strained – does the text's significance become clear. At the same time that the guilds and the Citizenry were seeking ways to undermine the authority of the Senate, Roosen was doing the opposite.

While the confessional character of assertions of obedience receded into the background in Roosen's text of 1695, the confessional polemics

---

te hebben; ziende dat wy niet meer alzulke Godloosen waren. Maar die wegens ons comportement/ alle vroome Magistraten, Leeraars, Burgers en Boeren laten getuyge zijn.'

[46] G[eeritt] R[oosen], *Nutzbahrer und Gründlicher Unterricht* (Hamburg, 1695), p. 3: 'Vielgeehrte und Geliebte Mit-Bürger'. The text is found in StAHbg, Sammelband 84, (12).

[47] Ibid., p. 48: '. . . absonderlich wan ich E.E. Hoch- und wolweisen Rath darinnen zu Dienste sein kan . . .'.

which had already initiated public defences by Winckler and an anonymous Mennonite author were by no means over. During the years leading to the collapse of Senate authority, public debates about Mennonitism and adult baptism continued. The contributions to the pamphlet war included a second text by Johann Winckler, *Vertheidigung Seines Gründlichen Beweises Der Kinder-Tauffe Gegen Die Einwürffe Etlicher Holländischen Wider-Täuffer* (Defence of his Thorough Proof of Child Baptism against the Charges of Some Dutch Anabaptists), published in 1696. In the dedication to his readers, Winckler again explained the circumstances of the Boudt family conversion several years earlier. He also explained that his original sermon on Mark 10: 14 defending child baptism had been attacked twice: first, by his one-time associate Johann Wilhelm Petersen, whom Winckler in 1686 had suggested as a candidate for the position of head pastor in the St Jacobi parish which Mayer later accepted;[48] and, secondly, in the *Grondig Bewijs* of 1693. Petersen, *Superintendent* in Lüneburg until he was suspended in 1692, became, along with his wife, one of the leading figures in separatist Lutheran Pietist circles around the turn of the eighteenth century. Soon after becoming aware of Petersen's attacks, Winckler read a copy of the Dutch Mennonite *Grondig Bewijs*. Daniel Severin Schultze, a junior Lutheran preacher from Hamburg, began a response to the Dutch pamphlet, but, on the advice of colleagues, Winckler in 1696 penned his own counter-attack, the *Vertheidigung*. In it he accused Mennonites of crimes and heresies such as Socinianism,[49] the antitrinitarian principles which were outlawed in several European jurisdictions. While the Mennonites claimed to lead godly lives, they did so on the basis of a corrupt faith and were therefore to be denounced vigorously.[50]

The elderly Geeritt Roosen took it upon himself to respond to Winckler. Soon after Winckler released his second anti-Mennonite booklet, Roosen composed 'bekentenis van onse onvervancklycke grondt geloofs' (Confession of our Irreplaceable Foundation of Faith).[51] He did not date the text, which consisted of twelve articles and was probably modelled on the confessions of faith in the Zonists' *Algemeene Belydennissen*. The original manuscript version includes a comment in the top corner of the first page: 'This was written in order to be printed against Winckler's accusation.'[52] It was not until 1702 that Roosen had this confession of

48 Rückleben, *Die Niederwerfung der hamburgischen Ratsgewalt*, p. 57.

49 Winckler, *Vertheidigung Seines Gründlichen Beweises Der Kinder-Tauffe*, p. 238.

50 Ibid., pp. 246–7.

51 StAHbg/MG, 248, vol. 4.

52 Ibid.: 'dit was opgeset om drucken te laten teg. wincklers beschuld 1697'. The passage may mean that Roosen was responding to a text Winckler released or sermon he gave in 1697. It may also mean that Roosen composed the confession of faith in 1697. The latter

faith printed in a German translation in a volume entitled *Unschuld und Gegen-Bericht der Evangelischen Tauff-gesinneten Christen/ so Mennonisten genandt werden* (Innocence and Protestation of the Evangelical Baptist-Minded Christians Who Are Called Mennonites).

Winckler's charges may have been the immediate reason for Roosen to write parts of the *Unschuld*, but they were not the only reason. Near the turn of the eighteenth century, Lutheran and Calvinist spokesmen throughout German- and Dutch-speaking territories were taking anti-nonconformist positions very similar to Winckler's. The pamphlets printed in 1702 in *Anabaptisticum et Enthusiasticum Pantheon* (Pantheon of Anabaptists and Enthusiasts) are an example. The *Pantheon* included attacks against all religious groups that may have seemed suspect from a strict Lutheran point of view. Among the texts in the compendium were *Quäcker-Grewel* (The Quaker Abomination) and *Quäcker Quackeley* (Quaker Quackery), which had both been released by Hamburg's Ministry in the early 1660s.[53] The same section of the *Pantheon* also included Thomas Müntzer's Prague Manifesto of 1521, a picture of Menno Simons, a Prussian Mennonite confession of faith from 1660, and an anonymous Mennonite catechism which was dated 1690 and consisted of thirty-five questions and answers.[54] The point of including all these texts was to emphasize the connection between Mennonites and early Reformation rebels. While Roosen did not refer to the anti-Mennonite propaganda of the *Pantheon*, which was almost certainly released after he finished writing and editing *Unschuld und Gegen-Bericht*, he was aware of other earlier attacks against his co-religionists. In 1687 Frederick Spanheim, a Reformed theologian and professor at the University of Leiden, had published a text in which he asserted that Mennonites were the offspring of the rebellious Anabaptist hordes of early sixteenth-century Münster.[55] Spanheim included in his work an attack on a contemporary of his, the Dutch Zonist

reading would place the writing of the confession around the same time that Riewart Dircks was forced to return to the Netherlands. On Dircks, see the further discussion in the section of this chapter which follows.

53 According to Bolten, *Historische Kirchen-Nachrichten von der Stadt Altona*, i, p. 186, n. 116, the author of *Quäcker-Grewel* was Johann Müller, an already well-practised anti-minority polemicist from Hamburg.

54 The anonymous catechism in this text was reprinted in the eighteenth century by Mennonites who mistakenly attributed it to Geeritt Roosen. See Michael Driedger, 'The Extant Writings of Geeritt Roosen', *Mennonite Quarterly Review*, 74 (2000), pp. 159–69.

55 This work was entitled *Controversiarum de Religione Elenchus historico-theologicus*. Frederick Spanheim (1632–1707) followed in the footsteps of his father Frederick, Senior (1600–49) who was also a Reformed theologian, professor at Leiden, and supporter of the thesis of Münsterite origins of Anabaptism. The elder Spanheim was the author of the anti-Mennonite tracts *Variae disputationes anti-anabaptisticae* (1643–48) and *Diatribe Historica de Origine, Progressu et Sectis Anabaptistarum* (1645; 2nd edn 1656).

Mennonite preacher Engel Arentsz van Doorgeest. Van Doorgeest replied publicly in 1693, the same year the *Grondig Bewijs* appeared. The controversy continued during the following year when Spanheim had his volume reprinted and van Doorgeest's response was translated from Dutch into German. The controversy did not end there. Mennonite leaders, perhaps concerned about a new wave of persecution against Anabaptists in Switzerland, printed van Doorgeest's defence a third time in 1700, only two years before *Unschuld und Gegen-Bericht* appeared, together with an open letter by the Zonist leader Hermannus Schijn.[56] Polemical tensions were growing.

Roosen's *Unschuld und Gegen-Bericht*, like the Lutheran polemical work *Anabaptisticum et Enthusiasticum Pantheon*, was a compendium containing a variety of texts. In addition to the confession of faith mentioned above, there were German translations of three of Menno Simons's writings,[57] a sermon by Roosen's preaching colleague and son-in-law Pieter Verhelle,[58] and Roosen's own reflections about the history of his local congregation. Some volumes also included a version of Tieleman Tielen van Sittert's 1664 apology explaining the early sixteenth-century history of the Anabaptist tradition. Each of the individual parts was intended to strengthen a central theme: there was no connection or affinity whatever between the followers of Menno Simons and the sixteenth-century Anabaptist kingdom at Münster.

To support his claim, Roosen provided a history of the separate origins of the Münsterites and Mennonites.[59] The anti-Christian Münsterites were almost exclusively a social phenomenon restricted to the countryside around Westphalia at the beginning of the sixteenth century. One of their leaders, Jan van Leiden, had come from the Netherlands and may have tricked a small number of Mennonites to follow him to the heretics' Westphalian heartland. Nonetheless, this in no way proved a connection between Münsterites and Mennonites. From Roosen's point of view, it made as much sense to draw historical connections between Münsterites and Mennonites as it did to draw connections between Münsterites and

---

56 After Roosen's *Unschuld* was published, Schijn attacked Spanheim again in 1711 in a separate book.

57 These texts are *Glaubens-Bekänntniß Von der Heiligen Gottheit* (*Confession of the Triune God*) (1550); *Wehmühtige und Christliche Entschuldigung* (selections from *Reply to False Accusations*) (1552); and *Menno Simonis Ausgang aus dem Pabstthum* (selections from *Reply to Gellius Faber*) (1554).

58 The subject of this sermon was the Christian's freedom from sin and death. Pieter preached about Christ's sacrifice, which released believers from the wages of sin and allowed them to become sanctified before God. At the End of Days the bodies of the saved would rise from the dead and live with Christ. As Robert Friedmann notes in *Mennonite Piety through the Centuries*, p. 151, the sermon contains very conventional Protestant themes.

59 See Roosen, *Unschuld und Gegen-Bericht*, pp. 7–29.

Lutherans. After all, had not Bernhard Rothmann, the rebellious preacher at Münster, been a Lutheran preacher gone astray? Both suggestions of historical connections were equally preposterous. While there may have been individual Mennonites from the Netherlands who were tricked into going to Westphalia, the Mennonites' brand of adult baptism had an ancient Christian pedigree, which was one of several characteristics that set it apart from the Münsterite heresy. Roosen wrote, citing the authority of Jacob Mehrning,[60] that the true baptismal ordinance was 'begun by Christ himself, taught by the Apostles, and practised in the first churches . . .'.[61] Furthermore, it

> had continued to be practised in each century thereafter, although it was suppressed by the Roman Church; nonetheless, this holy baptismal ordinance began to flourish again to an extent around 1200 through the activities of the famous Peter Waldo at Lyon in France, although only for a short time, for the Papists could not be pacified until they had made this Peter Waldo a hated man. . . .[62]

The followers of Waldo, Roosen continued, who dared to live as Christ had, were scattered throughout Europe. Like the Waldensians and other suffering bearers of the apostolic torch, Mennonites in their Dutch homeland, far away from the heretical territories of Westphalia, continued the time-honoured and Christ-sanctioned baptism, even though the majority of Christians had turned away from Christ's ways and preferred mistakenly to baptize children. While the Münsterites claimed to be true baptists, they showed by their actions that they did not fear God. They rejected properly established governmental authority, promoted robbery through the institution of the community of goods and practised a recently instituted, illegal and anti-Christian form of rebaptism. Nothing could be further from the way of life of the Mennonites, who obeyed government, respected private property, helped the needy through mutual aid and rejected both child baptism and rebaptism in favour of believers' baptism.

In addition to Mehrning, Roosen also cited the authority of scholars and churchmen like Thieleman Jansz van Braght, Engel Arentsz van

---

60 For background on Mehrning, see Ch. 2.

61 Roosen, *Unschuld und Gegen-Bericht der Evangelischen Tauff-gesinneten Christen*, p. 25: 'von Christo selbst eingesetzet/ von den Aposteln gelehret/ und in der ersten Kirchen im Gebrauch gewesen . . .'.

62 Ibid.: 'daß die heilige Tauffe auff eigenen Glaubens Bekäntniß von Christi Zeit ab durch alle 100 jährige Zeiten im Gebrauch (wiewol durch die Römische Kirche gedrucket) ist gewesen; Demnach hat diese heilige Tauff-Ordnung durch den bekandten Petrus Waldus zu Lyon in Franckreich im 1200sten Jahre nach Christi Gebuhrt einiger massen wieder angefangen zu floriren/ wiewol nur eine kurtze Zeit/ dann die Papisten kunten dabey nicht geruhig seyn/ biß daß sie diesen Petrum Waldum verhasset gemacht . . .'.

Doorgeest, Johann Montanus,[63] Philipp von Zesen,[64] Pieter Valckenier,[65] Heinrich Ludolph Benthem[66] and Gottfried Arnold.[67] These Protestants were impartial preachers and professors, for they acknowledged the truth, claimed Roosen. Fortunately, in his view, there were also impartial rulers. 'Christian governors in many places'[68] accepted the Mennonites' confessions of faith as the statements of good residents. For example, Roosen wrote that Bartholomäus von Ahlefeldt, the lord of Fresenburg in Holstein, had offered shelter to Menno Simons and his co-religionists in the mid-sixteenth century,[69] and the King of Denmark welcomed the Mennonites on his territory in places like Altona.[70] Even the Catholic king of France, after careful investigation, had agreed that the Mennonites, who lived under his authority for a short time after the French invasion of the United Netherlands in 1672, were in no way related to 'Quakers and night-runners' (*Quäcker und Nacht-läuffer*). The latter groups were

63 Although Roosen wrote of 'Johann Montanus', he almost certainly meant Hermann Montanus. Hermann Montanus was a Reformed nonconformist at the beginning of the seventeenth century. After falling out with Remonstrant colleagues, he accepted baptism by immersion in 1639 at the hands of Collegiants at Rijnsburg. Before he died in 1640, he wrote a tract which was later published in 1647 and 1648 in Amsterdam under the title *Nietigheydt Van den Kinder-doop* (The Invalidity of Child Baptism). Montanus's manuscript helped inspire Jacob Mehrning. Despite the pro-baptist message of his book, Montanus was not at all as concerned as Mehrning to defend the historical and ethical legacy of his Mennonite contemporaries. On Montanus, see van Slee, *De Rijnsburger Collegianten*, pp. 72–8.

64 Von Zesen (1619–89), considered the first professional German-speaking poet, founded the *Deutschgesinnte Gesellschaft* in 1643 for the promotion and preservation of the German language. The text of von Zesen to which Roosen referred was *Wider den Gewissenszwang* (1665). For more on the history of this text, see Peter Bietenholz, 'Philipp von Zesens Schrift *Wider den Gewissenszwang* und die Schweizer Täufer', in Michael Erbe et al. (eds), *Querdenken: Dissens und Toleranz im Wandel der Geschichte. Festschrift zum 65. Geburtstag von Hans R. Guggisberg* (Mannheim, 1996), pp. 305–17.

65 Valckenier (1638–1712) was the author of *'t Verwerd Europa* (1668). The text went through several Dutch and German versions. Roosen was referring to a German translation of the 1675 Dutch edition.

66 Benthem (1661–1723), a Lutheran preacher from Celle who sometimes worked in Harburg near Hamburg, published *Holländischer Kirch- und Schulenstaat* in 1698. This book included a copy of the Dordrecht Confession, and the author argued that the Mennonites deserved to be judged on the basis of their confessions of faith.

67 Arnold (1666–1714), a Lutheran Pietist, was of interest to Roosen because he was the author of the *Unparteiischen Kirchen- und Ketzerhistorie* (Frankfurt, 1699–1700), a work in which the sixteenth-century Anabaptists were classed among the true followers of Christ. See Ursula Kreuder, 'Gottfried Arnolds Sicht der Täufer', in Dietrich Blaufuß and Friedrich Niewöhner (eds), *Gottfried Arnold (1666–1714)* (Wiesbaden, 1995), pp. 165–77.

68 Roosen, *Unschuld und Gegen-Bericht*, p. 84: 'die Christliche Obrigheit an vielen Oertern . . .'.

69 On Fresenburg and the Mennonite experience in Holstein, see Goverts, 'Das adelige Gut Fresenburg und die Mennoniten'; also see Roosen, *Unschuld und Gegen-Bericht*, pp. 97–103.

70 Roosen, *Unschuld und Gegen-Bericht*, p. 104.

punished; the former lived without undue fear of worldly law, for they conformed to it.[71] The Quakers were a dangerous lot, but the Mennonites were nothing like them. According to Roosen, those people who were properly classified as Mennonites were among the best-behaved subjects in any territory.

A pattern is evident in the Mennonite–Lutheran polemics of the 1690s. Men embroiled in controversy and labelled as dissenters, even heretics and criminals, worked aggressively to clear their public image and the image of their allies or co-religionists. They did this by loudly professing not only their Christian orthodoxy but also their loyalty and obedience to secular rulers.

The institutional consequences of interconfessional polemics

The structural parallels between Lutheran and Mennonite defensive strategies are even stronger. When Johann Winckler was attacked by his conservative Lutheran colleagues for sympathizing with heretics, he attacked heretics. Similarly, Geeritt Roosen, one of the spokesmen for those 'heretics', tried to rebuff attacks not only by refuting Lutheran charges but also by attacking those he perceived to be guilty of the crimes with which he had been charged. The target of Roosen's attacks was a new preacher in the Flemish congregation named Riewart Dircks, and Roosen's reactions led to a major institutional reform among Mennonites in Hamburg and Altona.

Riewart Dircks was originally a preacher from Molkwerum in the Netherlands. From May to July 1695 he delivered some sermons and administered one baptismal service as a guest preacher in Altona. There is no record that his initial appearance in the congregation sparked any controversy. In fact, in May 1697 he returned to Altona to become a permanent addition to the Flemish congregation's preaching staff. But his second stay in Altona was not so happy.

Dircks's preaching of the nature of the Trinity during his second period in Altona upset some leading members of the congregation, most notably Geeritt Roosen. Sometime during 1697 Roosen recorded his concerns and objections in a manuscript entitled 'Ontdeckinge van Eenige suptyle en dubbelsinnige neepen' (Discovery of Some Subtle and Ambiguous Deceptions).[72] Roosen's concern was that Christ was being described as

---

71 Ibid., pp. 87–91. This passage from Roosen's text is based on Valckenier.

72 StAHbg/MG, 248, vol. 1. Although Roosen discussed religious tricksters in nothing more than broad and general terms in the main text, it is clear that he was thinking specifically of Dircks. In only one difficult-to-find place in the text is Dircks mentioned by name. The original page (fol. [3]^{v}) has been replaced by an extra sheet fastened with wax to the earlier

God's Son who existed with God in eternity but who was created after God. The implication of these teachings was that God was the Father only after the birth of the Son to Mary, and also that the Son was inferior to the Father.[73] While the defenders of this heretical position claimed to be confessing Mennonites, wrote Roosen, they were actually leading their listeners dangerously astray from a simple and trusting faith in the truth. On 16 August, less than three months after his arrival, Dircks returned to the Low Countries. He had been ostracized although not officially expelled by Altona's Flemish Mennonites. Despite Roosen's clear condemnation of views he considered heretical, not everyone seemed to share his disgust with Dircks. Those who wanted Dircks to leave had their way, but Roosen wrote in the membership book that 'many people were greatly displeased that no effort was made to keep him here, so that it was a close thing that a schism was averted . . .'.[74]

Upon Dircks's departure, the congregation was left with an old problem: it had a shortage of ordained preachers. To deal with this problem as well as the disquiet caused by Dircks's forced departure, five visiting preachers from the Netherlands and Friedrichstadt acted as temporary replacements between August 1697 and the beginning of 1698.[75] Geeritt Roosen, Pieter Verhelle and Jan de Lanoy, although nominally the leaders of the congregation, apparently did not carry out their preaching duties during these months. Roosen was nonetheless busy.

At about the same time (late 1697) that he was writing a letter to Anabaptists in the Alsace, in which he advised them to take a moderate and conciliatory approach to ongoing disputes among believers there,[76] Roosen was also preoccupied with finding a settlement to local disputes. On 20 November 1697 he wrote a congregational ordinance entitled 'Dienaarlyke Overweeginge tot veroffeninge der gereezene Verschillen in de Gemeente' (Ministerial Considerations towards Settling the Growing

---

version. On the reverse of the new, loose page (fol. [3]v) is part of a different document which names Dircks directly. Also see Roosen's undated manuscript entitled 'over de menschwerdinge Jesu Christy . . .', which is found in StAHbg/MG, 248, vol. 1. Judging from the quality of his handwriting, this manuscript was probably written in the last years of the 1690s and may have been inspired by the christological controversies surrounding Dircks's 1697 preaching. No texts by Dircks survive in Hamburg's archives.

73 These beliefs had been condemned at the anti-Arian Council of Nicaea in 325.

74 StAHbg/MG, 147, vol. 1, p. 156: 'maer veelen tot groot misnaegen, dat men hem hier niet socht to houden soo dat shier een scheuring uytsou ontstaen hebben . . .'.

75 See StAHbg/MG, 246b, 'Notitien vande predicatien'.

76 'Gerhard Roosen to friends in Alsace', in *Letters of the Amish Division: A Sourcebook*, ed. and trans. John D. Roth, with the assistance of Joe Springer (Goshen, 1993), pp. 67–71. Roosen did not indicate when in 1697 he wrote his letter. He did, however, refer to arrangements agreed to under the Treaty of Ryswick (that is, Strasbourg and the Alsace being granted to France). The Treaty was signed in September 1697.

Disputes in the Congregation).[77] Roosen gave two reasons why the ordinance was necessary: dissatisfaction over Dircks's arrival and then departure; and further dissatisfaction over a decision not to call Matthys Diepenbroek from Haarlem to be a preacher in the congregation (article 1). The majority of the two-page document outlined the means of avoiding similar disputes in the future. The model for his proposals was the *Oprecht Verbondt van Eenigheydt* (see Ch. 3). Preachers new to the congregation would have to accept the principles and confessions in the *Verbondt* before they could preach or administer the sacraments (article 2). If ever a preacher from another Mennonite congregation arrived in Altona unannounced, he should be questioned before being admitted to the pulpit, just as Galenus Abrahamsz was questioned two decades earlier; all preachers sympathetic to Socinian principles would be asked to leave (article 3). Important resolutions concerning congregational government would be brought before members for discussion and voting (article 4). But in no case could a decision (even a majority decision) run contrary to the principles in the *Verbondt* or the confessions, which provided the guidelines for avoiding and overcoming disturbances (article 5). On 28 November, a week after he composed it, Roosen's ordinance was read to the congregation's members.

Just over one month later, on 12 January 1698, Roosen issued a memorial[78] to his congregation which was reminiscent of his 1669 grant of land (see Ch. 3). Like the 1669 document, the new one condemned all innovations in matters of faith. In the 1698 text Roosen's specific targets were 'Collegiants or Socinians' who denied Christ's divinity, 'just like Socinus and now his followers'.[79] Again like in 1669, Roosen promised financial assistance from his substantial inheritance only to those who remained faithful to the articles outlined in approved confessions of faith.[80] A week later a scribe wrote the first entry in the congregation's new protocol book. This was the book in which from then on decisions taken at council meetings were recorded. Before 1698, recordkeeping during council meetings had been much less systematic, and few of those earlier records survive. Largely at Roosen's initiative, the 1697 controversy had forced a re-evaluation of the processes of congregational government.

To summarize developments described in this and the preceding section: In 1696 Johann Winckler repeated several serious charges against the

77 StAHbg/MG, 4.

78 StAHbg/MG, 193/14.

79 Ibid.: '. . . gelyck de van socinus doen en nu syn aanhanck dryven . . .'.

80 In this particular case he did not refer to the *Verbondt* but rather the congregational songbook (see Visser, 'A Checklist of Dutch Mennonite Confessions of Faith', II.J.), which included a version of two Dutch confessions, the Jaques Outerman confession and the *Olijftacxken*.

Mennonites, including that they were guilty of the antitrinitarian heresy of Socinianism. Soon thereafter, Geeritt Roosen wrote a first draft of the confession of faith which would later be published as part of *Unschuld und Gegen-Bericht*; on that draft, he indicated that he intended the text as a refutation of Winckler's charges. In 1697 the Flemish congregation, led by Roosen, pressured Riewart Dircks to leave after he had preached apparently heretical ideas about the Trinity. In order to avoid heterodox preaching of this sort from casting a shadow on the Mennonites' Christian orthodoxy, Roosen codified clear rules governing congregational life, the first of their kind in Hamburg and Altona. Socinian heresy was condemned in this congregational ordinance, which was soon followed by further regulative measures. In short, while under increased scrutiny by Lutheran clergymen at a time when Hamburg was in political turmoil, the Mennonites were voluntarily tightening institutional controls on their actions.

Broader implications

Among the reasons that the developments described in this chapter are significant is that they are typical of a social dynamic fundamental to the formation of early modern Mennonite identity. Put in straightforward terms, the loudest and clearest public statements of Mennonite identity were often made either as direct rebuttals to anti-Mennonite propaganda or as pre-emptive defences against anticipated libels. In other words, we should think about expressions of group norms primarily in terms of strategic and therefore contingent interactions between Mennonites and others, not in terms of a pure, permanent character. This defensive assertion of identity was characteristic of Mennonitism 'from the very beginning', that is, by the years after the mid-1530s when Menno Simons and colleagues tried to rescue fellow believers from the dangerous charge that the criminal excesses of the Münsterite kingdom were natural consequences of Anabaptist belief and practice. Polemics and the defence against them were a key animating spark of Mennonite identity through many generations. These ingredients are crucial for understanding Hans-Jürgen Goertz's thesis about early modern Mennonite self-policing and self-regulation.

While self-regulation and identity asserted amid polemics were key characteristics of Mennonite life in most early modern northern European territories, they were not exclusively Mennonite characteristics. In his survey of early modern Jewish life, Jonathan Israel writes:

[81] Jonathan Israel, *European Jewry in the Age of Mercantilism, 1550–1750* (3rd edn, London and Portland, Ore., 1998), p. 162.

> The universal precariousness of Jewish life militated strongly in favour of subjection to discipline and authority. It was not simply a question of upholding the Torah and pursuing the moral ideals of Judaism. Anything likely to exacerbate the ever-present reality of popular hatred was deemed a threat to the community. Unseemly conduct, licentiousness, extravagance, the presence of too many beggars, any sort of provocative behaviour was liable to be promptly suppressed. The boards of the elders kept a vigilant eye on costume, morals, and every aspect of life-style and this congregants had no choice but to accept.[81]

It was the precariousness of minority life more than any unique religious principles which motivated self-policing. Quakers, Mennonites, Lutheran Pietists, Jews and other groups in politically vulnerable circumstances who nonetheless wanted to be recognized as legitimate members of mainstream society, despite their nonconforming religious beliefs, all provide examples of self-regulation promoting social order and stability.

One point deserves special emphasis. These examples of a religious community's self-regulation promoting stability are not evidence of 'social discipline' as the term is normally understood. It is good to avoid labelling this form of community self-regulation 'social discipline' because, even though (as Goertz argues) governments could be indirect beneficiaries of the resulting Mennonite obedience, government agents did not initiate changes and did not even require that the Mennonites be any more obedient than they already were.[82] Johann Winckler and Geeritt Roosen both volunteered their obedience to the same weakened secular authorities. In the words of Georg Simmel, an early twentieth-century pioneer in the then emerging field of sociology, conflict could in some circumstances act as 'an integrative force'.[83]

These historical and sociological patterns have some implications for debates about the confessionalization paradigm. The definition of confessionalization primarily as an early form of social discipline is narrow and constricting. This is not an argument made on the basis of evidence from Mennonite history alone but is also a conclusion emerging more clearly in other recent historical studies.[84] By emphasizing alliances between

---

82 This conclusion also holds for governmental legislation on oath-swearing from the 1690s, which is discussed in Ch. 6.

83 Georg Simmel, *On Individuality and Social Forms*, ed. and intro. Donald N. Levine (Chicago and London, 1971), p. 74.

84 See Schmidt, 'Sozialdisziplinierung?'; and Schindling, 'Konfessionalisierung und Grenzen von Konfessionalisierbarkeit'. Also see Randolph Head, 'Catholics and Protestants in Graubünden: Confessional Discipline and Confessional Identities without an Early Modern State?' *German History*, 17 (1999), pp. 321–45; and Marc R. Forster, *The Counter-Reformation in the Villages: Religion and Reform in the Bishopric of Speyer, 1560–1720* (Ithaca, NY, 1992). Isabel V. Hull, *Sexuality, State and Civil Society in Germany, 1700–1815* (Ithaca, NY and London, 1996), pp. 54–6, even doubts the value of the social discipline model as applied to the setting it was meant originally to apply to – the eighteenth century.

secular rulers and church leaders, the standard paradigm not only loses sight of religious groups not allied or working officially with rulers but also churches that consolidated their collective identities in opposition to rulers. In Hamburg, for example, an intensification of orthodox Lutheran identity led to rebellion, and this case is certainly not as famous as the examples of early modern Reformed theories of political resistance. In short, when confessional identity formation led to social order, it could do so through mechanisms other than social discipline; and, in addition to promoting order, it could also do the opposite.

There is a straightforward solution to problems of definitions. Rather than proposing a new meaning for the concept of confessionalization, it would be best to return to an older, more basic meaning to which almost everyone can agree: confessionalization is the process of religious identity formation which was so typical of the generations after the Reformation. Anything more serves only to complicate matters unnecessarily. In other words, 'confessionalization' and 'confessionalism' need not be taken to mean anything very different. Accepting this reduced definition does not amount to an outright rejection of the work of those scholars who have emphasized the link between government-directed social discipline and confessionalism. The reason is that the reduced definition leaves room for the possibility of government-directed action, while avoiding putting it at the centre. This is appropriate at a time when even some of the staunchest promoters of the older, state-focused model are starting to wonder out loud about the outmoded theory of power and authority (as something concentrated in the hands of rulers) it assumes.[85]

In addition to supporting the calls to weaken the connection between confessionalization and social discipline, there is a further implication of the evidence in this chapter which is worth highlighting. It concerns the dominant structural-functionalist approach to confessionalization studies, which concentrates attention on collective actors like 'the church' or 'the state'. By focusing excessively on the study of such institutional structures, we risk losing sight of the individual men and women whose actions and beliefs gave substance to otherwise abstract categories.

---

85 See the concluding statements by François, Schmidt, Schilling and Reinhard in Reinhard and Schilling (eds), *Die katholische Konfessionalisierung*, pp. 453–5. Also see Reinhard, 'Sozialdisziplinierung – Konfessionalisierung – Modernisierung', p. 55: 'So scheint unter anderem auch in der Geschichte der "Sozialdisziplinierung" die Vorstellung eines einheitlichen und allein von der Obrigkeit betriebenen Prozesses mehr und mehr verloren zu gehen. . . . Möglicherweise hatte Michel Foucault recht, als er die Disziplinierung der frühneuzeitlichen Gesellschaft keiner Zentralinstanz mehr zuschrieb, sondern dezentralen Vorgängen an verschiedenen Punkten der Gesellschaft, die keineswegs nur mehr durch Normen und den Einsatz von Macht zu deren Beachtung gesteuert werden, sondern durch neuartige kognitive Prozesse, die Lernfähigkeit einschließen.'

The way forward in confessionalization research is not to continue to make broad generalizations about collective actors. There is an alternative. Instead of studying institutions in a general way, historians can and are examining patterns of interaction involving individual and identifiable early modern believers, religious leaders and government officials.[86] 'Mennonite confessionalization' is a legitimate subject of this ongoing research. The following chapters provide further examinations of patterns of interaction involving Mennonite men and women.

86 A strong theoretical foundation upon which to establish future studies would be Georg Simmel's sociology, as outlined in his *Soziologie* (Frankfurt, 1995 [1908]). Heinrich Richard Schmidt has recently suggested using Anthony Giddens's structuration theory as a sociological foundation for a reconceived confessionalization paradigm. Both Simmel's and Giddens's work would focus greater attention on dynamic interactions and processes.

CHAPTER FIVE

A Conformist Brand of Non-resistance: Controversies and Silences

No study of Mennonites and political order would be complete without an examination of the ethical principle of non-resistance (*Wehrlosigkeit*). In the early modern era following the fall of the Anabaptist regime at Münster, the rejection of violence and the refusal to bear arms had been part of the constitution or ideological core of almost all Mennonite communities.[1] Today, non-resistance remains central to Mennonite self-definitions, but it has taken on the meaning of active 'peacemaking',[2] which early modern Mennonites would have found foreign and even absurd.

In this chapter, there are two goals. One is to look closely at the assumptions that Geeritt Roosen and other Mennonite leaders made while discussing non-resistant faith. They usually made an issue of non-resistance amid controversies with dissident believers. However, there are some aspects of the subject which they did not address and seem rather to have been taken for granted. These silences are as noteworthy as the controversies. The other goal is to show that an understanding of official and publicly stated standards alone, no matter how much we are aware of unstated assumptions, will give an incomplete picture of Mennonite life. By focusing too narrowly on official statements, we risk overlooking the tensions that existed between rhetoric (important though it was) and actual lived experience.

Coping with the dangers of merchant shipping in wartime

Mercantile activity was one area of life in which practical aspects of non-resistant principles were especially pressing for congregation members involved in whaling and shipping in northern European waters. At no

---

[1] Germany in the 1930s and 1940s is the best-known example of a period when congregational leaders rejected the principle in favour of the then dominant militarist ideology of the Nazis. See Hans-Jürgen Goertz, 'Nationale Erhebung und religiöser Niedergang', in Hans-Jürgen Goertz (ed.), *Umstrittenes Täufertum* (2nd edn, Göttingen, 1977), pp. 259–89.

[2] This is especially true of post-1960s North America. See Leo Driedger and Donald B. Kraybill, *Mennonite Peacemaking: From Quietism to Activism* (Scottdale, Pa., and Waterloo, Ont., 1994).

time was this truer than during the 1690s, when Hamburg was experiencing political uncertainty and many of Europe's governments were at war.

The Nine Years War (1688–97) against France complicated travel on the waters near the mouth of the Elbe River, the North Sea, the English Channel and the Arctic Ocean. The Dutch, Swedes, Danes, French and English all had warships on patrol. The actions of the Danish crown provide many examples of how merchant shipping was made more difficult during these years of war. Because of Hamburg's commercially important position near the mouth of the Elbe, Denmark had wanted for some time to make the city a dependent territory; control of Hamburg as well as Glückstadt and Altona would have translated to effective dominance over trade along the Elbe. An impediment to the Danish plan was that Hamburg belonged loosely to the Holy Roman Empire. Danish armies had approached the city twice in recent decades, but in both 1679 and 1686 troops from the Duchy of Braunschweig-Lüneburg had come to the city's rescue.[3] Tensions between Denmark and Hamburg again increased during the Nine Years War. At the beginning of 1690 Christian V of Denmark was negotiating with Emperor Leopold I (1658–1705). In exchange for joining the campaign against France, Christian asked for the right to charge massive tolls at Glückstadt. Such tolls would have been a very serious blow to Hamburg's trade, for ships had to pass there on their way to open waters. The negotiations came to nothing, and in 1691 Denmark declared its official neutrality in the conflict against France. Yet the Danes remained determined to assert their sovereignty over the Elbe waterway. Soon after the failed negotiations with the Empire, Christian raised the stakes in his bid to control the region. On 25 February 1691 he issued a mandate forbidding Hamburg's whalers to fish around Spitsbergen Island in the Arctic Ocean. By the summer of that year the Danes were actively stopping ships to check passports and levy fines against merchants and whalers from Hamburg.[4] A treaty between Hamburg and Denmark was concluded in August 1692, but Danish forces continued, in contravention of the agreed resolution, to assert their alleged rights to charge a fine on ships owned by businessmen from Hamburg.[5]

Merchants and whalers tried as best they could to cope with Danish hostility. One method in particular was common and usually effective: shared ownership of vessels and goods. In itself, this kind of cooperative enterprise was a business convention, even long before the 1690s. On any given ship, cargoes were usually owned by several, even many, businessmen.

---

3 Loose, 'Das Zeitalter der Bürgerunruhen', p. 307.

4 See Rückleben, *Die Niederwerfung der hamburgischen Ratsgewalt*, ch. 3 and appendices 2–5.

5 See Loose, 'Zeitalter der Bürgerunruhen', pp. 302–3; and Brinner, *Die deutsche Grönlandfahrt*, pp. 212–17.

In 1646, for example, three Mennonites (Hans Plus, Paul Roosen and Pelgrim Milder) were among the forty-five businessmen who owned portions of the cargo on a ship returning from Archangel to Hamburg.[6] By way of comparison, in 1695 the ship *Vergüldeter Elefant* (Gilded Elephant)[7] had cargo belonging to nine parties. The largest share of cargo (eleven-sixteenths) belonged to four groups from the de Vlieger family. Not only the transportation of cargoes but also ship ownership itself was often a cooperative business. The ship *Vergüldeter Elefant* can again serve as an example. Nine-sixteenths of the ship was owned by members of the de Vlieger family, and the rest was divided between four men (Ahasverus and Conrad Köhn [Koen], Gerhard Raecke and Andreas Leser), the first two of whom were, like the de Vliegers, members of the Flemish Mennonite congregation in Hamburg and Altona.[8] Businessmen who placed all their goods on one ship were taking a tremendous risk, for to do so was to bet that the vessel would not sink nor be arrested. By sharing cargo space and the ownership of boats, merchants were trying to reduce their chances of being bankrupted by a single misfortune.

The practice of multiple ownership took on added significance during the Danish blockade in the 1690s. Until 1691, residents of Danish Altona were in theory exempt from the penalties imposed by their monarch against whaling and merchant ships registered in Hamburg. Hamburg-based businessmen sometimes tried to avoid Danish fines and confiscations by registering their ships and cargoes under the name of a Danish subject from Altona, who would be made a business partner. In such cases the Altona-based ship director would arrange a Danish passport for the ship and cargo, even though the majority interests in the ship may have been held by businessmen from Hamburg.[9]

This juggling of ownership was tempting for all merchants, Mennonites included. Hamburg-based Mennonites who wanted to arrange Danish passports for their ships had an advantage, for their networks of family, church and business contacts extended across the jurisdictional boundary separating Hamburg from Altona. Of course there was a complication. The ease with which Mennonites from Hamburg could arrange Danish passports was only an advantage as long as they were not detected or, if detected, Danish authorities had no objections to the practice. As of 20 June 1691 Danish authorities had orders to stop at Glückstadt all ships in which residents of Hamburg had shares, even if a Danish subject held the

[6] Martin Reißmann, *Die hamburgische Kaufmannschaft des 17. Jahrhunderts in sozialgeschichtlicher Sicht* (Hamburg, 1975), p. 63.

[7] Landesarchiv Schleswig, Abt. 11/Nr. 493, 12 December 1695.

[8] StAHbg/MG, 147, vol. 1, p. 66; ibid., 148, vol. 1, p. 4.

[9] My thanks go to Anke Martens for making me aware of this practice.

passport. Bond (*Kaution*) charges for offenders were as high as 4000 Reichstaler.[10]

One of the ships seized by the Danish patrols during the summer of 1691, when the government began taking stricter measures against Hamburg's merchants and whalers, was the *Rathaus von Altona* (Altona City Hall). The ship's director, the Mennonite Herman Goverts, was required to pay a 2000 Reichstaler bond. He raised the money with help from his father-in-law Geeritt Roosen as well as Carel de Vlieger.[11] In August 1692, two further members of the Goverts family – Pieter, since 1689 a deacon in the Flemish congregation, and Paul, since 1688 a Lutheran[12] – were unlucky enough to be caught and fined by Danish authorities for the offence of cooperating with colleagues from Hamburg. Pieter had obtained a Danish passport 'using the oath given in Mennonite fashion' (presumably the formula *bei Mannen Wahrheit* – see Ch. 6) to attest to the truth of his claims. What he failed to mention was that the majority of the ship's shareholders were from Hamburg.[13]

Although they could be severe, fines and confiscation were not the worst of worries facing Elbian merchants. Merchants could also become casualties of war. By January 1690, sixteen Hamburg-based merchant ships had already been lost in the hostilities of the Nine Years War.[14] Hamburg's civic officials were unable to do much to prevent such losses. The problem had been a long-standing one. In response to requests in the early 1660s from Hamburg's whalers and Archangel traders, some of whom were Mennonite, the Senate had agreed to pay for the costs of protection. Where it was feasible, it provided soldiers and arms to man merchant vessels. By the end of the 1660s, the city also owned two warships – *Leopoldus Primus* and *Wapen von Hamburg* – for use as convoyers in open waters beyond

---

10 Rückleben, *Niederwerfung*, p. 44.

11 Landesarchiv Schleswig, Abt. 11/Nr. 488I. Herman Goverts married Sara Roosen in 1676. I am not sure whether the Carel de Vlieger in question was the father or the son.

12 StAHbg/MG, 147, vol. 1, p. 55.

13 See Brinner, *Grönlandfahrt*, p. 216. Pieter Goverts had given a 'nach menonitischer [*sic*] arth gethanen eydt'. The original, which I have not been able to check, is at Landesarchiv Schleswig, Abt. 11/Nr. 488I, 22 July 1692. The ship was called *Friede* (Peace). This was one of several incidents of its sort in the early 1690s. Heinz Münte, *Das Altonaer Handlungshaus van der Smissen 1682–1824. Ein Beitrag zur Wirtschaftsgeschichte der Stadt Altona* (Altona, 1932), p. 7, n. 24, speculates that Daniel van der Smissen, a citizen of Danish Glückstadt who was related to members of Altona's Flemish congregation, organized several ships owned by Hamburg residents between 1690 and 1691 in order to take advantage of his Danish residency during the Danish ban on Hamburg whalers. For further references to the abuse of passport privileges by Altonaers, see J.S. Bromley, 'The North Sea in Wartime, 1688–1713', independently paginated chapter in *Corsairs and Navies, 1660–1760* (London, 1987), pp. 54–5.

14 Rückleben, *Niederwerfung*, p. 31.

the mouth of the Elbe.[15] Despite their best efforts, Hamburg's convoy ships were unable to provide protection for all of the city's ships. For example, the convoyers were not available or were unable to help several Hamburg-based ships returning to their home port in 1690. In August of that year the famous French naval officer and privateer Jean Bart had positioned ships in the waters off the island of Helgoland about 50 kilometres outside the mouth of the Elbe River. In the space of a week his crews captured three merchant ships and nine whaling ships. The nine whaling ships were returned only after very high ransoms were paid – in total, 106,500 livres.[16] At least two of the ransomed ships – *Witte Baer* (The White Bear) and *Goude Vlieg* (The Golden Fly) – were owned by the Flemish Mennonite Carel de Vlieger Senior or his son Carel Junior.[17] Two other ships – *de Sonn* (The Sun) owned by a Peter Peters and *de Koning Davidt* (The King David) captained by another (or the same) Peter Peters – may have had a Mennonite connection.[18] It is difficult to know if any of the ransomed ships were armed.

Officials in Altona likewise could do little to protect Danish subjects from wartime losses. On 28 April 1691 the Mennonite businessmen Dominicus Kipping, Pieter Pieters and Herman Pauls Roosen (Geeritt Roosen's brother) sent a letter to the Danish king asking for protection and assistance against privateers in the waters around Vlissingen and Middelburg. Between May and December 1690 they had lost a number of ships in this region. They included another document listing their losses,

15 See Ernst Baasch, *Hamburgs Convoyschiffahrt und Convoywesen: Ein Beitrag zur Geschichte der Schiffahrt und Schiffahrtseinrichtungen im 17. und 18. Jahrhundert* (Hamburg, 1896); and Joachim Ehlers, *Die Wehrverfassung der Stadt Hamburg im 17. und 18. Jahrhundert* (Boppard am Rhein, 1966), pp. 9–10.

16 For a list of the captured and ransomed ships, see Brinner, *Grönlandfahrt*, p. 163, n. 1; and Archives Nationales (Paris), Marine, Series B4, vol. 12, fols 473–6, 'Extract des Reg[ist]res du Con[sei]l d'Etat', Arrêt du Conseil, à Versailles, 11 December 1690. Captain Caspar Tamm of the *Wapen von Hamburg* was returning to Hamburg with a convoy of ships from the Iberian Peninsula around the time of Bart's attacks. See Tamm's journal: StAHbg, Senat, Cl. VII Lit. Ca Nr. 3 Vol. 7c (6), (31)–(33). I should like to thank Prof. James Pritchard for providing the archival information from Paris.

17 Carel de Vlieger Senior was active together with Hinrich Pender and Geeritt Roosen in the whaling business as early as 1669 and became a deacon in 1689; see StAHbg/MG, 147, vol. 1, p. 9. Carel Junior became a deacon upon his father's death in 1695; see StAHbg/MG, 147, vol. 1, p. 95.

18 There were two Pieter Pieters in the Flemish congregation. Pieter Pieters Windt (StAHbg/MG, 147, vol. 1, p. 73) was listed as a sailor who died overseas in 1692. The second Pieter Pieters (ibid., pp. 98 and 163, and StAHbg/MG, 6, vol. 1, pp. 7–8) seems to have been prone to violence and confrontation; he was the subject of disciplinary proceedings in 1696 and 1699. Because the name was so common in Dutch circles, it is impossible to tell if the man (or men) named Peter Peters who had connections with the ransomed ships also had ties to the Mennonite community.

which they recorded as reaching the enormous total of just over 98,170 mark *lübsch*. The ships' cargoes included such products as vitriol (a dyeing agent for cloth) and French wines.[19]

After the defeat of the French at sea in the Battle of La Hogue in May 1692 the French naval presence in northern European waters diminished somewhat. Yet the dangers to merchant shipping remained. In November 1692 a convoy of approximately forty merchant vessels left Hamburg for the annual voyage to the Iberian Peninsula. The fleet was escorted by Hamburg's two warships led by captains Schröder and Marisen. The convoyers did manage to fend off an attack in the English Channel by six privateering ships flying British flags, but the fleet could not withstand the effects of a storm that followed the battle. The Hamburg merchants had to dock in south-eastern England. After the signing of the Grand Alliance against France in 1689, Hamburg, as an ally of the Empire, was also nominally an ally of the English. Perhaps in revenge for Hamburg's initial reluctance to enter the war or perhaps because of opportunism on the part of locals towards the Germans, the fleet was prevented from leaving after the storm. Some of the ships' cargoes were even unloaded. Despite the Senate's protests to Imperial officials, the ships remained under English control at least until the middle of 1693. At the end of May 1693 Captain Schröder sailed from Portsmouth with the merchant fleet, which was still destined for Iberian ports. The German convoy did not sail alone. It was joined by Dutch and English ships. At one point in June the fleet was approximately 150 ships strong, among them twenty warships. In the middle of June the fleet came under attack by French forces. Part or all of the fleet was forced to stop at the French port of Toulon, where the merchants' goods were confiscated. Mennonite merchants were among those from Hamburg entangled in the unlucky events of 1692 and 1693.[20]

Merchants, in response to the dangers of wartime shipping, may have organized private warships to supplement Hamburg's convoyers. This, at least, is the conclusion of the historian Wanda Oesau.[21] Oesau suspects that the whaling ship *König Salomos Gericht* (King Solomon's Court)

19 Landesarchiv Schleswig, Abt. 65.1/Nr. 1729a.

20 For general details about the events of November 1692 to summer 1693, see Baasch, *Convoyschiffahrt*, appendices 24 and 25, pp. 454–8; and Rückleben, *Niederwerfung*, p. 35. At the very end of the seventeenth century the Imperial Cameral Court in Wetzlar was presented a case resulting from the series of catastrophes beginning in November 1692. In a document dated 28 March 1698, Jacob de Vlieger (son of the Mennonite deacon Carel de Vlieger Senior) and other signatories described the issue at stake in the case as follows: 'wer die unkosten tragen soll, so da gemacht, wegen einiger in Engelland aufgebrachten, und nach der befreyunge wieder verunglückten kauffschiffe' (StAHbg, Reichskammergericht, B1b, Lit. F., fol. 1^{v}).

21 Oesau, *Hamburgs Grönlandfahrt*, pp. 111 and 288.

was used from time to time during years of war (1679 and 1691 to 1693, years when it was not listed among the whaling fleet) as a private convoy ship. It is known to have been armed with thirty-four cannons.[22] The ship had first appeared in whaling records in Hamburg in 1672, and for most of its time in Hamburg its listed owner was Gerd Harmsen Baker. In 1694, the last year the ship was included in the city's whaling records, its owner was listed as Herman Geertz Baker Junior. None of this would be particularly noteworthy if it were not for the claim by the historian Joachim Münzing that the ship's owners were Mennonites.[23]

Münzing's claim is almost certainly based on an assumption made in the course of reading Ludwig Brinner's early twentieth-century standard work on the history of the German whaling industry. In his book Brinner noted that members of the Baker (Backer) family who were involved in Hamburg's whaling industry were Mennonites.[24] The Bakers were Mennonites; *König Salomos Gericht* was owned by Bakers; therefore, or so the logic goes, *König Salomos Gericht* was owned by Mennonites. Although local Mennonites may indeed have armed their merchant vessels at this time (see below), we should be cautious about using Münzing's statement as evidence.

There was a Baker (Backer) family (or families) in Altona's Flemish congregation,[25] but the family name was common. For example, it was also found in Altona's Calvinist community. A Herman Gerritsen Baker was married in Altona's German Reformed church in 1652.[26] Perhaps speaking for the possibility that the people in question were Mennonites is the fact that there was at least one Dutch Mennonite named Gerrit Harmensz Backer, a name very similar to that of the long-time director of *König Salomos Gericht*. At the anti-Galenist Leiden Synod in 1660 he had acted as a representative for the Flemish congregation in Alkmaar.[27]

---

22 Ibid., pp. 164–6. Oesau describes a large painting of Hamburg's harbour and skyline by Elias Galli from around 1680 which shows *König Salomos Gericht* firing its cannons. The painting can still be found in the Museum für Hamburgische Geschichte.

23 Münzing, *Die Jagd auf den Wal*, p. 29.

24 Brinner, *Grönlandfahrt*, p. 340.

25 For information about the male members of the Ba(c)ker family (or families) in the Mennonite congregation, see StAHbg/MG, 147, vol. 1, pp. 13, 49, 66, 100, 122, 159 and 107. At least one of these men, Frans Hindericksen Baker, was a captain of whaling ships. These ships were *Dolvin* (Dolphin) from 1671 to 1677 and *groene Papagei* (Green Parrot) in 1680, both of which were owned by another Mennonite, Pouls Jansen Schoemaker. See Oesau, *Hamburgs Grönlandfahrt*, pp. 281–4. On Schoemaker, see StAHbg/MG, 147, vol. 1, p. 47.

26 See Franz Schubert (ed.), *Trauregister aus den ältesten Kirchenbüchern Hamburgs: Von den Anfängen bis zum Jahre 1704* (Göttingen, 1997), p. 67.

27 See *Verhaal Van 't gene verhandelt ende besloten is, in de By-Een-Komste Tot Leyden* (Amsterdam, 1661), p. 6.

In other words, although not a member of Geeritt Roosen's congregation, he, like Roosen, was a supporter of the confessionalist strategy of achieving Mennonite unity. It is difficult to draw conclusions based on this information. While based only on the weakest of circumstantial evidence, it is a possibility that Gerrit Harmensz Backer from Alkmaar and Gerd Harmsen Baker in Hamburg were one and the same person; just as likely, judging from available evidence, is the possibility that Gerrit Harmensz Backer from Alkmaar never had any close contacts with Hamburg. However, what is beyond speculation is that there never was a Baker or Backer family member in Hamburg and Altona's Flemish Mennonite congregation with the first initials 'G.H'. or 'H.G'.

There is good reason to suspect that Gerd Harmsen Baker of Hamburg, the whaler and warship owner, was in fact not only not a member of the local Flemish Mennonite congregation but also that he was not a member of any Mennonite community. Both Gerd Harmsen Baker and Herman Geertz Baker Junior were members of Hamburg's *Handelskammer* (chamber of commerce).[28] In eighteenth-century Hamburg, Mennonites very rarely held minor public offices, but in the seventeenth century such an arrangement was as good as unimaginable. Until we find further evidence, it would be hasty to assume, as Münzing did, that *König Salomos Gericht* was a Mennonite warship.

Whatever the status of *König Salomos Gericht*, we can be certain that local Mennonites did arm their ships in decades both before and after its active service in Hamburg. In August 1658, during the Northern War between Sweden and Russia, the Mennonite Hans Plus (see Ch. 6) had organized two merchant ships to carry goods to Archangel. Both were armed, the first with five cannons and the second with twelve. Plus himself travelled with the first ship.[29] Roosen, who had been keeping congregational records since the mid-1650s, made no note about Hans Plus's involvement with an armed ship. There is no evidence that Plus was punished or even chastised in private conversations by his Mennonite peers. It is entirely possible that no Mennonite leader knew about his activities. And it is also possible that they did know about them but at the time did not see his actions to be particularly noteworthy nor morally questionable.

---

28 See Ernst Baasch, *Die Handelskammer zu Hamburg*, 2 vols (Hamburg, 1915), ii, p. 900.

29 See A.V. Dëmkin, '"Rospisi korablem" zapadnoevropeiskikh kuptsov, sospavlennie v Arkhangel'ske v 1658 g.', *Issledovaniia po istochnikovedeniiu istorii rossii dooktiabrskogo perioda: sbornik statei* (Moscow, 1987), pp. 89–113. The source also indicates that Herman Goverts, a Mennonite deacon in Altona, sent an unarmed ship to Archangel in 1654. Because these were war years, Russian officials kept careful records about armed vessels. I am indebted to Anke Martens for providing me with this information. On Herman, see StAHbg/MG, 147, vol. 1, p. 3.

There were also armed Mennonite merchant vessels in the eighteenth century. In 1712, the year after Geeritt Roosen died, a scribe mentioned in a protocol entry that the congregational members Lorenz Kramer and Hinrich van der Smissen were threatened with disciplinary action if they did not relinquish their shares in an unnamed ship armed with an unspecified number of cannons. The preacher Jan de Lanoy was able to persuade the two men to give up their connections with the vessel and thus avoid punishment.[30] Beyond threatening actions, no disciplinary measures were taken. In the first part of his *Geschichte der Mennoniten-Gemeinde* (History of the Mennonite Congregation) (1886), Berend Carl Roosen used the 1712 episode to establish the non-resistant credentials of his predecessors in congregational office.[31] A century before Roosen's book, Johann Adrian Bolten, the Lutheran historian of churches in Altona, offered a competing interpretation of the episode. Commenting on the 1712 incident, he wrote: 'now [1790], without second thoughts, the local Mennonites carry such guns on trips where they are felt to be necessary'.[32] Bolten's claim is confirmed by other evidence. In the late eighteenth century the merchant Berend III Salomons Roosen (1757–1820), a Mennonite deacon from 1805 to 1810 and 1811 to 1819, owned at least three ships that sailed with cannons on board.[33] Non-resistance remained an ethical

30 StAHbg/MG, 6, vol. 1, p. 36. Lorenz Kramer was the ship's owner and Hinrich van der Smissen the captain. Oesau, *Hamburgs Grönlandfahrt*, pp. 293–6, indicates that an H.v.d. Schmissen was active as a whaling captain for the ships *Vreede* (Peace) from 1714 to 1717, *Morgensteer* (Morning Star) in 1718 and *Olyvboom* (Olive Tree) from 1721 to 1724. The owner of all three of these ships was the Flemish Mennonite deacon Ernst Pieters Goverts (StAHbg/MG, 147, vol. 1, p. 161). In the early eighteenth century, there were two congregational members with the name Hinrich van der Smissen. Both were involved with the whaling business. The younger Hinrich (1677–1726) (StAHbg/MG, 147, vol. 1, p. 167) is the most likely person to have been involved in this incident, since his older uncle (1662–1737) (ibid., p. 104) had been an owner of whaling ships since the 1680s. As an entrepreneur the older Hinrich may have had less time and interest in the hands-on aspects of this line of work. On the activities of the elder Hinrich van der Smissen, see Münte, *Das Altonaer Handlungshaus van der Smissen*; also see Brinner, *Grönlandfahrt*, pp. 443–4.

31 Roosen, *Geschichte der Mennoniten-Gemeinde*, part 1, p. 66.

32 Bolten, *Historische Kirchen-Nachrichten*, i, p. 289: 'jetzt wird von den hiesigen Mennoniten solches Geschütz auf Reisen, die es nothwendig machen, ohne Bedenken geführet'.

33 See Kresse, *Materialien zur Entwicklungsgeschichte*, p. 13. Also see G.A. Roosen, 'Die Familie Roosen und ihre Anverwandten', pictures between 72 and 73; copies of his text can be found at the Staatsarchiv Hamburg, as well as the libraries of the Museum für Hamburgische Geschichte and the Genealogische Gesellschaft, Sitz Hamburg. In 1835 Jens Jacob Eschels published his *Lebensbeschreibung eines Alten Seemannes*, in which he described his work with the Mennonite Christian Roosen, who until 1781 was the captain of the ship on which Eschels sailed. As though it were not at all out of the ordinary, the Lutheran Eschels mentioned (p. 128) that the ship, which was owned by the van der Smissen family, was armed with ten cannons.

precept of the congregation,[34] but there is no record of any leader ever voicing objections to local members who armed their ships in that period. Berend Carl Roosen was unaware of or was reluctant to discuss the complexities of the issue. Not all early modern Mennonites were against protecting their material goods with the force of arms.

A controversy in the 1690s about arming merchant ships

Officially, early modern Dutch Mennonites prohibited believers from committing violence or bearing arms. Mennonites in Germany also held this ethical position.[35] In a 1628 letter to Amsterdam, local leaders wrote: 'Concerning revenge we believe and confess, following Matthew 5: 39, that a Christian may not resist evil.'[36] Several decades later, in a confession of faith composed for the volume *Unschuld und Gegen-Bericht* (1702), article 10 stated: 'We are required (so that we may have and maintain a good conscience before both God and men) to practise revenge against no one and to refuse to resist evil with arms; rather, we should suffer and tolerate the injustice practised against us, valuing our neighbour's blood more highly than our earthly possessions.'[37]

Occasionally Mennonites in Altona and Hamburg would be disciplined by preachers and their peers for violating the ethical norm of non-resistance. Between 1660 and 1700 there were fourteen recorded incidents in the congregation's membership book (see App. 9). These members, all men,

34 A late eighteenth-century controversy highlighting the importance of non-resistance involved local concern about the Dutch Mennonite preacher and militia leader Franciscus Adriaan van der Kemp. On the controversy, see Roosen, *Geschichte der Mennoniten-Gemeinde*, part 2, p. 55; *Stats-Anzeigen*, ed. August Ludwig Schlözer, vol. 7:25 (1785), pp. 71–85; undated drafts of the letters of protest from Hamburg-Altona to the Netherlands, StAHbg/MG, 8; and StAHbg/MG, 201, 'Hantekening van 't Voorgevallene op de Societiets-Vergadering' (6 May 1789). On van der Kemp, see Helen Lincklaen Fairchild, *Francis Adrian van der Kemp, 1752–1829: An Autobiography together with Extracts from his Correspondence* (New York and London, 1903).

35 Like his Flemish colleagues in Altona and Hamburg, the Dompelaar preacher Jacob Denner also emphasized the Christian duty to obey secular rulers, although he did not put any great stress on the principle of non-resistance. See Denner, *Christliche und erbauliche Betrachtungen*, pp. 70, 216, 885–6.

36 Universiteitsbibliotheek Amsterdam, Handschriften, XXVII, 567, fol. 6v: 'De weder wrake belangende gelouen ende bekennen wy gerrne dat een Christen den quaden niet wederstaen mach gelick Mat 5.39 . . .'.

37 'Evangelisches Glaubens-Bekändtniß', p. 35, in Roosen, *Unschuld und Gegen-Bericht*: 'Werden also aus allem diesem gezwungen (damit wir beydes vor GOtt und Menschen ein gut Gewissen haben und behalten mögen) gegen niemand Rache zu üben/ oder mit gewaffneter Hand dem Ubel zu widerstehen/ sondern sollen vielmehr das uns angethane Unrecht leiden und dulden/ unsers Nechsten Blut theuerbarer als unsere zeitliche Güter achtende . . .'.

had either assaulted others physically, been caught carrying weapons or had accepted employment as soldiers. Although all violent sinners were expelled, many were readmitted to the congregation soon after their punishment had begun.

However, one of the noteworthy things about these expulsions is that none involved the arming of merchant ships. Before 1712, there are not even any recorded cases of official warnings given to individual members who armed their ships. This is significant in the light of a manuscript written by Geeritt Roosen in April 1694. It was entitled 'Schriftuerlycke Bedenckinge over het reeden en uytsenden van scheepen met geschut tot defencie' (Scriptural Thoughts on the Ownership and Sailing of Vessels with Cannons for Defence).[38] The manuscript indicates that the issue of arming merchant vessels was very current during the Nine Years War, but the author never named specific individuals as being responsible for moral transgressions. Around the same time that Roosen's manuscript appeared, Dutch Zonists were confronting a similar issue. At the May 1689 meeting of the Zonist Society in Amsterdam delegates resolved to hold fast to the principle of non-resistance, and at the following year's meeting they restated this position, adding their objections to Mennonites arming their ships. In June 1694 the Society's delegates, which did not yet include any members from Hamburg and Altona, again addressed the issue of armed merchant vessels. All their resolutions from previous years seem to have achieved no satisfactory results, for they passed a motion in 1695 to place under the ban all who violated resolutions against arming ships.[39] While there was a consensus among Mennonite preachers against the arming of merchant ships, this consensus did not extend to all Mennonites in seventeenth-century northern Germany and the Netherlands. Although it is difficult, because of a paucity of surviving sources, to provide exact details, there were apparently some congregational members who violated the injunctions.[40]

38 The manuscript survives in two copies, one in Roosen's hand and the other in the hand of an unknown scribe: StAHbg/MG, 246b; and StAHbg/MG, 248, vol. 4. All of the references that follow are to the first of these manuscripts, Roosen's autograph.

39 Gemeentearchief Amsterdam, PA 565, A 941 I, pp. 72, 78, 83, 102, 111 and 113.

40 The arming of merchant ships had been an issue of much debate among Waterlander Anabaptists in the first half of the seventeenth century. As in Hamburg and Altona at the end of the century, official statements were made against it, often to little avail. See Mary Sprunger, 'Waterlanders and the Dutch Golden Age: A Case Study on Mennonite Involvement in Seventeenth-Century Dutch Trade and Industry as One of the Earliest Examples of Socio-Economic Assimilation', in Alastair Hamilton, Sjouke Voolstra and Piet Visser (eds), *From Martyr to Muppy (Mennonite Urban Professionals): A Historical Introduction to Cultural Assimilation Processes of a Religious Minority in the Netherlands: The Mennonites* (Amsterdam, 1994), pp. 133–48; and ead., 'Rich Mennonites, Poor Mennonites: Economics and Theology in the Amsterdam Waterlander Congregation during the Golden Age' (Ph.D. diss., University of Illinois at Urbana-Champaign, 1993), ch. 3.

Gerritt Roosen's April 1694 manuscript is fascinating and important on two counts. First, it contains a 'hidden transcript'[41] of resistance to the official moral dictates of the community. The local Mennonites who wanted to arm merchant ships (and may indeed have done so in the 1690s) did not record their own views, so Roosen's refutation provides evidence of attitudes that would otherwise have disappeared without a trace. Secondly, the manuscript also gives a clear restatement of the official Mennonite position. This position is worth examining in some detail to show the range of meanings and implications borne by the early modern Mennonite principle of non-resistance.

Roosen's main theme was practical and ethical problems for Mennonite merchants arising from wartime circumstances. One of these included 'travelling with passports from foreign potentates'.[42] Roosen disapproved of this practice, the negative consequences of which he knew from personal experience (see above). Although oath-swearing was connected with the issue of arranging passports, Roosen did not address this matter. However, as the manuscript's title makes clear, the author devoted by far the most space to the question of whether Mennonites could take active measures to protect their merchant ships. His conclusions were threefold: cannons on board did not provide real protection; God-fearing Mennonites were prohibited from using them; and their use infringed on the Mennonites' duties as citizens.

Concerning the first issue, Roosen told his readers that they should know from experience that even armed merchant ships were easy prey for better-equipped privateers and warships. Weapons on board certainly did not stop the capture of ships and probably, he contended, led to greater damage being suffered by the Hamburg-owned vessels.[43] His main example was the damage suffered by 'our winter fleet' (*onse winter vloot*) of 1692.[44]

Furthermore, the decision of ship owners to arm their vessels was contrary to God's will and the Mennonites' own promises made upon baptism into the community of faith. Roosen asked his readers rhetorically:

> What might others who know of our confessions of faith think of us? We confess to be defenceless, weaponless Christians. We realize and teach that, like sheep and lambs, we must suffer and be non-resistant, never taking revenge. But to what avail are our confessions of faith if

---

41 For more on this concept, see James C. Scott, *Domination and the Arts of Resistance: Hidden Transcripts* (New Haven, 1990).

42 StAHbg/MG, 246b, 16 April 1694, fol. [5]^{r}: 'met vreemde potentaten seebrieven voeren . . .'.

43 Ibid., fols [4]^{v}–[5]^{r} and [8]$^{r-v}$.

44 Ibid., fol. [5]^{r}.

> we oppose them with our deeds and – with daggers, pistols and other murderous weapons – appear to be snapping, tearing beasts like bears, wolves and lions?[45]

Mennonites who armed their ships were guilty of living lives empty of any meaningful religious commitment, which contrasted sharply with the example of 'the pious martyrs who, true to the confessions, sealed their faith with death'.[46] Unlike the martyrs of old, Mennonites who desired to use weapons were poor followers of Christ. Rather than entrusting their safety to God's care, the sailors were relying on their own inadequate abilities in an attempt to satisfy their longings for worldly wealth.[47]

According to Roosen, Mennonites owed their safety in this world first and foremost to God, but the government also played an essential role. In other words, Roosen's impassioned defence of non-resistance in no way amounted to a rejection of the authority of the local government. Quite the contrary, he was as concerned to defend virtues of civil obedience and citizenship as he was to defend biblical non-resistance. He wanted to emphasize that confessing Mennonites should in no way actively resist evil by defending themselves, by helping to defend others, or even by hiring armed vessels manned by non-Mennonites. This was unscriptural. What is more, Mennonites who took such action were not simply acting contrary to God's word; they were also 'encroaching on the authority of rulers'.[48] This conclusion is similar to that found in another of Roosen's manuscripts, an undated one on the sin of greed. Mennonite profit-seekers, like those who wanted to arm merchant vessels, strove 'not only against God's law but also against civic morality and modesty, and, thus, furthermore against the public order or laws of the temporal authorities in the country and in cities'.[49] Without

45 The quotation is taken from the second written side of an insert Roosen included in his own handwritten copy of the manuscript. The original reads: 'wat mogen ander luyden dencken die van onse belydenissenisse [*sic*] kennisse hebben dat men een weerlooß wapenloos christen doen belyt, verstaet en leert dat men lyden moet en weer loos en wraeklos syn moet als schapen en lamren wat helpt en wat baet sulcken belydeniß als men met werck en doet het contra stet en dat men sich so als bitse verscheurende dieren met degens en pistolen, mordtdadige wapen en als beiren wolven en leewen ten voorschyn kompt.'

46 StAHbg/MG, 246b, 16 April 1694, fol. [2]^{v}: 'der vrome martelaeren, die volgens die belydenisse haer gelove met de doot besegelt . . .'. In this part of his text, Roosen referred to a German-language confession of faith, which was almost certainly Tieleman Tielen van Sittert's 1691 edition of the 1632 Dordrecht Confession. Roosen included the historical appendix to this edition of the Dordrecht Confession in several copies of his book, *Unschuld und Gegen-Bericht* (1702).

47 StAHbg/MG, 246b, 16 April 1694, fols [4]^{v}–[5]^{r} and [8]$^{r-v}$.

48 Ibid., fol. [7]^{r}: 'soo wort oock daermet in het overicheytlycke ampt gegreepen'.

49 StAHbg/MG, 248, vol. 1, 'bedenckinge over onversadelycke begeerte tot gelt goet en aerse schatten die 1 tim 6 v 10 giricheyt oft geltgiricheyt genoemt wort', fol. [5]^{r}: 'niet alleen strydende teegen de wet godts maer oock teegens d' borgerlycke seeden en bescheydenheit en daerby oft beneffens tegen de polesye oft wetten van de wereltlycke overicheeden, van landen en steeden . . .'.

using the word itself, he was hinting that greedy, defence-minded Mennonites were guilty of political rebellion.

There is no surviving text written by Roosen's congregational opponents in the controversy over arming ships. Roosen did, however, mention a series of examples used by his unnamed opponents to justify their position(s). Mennonites, it was true, paid money to the government in exchange for armed protection. There were protection tributes, convoy taxes and contributions to support the civic militia. On this last issue Roosen's text is especially interesting. Most male citizens and residents of Hamburg were required by law to serve in the civic militia. This usually entailed active service on street patrols and at guard posts. However, through the seventeenth century more and more individuals – Lutherans and non-Lutherans alike – were able to pay for replacements, usually young guild workers who could not obtain citizenship.[50] For example, Roosen wrote that Mennonite residents in Hamburg 'pay watch money to civic captains so that they can hire a man in our place (so they say) who will go to the wall with his gun'.[51] He in no way condemned these payments. In other words, at the same time that Hamburg's Senate was having difficulty arranging taxes from the Citizenry in order to pay the civic militia (see Ch. 4), Roosen was acknowledging the duty of Mennonites to pay for such services. Those Mennonites who wanted to arm ships apparently claimed that there was little difference between paying governments for this kind of protection and privately hiring non-Mennonite soldiers to protect commercial goods. In both of these cases Mennonites did not themselves operate the weapons.[52] From the point of view of Roosen's opponents, they were in no way rebels against secular and divine authority but simply responsible businessmen doing their best, within the bounds of the law and Mennonite practice, to promote their enterprises during difficult and dangerous times.

Roosen rejected this kind of argument. Accepting protection from government troops was entirely different from privately organized defensive measures, or so he contended. The money which Mennonites paid the government was certainly used to resist evil, often to the Mennonites' advantage, but defending citizens was the government's God-given duty.

---

50 See Ehlers, *Die Wehrverfassung der Stadt Hamburg*, pp. 91–6. For further background, see Walter Klaassen, *Mennonites and War Taxes* (Newton, Kans., 1978), pp. 14–19.

51 StAHbg/MG, 246b, 16 April 1694, fol. [3]^{v}: 'aen borger cappiteyns wachtgelt betaelt, daervoor sy in onse plaets (soo sy seggen) een man voor hueren, die met syn geweer te wal gaet . . .'. Also see ibid., fol. [7]^{v}–[8]^{r}. Roosen, *Geschichte der Mennoniten-Gemeinde*, part 1, pp. 58–9, writes that during the Danish siege of Hamburg in 1686 Mennonites trapped in the city were allowed to serve in noncombatant roles as firefighters. I have not been able to find a source confirming this assertion.

52 StAHbg/MG, 246b, 16 April 1694, fol. [3]$^{r-v}$.

Paraphrasing Romans 13: 6–7, Roosen wrote that 'it is our duty to be subservient to the authorities and also to pay tolls, excises and tributes to them'.[53] This was a necessity of living in cities and did not violate Christ's commandments. After all, Christ himself had lived under the protection of worldly rulers while on earth,[54] which was not difficult to understand, since government authority was founded in God's authority.[55] As long as non-Mennonite government employees were the ones using weapons to protect God-fearing citizens against enemies, Mennonites and others had no right to object. But as soon as Mennonites took their own initiatives to hire non-Mennonite mercenaries, they had gone too far. Mennonites should fulfil their duties and the government its duty.[56] Roosen's position was that arming ships was not wrong in itself; it was only wrong for Mennonites. In effect, by delegating responsibility for maritime defence to secular authorities, he combined his strategy of preserving a brand of conservative, non-resistant, confessional Mennonitism with the strategy of promoting a kind of political conformity.

A similar combination of themes is found in other local seventeenth-century Mennonite texts. In the 1628 letter to Amsterdam (mentioned at the beginning of this section), leaders in Hamburg and Altona wrote that they believed secular rulers were like fathers who corrected the wrongs of disobedient sons. And in the confession of faith included in Geeritt Roosen's *Unschuld und Gegen-Bericht* (1702), the article on non-resistance was followed immediately by another on government, which stated in no uncertain terms

> that government is from God, and those who oppose government oppose God's order; therefore, we require ourselves to be obedient to our rulers for the sake of the Lord and our conscience, not because of the threat of punishment. . . . To them we are required to pay tolls and meet other requirements, while also showing them obedient respect, they being not just kings alone but also rulers of lesser orders, as well as those who have been given particular sovereignty over cities and territories.[57]

---

53 Ibid., fol. [3]^{v}: 'nu wort ons belast de overheyt onderdanich te syn, en oock aen haer tol, acsys, en schattinge te betaelen . . .'.

54 Ibid., fol. [5]^{v}.

55 Ibid., fols [3]^{v} and [6]^{r}.

56 Ibid., fols [4]$^{r-v}$ and [6]^{v}–[7]^{v}.

57 'Evangelisches Glaubens-Bekändtniß', pp. 36–7, in Roosen, *Unschuld und Gegen-Bericht*: 'daß das Ampt der Obrigkeit von GOtte sey/ und diejenigen so sich der Obrigkeit widersetzen/ der Ordnung GOttes widerstreben/ dahero wir uns verpflichtet halten/ derselben um des HErrn Willen unterthänig zu seyn/ nicht um der Straffe sondern üm des Gewissens willen . . ./ welchen wir schuldig seyn Schoß/ Zoll und andere Verordnungen/ zu bezahlen/ wie auch ihnen alle Ehre in aller Unterthänigkeit zu erweisen; Nicht aber den Königen allein/ sondern auch/ die in geringerem Stande und Beschaffenheit/ wiewol in besonderer Hoheit/ über Städte und Länder gesetzet seyn.'

There was a small qualification. Believers would have to obey God's law if rulers tried to force Mennonites to break that law. Compared with the strong statement on obedience to divinely instituted secular rulers, the qualification seems hollow. The statement included none of the uncompromising rhetoric of earlier Anabaptist confessional statements, which had sometimes declared secular authority to be within the realm of the Antichrist. In any case, in neither Hamburg nor Altona did Mennonites seem to think there was any obvious conflict between God's law and secular law. For Flemish Mennonites in Hamburg and Altona, as elsewhere, non-resistance and obedience to government were part and parcel of the same ethic.

Gunpowder production and the conformist ethic of non-resistance

Geeritt Roosen's relatives made gunpowder. Wasn't this a violation of the principles Roosen trumpeted? The answer helps further to highlight the politically conformist interpretation Mennonites gave to the principle of non-resistance throughout the early modern period.

While Geeritt Roosen was a firm supporter of non-resistance, he seems to have had no problems with his family members producing gunpowder; he discussed it as though it were completely normal without once raising moral reservations. The earliest narrative source with information about Roosen family gunpowder-making is Geeritt Roosen's family chronicle, written in the 1680s.[58] According to Geeritt Roosen, the first of his forefathers to settle in Holstein was Cord Roosen (d. 1553 or 1554). The date was 1532, a few years before the infamous Anabaptist regime in Münster (1534–35) and Menno Simons's conversion to Anabaptism (1536). Cord had left his pregnant second wife in Westphalia. Her parents had apparently forbidden her to travel northward with her husband. Geeritt Roosen wrote that the reason for Cord's journey was to find a territory where he could live his life in obedience to God without fear of persecution. Roosen also claimed that Cord, before he left for Holstein, had been an Anabaptist in the non-resistant tradition of Menno Simons. We should treat these claims – that he was an Anabaptist and believed in non-resistance – with caution. In the early 1530s Menno was still a Catholic priest who was only sympathetic to northern European Anabaptist groups but not yet an active leader among them. Furthermore, in 1532 in Westphalia opposition to child baptism was much more widespread than the actual

58 [Geeritt Roosen], 'Geeritt Roosen und seine Geschichte der Kriegsereignisse seiner Zeit', pp. 365–70. A copy of this difficult-to-find journal article is found at StAHbg. Also see StAHbg, Genealogische Sammlungen, Roosen, 'Notitie of Geslachtregister opgesteld door Gerrit Roosen Ao. 1683'; and StAHbg/MG, 242.

practice of adult baptism. The most important Anabaptist leader in northern Germany between 1530 and 1533 was Melchior Hoffman. Because of violent persecution, Hoffman told his followers in 1531 to suspend the practice until the End Time, which he expected would begin on Easter 1533. Until the surprising Anabaptist successes of early 1534 in Münster, Anabaptists and adult baptism were rare in Westphalia. In 1532 Cord Roosen was probably a Protestant opposed to child baptism. But it is unclear if he ever accepted adult baptism. While Cord Roosen may not himself have been a Mennonite, his son borne by his second wife certainly was. When this son, Geerlinck (1532–1611), reached adulthood, he had moved to live with his father in Holstein, where he probably converted. According to Geeritt Roosen, Geerlinck learned the skills of farming and gunpowder-making from his father, who in turn had learned the skills before moving to Holstein. In other words, Cord learned the skills during or before the early 1530s, when there was still no theological or ethical consensus among northern European Anabaptists on the issue of the use of force by Christians.[59]

This consensus developed first in the wake of the failure of the Anabaptist regime in Münster, when Menno Simons was one of the leading figures among Anabaptists. Geerlinck Roosen lived and worked in the region where Menno Simons was based during much of the last part of his life (*c.* 1546–61).[60] Unfortunately, the records of the Fresenburg congregation near Oldesloe, which might have provided some insights into early German Anabaptist beliefs and practices, were destroyed during a campaign of the Thirty Years War.[61] We therefore have to draw inferences from other sources. Among surviving sources, perhaps the most useful is the Wismar Articles of 1554, signed by Menno Simons and several other Anabaptist leaders. The wording of article 8, the most relevant article, is disputed. A conservative version reads:

> Article 8: On Weapons. The elders cannot regard it as impure if a believer while on a journey carries an honorable staff or a sword over his shoulder in accordance with the customs of the country. But the elders declare it impermissible to display or show weapons of war at the command of the government, unless it is a question of unweaponed service.[62]

---

59 See Stayer, *Anabaptists and the Sword*; and Deppermann, *Melchior Hoffman*, particularly ch. 10, sect. 2.

60 For a narrative of Menno Simons's activities in Holstein, see Harold Bender's 'Brief Biography' in *The Complete Writings of Menno Simons, c. 1496–1561*, ed. John Christian Wenger (Scottdale, Pa., 1956), pp. 21–8.

61 See Roosen, *Unschuld und Gegen-Bericht*, p. 103.

62 Quoted from Stayer, *Anabaptists and the Sword*, p. 323. The original is found in *Bibliotheca Reformatoria Neerlandica: Geschriften uit den tijd der hervorming in de Nederlanden*, ed. S. Cramer and F. Pijper, 10 vols (The Hague, 1903–1914), vii, p. 53. It

The first part of the passage is not so controversial. Carrying customary weapons would have helped believers go undetected by those police forces looking for them in an era when they were still considered criminals in many jurisdictions.[63] What is controversial is the question of unarmed service (*unweerlicke knechten*). As translated, it means that it was not acceptable for believers to serve in a militia, but they could serve rulers. However, the early twentieth-century Dutch historian Karel Vos thought this interpretation was based on a mistake, because the phrase in question only appears in a few versions of the text. In other versions the phrase reads as 'armed service' (*weerlicke knechten*). For Vos this was evidence that Menno Simons and other leading Anabaptists were willing to allow believers to become soldiers. In other words, according to Vos, in 1554 Simons was not yet a supporter of non-resistance.[64]

Vos's interpretation is problematic. In 1554 or 1555, around the same time he signed the Wismar Articles, Menno Simons had the text *Van't Kruys Christi* (The Cross of Christ) published in Holstein.[65] In it he paraphrased a famous passage from the Bible (Isa. 2: 4): 'For we have, by the grace of God that has appeared to us, beaten our swords into plowshares, and our spears into pruning hooks, and we shall sit under the true vine, that is, Christ, under the Prince of Eternal Peace, and will never more study outward conflict and the war of blood.'[66] This passage is an expression of a consistent set of positions on non-resistance which Menno Simons held throughout his career as an Anabaptist. In all his writings he was against the use of weapons by believers. However, unlike the Swiss Brethren of the early sixteenth century, he did not advocate the idea that Christians should avoid absolutely all dealings with governments. The conservative translation above, not the version of the Wismar Articles suggested by Vos, conforms to the consistent character of Menno's writing on the subject.[67]

---

reads: 'Item ten 8. van de vvapenen, wanneer die ghelouighe ouer de wech reyst nae de gelegentheyt des landts, een eerbaer stock ofte rapier ouer die schouderen te hebben nae des Landts maniere ofte ghevvoonte, kunnen die Oudste niet voor onreyn aensien. Maer die gheweerlicke wapens nae de Ouericheyt beuel te laten besien ofte te tonen, stellen die Oudste onvry te syn, ten sy dattet die onweerlicke knechten gheschiet.' The translation in *The Complete Writings of Menno Simons*, p. 1042, is unreliable.

63 Stayer, *Anabaptists and the Sword*, pp. 323–4.

64 Karel Vos, *Menno Simons 1496–1561: Zijn leven en werken en zijn reformatorische denkbeelden* (Leiden, 1914), p. 126, n. 2: 'Het leerstuk der weerloosheid werd in 1554 derhalve nog niet beleden.'

65 See P. Valkema Blouw, 'Drukkers voor Menno Simons en Dirk Philips', *Doopsgezinde Bijdragen*, new ser. 17 (1991), p. 73 (H70); and Keyser, 'The Fresenburg Press'.

66 Quoted from *The Complete Writings of Menno Simons*, p. 603.

67 I am following the conclusion of Stayer, *Anabaptists and the Sword*, pp. 323–4, who summarizes other relevant literature.

Seen in the light of the Wismar Articles and Menno Simons's writings, there would have been little reason for gunpowder production to have become a cause for scruples, so long as believers did not themselves use the gunpowder in weapons of war. This would have been an example of 'unweaponed service'. Thinking in terms of the Wismar Articles, it might even have been acceptable for territorial rulers like Bartholomäus von Ahlefeldt (see Ch. 1) to hire the Anabaptists, whom he protected, to make gunpowder. It is in fact likely that gunpowder was produced on Ahlefeldt's territory of Fresenburg in Holstein. In the late nineteenth century, Berend Carl Roosen wrote that there still existed traces of a long abandoned and nearly forgotten gunpowder mill along a stream which used to be called Pulverbek (Powder Creek). Roosen assumed that his Anabaptist ancestors built and operated that mill.[68]

Into the early eighteenth century, long after Menno Simons was dead, members of the Roosen family remained active in the trade of gunpowder-making. For example, Paul Roosen (d. 1649), Geeritt Roosen's father, had made gunpowder in the early seventeenth century in Holstein, before his relocation to Altona (1611) and the birth of his son Geeritt (1612).[69] He did not break off all connections with the trade once in Altona. In 1646 Paul Roosen, then a deacon in Altona's Flemish congregation,[70] was trading in saltpetre, the major ingredient in gunpowder.[71] Hamburg was a major centre of the European weapons market before, during and after the Thirty Years War,[72] and resources like saltpetre were much in demand as strategic resources. Selling it was lucrative business. By the beginning of the eighteenth century, when the small-scale production methods used by the Roosens were replaced by more modern and efficient industrial methods, the economic benefits to be gained by family members from the trade had diminished. The last Roosen gunpowder producer in the early

68 See Roosen, *Geschichte unseres Hauses*, pp. 14 and 19–20. Also see Hubertus Neuschäfer, *Schlösser und Herrenhäuser in Südholstein* (Würzburg, 1985), pp. 161–2; Hinrich van der Smissen, *Mennostein und Mennolinde zu Fresenburg: Zur Erinnerung an den 16. September 1922* (n.p., n.d.), picture between pp. 22 and 23; and StAHbg/MG, 27, 'Festspiel zum 50jährigen Amtsjubiläum des Herrn Pastor B.C. Roosen, aufgeführt am 13. Oktober 1895'.

69 See [Roosen], 'Geeritt Roosen und seine Geschichte'.

70 Paul Roosen was a deacon in Altona in 1628 when his congregation sent a letter (referred to in the text above) to Mennonites in Amsterdam outlining the principles of their faith, which included non-resistance and obedience to rulers.

71 StAHbg, Cl. VII Lit. Eb No. 1 Vol. 1, letters dated 16 and 24 February 1646. Also see Landesarchiv Schleswig, Abt. 11/Nr. 703c. I am indebted to Anke Martens for making me aware of these sources. For information on King Christian IV's involvement, see Wichmann, *Geschichte Altona's*, p. 50.

72 See Ernst Baasch, 'Der Verkehr mit Kriegsmaterialien aus und nach den Hansestädten vom Ende des 16. bis Mitte des 17. Jahrhunderts', *Jahrbücher für Nationalökonomie und Statistik*, 137, 3rd ser. 82 (1932), part II, pp. 538–43.

modern period was probably David Roosen.[73] He was twice given assistance as part of the Altona Flemish congregation's programme of poor aid. A portion of the assistance consisted of clothes and money distributed in November 1705.[74] David had also been granted 100 mark *lübsch* in 1704 for the construction of a storage house near his gunpowder mill.[75] As far as can be determined from the surviving record, there was no controversy about helping to finance David Roosen's enterprise.

In his family chronicle, Geeritt Roosen never discussed what his forebears did with the gunpowder they produced. While it is possible that they used it only for such mundane activities as hunting, mining and stump-clearing, we would expect Roosen to have emphasized this point were he worried about the moral status of the trade. The best clue we have from his text about the use of the gunpowder is that the family (at least Geeritt Roosen's father, Paul) made high-grade powder (*fyn pulver* or *buskruyt*), the type which was used in the most advanced and accurate firearms of the day.[76]

Besides members of the Roosen family, other local Mennonites also traded in strategic goods and even weapons at the beginning of the eighteenth century. In 1703 Hinrich van der Smissen sent a shipment of rapiers and muskets on a vessel (the destination of which I am not aware) owned by Hinrich Dircks.[77] That same year Hinrich van der Smissen (probably the same man) sent a shipment of Swedish copper – material used in the weapons industry but also for coin and utensil production – from Altona to Archangel. He was working as an agent for the Amsterdam-based businessman and Anabaptist Egbert Thesingh. Egbert Thesingh, his brother Jan Thesingh and Christoffel Brants were business partners in the weapons trade with Russia in the late 1690s, and for these enterprises

---

73 There are two David Roosens listed in the congregation's membership book. Neither seems to have been closely related to Geeritt Roosen. The entry of the most likely candidate for the person in question is found at StAHbg/MG, 147, vol. 1, p. 104. The other person, David Pauls Roosen (ibid., p. 186), was baptized in 1707 and was therefore probably too young to be receiving financial support from the congregation. In 1723 this latter David was expelled for becoming a soldier.

74 StAHbg/MG, 6, vol. 1, p. 29.

75 Ibid., p. 21: 'Geresolveert om aan david Roosen assistentie te doen tot het bouwen van een drooghuys by syn pulver meulentie tot op eenhundert marcklubs.' In 1674 Jan Neybuer had drowned in a pond near a 'powder house' (*pulverhuyß*), presumably in Altona; see StAHbg/MG, 147, vol. 1, p. 81. Gunpowder (*Schießpulver*) was often referred to simply as powder (*Pulver*).

76 On the process and technology of gunpowder-making in early modern Europe, see Ottomar Thiele, *Salpeterwirtschaft und Salpeterpolitik: Ein volkswirtschaftliche Studie über das ehemalige europäische Salpeterwesen* (Tübingen, 1905), pp. 41–7.

77 See Niedersächsisches Staatarchiv Stade, Rep. 5a Fach 289 Nr. 19, fol. 82. My thanks again to Anke Martens for making me aware of this source.

they had the help of unnamed contacts in Hamburg.[78] Mennonite leaders may not have known about this activity, but, even if they had known, they may very well have treated it in the same way as gunpowder production – that is, not thought much of it.

It may seem surprising that Geeritt Roosen failed to acknowledge non-resistant convictions, even if only in passing, when discussing the practice of gunpowder-making. In the light of his politically conformist brand of non-resistance, however, the silence need not seem so remarkable. In fact, it makes sense in the context of controversies of the day. These controversies did not result in a blanket rejection of the use of arms but only a rejection of the use of arms by Mennonites, who lived, Roosen claimed, according to principles different from their neighbours. Geeritt Roosen acknowledged explicitly that rulers were expected to use force to protect their subjects, among whom were good Mennonite taxpayers. During controversies about non-resistance, the trade in weapons, gunpowder or other strategic materials was never mentioned. As long as Mennonites continued to observe strictly the injunction against using arms themselves and refused to take any actions which might suggest they were trying to usurp the authority of secular rulers, there is no good historically grounded ethical reason for us to suspect that a controversy should have arisen.

Conclusion

The longevity of the intimate link between non-resistance and obedience is illustrated by a striking example from the later nineteenth century. In a passage from the second part of *Geschichte der Mennoniten-Gemeinde* (1887), B.C. Roosen wrote that his congregation in the early modern period 'held fast to the principle of non-resistance'.[79] This is the topic sentence for a paragraph devoted to a description of eighteenth-century celebrations of royal authority. In 1719 Mennonites in Hamburg and Altona gave thanks during a church service for a major Danish victory in the Great Northern War. And in 1746, upon hearing of the death of Denmark's

[78] See J.W. Veluwenkamp, '"N Huis op Archangel": De Amsterdamse koopmansfamilie Thesigh', *Jaarboek Amstelodamum*, **69** (1977), pp. 123–39, at pp. 131–2. Although a conclusive statement is impossible, the Hinrich van der Smissen in question was probably the elder of the two discussed earlier in this chapter. I do not know to which Amsterdam congregation Egbert Thesingh belonged. Since the early seventeenth century the Brants family had been affiliated with Amsterdam's Waterlander congregation. See Bert Westera, 'Mennonites and War in the Seventeenth and Eighteenth Centuries: The Brants Family between Pacifism and Trade in Guns', in Hamilton, Voolstra and Visser (eds), *From Martyr to Muppy*, pp. 149–55.

[79] Roosen, *Geschichte der Mennoniten-Gemeinde*, part 2, p. 20: 'An dem Grundsatze der Wehrlosigkeit hielt die Gemeinde fest.'

King Christian VI, the congregation's preachers decided to drape the pulpit with a black cloth as a sign of mourning, a tradition which continued throughout the rest of the century with the death of a monarch. Besides discussing these two cases, B.C. Roosen included no other examples of non-resistant behaviour in this part of his text. Nor did he make any comment which might suggest in the slightest way that his topic sentence and evidence did not belong together. The link between non-resistance and political obedience seemed as obvious to Berend Carl Roosen in the nineteenth century as it had to Geeritt Roosen in the seventeenth century.[80]

While preachers accepted the conformist brand of non-resistance to such an extent that they never considered gunpowder-making problematic, not all congregants shared the convictions leaders sometimes stated publicly. That some Mennonite merchants in the seventeenth century armed their ships with cannons makes this clear. At least one thing needs to be remembered when thinking about this act of nonconformity to officially stated norms. Official norms of non-resistance did not apply with constant intensity. Official concern among preachers about the arming of ships by Mennonite merchants seems to have diminished during the eighteenth century, but even for the period before Geeritt Roosen's campaign of the 1690s to reinvigorate the principle of non-resistance there is evidence that sailing with armed ships was not always contentious. Occasionally, a tension between official principle and everyday practice was brought into clear relief. However, whether because of preachers' lack of knowledge of congregants' actions or because of lack of concern, this tension was intermittent at best. The high points of controversy provide an important but incomplete picture of the lives led by Mennonites, lives which were not always led according to clearly articulated, official principles.

80 For more on the nineteenth century, see Michael Driedger, 'Kanonen, Schießpulver und Wehrlosigkeit: Cord, Geeritt und B. C. Roosen in Holstein und Hamburg 1532–1905', *Mennonitische Geschichtsblätter*, 52 (1995), pp. 101–21.

CHAPTER SIX

The Non-swearing of Solemn Oaths: Official Accounts versus Everyday Behaviours

Issues of identity and obedience arose for Mennonites not only because of their non-resistant faith. As was also the case with adult baptism and the refusal to bear arms, the non-swearing of oaths had been a radical act in the first generation of the Reformation. Those who took such steps were protesting against the established authority of the state and the official church. However, from the mid-sixteenth century to the early seventeenth century, informal and even legal arrangements had begun to emerge in a number of northern European jurisdictions which allowed Mennonites, no longer religious protesters, to practise their nonconforming faith with the tacit approval (or at least without the repressive intervention) of established authorities. Many such arrangements were worked out in the sixteenth and seventeenth centuries.[1] An examination of the issue of oath-swearing provides further glimpses into the ways in which government agents, congregational leaders and rank-and-file Mennonites dealt with the tensions between official standards and the daily practice of faith.

The trials of Hans Plus

The trials of the Hamburg-based Mennonite merchant Hans Plus are among the best-documented and most intriguing examples of seventeenth-century public debate about Mennonite identity. In 1661 Plus was charged in the Imperial Cameral Court (*Reichskammergericht*)[2] in Speyer with being a member of the illegal sect of Anabaptists (*Wiedertäufer*). Anabaptism (that is, rebaptism) was illegal in Hamburg, just as it was in the rest of the Empire. In the early modern period most secular governments expected their subjects and citizens to participate in the rites of established parish churches, which included child baptism. Thus, a parent's

[1] One reason we know so much about these early modern legal complexities is that German and Dutch Mennonites in the late nineteenth century did a survey of the historical record. They were searching for precedents that would help them to negotiate with their national governments. See [Jan] ten Doornkaat Koolman, *Die Verpflichtung der Mennoniten an Eidesstatt* (Berlin, 1893); J. Dyserinck, *De vrijstelling van den eed voor de Doopsgezinden* (Haarlem, 1883). Also see the documents in StAHbg/MG, 7.

unwillingness to have an infant baptized could be equated with an unwillingness to submit to legitimate political authority, and a second baptism was interpreted almost universally as an act of open rebellion.

It may therefore seem surprising that a secular government, the Senate of the city of Hamburg, was the co-defendant in the case against Plus. The city was accused of having given protection to a criminal. The arguments before the court in Speyer focused on two issues. Had Plus sworn an illegal oath before a court in Hamburg? And were Mennonites Anabaptists? Lawyers representing Plus and the city of Hamburg spent a good deal of energy trying to prove that the categories 'Mennonite' and 'Anabaptist' identified two completely distinct groups, each with a different status under the law. The stakes were high, for if Mennonites were in fact Anabaptists and Plus was convicted, Hamburg's Senate would also be held to account. In short, intertwined in the case were questions of government authority and confessional identity.

The High Court trial in Hamburg

Events associated with the trial began in 1655, when Hans Plus sailed to the northern Russian port of Archangel. This was not his first time travelling there. Already as a teenager he had been on many trips to northern Russia with his father Pieter. Hans continued to trade with Archangel after his father's death.[3] Toll records in Hamburg from 1645 indicate that his business was lucrative, for that year he declared at least 45,900 marks *lübsch* in sales. In the following year he was among several merchants, including the Mennonites Pelgrim Milder and Paul Roosen (Geeritt Roosen's father), who had shares in a ship returning to Hamburg from

2 Other cases before the Imperial Cameral Court involving Mennonites from Hamburg and Altona (although not focused to the same degree as Plus's case was on the legal status of Mennonites) were StAHbg, Reichskammergericht: E15, F11, J2, J3, J18 and M28, all of which involved Abraham Stockman, his associates and heirs; B1b and V9, which involved members of the de Vlieger family; S37, in which François Noë had a small role; S84, which included a statement by Peter Goverts's widow; S172, in which the eighteenth-century businessman Berend Roosen was involved. In the eighteenth century probably the most lively case surrounding a Mennonite was the dispute over Ernst Pieters Goverts's estate. See StAHbg, Reichskammergericht, R25; StAHbg, Familienarchive, Goverts, 44; and Landesarchiv Schleswig, Reichskammergericht, 72.

3 StAHbg, Genealogische Sammlungen, Roosen, 'Notitie of Geslachtregister opgesteld door Gerrit Roosen Ao. 1683', p. 8. For other examples of merchant travel during this period, see StAHbg/MG, 242, pp. 27–8, which records trips Herman Roosen made to Russia and elsewhere in 1653, 1655 and 1657. Also see Johannes Block, *Muscovien-Fahrt/ Das ist: Kurzer und umbständlicher Bericht/ von der Schiffarth aus Hamburg nach Archangel* (Hamburg, 1683); and Roosen, *Geschichte unseres Hauses*, pp. 60–62.

Archangel. Plus's share of goods on board totaled 13,600 marks *lübsch*.[4] Probably because Plus was experienced in trade with Russia, a Lutheran colleague named Johann Jacob Hübner hired him in 1655 as an agent to sell and buy goods at the summer market there. In the summer on the trip to Archangel Plus brought incense, gold foil and lavender oil, among other goods, to sell on Hübner's behalf. These items may well have been intended for sale to Russian Orthodox buyers for use in religious ceremonies. In the autumn he returned with rolls of prepared leather for his employer. Several months later, on 7 May 1656, Plus gave Hübner the records of sale and purchase.[5] That is when the trouble began.

On 28 January 1657 Hübner's lawyer started proceedings against Plus before the High Court (*Obergericht*) in Hamburg.[6] The charge was that Plus had not acted in his client's best interest. Market conditions were favourable, Hübner claimed, and, had Plus taken more care, he should have been able to have earned an extra 800 Reichstaler from the sale of his client's goods. In response Plus's lawyers said that Hübner's charges were libellous and not deserving of a response. Plus was nevertheless forced eventually to appear before the court.

The High Court case against Plus lasted for four full years. This was not because it involved complicated, exhausting legal arguments. The delay owed more to Plus's reluctance to appear before the court to swear an oath. Plus was a member of Altona's Flemish Mennonite congregation. In the seventeenth century there was no consensus among northern European Anabaptists on the subject of oath-swearing, but, like most Mennonite groups, the local Flemish Mennonites were opposed in principle to swearing solemn oaths, which required a defendant to call upon God as a witness to the truth of testimony. Thus the corporal oath (*körperlicher Eid*), so called because a person swore it while holding a holy object like the Bible or a cross, was generally unacceptable to them. The civil, non-religious alternative Mennonites throughout northern Europe used most often in

4 Reißmann, *Die hamburgische Kaufmannschaft*, pp. 62–3 and 381.

5 Two copies of the records are found amid the papers concerning the Cameral Court proceedings: StAHbg, Reichskammergericht, H177, (7) and (13). For more on the business dealings between Plus and Hübner, see Elisabeth Harder-Gersdorff, 'Lübeck und Hamburg im internationalen Handel mit russischem Juchtenleder in der Frühen Neuzeit (1650–1710)', *Zeitschrift des Vereins für Lübeckische Geschichte und Altertumskunde*, 67 (1987), pp. 123–5. On p. 122 is a picture of a notarized copy from 1661 (not 1667 as Harder-Gersdorff claims) of the bill Plus gave to Hübner in 1656.

6 The following summary is based on references to the High Court case in the Imperial Cameral Court proceedings. See StAHbg, Reichskammergericht, H177, (2), (3), (4), (6), (12), (14) and (25). Records from High Court proceedings in Hamburg have not survived for this as well as many other cases. It is also difficult to learn in detail about Senate reactions to this case, for many early Senate documents were destroyed when large regions of Hamburg burnt to the ground in 1842.

the seventeenth century was testimony *bei Mannen Wahrheit* (by the truth of men), which replaced the common and solemn appeal to God the Almighty. The cooperation of government officials was necessary, of course, if this option was to have legal validity. Hamburg was one jurisdiction where officials did cooperate.

By 1660 the pressure was increasing on Plus to attest to the accuracy of the record of sale he submitted to Hübner and the propriety of his business dealings. In the absence of decisive evidence and witnesses, Plus's solemn oath or the equivalent was crucial for the court's decision. In late November 1660 it was decided in the High Court that Plus could make his statement using the formula *bei Mannen Wahrheit* in place of the solemn oath. Hübner's lawyer Casper Bernhardi tried to stop the use of the special formula, threatening to appeal to a higher court if it was used. Bernhardi's protests were in vain. On 28 November, immediately upon his return to Hamburg from his travels that year, Hans Plus appeared before civic officials on the recommendation of his lawyer. After officials warned him about the severe penalties for perjury, he made the following statement: 'I, Hans Plus, swear *bei Mannen Wahrheit* that the bill submitted on 7 May 1656 is correct and that I have applied all possible diligence in the sale of goods, without any deception or grudge.'[7] Hübner's demand for 800 Reichstaler in reparations was rejected. But his lawyer lived up to the threat to send the case to a higher court.

The Imperial Cameral Court trial in Speyer

The Cameral Court in Speyer was one of two high courts in the Empire.[8] The Emperor himself had no direct influence in its operation, because the

7 StAHbg, Reichskammergericht, H177, (3), fol. 2r; ibid., (4), fol. 2r; and ibid., (6), fol. 2r: 'Ich Hannß Plüß schwere bey Mannen warheit, daß die am 7. May Anno 1656. sub Lit. A. producirte Rechnung richtig, und ich in verkauffung der wahren allen möglichen vleiß angewendet, sonder list und gefehrde.'

8 The other high court was the Imperial Aulic Council (*Reichshofrat*), which was directly under the Emperor's control. On the two courts, see Rudolf Smend, *Das Reichskammergericht: Geschichte und Verfassung* (Aalen, 1965 [1911]); Wolfgang Sellert, *Über die Zuständigkeitsabgrenzung von Reichshofrat und Reichskammergericht* (Aalen, 1965); Michael Hughes, *Law and Politics in Eighteenth Century Germany: The Imperial Aulic Council in the Reign of Charles VI* (Woodbridge, 1988), ch. 2; Martin Heckel, 'Die Religionsprozesse des Reichskammergerichts im konfessionell gespaltenen Reichskirchenrecht', *Zeitschrift der Savigny-Stiftung für Rechtsgeschichte, Kanonistische Abteilung*, 77 (1991), pp. 283–350; and books in the series *Quellen und Forschungen zur Höchsten Gerichtsbarkeit im Alten Reich*. In a 1618 Imperial Cameral Court case Hamburg had been declared to be within Imperial jurisdiction, but its status as an Imperial city was not recognized fully until 1768. Denmark disputed the Imperial claim by legal and extra-legal means.

Court was for the most part funded (or underfunded) and controlled by territorial princes. Cases brought before the Imperial Cameral Court were conducted by specially trained lawyers who submitted evidence in written petitions rather than by calling witnesses to appear in person. Appealing to the Court's authority seemed the logical next step for Hübner's representatives in their attempt to force Plus to concede 800 Reichstaler. Because of the changed context and the further interests involved, however, the case was now transformed into one about more than just money.

There were four lawyers involved in Hübner's case against Plus, two working for the prosecution and two for the defence. Lieutenant Ulrich Daniel Kühorn represented Johann Jacob Hübner in Speyer, while the *advocatus fisci*, a prosecutor who remained unnamed in the court documents, represented the Empire.[9] Their opponents were Dr Paul Gambs, representing Hans Plus, and Dr Johann Carl Müeg, representing the Senate of Hamburg.

Hübner's lawyer introduced his case first on 17 June 1661.[10] Kühorn's case was in many respects an elaboration on the arguments Caspar Bernhardi had made in Hamburg. According to Kühorn, Plus's delay in swearing an oath confirmed Hübner's charge of inappropriate business practices; Plus must obviously have had something to hide. When Plus did eventually attest to the accuracy of his bill and the propriety of his actions, he had used mere words. Because Plus's testimony was the decisive evidence in the High Court case, it was absolutely essential that his statement be credible. But in the eyes of Hübner's lawyers Plus had committed a second crime, perjury, in the course of the trial, which he only partly disguised with an illegitimate oath.

Kühorn charged Hamburg's Senate with complicity in Plus's alleged perjury. The oath *bei Mannen Wahrheit* was 'completely invalid' (*gantz nichtig*), but the court in the city had decided nonetheless 'to approve such a nullity' (*solche nichtigkeit approbiren*).[11] The oath had no legitimate legal standing in Hamburg, since the Senate had not given formal recognition to this type of testimony. What is more, it was in violation of Imperial law. The formula *bei Mannen Wahrheit* was an Anabaptist oath, and Anabaptism was illegal in the Empire. Given all these considerations, Kühorn asked that the High Court decision be overturned and that Plus be required to pay Hübner 800 Reichstaler with interest added.

---

9 On the *Fiskalamt*, see Smend, *Reichskammergericht*, sect. II, ch. 5.

10 See StAHbg, Reichskammergericht, H177, (1)–(9), esp. (3) and (4). Andreas Ebert-Weidenfeller, *Hamburgisches Kaufmannsrecht im 17. und 18. Jahrhundert: Die Rechtsprechung des Rates und des Reichskammergerichtes* (Frankfurt, 1992), pp. 86–8, briefly discusses the legal implications of the case Hübner v Plus.

11 StAHbg, Reichskammergericht, H177, (4), fol. 2r.

The second lawyer to address the Court was the Imperial prosecutor. On 26 June this man elaborated on some of Kühorn's arguments.[12] In the Imperial mandates of Speyer from 1529 and 1544 and Augsburg from 1551 it had been decided 'that no one belonging to the seditious sect of Anabaptists shall be tolerated or permitted anywhere in the Holy Roman Empire; but rather he shall be rooted out with fire or sword or the like, depending on individual circumstances'.[13] By allowing Plus to swear an illegal oath and by giving him protection, officials in Hamburg had neglected their duty to uphold the law. The Imperial prosecutor therefore asked the Court 'to confiscate publicly the possessions of such Anabaptists as heretics . . . and furthermore to fine the authorities who knowingly provide such sectarians shelter and protection six and two-thirds pounds of pure gold'.[14] The case had taken on a new, more dramatic dimension.

Plus's defence began on 19 August 1661. His representative, Dr Paul Gambs, responded in detail to most of the charges directed against his client.[15] Hübner, not Plus, had lied under oath, and Hübner's charges thus served only to waste the Court's time as well as damage Plus's good reputation. After all, Plus had acted honestly and in good faith in 1655 when Hübner had employed him. It was true that Plus had not appeared before Hamburg's High Court immediately upon being requested to do so, but the reason was that he had been delayed returning from his yearly trip to Archangel. He had answered the Court's request to provide a testimony as soon as he could.

Gambs also rejected the new and more serious charges Kühorn had introduced in Speyer. Plus was not an Anabaptist but rather a Mennonite (*Minist*). Unlike Anabaptists, Mennonites were Christians. They also brought prosperity (*große nahrung*)[16] to Hamburg through their commercial activities and were obedient to magistrates. Plus, for example, had become a legally recognized resident in Hamburg in the legally recognized way – he had arranged a *Kontrakt* with city officials, which included paying recognition or protection money (*Schutzgelder*) and

12 See StAHbg, Reichskammergericht, H177, (10).

13 Ibid., fol. 1r: 'daß keiner der auffrührischer sect der widertäuffer zugethan, im hey Röm Reich irgendwoh gedüldet noch gelitten: sonderen wider dieselbe mit fewr, schwerd, oder dergleichen nach gelegenheit der persohn verfahren . . .'. Also see *Corpus Constitutionum Imperialium* (Regensburg, 1675), pp. 1429–40.

14 StAHbg, Reichskammergericht, H177, (10), fol. 1v: 'die gütter solcher widertäuffer alß kätzer öffentlich zu confisciren . . . vnd annebens die Obrigkeit, welche sothanen sectarys wißentlichen vnderschleiff, schütz vnd schirm gibt, sonderlich aber denen verschönet, mit zehenmarck löttiges golts zu bestraffen . . .'. 'Zehenmarck löttiges golts' would translate to approximately 6.67 pounds of pure gold.

15 Ibid., (12)–(14), esp. (12).

16 Ibid., (12), fol. 10r.

vowing to do good by the city.[17] The Mennonites had used the formula *bei Mannen Wahrheit* 'from time immemorial' (*von Vndenklichen iahres her*),[18] and it was the only form of testimony which Plus could use with a good conscience, his lawyer claimed. The use of the formula *bei Mannen Wahrheit* did not violate Imperial law and was acceptable in Hamburg. An article of the city's legal code allowed people to give testimony using an alternative to the solemn oath, provided that the solemn oath injured their conscience and that the resulting alternative testimony was deemed sufficiently believable. Testimony *bei Mannen Wahrheit* was not mentioned specifically, for the statute was clearly intended to apply to a broader range of cases than Mennonite defendants alone.[19] In any event, Gambs's point was that Mennonites were not required by law to swear a solemn oath. Since the charges had no merit, Gambs called for Plus to be acquitted without having to pay court fees.

Dr Johann Carl Müeg, the lawyer for Hamburg's Senate, was the last to present his client's case on 25 September.[20] Like the Imperial prosecutor had done following Kühorn's introduction, Müeg elaborated on an important element of Gambs's presentation. Müeg conceded that Anabaptists were an illegal group under Imperial law. However, because Plus denied being an Anabaptist, the Imperial prosecutor's charges against Plus and the Senate were meaningless, unless it could be first established that Plus was in fact a member of an illegal sect. The burden of proof lay with Plus's accusers.

In the trial's later stages the lawyers focused on the issues of the legality of Plus's testimony and Plus's confessional identity, the new and more serious issues that had been raised in Speyer. Two documents became central in Gambs's and Müeg's further arguments on these issues: *Ernstliche Verwar- und Vermahnung an alle/ Die unrechte falsche Eyde schweren* (Earnest Warning to all those who Swear False Oaths); and a 1662 edition of the *Olijftacxken* (Little Olive Branch), a Mennonite confession of faith (see Ch. 3).

17 See StAHbg, 'Die Fremden in den Rechnungsbüchern der Wedde und Kämmerei von 1600–1700' (unpublished reference book in the archive's reading room), section G, 'Die Fremden der Kämmerei', p. 246. There is no indication in the surviving records of what kind of oath or alternative formula Hans Plus used to seal his agreement.

18 StAHbg, Reichskammergericht, H177, (12), fol. 9^r.

19 *Der Stadt Hamburg Statuten und Gerichts-Ordnung* (Hamburg, 1771), p. 101 (Part. I, Tit. 34, Art. 4): 'Da auch der Beklagte sein Gewissen mit Beweisung vertreten wollte, und könnte; ist er den Eid zu leisten nicht schuldig, sondern mag sich der Beweisung gebrauchen: und da er keine gnugsame Beweisung führen könnte, mag er gleichwol den deferirten Eid nochmals schweren.' This statute is referred to in StAHbg, Reichskammergericht, H177, (12) and (36).

20 StAHbg, Reichskammergericht, H177, (16).

Müeg introduced *Ernstliche Verwar- und Vermahnung* into evidence twice on the same day, 11 April 1662, and Gambs referred to the text again on 28 April 1662.[21] Both lawyers wanted to use it to refute the prosecution's allegation about the illegality of testimony *bei Mannen Wahrheit*. Kühorn had claimed that it was unlawful, 'since the formula in question contains no appeal to God's name (such as is demanded in all legitimate oaths)'.[22] Müeg did not see this as a serious objection. The Senate in Hamburg permitted no one, including Mennonites, to swear meaningless oaths or commit perjury.

> In particular they [defendants] are told in advance, as outlined in the *Verwahrnung* [*sic*], of the serious punishment for perjury, and they must declare that they submit to the divine retribution and governmental punishment outlined in the *Verwarnung*, if they swear falsely. They must therefore give their accustomed oath with raised fingers, like everyone else.[23]

Kühorn was right to note that God's name was not mentioned in the words of Plus's testimony. Nonetheless, Müeg continued, Plus agreed to the terms of the legal warning, which he indicated by holding up his right hand in the prescribed manner when he gave his testimony: he raised his thumb as well as his index and middle fingers while folding in his last two fingers. The thumb represented God the Father; the index finger God the Son; the middle finger God the Holy Spirit; the last two fingers the souls and material bodies of humanity.[24] Having done this, if he lied to the

---

21 Ibid., (22), (24) and (29). At about this time there was a similar case before the Court in Speyer in which Gambs was active. In 1649 Jacques Budier, a wealthy and influential merchant, had begun proceedings against Duarte de Lima before the Territorial Court (*Landesgericht*) in Holstein. The following year the case was referred to the Imperial Cameral Court where the Duke of Holstein and the Senate of the city of Hamburg were co-defendants. The charge was that a Jewish oath had been preferred to a Christian one. At the very end of the trial, in 1662, Paul Gambs acted as the lawyer for de Lima. See Hans-Konrad Stein-Stegemann, *Findbuch der Reichskammergerichtakten* (Schleswig, 1986), pp. 72–3.

22 StAHbg, Reichskammergericht, H177, 17 June 1661, (4), fol. 2r: 'indem erwehnte formula keine Invocationem Nominis Divini et advocationem Dei in testem (wie in allen legitimis juramentis erfordert wird) in sich begreiffet . . .'.

23 Ibid., 11 April 1662, (20), fol. 2r–v: 'besondern es wirt ihnen die in Copia beygelegte gewöhnliche Verwahrnung für der schweren Straffe deß Mein Eydes zuvor vorgelesen, vnd müßen sich erklären, daß Sie der in der Verwarnung benandten Göttlichen Zorn vnd Rach, auch Obrigkeitlicher Straff vnterworffen sein wollen, sofern Sie falsch schweren. Müßen auch deßwegen allsolchen ihren gewöhnlichen Eydt mit abgerichteten Fingern wie sonsten gebrauchlich abstatten.'

24 For more details about the Trinity symbol used in oath swearing, see André Holenstein, 'Seelenheil und Untertanenpflicht: Zur gesellschaftlichen Funktion und theoretischen Begründung des Eides in der ständischen Gesellschaft', in Peter Blickle with André Holenstein (eds), *Der Fluch und der Eid: Die metaphysische Begründung gesellschaftlichen Zusammenlebens und politischer Ordnung in der ständischen Gesellschaft* (Berlin, 1993), pp. 11–63, at pp. 34–5. The *Verwarnung* includes an illustration of a hand held in the

court he would in effect be asking God to remove divine protection and grace from him, the criminal-sinner, and to count him among the damned when the Last Judgement came. *Bei Mannen Wahrheit*, when combined with the symbolic gesture, was not a meaningless formula, asserted the defence. It weighed as heavily upon the conscience and therefore had all the necessary religious safeguards of the conventional solemn oath. In effect, although the civic statutes allowed for defendants to use alternatives to the solemn oath if their conscience required, the magistrates nonetheless insisted on an element of solemnity in all testimony. It was not at all important from Müeg's point of view to consider whether or not these conditions conformed to the strictures of orthodox Mennonite teachings. The question was moot; he did not raise this issue in his presentations before the Court. The Mennonite Plus had agreed to give his testimony in this legitimate form. That was sufficient.

Kühorn and the Imperial prosecutor of course rejected these arguments. They continued to assert that Imperial law, not Hamburg's civic law, applied in this case. Hamburg's law was irrelevant; because Plus was a Mennonite, he was a criminal, pure and simple. On 13 November 1661 and 10 January 1662,[25] in their second presentations to the Court, Kühorn and the Imperial prosecutor proclaimed that there was no important difference between Mennonites and Anabaptists. Both groups rejected child baptism, whereas all obedient Christians accepted it as part of the foundation of a well-ordered society. The Imperial prosecutor wrote that 'Plus is from the same abominable sect, none of whose members pay homage to governments.'[26] This type of argument minimized the importance of the charges that Plus had acted improperly in Archangel; even if he was innocent of the original charges of business impropriety, he remained an Anabaptist and a criminal.

In addition to having to establish Plus's honesty and propriety and the legality of testimony *bei Mannen Wahrheit*, Gambs and Müeg therefore had to concentrate more effort on showing that Mennonites were not Anabaptists. In his second series of presentations on 18 and 28 April 1662 Gambs tried several strategies to clear his client's name.[27] He repeated the assertions that Plus was a resident in good standing in Hamburg, and that the Mennonites were an economic asset to Hamburg as well as other areas

---

required position. This illustration is an almost exact copy of one that appeared many decades earlier on the front cover of M. Besszler, *Einfeltiger Bericht ausz Gottes wort vom eidschweren was es sey* (Nuremberg, 1554). On the early history of southern Anabaptist oath-swearing, see Edmund Pries, 'Anabaptist Oath Refusal: Basel, Bern and Strasbourg, 1525–1538' (Ph.D. diss., University of Waterloo, 1995).

25 StAHbg, Reichskammergericht, H177, (17), (18) and (19).

26 Ibid., (19), fol. 2^v: 'Plus von dergleichen verworffener Sect seye, so insgemein keiner Obrigkeit hüldigen wollen.'

27 Ibid., (26) and (28).

of the Empire in which they lived and travelled. He also restated his charges against Hübner: he had been motivated 'by nothing but unfavourable, vengeful wishes' (*nur auß misgünstigen vnnd rachgierigen gemüeth*).[28] On the broader question of the legal status of Mennonites, Gambs submitted handwritten, translated excerpts from the latest edition of the Mennonites' *Olijftacxken* confession of faith.[29] Gambs's document included a copy of the Apostles' Creed, in addition to portions of two of the *Olijftacxken*'s fourteen articles. The article on baptism, which Gambs included in its entirety, emphasized the Christian responsibilities that came with entry into the community of the godly but said nothing about rejecting child baptism. The excerpt Gambs presented to the Court concerning government paraphrased the well-known and widely accepted commandments in Romans 13: 1–7: subjects should obey rulers.

In 1663 Kühorn and the Imperial prosecutor presented their own counter-evidence, which was intended to strengthen the link between Mennonites and Anabaptists. This included excerpts of articles about baptism and government taken from a version of a Mennonite confession of faith printed in Hoorn in 1620.[30] The Imperial prosecutor submitted a translated and notarized copy of parts of this text to the Court on 27 March 1663, thus doing one better than Müeg, who in 1662 had only submitted a translated copy of the *Olijftacxken* to the Court. The excerpt the Imperial prosecutor chose on baptism stressed that Mennonites held child baptism to be 'a human law in the realm of the Antichrist'.[31] On the subject of government the excerpt asserted, among other things, that human laws, including Imperial law, held a lower status than Christ's law.[32]

These principles were clearly stated by the Mennonites themselves, argued Hübner's lawyers. How could Hamburg's magistrates tolerate groups with such obviously seditious views? Hamburg's officials could not claim ignorance of these heresies. Kühorn and the Imperial prosecutor mentioned several texts by leading church scholars, including Lutheran clergymen from Hamburg, which showed that all residents of Hamburg had been warned of the grave dangers of Anabaptism.[33] One of these

28 Ibid., (26), fol. 3ʳ.

29 Ibid., (27). A copy of the 1662 edition of the *Olijftacxken* is found at StAHbg, Cl. VII Lit. Hf Nr. 4 Vol. 1a (10).

30 StAHbg, Reichskammergericht, H177, (37). For background on this confession of faith, see Archie Penner, 'Pieter Jansz. Twisck – Second Generation Anabaptist/Mennonite Churchman, Writer and Polemicist (Ph.D. diss., University of Iowa, 1971), pp. 256–61.

31 StAHbg, Reichskammergericht, H177, fol. 1ʳ: 'ein menschen gesatz in dem Reich des Ante Christ'.

32 This confession of faith was not among those included in the *Algemeene Belydennissen* (1665), the canonical collection of Zonist Mennonite confessional texts.

33 StAHbg, Reichskammergericht, H177, (17), (30), (31) and (34). Around this very time, in April 1663, Imperial representatives published a mandate against Wilhelm Thomas,

books, *Anabaptismus. Das ist: Wiedertauffer Irthumb* (Anabaptism, or, the Error of the Rebaptizers) (1645), by Johann Müller, the head pastor of Hamburg's St Petri parish, was a detailed attack on the very confession of faith that the Imperial prosecutor had presented as evidence in Speyer.

On 2 September 1663 Müeg responded to the prosecution's claims about the Hamburg government's leniency towards Anabaptists. 'Evidence that the council of the city of Hamburg does not tolerate seditious Anabaptists is found in the recent capture and expulsion of some such people from this city and its territories.'[34] He did not provide many details, but he was almost certainly referring to the 1660 banishment of three Quakers, Cornelis Roelifs, Heinrich Deen and Peter Heinrichs. The legal foundation for the banishment of Quakers was a mandate dated 24 June 1660 (see Ch. 3).[35] Significant by its absence in this mandate was any mention of Mennonites or even Anabaptists. Magistrates avoided what seems in retrospect to have been a prime opportunity to make a connection between all kinds of sectarians, whether Anabaptist or spiritualist, for one of the expelled Quakers (Cornelis Roelifs) was a former Mennonite. One explanation may have been a lack of knowledge about a Mennonite–Quaker connection. Another may have been lack of interest in making a connection. Was the failure in 1660 to make a connection between Quakers and Anabaptists part of a conscious strategy in anticipation of a heresy trial in Speyer? Such foresight on the part of magistrates is unlikely, for not even lawyers for the prosecution during Hans Plus's trials seem to have been aware of a possible link, whether theoretical or real, between Quakers and Mennonites. Whatever the case, the magistrates' failure in 1660 to notice a link between Quakers and Mennonites was advantageous several years later when lawyers for Hans Plus and the city of Hamburg insisted before the Imperial Cameral Court in Speyer on a legal distinction between Mennonites and sectarians.

Baron von Quadt in Wickrath, a territory in Jülich in the Rhineland. In the mandate the Baron was charged with the same crime as the Senate in Hamburg, that is, giving protection willingly to members of the illegal sect of Anabaptists. If he did not expel sect members from his territory immediately, he would face a trial before the Imperial Cameral Court. Officials in Hamburg were aware of this ultimatum. Two copies, one printed and the other handwritten, were saved in the Senate's files. See StAHbg, Senat, Cl. VII Lit. Hf Nr. 4 Vol. 1a, (11) and (12). I have been unable to find further details about this case in the files on Wickrath in the Hauptstaatsarchiv in Düsseldorf.

34 StAHbg, Reichskammergericht, H177, (40), fol. 1r: 'daß [der Rat der Stadt Hamburg] keine Auffrührische Wiedertäuffer in ihrer Stadt vnd gebiete gedulden, bezeüget die newlich beschehene Stadt- vnnd Landkündige Captivirung vnnd Außweisung etzlicher Auffrührischen Wiedertäuffer auß dieser Stadt vnnd dero Gebiete . . .'.

35 Also see a mandate dated 12 April 1658 and written against Anabaptists and Sacramentarians; *Sammlung . . . der Gesetze und Verfassungen*, ed. Blank, i, pp. 152–4.

Müeg's point in 1663 was clear and simple. Hamburg's Senate knew how to identify and deal with seditious sectarians, but Mennonites did not number among these. To further refute the case of the prosecution, Müeg resubmitted on 2 September 1663 the same selections from the *Olijftacxken* he had presented more than a year earlier to the judge, this time copied by a notary from the original Dutch and translated twice into German.[36] Plus's lawyers claimed that these were the principles of faith that Plus held and that these principles demonstrated the Christian orthodoxy and political harmlessness of the Mennonite faith.

The trials' implications and outcome

Constant escalation characterizes Plus's trials in Hamburg and Speyer. The trials unleashed pressures which transformed an apparently minor dispute among former business colleagues into a major controversy among representatives of powerful political institutions about legal and constitutional categories and about heresy and obedience. A local conflict was ascribed universal implications.

Because Plus showed so little interest in taking part in the public discussion about what kind of a person he was, we can only follow attempts by others to define him. The arguments of the prosecution and defence reveal some striking divergences and parallels. First, the Court in Speyer was presented with two diametrically opposed pictures of Hans Plus 'the Mennonite'. On the one hand, he was a legal resident of Hamburg who, as an archetypal Mennonite, could not for the sake of his conscience swear a solemn oath; on the other hand, he was an archetypal heretic appealing to his religious affiliation merely to delay having to perjure himself. But, secondly, in one noteworthy regard, the picture of Hans Plus the Mennonite presented by both sides was an equally exaggerated, depersonalized picture. The longer the trial lasted and the more lawyers tried to impose their competing arguments, the less both sides treated Plus as an individual. It was ultimately he who would suffer the legal consequences of a conviction, but the concrete details of his life became less and less important for deciding his guilt or innocence. Officials in Speyer, even Plus's own lawyers, seemed unacquainted with flesh-and-blood Mennonites. Such familiarity was unimportant for them. The crime of Anabaptism had already been defined in Imperial law books and ecclesiastical ordinances from the early sixteenth century. In the middle of the seventeenth century many of these texts were still being used as normative measures for possible social deviations. For example, no one, not even Plus's lawyers, raised doubts

36 StAHbg, Reichskammergericht, H177, (41), (42) and (43).

about the denunciation of rebaptism as a criminal act under Imperial law. Plus's lawyers insisted only that their Mennonite client was in no way an Anabaptist and therefore not subject to anti-Anabaptist Imperial mandates. He became little more than a supposedly representative example of abstract classes or kinds of people, and his fate began increasingly to depend on an evaluation of these classes.

In the Cameral Court the abstract question – were Mennonites in fact and in law Anabaptists? – had taken on a real significance when fines and the confiscation of property were threatened. If Hübner's faction had been able to force its paper version of Anabaptism on Plus's defenders, the consequences could have been far-reaching for government officials and flesh-and-blood Mennonites in and around Hamburg. In a short time Mennonite identity was transformed from a mundane, everyday issue of little public significance into a controversial matter involving constitutional authority and political power. The charges that Mennonites were seditious sectarians gained credibility from the weight of the social, legal, religious and political resources used to support them. For a short time, these were immense.

While the trial seemed for a short while to hold the potential of far-reaching consequences, abstract and legal dangers never extended beyond the courtroom. Despite the gravity of the trial, lawyers' interest and activity in the case weakened in the course of the 1660s. Like so many cases brought before the Imperial Cameral Court, Hübner's request for compensation and his charge of Anabaptism against Plus were never resolved. On 17 June 1663 Gambs submitted a letter he had received from Plus's legal representative in Hamburg, Henrich Schröder.[37] In an effort to counteract the depersonalized and decontextualized treatment of his client (or, as opponents charged, in an effort to stall for time), Schröder requested that Plus be asked to tell the Court what his own personal beliefs were. This, after all, was important in a case which had become focused on confessions of faith. Before he could provide this information, however, Plus would have to return from Russia. Schröder expected his client would return to Hamburg late in 1663. This did not happen. On 23 November 1663 Gambs asked for a further postponement of the case. Plus had apparently remained in Russia to collect debts owed him. It was not certain when he would return.[38] On 4 December the Imperial prosecutor answered Gambs's petition by charging that Plus had moved from Hamburg to Moscovy to avoid legal consequences. The Court should order officials in Hamburg to seize Plus's assets in the city until the matter was settled. Gambs immediately protested against a possible seizure of his client's property.

---

37 Ibid., (39). Schröder's letter is dated 22 April 1663.

38 Ibid., (44).

On 8 December 1663 the case Hübner v Plus was considered briefly for the last time in Speyer.[39] But no decision was reached. On 26 November 1671 Hans Plus died in Moscow.[40] The Imperial Cameral Court case against him was from then on meaningless. Without a concrete person to charge or defend, the grand accusations against or praises for the class of people known as Anabaptists or Mennonites had no legal foundation. Other than forcing Plus into exile in Russia, there were no lasting results to the trial.

There were mainly political reasons why a final legal decision concerning Plus's identity was not arranged in the 1660s. As soon as Caspar Bernhardi transferred Hübner's complaints to the Imperial Cameral Court, the case was transformed from a routine commercial trial into a much more serious one. Hübner's chances of a favourable decision seemed greater if he could bring the Imperial bureaucracy onto his side and if his opponent was seen to be a heretic rather than a merchant. Faced with this strategy, Imperial representatives had to fulfil their duty by defending the final authority of Imperial law over the laws of Hamburg. The situation made close allies out of the lawyers defending Hans Plus and the city of Hamburg. As long as Mennonites were known to be good subjects, the Senate of the city of Hamburg could be considered to be a responsible government. The competing categories – seditious heretic versus good subject – had much to do with the various interests of the Empire and Hamburg. In order to establish a clear definition of Mennonites (or of Hans Plus alone), it would have been necessary for lines of authority to be drawn indisputably in favour of one side. This was not the case. There was a rough balance of opposing legal and political forces and the matter was not important enough for the Empire to enforce its will with military force. A legal and political stalemate made an indefinite continuation of these efforts unproductive for both sides.

It is curious that Mennonites seem to have remained relatively passive throughout the course of the trial, when others tried to define and restrict their public identities and behaviour. As far as can be determined from available documents, no Mennonite leader used public means to try to influence government officials during the trials in Hamburg and Speyer. Judging from Mennonite records in Hamburg and Altona, the trials never took place. What might explain this? Hans Plus's original objections to the solemn oath sparked a long and detailed investigation of Mennonite beliefs by Imperial officials, even if only from a distance. The risk of further unwanted and potentially dangerous scrutiny was best avoided. The need

39 For details about events in December 1663, see the notebook at the beginning of the file (StAHbg, Reichskammergericht, H177) on the case Hübner v Plus.

40 StAHbg/MG, 147, vol. 1, p. 14; and StAHbg, Genealogische Sammlungen, Roosen, 'Notitie of Geslachtregister opgesteld door Gerrit Roosen A° 1683', p. 8.

for a low profile ruled out lobbying efforts connected with Plus's case. The early 1660s were also a period of infighting among Mennonites in Germany and the Netherlands, which may have further diminished Mennonite leaders' interest in confronting the difficult issues of the trials. As for Hans Plus himself, he seems to have been satisfied to let others represent him on paper in court, where he was treated as a member of abstract, collective categories, not as an individual. The result, perhaps surprising given all the attention devoted to finding out what kind of person he was, is that we have very little information about his beliefs from his own point of view.

Solemn oaths and alternatives in the 1690s

The two trials of Hans Plus in the 1650s and 1660s did not lead to any significant legal reform in Hamburg. Anabaptism (*Wiedertäuferei*) remained a crime in the Empire and in Hamburg, and accusations that Mennonites were heretics and criminals by their very membership in an Anabaptist group were heard occasionally from Hamburg's Lutheran pulpits. Nonetheless, commercial and legal affairs conducted between Mennonites and secular officials continued on a more or less cordial basis. Appealing to the relevant article in Hamburg's civil statutes (see above), tolerated religious nonconformists like the Mennonites could still provide testimony in court cases or in other civic or commercial matters by using an approved alternative to the solemn oath. For Mennonites this probably[41] meant the formula *bei Mannen Wahrheit* (by the truth of men). For example, on 14 June 1675 the Mennonite entrepreneurs Focke van Laer, Hans van Laer and Carel de Vlieger accepted or renewed their citizenship in Hamburg after paying a contribution of 40 marks each and after pledging their loyalty to the city using the formula *bei Mannen Wahrheit*.[42]

---

[41] For general remarks about the standard practice of swearing an oath of citizenship, see StAHbg, Claus Stukenbrock, 'Der Hamburger Bürgereid im 19. Jahrhundert' (internal research paper, 15 October 1959). It is difficult to say with certainty how common the use of Mennonite alternatives to the solemn oath were. When Mennonites accepted citizenship in Hamburg, the form of testimony used was usually not recorded. Scribes did not even record as a matter of course the confessional affiliation of a new citizen. Perhaps some Mennonites became citizens without revealing their confessional affiliation, choosing instead to swear the conventional oath; perhaps some civic officials were not at all interested in such questions and therefore did not record what to us might have seemed to be noteworthy cases. It is similarly difficult to say with any certainty how oaths and testimony were handled in other matters such as commercial transactions.

[42] StAHbg, Staatsangehörigkeitsaufsicht, A I a5, p. 100. Also see StAHbg/MG, 147, vol. 1, pp. 9 (Carel de Vlieger), 45 (Hans van Laer) and 120 (Focke van Laer).

Evidence that alternative testimony did not always proceed according to the formula *bei Mannen Wahrheit* comes from two letters written in 1690, when the council of the Flemish Mennonite congregation asked Hamburg's Senate to address the issue of Mennonite alternatives to the oath. The first letter was written sometime in January 1690.[43] In it the congregational council said it wanted to have a fully standardized formula for Mennonites to use when giving testimony before the authorities. The formula, the Mennonites stated, should not violate their religious objections to oath-swearing. It should also help to avoid legal inconveniences. The author of the letter, who remained unnamed, mentioned the cases of at least one congregational member (also unnamed) who had been brought to court by men hoping to win a case quickly against him because he would be forced for conscience sake not to swear an oath. In other words, these men were trying to win a case on the same terms that Johann Jacob Hübner had tried several decades earlier against Hans Plus.[44] Such problems could be resolved, the letter's author claimed, if a statute were passed giving full public and legal recognition to a special formula for Mennonites. The rights and responsibilities of all parties in disputes involving Mennonites would thus be clear. The author thanked the Senate for having spared Mennonites in the past the necessity of swearing by God's name when arranging citizenship, maritime passports and commercial shipments. According to the author, each of these matters was concluded with a simple verification of the truth; that is, a simple 'yes' was used in answer to a question of fact. He requested that this practice not be changed, but he also realized that the Senators themselves held no united opinion about whether anything other than the commonly used solemn oath had legal legitimacy. Therefore, the Mennonite letter writer asked that the Senate arrange a committee to investigate how best to codify a special Mennonite formula for use in all legal matters.

The second letter from the Mennonites to the Senate is dated 17 February 1690.[45] Unlike the January letter, this one was signed. Its authors were

43 StAHbg/MG, 7, 'Unterthänigste Supplic'.

44 Ibid.: 'Zumahlen da wir ja ohne Ruhm gegen Ew. Wohledl. Hochw. Raht und gemeinen besten unß je und allewege unserer schuldigkeit auch sonsten gegen Jeder männiglich unserer Mitbürger und Einwohner also bezeiget und verhalten, daß dem vermuhten nach niemand über unser comportement mit Recht sich zu beschwehren haben wird, dan bey so gestalten Sachen sich böse leute genug finden dürfften, welche unß in unrechtmäßigen Sachen zu gerichte ziehen und sodan leichtlich erhalten möchten daß wir unß Eydtlich zu purgiren oder die Sache verlustig zu sein, gewärtig sein müsten, gestalten deßen schon Exempel am tage daß solches gegen einem auß unserer gemeine gesuchet, Einem andern aber es schon würcklich angemuhtet werden wil . . .'. Although it is ambiguous, this passage may be the only recorded reference a member of the local Mennonite congregation ever made to Hans Plus's trials of the 1650s and 1660s.

45 StAHbg/MG, 7, 17 February 1690.

Geeritt Roosen and Carel de Vlieger Senior. They were writing in response to an earlier Senate decree (perhaps from 7 February)[46] which they judged unsatisfactory. In the decree the Senate had apparently recognized the use of the special Mennonite formula of testimony *bei Mannen Wahrheit* in limited circumstances like the arrangement of commercial contracts and customs matters; the Senate's decree did not, however, mention testimony in matters before the courts. The authors of the letter suggested again that a single formula apply to all legal arrangements. However, Roosen and de Vlieger also wanted to convince the Senators that there was a much more appropriate way than testimony *bei Mannen Wahrheit* of satisfying a Mennonite's conscience in place of a corporal oath: 'In Holland it is not the custom among our co-religionists to give declarations *bei Mannen Wahrheit* in place of an oath but rather to testify with *true words*.'[47] Compared with the previous letter, the Mennonites were much clearer about how testimony should be arranged. Their proposal consisted of a simple question and answer, applicable to all situations. An official would ask an individual if a straightforward statement of fact was true in all counts, 'to which he could answer clearly and from his heart "yes"'.[48] The reason they gave for suggesting this approach was that the questions posed by officials were sometimes so strange 'that one hardly knows how one is supposed to respond'.[49] They gave no examples. What was clear, however, was that traditional solutions were not working. Carel de Vlieger was now rejecting the formula of testimony he had used in 1675 to affirm his allegiance to the city of Hamburg.

Mennonite claims from 1690 need to be seen in a broader perspective. When, in their February 1690 petition to the Senate, Geeritt Roosen and Carel de Vlieger stated that the civil formula *bei Mannen Wahrheit* was not used by Mennonites in the Netherlands, they were in error. In fact, it was probably the most common form of civil testimony used by northern European Mennonites in the seventeenth century. What is more, it probably had its origins in the Low Countries. It was in use there (in Catholic

---

46 In the nineteenth century Roosen, *Geschichte der Mennoniten-Gemeinde*, part 1, pp. 97–8, wrote that the Senate replied on 7 February to an earlier congregational petition. According to Roosen the Senate agreed to accept Mennonite testimony *bei Mannen Wahrheit* in commercial matters only. The Senate letter to which Roosen referred cannot be found or has not survived. His very brief account of the reply does, however, seem plausible, especially when compared with the two surviving letters from the Mennonite congregation, both of which Roosen does not seem to have read at the time he wrote his text.

47 StAHbg/MG, 7, 17 February 1690: 'in hollandt ist eß midt den unserigen nicht dem brauch, an Eidts staadt sich by mannen wahrheidt zu Erklehren, sunderen eß zu bezeugen midt *waeren woorten*'.

48 Ibid.: 'daß man dan deudtlich undt van hartzen Ja dahrauf saegen kondte'.

49 Ibid.: 'den eß wierdt zu weilen, durch einige herrn beim *attestieren* soo seldtsaem gefraegt, daß man Vast nicht weis, wie man recht zur sache andtwohrten soll'.

Spanish-controlled territory, no less) as early as August 1570 and was probably recognized officially in the northern province of Holland sometime between 1578 and 1581.[50]

There were also other alternatives to the common solemn oath in use in the Netherlands. In 1632 the States of Groningen and Ommelanden passed a resolution allowing Mennonites to make binding obligations with a handshake. Instead of Mennonites reciting a solemn oath themselves, an official would read one to them in the second person. The example provided in the resolution ended with the phrase 'so help you God'. The handshake sealed the obligation.[51] Mennonites who made obligations on this basis were themselves not swearing an oath actively, but the line between a solemn oath and civil testimony was especially unclear in this case.

A similar arrangement seems to have applied in or around Hamburg. In 1692 merchants from Hamburg requested that the council of the town of Stade apply a Mennonite model of testimony to all shippers dealing with officials in the Swedish-controlled port. According to the historian Claus Tiedemann, this involved nothing more than sealing a commercial or customs arrangement with a handshake.[52] There is no indication how long previously handshakes had been used along the Elbe. This model may have been what Geeritt Roosen and Carel de Vlieger were referring to when they told the Senate of the city of Hamburg in February 1690 that Mennonites simply affirmed the truth of their statements. The exact procedure used in such cases around Stade is also unclear, so there is no way of knowing whether or not the arrangements in Stade included a solemn element similar to that used in Groningen and Ommelanden.

The Dutch example of a handshake following a second-person reading of the solemn oath was a hybrid of forms. The testimony Hans Plus had given in 1660 is another example of such hybrids. From a Mennonite point of view one could say he had given civil testimony, making no reference to the name of God; from the point of view of officials in Hamburg, one could say he had provided solemn safeguards while giving

---

50 See Dyserinck, *De vrijstelling van den eed voor de Doopsgezinden*, pp. 36 and 67–72. Dyserinck (pp. 67–9) includes a transcription of a March 1588 privilege from the Court of Holland, which is the earliest surviving document entrenching the rights of Dutch subjects to use the formula in place of any invocation of God's name. Also see C.W. Bruinvis, 'Oude rechtstoestand der Mennisten in Holland', *Doopsgezinde Bijdragen*, 39 (1899), pp. 181–4; and the headings 'Eed' and 'Mennogezinden' in Eduard van Zurck, *Codex Batavus, waer in het algemeen Kerk- publyk en Burgerlyk Recht van Holland, Zeelant, en het Ressort der Generaliteit Kortelyk Is Begrepen* (2nd edn, Delft, 1727).

51 Dyserinck, *Vrijstelling van den eed*, p. 48: 'Dat u Godt soo helpe'.

52 Claus Tiedemann, *Die Schiffahrt des Herzogtums Bremen zur Schwedenzeit (1645–1712)* (Stade, 1969), p. 25.

his civil testimony, because he had raised his hand in the symbolic way required. The distinction between the solemn oath and civil alternatives acceptable to Mennonites was ambiguous.

Clear distinctions were sometimes also difficult to draw between the two main kinds of civil testimony – *bei Mannen Wahrheit* and simple affirmation with true words. Among the Zonist-aligned Flemish Mennonites in Rotterdam, swearing a solemn oath generally led to expulsion from communion. This was the fate suffered by Bastiaan van Weenigem,[53] the Rotterdam preacher who had been such a strong ally of Geeritt Roosen during the disputes with the Dompelaars in the 1660s. In 1694 he accepted a public office in Rotterdam after swearing a solemn oath, and soon thereafter his congregation put the elderly preacher under the ban. There was a great irony to this situation. In 1684 van Weenigem himself had negotiated an arrangement with the city of Rotterdam, whereby Mennonites could conduct all business with the government without having to swear a solemn oath or raise a hand in a solemnly symbolic way. They were permitted to make commitments simply 'according to the truth of men or women, using the word "yes"'.[54] In making their unsuccessful case in 1690, Geeritt Roosen and Carel de Vlieger had said that in the Netherlands Mennonites made a clear distinction between simple affirmation and testimony *bei Mannen Wahrheit*. However, in his negotiated agreement of 1684 van Weenigem had made no such differentiation.

These examples show two things: legal practice surrounding Mennonite oath swearing or the non-swearing of oaths varied from jurisdiction to jurisdiction as well as over time; and the knowledge which Mennonites or magistrates did have about the current state of accepted practice was hardly perfect – or this knowledge was kept private for tactical reasons.

Dutch practices of giving testimony were too varied to provide a single model for northern German practice, but Dutch religious opinion may nonetheless have played a small role in the timing of the 1690 petitions. In 1688 Klaas Toornburg, a young doctor and newly ordained preacher among the Waterlander Anabaptists in Alkmaar, had written a two-part examination of Christian ethics, focusing on the use of weapons to resist evil as well as on oath-swearing. He had principled objections to both. Take his statement on the latter: 'We understand that the Lord Jesus forbids,

---

53 See Karl Vos, 'Bastiaan van Weenigem en het eedvraagstuk', *Nederlandsch Archief voor Kerkgeschiedenis*, new ser. 6 (1909), pp. 121–38.

54 Dyserinck, *Vrijstelling van den eed*, p. 67: 'by haer mannen- ofte vrouwen waerheit, en sulcx op 't woord van jae'. Also see Vos, 'Bastiaan van Weenigem'. The decision at the June 1695 Zonist Society meetings (Gemeentearchief Amsterdam, PA 565, A 941 I, p. 115) to hold to the accepted confessional statements concerning oath-swearing may have been related to Bastiaan's actions.

without any exception whatever, his followers to swear an oath.'[55] He read Matthew 5: 33–7 in a literal way to mean that the only replacement for the oath that could be acceptable to Christians was a simple 'yes' or 'no'. Nowhere in his text did Toornburg mention testimony *bei Mannen Wahrheit*, which a reader could take to mean that it too was illegitimate in the eyes of God under the covenant established in the New Testament. Geeritt Roosen also compiled a confession of faith, 'Schriftuerlycke Belydenis Getrocken uyt Eenige predicadien' (Scriptural Confession Taken from Some Sermons),[56] in the same year that Toornburg's text appeared in print. Like Toornburg, Roosen asserted that Christ's command in Matthew 5: 33–7 meant 'that oath-swearing is forbidden as clear as can be';[57] rather, it was a Christian's duty to tell the truth in all circumstances. Roosen too did not mention alternative forms of testimony. And he did not cite Toornburg. The two authors may never have met nor known of the other's work, but both men had learned either through reading and reflection or contacts with like-minded co-religionists to take the same strong, principled position against oath-swearing.

It is also important to understand the political climate when trying to explain the timing of the petitions. The author of the January 1690 letter to Hamburg's Senate had raised concerns about legal charges made by ill-minded people against Mennonites simply because they did not swear a solemn oath. Another trial like the one Hans Plus had faced in the Imperial Cameral Court would have been equally as unwelcome or even dangerous in 1690 as it had been in the 1650s and 1660s. It is true that in Hamburg's statutes there were general provisions for witnesses to use alternatives to the solemn oath when giving testimony, but, in circumstances where the law did not mention Mennonites specifically, ambitious litigants could use the threat of an appeal to old Imperial legislation to intimidate defendants who planned to use the formula *bei Mannen Wahrheit*. If there happened to have been threats of a new heresy trial, this would have been reason enough for Geeritt Roosen and Carel de Vlieger to lobby the Senate to codify a standard civil alternative to the solemn oath for Mennonites in

55 Klaas Toornburg, *Schriftuurlijcke Verhandelingh Tegens het Eed-zweeren* (Alkmaar, 1688), p. 9: 'Wy verstaen dan dat de Heere Christus de sijnen alhier het Eedt-zweeren sonder eenige exceptie of uytnemingh/ geheel en al verbiet . . .'. Towards the end of the sixteenth century Toornburg's Waterlander predecessors did not have serious qualms about believers swearing oaths by God's name, so long as they were always telling the truth. See two articles by Dyck, 'The First Waterlandian Confession of Faith' and 'The Middelburg Confession of Hans de Ries'.

56 StAHbg/MG, 246b, 'Schriftuerlycke Belydenis'. The text of this confession of faith is based on the sermons which Geeritt Roosen, since his July 1663 ordination, had preached prior to baptismal and communion services.

57 Ibid., p. 46: 'soo dat hiermet het Eedsweeren teenemael, Ja naeckt en klaer, afgeleert en verbooden is . . .'.

1690. Concern about the repercussions of legal ambiguity may thus have encouraged Mennonite lobbying efforts to be directed against a form of testimony that earlier had been accepted by such prominent Mennonite leaders as Bastiaan van Weenigem in Rotterdam and Carel de Vlieger locally.

Those efforts would have become more difficult after March 1690. The middle of March was when *Senior* Samuel Schultz of Hamburg's Ministry first proposed an oath of religious orthodoxy to his fellow Lutheran clergymen (see Ch. 4). The move raised the issue of Lutheran religious unity to the centre of attention in Hamburg. Probably at least partly because of concerns about the impact orthodox attacks on 'heretics' would have on the city's economic prosperity, the Senate, which at this time was not only negotiating with the Mennonites but also with Calvinists,[58] rejected the Ministry's plans to further entrench Lutheran unity. With tensions raised between the Ministry and Senate, circumstances were no longer so favourable for Mennonite–Senate negotiations.

The issue of alternatives to the solemn oath was raised at least once more several years later. In a mandate from 24 January 1694, given in response to the petition of a Flemish congregational member named Lorenz Claesen,[59] Hamburg's Senate instructed civic officials to acknowledge testimony *bei Mannen Wahrheit* 'as if a corporal [that is, solemn] oath had actually been given'.[60] These provisions applied to any Mennonite seeking citizenship or appearing before court officials. In the document, no mention was made of testimony in commercial matters, perhaps on the assumption that such arrangements had already been formalized by law in February 1690. There was also no mention of any necessity for solemn symbolic gestures of the kind Hans Plus had been required to use to secure the validity of the formula of civil testimony. Under the terms of the 1694 mandate Mennonites could give strictly civil testimony freed of all solemn trappings. In contrast to the more legally ambiguous situation Plus had faced around the middle of the century, Mennonites could now

58 See Rückleben, *Die Niederwerfung der hamburgischen Ratsgewalt*, p. 83, n. 138, and p. 113, n. 278.

59 On Claesen (Clawsen), see StAHbg/MG, 147, vol. 1, p. 70; and StAHbg, Staatsangehörigkeitsaufsicht, A Ia 5, p. 10 (entry from 27 January 1665). I have been unable to find Claesen's original petition.

60 Quoted from ten Doornkaat Koolman, *Die Verpflichtung der Mennoniten an Eidesstatt*, p. 30: 'alß wan ein Cörperlichen-Eydt würklich abgestattet wäre'. The mandate survives, as far as I am aware, only in ten Doornkaat Koolman's nineteenth-century transcription. The timing of this mandate is noteworthy. 24 January 1694 was just a few days after what the historian Hermann Rückleben, *Die Niederwerfung der hamburgischen Ratsgewalt*, pp. 204–10, indicates was a high point of mob violence in Hamburg during which access to government buildings was being denied to officials. The issuance of the mandate is evidence that the operation of government was not entirely blocked by events.

appeal to unambiguous statutes when seeking to be freed from swearing a solemn oath in Hamburg. The arrangements established in the early 1690s became the legal norm in Hamburg until at least the latter part of the eighteenth century.[61]

However, practice in and around Hamburg remained varied. In May 1695 the ship *Vergüldeter Elefant* (see Ch. 5) was arbitrarily impounded by Danish customs officials at Glückstadt. Its owners, a group of Mennonite and non-Mennonite business associates from Hamburg, were expected to pay a fee before it would be released. In December 1695, as part of their efforts to free their ship from custody, they gave testimony before Hamburg's magistrates: their business dealings had been blameless and were not deserving of punishment by the Danes. Thereafter the magistrates wrote a letter on the businessmen's behalf to Danish officials. Among the Mennonites involved were several de Vliegers: Jacob, son of Carel de Vlieger Senior, Salomon, Berend and another Jacob. While the non-Mennonites used solemn oaths before Hamburg's magistrates, the Mennonites gave their testimony using the formula *bei Mannen Wahrheit*.[62] The de Vliegers' December 1695 declaration *bei Mannen Wahrheit* is in itself hardly remarkable. After all, they were merely complying with the newly codified but long-standing practice used by many Mennonite merchants. However, a short while later two of the de Vliegers chose to comply with another older legal convention: testimony using a solemn oath. In the mid-1690s Berend and Jacob de Vlieger[63] were part of a consortium of insurance agents for a merchant ship which became the victim of an attack in the English Channel. They and the other agents refused to honour the insurance claim of the ship's owners. The reasons included that the ship had left the Elbe River without an armed convoy and had taken a route different from the one planned. To try to secure their claim, the ship's owners took their case to Hamburg's Admiralty and High Court, and finally to the Imperial Cameral Court from 1698 to 1701. As part of their defence, Berend and Jacob signed a document submitted to the Cameral Court (then located in Wetzlar) in which they used an

61 See Klefeker, *Sammlung der Hamburgischen Gesetze und Verfassungen*, viii, p. 411. For a reference to oath-swearing in an eighteenth-century Mennonite sermon, see Gerrit Karsdorp, *Lyk- en Gedachtenis-Reeden . . . op het hoogstsmertelyk Overlyden van Syne Koningl. Majesteit Federik de Vyfde* (Hamburg, 1766), p. 29.

62 Landesarchiv Schleswig, Abt. 11/Nr. 493, 12 December 1695. My thanks go to Anke Martens for providing a transcription of this document.

63 Entries on Berend de Vlieger in the congregation's membership book is found at StAHbg/MG, 147, vol. 1, p. 95. The identity of Jacob is difficult to determine, for there were three men with that name in the congregation: Jacob Jans de Vlieger (ibid., p. 18); Jacob Carels de Vlieger (ibid., p. 86); and Jacob Jacobs de Vlieger (ibid., p. 132). The last of these had married a Reformed woman in 1691, but she was baptized into the Mennonite congregation in 1693.

entirely conventional solemn oath without any kind of Mennonite modification.[64] Geeritt Roosen nor any other leader or member of the Flemish congregation is recorded to have objected to the de Vliegers' actions. Perhaps no one else knew? The question is not very relevant. What is important is that, despite public statements by leaders to the contrary, Mennonites occasionally swore solemn oaths in addition to giving testimony *bei Mannen Wahrheit*.

In his 1694 manuscript on the defence of merchant ships (see Ch. 5) Geeritt Roosen had written little about oath-swearing. He wrote more on the issue in his pamphlet from 1695, *Nutzbahrer und Gründlicher Unterricht Von dem jetzo gewöhnlichen Brauch and Art Der Unrahtsahmen Kachel-Ofen* (Useful and Fundamental Lesson about the Current Custom and Type of Inadvisable Tile Oven).[65] When presenting his proposals for oven design (see Ch. 4), he wrote not as a Mennonite and preacher but simply as someone concerned for the welfare and common good of the city. According to his own statement in the pamphlet, he was a legally registered resident (although not a citizen) of Hamburg.[66] He remarked that in 1640, the same year he married and established a household in Hamburg, he had accepted the status of an official resident after he 'committed with hand and mouth to do my best to seek the best for the city'.[67] It is not absolutely clear from the text to which form of oath or testimony the phrase 'with hand and mouth' refers. But knowing the details of his earlier pledge are not important here. What is most

64 The relevant section of the document – StAHbg, Reichskammergericht, V9 (7) – reads: 'Und dann wir Endts Unterschriebenen an erwehnten Käyserl. Cammer-Gericht in Rechtlichen Process und Streit gerathen/ dannenhero dergleichen wohlverordneten Eyd abzustatten uns nichts weniger/ als andere gehalten wissen/ die Wichtigkeit was solcher Schwur an- und auff sich habe/ und nach sich führe/ uns genugsam bekannt und wissend/ daß nehmlich diejenige/ so zu dessen Abstattung verbunden/ den Allmächtigen GOtt Vatter und Schöpffer aller Creaturen/ der das Verborgene aller Menschen Herzen und Gedancken siehet/ Gott den Sohn/ und heiligen Geist/ als persönlich zugegen/ durch die Aufstreckung der drey Finger offentlich zu Gezeugen anruffen/ . . .'.

65 In Hamburg this text can be found in StAHbg, Sammelband 84, (12).

66 There is little independent evidence that his claim was in fact true. Specifically, Roosen is not listed in surviving citizenship registers nor in records of official residents. Records may of course have been incomplete. Whatever his status, civic officials did accept him as a witness for another Mennonite's application for residency rights. See StAHbg, Staatsangehörigkeitsaufsicht, A Ia 4, 1629–1663, p. 444; and StAHbg/MG, 147, vol. 1, p. 53 (Claes Peters).

67 StAHbg, Sammelband 84, (12), 48: 'Wann sie solchem nach in dieser Ofen Verbesserung/ meiner verlangen/ absonderlich wan ich E.E. Hoch- und wolweisen Rath darinnen zu Dienste sein kan/ wie ich mir dann bey Annehmung zum Einwohner Anno 1640. *mit Hand und Mund verpflichtet habe/ bestmüglich/ der Stadt Bestes zu suchen/* wie ich darinnen/ ohne Ruhm zu melden/ mir auch als einen redlichen Bürger wolanständig stets fleißig erzeiget habe/ und so ferner verharren werde/ zu sein. Dero Dienstschuldigster Geeritt Roosen.' I have translated the italicized portion of the text.

noteworthy about the reference to the 1640 pledge is that in 1695, five years after insisting that Mennonites gave official statements not with an oath nor with testimony *bei Mannen Wahrheit* but rather with a simple affirmation of the truth, Roosen was not very concerned about the finer points of such questions. What was crucial to him was that he was seen to be a good resident of Hamburg.[68] He was acting as a conformist patriot, not a confessionalist Mennonite.

Conclusion

The evidence discussed above is worth summarizing. In 1660 during his trial in Hamburg, Hans Plus insisted on using the Mennonite formula *bei Mannen Wahrheit* to avoid swearing a solemn oath, but also at the same time he used solemn gestures; in 1690 Geeritt Roosen and Carel de Vlieger Senior asserted that Mennonites did not use the formula *bei Mannen Wahrheit* or any other form of oath but simply testified to the truth, yet in previous years at least one of these men (de Vlieger) and possibly both had used the formula *bei Mannen Wahrheit*; and in the mid-1690s Jacob and Berend de Vlieger, like the Dutch confessionalist preacher Bastiaan van Weenigem, swore solemn oaths after earlier having used or defended the Mennonite formula *bei Mannen Wahrheit*. What these examples make clear is that Mennonite attitudes towards the sometimes contentious ethical issue of oath-swearing were not uniform and constant. Principles and practices varied.

Two further things connect examples from the trials of Hans Plus and the public discussions of the 1690s. First, the relationship between government institutions and political subjects is noteworthy. Thinking in terms of the model of social discipline (see Ch. 4), some historians might expect governments to have had a leading role in these cases. However, while government institutions were involved, their role was not a leading one. Hamburg's High Court and the Imperial Cameral Court would not have been at work on Hans Plus's case had the merchant Johann Jacob Hübner not filed a complaint. And, in the 1690s, Hamburg's weakened

68 Roosen certainly acted for much of his life as a local patriot in Hamburg. Before becoming a preacher he was, among other activities, an entrepreneur who sold socks. A picture of an engraving that came along with a package of his socks read 'A dozen good Hamburg socks'. In the centre of the engraving was a large rose, above it the gates of the city of Hamburg (the civic symbol), and below the rose a picture of the harbour and skyline of the city. See Schepansky, 'Mennoniten in Hamburg und Altona zur Zeit des Merkantilismus', pp. 65–6. The woodcut is an early example of an advertisement. The original was lost in the early 1980s. A photograph can be found in *Mennonitische Geschichtsblätter*, 38, new ser. 32 (1980), between pp. 49 and 50.

Senate twice passed rulings on the issue of Mennonite oath-swearing, each time following a request for action from the Mennonite congregation. In both cases, subjects took the initiative which started judicial and administrative activity in government institutions.[69]

The second point concerns the relationship between everyday behaviour and claims about it. In the 1660s and 1690s, Mennonite leaders and non-Mennonite officials alike painted a series of vastly simplified, abstracted and even inaccurate pictures of the way actual Mennonites behaved. Although portrayed as 'the way things really were', these claims about Mennonite life had a more important purpose: they were attempts to persuade others and thereby shape the future state of affairs. This helps explain why over time officials and representatives changed their story or lost interest in the business of categorizing and defining Mennonites. In new circumstances, old claims carried less weight or lost relevance altogether – they were no longer good tools for persuasion.

69 This finding confirms a key argument made by Schmidt, 'Sozialdisziplinierung?'.

CHAPTER SEVEN

Mixed Marriages and Social Change

In the early modern era, the boundaries separating confessional communities were reinforced from both sides. On the one hand, Mennonites, like Calvinists, Catholics and Jews, were not fully enfranchised members of northern German Lutheran society. And, on the other hand, although the Mennonite community was formally a voluntary one joined by adult believers, it was in practice a community into which individuals were born and in which they were raised to accept certain rights, responsibilities, disadvantages and beliefs.

But not all young Mennonites assumed their inherited roles as was expected of them. When they were baptized or disciplined and when they married and died, their actions were recorded in the congregation's membership book.[1] Rather than providing a simple picture of a stable and homogeneous community, the records in this source show that the decisions of young couples to establish their own households contributed to the weakening of older, exclusively confessional conceptions of community.

Marriages between Mennonites in the seventeenth century

Marriage practices, like so many other aspects of Mennonite life in the seventeenth century, were affected greatly by the experience of migration (see Ch. 1). In the early seventeenth century, when most Mennonites were settling for the first time in urban centres in northern Germany, congregational institutions were in formative stages, if they existed at all. One reason may have been that it took a while for the congregation to gather enough members to warrant permanent institutions. Another seems to have been the originally very limited privileges that Mennonites were granted in Altona. There they were not yet allowed to worship publicly until 1622. This had consequences for young Mennonite couples. For example, when Paul Roosen arrived in Altona in 1611 to marry and to establish a leather-tanning business on the street Große Freiheit, he could not find a Mennonite preacher to perform the marriage ceremony. He and his wife, Janneken Quins, were wedded in 1611 in Steinbek by Pastor

1 StAHbg/MG, 147, vol. 1.

Neve, a Lutheran. The case of Paul and Janneken was typical of Mennonite marriages before 1622.[2] Janneken Quins, a refugee from the Low Countries, and Paul Roosen, a migrant to Altona from Holstein's countryside, lived through a period of transition from open persecution against Anabaptists to limited toleration. Because they were afforded limited degrees of toleration in centres like Altona and even Hamburg, the Mennonites could begin to set down roots, while also maintaining ties with the Netherlands.

The experiences of the van der Meersch family provide another example of the kinds of ties linking seventeenth-century Mennonites in the Netherlands and northern Germany, as well as some of the pressures that kept groups at a distance from one another. Abraham van der Meersch (1643–1728), in his 1721 ethical will to his grandson,[3] wrote that his family had stayed in Hamburg from 1672 until June 1673 to escape the ravages of war in the Netherlands. Geeritt Roosen normally made notes in the Flemish congregation's membership book about new arrivals like the van der Meersch family, even if those families stayed briefly. But Roosen made no such record of the van der Meersch's stay during those years of war. Van der Meersch was a member of Galenus Abrahamsz's Lamist congregation in Amsterdam. While there are indications that by the late 1670s or early 1680s the Zonist-aligned Mennonites in Hamburg and Altona had made peace with the Lamist leader Abrahamsz (see Ch. 3), tensions arising from the 1664 Lamist–Zonist schism in Amsterdam were probably still fresh in people's memories. Although Abraham van der Meersch may have had contacts with Mennonites in Hamburg and Altona in the early 1670s, old factional tensions may explain why he never officially became a member of the congregation. He returned to Amsterdam as soon as it was safe, but he again went to Hamburg in September 1696. Once again Geeritt Roosen did not record his name, but this time for a different reason. Abraham had travelled to Hamburg with his son of the same name to help find an appropriate Mennonite woman for the young man to marry. Before finally marrying Catarina Outerloo in 1697 Abraham Junior received his baptism before the congregation in Altona. He was recorded in the congregation's membership book,[4] but his father, who was a mere visitor, was not. The young couple moved to Amsterdam soon after their marriage.

The van der Meersch–Outerloo marriage had several typical elements. In the seventeenth century, marriages normally took place between two

---

2 Roosen, *Geschichte der Mennoniten-Gemeinde*, part 1, pp. 11 and 37.

3 Abraham van der Meersch, '"De laatste vaderlijke lessen" (1721)', ed. P. Visser and S.B.J. Zilverberg, *Doopsgezinde Bijdragen*, 17 (1991), pp. 163–4.

4 StAHbg/MG, 147, vol. 1, p. 155.

Mennonites who had received parental consent and the approval of the congregation. This required that young Mennonites had to be baptized before they were considered eligible for an official marriage. Marriages usually occurred soon after baptisms; both were rites of passage into full adulthood. Certainly not all marriages involved a partner from other communities, but it was nonetheless common enough for marriages conducted in Altona to involve one person from a Mennonite congregation in Friedrichstadt, Lübeck, Prussia or the Netherlands. Some of these couples stayed in or around Altona, while others moved soon after marriage to the home territory of the foreign spouse. Such interregional marriages helped to expand the congregation's biological resources and cultural contacts.

Another strategy developed by socially conservative Mennonites to deal with the limited pool of eligible spouses was to build local family alliances through marriage. Multiple examples can be found in the Roosen and de Vlieger families, major factions of which were closely related through marriage. In 1679 Jan de Vlieger married Maria Roosen; in 1681 Carel de Vlieger Junior married Ester Roosen; and in 1685 Hans Roosen married Clara de Vlieger. All six were the children of either Carel de Vlieger Senior or Geeritt Roosen.[5] The tendency to marry a believer from the local congregation was especially strong among members of the congregation's most well-to-do families. As a consequence, some family names in early modern Hamburg and Altona were characteristically (although not necessarily exclusively) 'Mennonite': Goverts, de Jager, Kramer, Linnich, Münster, Roosen, van der Smissen, Stockman, de Vlieger, Voss. These families were not only among the most prominent in business life, but many of the congregation's leaders came from their ranks. For example, Carel de Vlieger and Geeritt Roosen were not only a deacon and a preacher respectively, but both had had long and successful careers in the shipping business and other commercial activities. Although such a close connection between business and congregational networks was typical of Mennonite social life throughout northern Europe,[6] it was not unique to Mennonite communities.[7]

A transcript of a model marriage ceremony survives from the latter part of the seventeenth century. It was remarkably simple and probably

5 See Roosen, *Geschichte unseres Hauses*.

6 The economic significance of these kinds of connections is emphasized by Schepansky, 'Mennoniten in Hamburg und Altona'. Sprunger, 'Rich Mennonites, Poor Mennonites', p. 110, writes of '. . . one of the most striking aspects of the Mennonite business world in the seventeenth century: the financial and marriage network to be found within each congregation'.

7 See Kurt Samuelsson, *Religion and Economic Action*, trans. E. Geoffrey French (New York and Evanston, Ill., 1961), ch. 4.3. For broad background, see Jack Goody, *The European Family: An Historico-Anthropological Essay* (Malden, Mass., and Oxford, 2000).

not unlike other Christian marriage ceremonies. In the presence of the congregation, the preacher first asked the groom and then the bride if they were free from personal attachments either within or beyond the congregation which would stop them from joining in marriage. They were then asked if each accepted the other willingly before God as husband and wife, and if they would love and be true to the other according to God's word, which meant that they would never separate until death. Finally, the preacher pronounced them married.[8]

Although marriages involving Mennonites were generally conducted according to the model described above, there were exceptions. The experiences of the preacher Jacob Jacobs de Vlieger provide some examples. De Vlieger was originally from Altona, but from 1662 to 1664 he preached in one of Friedrichstadt's Mennonite congregations. In 1664 he returned to Altona, where he joined the Flemish congregation's preaching staff. After the death of his first wife he travelled back to Friedrichstadt briefly in 1669 in order to marry for a second time. His wife-to-be, Mayken Wolters, was also his first cousin, and the preachers in Altona's Flemish congregation refused to perform the ceremony; colleagues in Friedrichstadt had fewer qualms.[9] De Vlieger continued, however, to work as a preacher in Altona – at least until 1671. That year he announced to the congregation that, because it was difficult for him to make a living as a lay preacher, he wanted to resign. Creditors' demands were among the difficulties he was facing. Bankruptcy could sometimes count as grounds for expulsion from communion in the Flemish congregation,[10] but with financial assistance

---

8 StAHbg/MG, 248, vol. 2, a loose sheet in the text 'afdeelinge om inde oeffeninge . . .': 'bewoordinge over het trou bevestiging/ met het voortreeden en presenteren uwer personen geeft gy te kennen dat gy in u voorneemen noch onverandert syt alsoo hebben wy u deesweegen deese vragen voortestellen/ 1 soo vragen wy u bruydegom NN oft gy deese uwe voorgenomen trouwe oock vry hebt van alle ander vrouws personen buyten en binnen de gemeynte uytgenomen deese uwe bruyt NN die aen uwe syde staet wat segt gy daerop/ antw Ja/ soo oock aen de bruyt – 2 soo vragen wy u bruydegom NN oft hy deese uwe vry beleeden trouwe hiermet vrywillich overgeeft aen deese uwe bruyt NN en haer daermet aenneemt voor uwe Echte wettige voor godt en deese gemeynte getroude huysvrou/ om haer liefde en trouwe te bewysen gelyck een Christelyck man naer uytwys van godts woort schuldich is te doen/ haer nimmer te verlaten in voorspoet noch tegenspoet tot dat godt u door den doot compt te schyden wat segt gy daertoe/ antwt Ja/ en soo oock tot de bruyt/ de heere is een hoorder uwer woorden ende de gemeente een getuyge dat gy u door de reeden uwes monts in den echten staet verbonden hebt . . .'. The document was recorded in Geeritt Roosen's handwriting. The text is undated.

9 For details about this and other marriages between first cousins, see App. 5.

10 For examples of disciplinary action against bankrupt members, see App. 8. For details on the treatment of bankrupt Mennonites in another jurisdiction, see Mary Sprunger, 'Faillissementen: Een aspect van geestelijke tucht bij de Waterlands-doopsgezinde gemeente te Amsterdam in de zeventiende eeuw', *Doopsgezinde Bijdragen*, new ser. 17 (1991), pp. 101–30.

from friends he was able to pay off his debts and thus remain a member of the congregation in good standing. In March 1674, less than half a year after the death of his second wife, de Vlieger again faced financial problems, this time of greater severity. He left Altona for Glückstadt, where he married a Calvinist woman and joined her church.

Marriages between cousins and marriages with members of non-Mennonites churches represent two very different trends. The latter (to be discussed at greater length in the sections below) encouraged local assimilation, while the former was an extreme form of endogamy. In addition to the 1669 marriage of Jacob Jacobs de Vlieger and Mayken Wolters, there were five pairs of first cousins who married without the approval of the congregation and its preachers in the last half of the seventeenth century.[11] In some of these cases, Geeritt Roosen noted explicitly in the membership book that the couple remained members of the congregation, and in no case was there ever any indication that such marriages resulted in disciplinary action. The Flemish were not in principle against such marriages. There are three examples. Two involved the first cousins Hans Stockman and Anna Maria Janss (married in 1674) and Focke van Laer and Elisabet van Laer (married in 1685).[12] The other, between the first cousins François and Maria Stockman, had taken place in 1665. A few years later word spread that the couple had had sexual relations before marriage. They were disciplined briefly for this sexual indiscretion, but their marriage, like the 1674 and 1685 cases, had been conducted before the congregation in Altona according to the usual procedure.[13]

The significant difference separating marriages between first cousins that were held in Altona's Mennonite congregation from those that were not is that the former were first approved by Danish authorities in Altona. Receiving this approval was the main concern of Flemish leaders. Because records for the seventeenth century are less than ideal, it is difficult to say whether the congregation consulted authorities in Altona only before marrying first cousins or whether they registered all marriages. The registration of all marriages would not have presented too many difficulties, for Mennonite preachers were already keeping such records for their own purposes.

While only fragmentary clues are available about Danish demands, a little more can be said about arrangements in Hamburg. Until the beginning of the eighteenth century, Hamburg's civil authorities apparently had made no demands of Mennonite leaders concerning the registration of marriages.

---

11 See App. 5.

12 See StAHbg/MG, 147, vol. 1, pp. 36, 52, 78 and 120.

13 Ibid., pp. 46 and 48.

This changed on 2 August 1703 when Albert Twestreng, one of Hamburg's senior civic officials in charge of internal affairs, sent a note to Mennonite representatives in the city.[14] In it he demanded that all Mennonite residents of Hamburg obtain a marriage licence before marrying. This demand was one of the central issues facing congregational council members during their meetings at the end of 1703. At the 9 September meeting the preacher Jan de Lanoy and the deacon Jan Beets were given the task of asking Reformed and Catholic leaders if Twestreng also sent them such a note. No results of their inquiries were recorded.[15]

Discipline, confessionally mixed marriages and conversions in the seventeenth century

The Mennonites' long-standing concern about maintaining the moral purity of their religious community is shown in the following example, one of many from the early modern era. Towards the end of 1703, around the same time that Albert Twestreng had requested that all marriages of Mennonites living in Hamburg be registered, the council of the congregation in Hamburg and Altona also addressed two disciplinary issues. Geeritt Roosen and the deacon Ryndert Jansen were assigned to speak with Sussanna Mirbeeck and Sara Trittouw, who had both married outside the congregation since the last communion. Council members also resolved to speak with three unnamed congregation members who had been missing from the congregation and had gone bankrupt. The offending members were told that if they did not improve their ways, they would be banned from the next communion.[16]

This kind of concern for moral purity dates back to the earliest years of the Mennonite movement in the sixteenth century. Compared with some other Anabaptist leaders in the middle of the sixteenth century, the main early Mennonite leaders (Menno Simons, Dirk Philips and Leonard Bouwens) all supported the strict use of discipline as a means to enforce the biblical ideal of a community 'without spot or wrinkle'.[17] The Mennonite congregation in Hamburg and Altona was in many regards

14 StAHbg/MG, 145. For a review of earlier mandates on marriage in Hamburg, none of which specifically concerns Mennonites, see *Sammlung der . . . Gesetze und Verfassungen*, ed. Blank, i, pp. 44–6 and 241.

15 The record of the 9 September 1703 meeting is found at StAHbg/MG, 6, vol. 1, pp. 18–19. Mennonite leaders discussed Twestreng's interest in congregational affairs twice more, on 4 October and 1 November 1703; ibid., pp. 19–20.

16 See ibid., pp. 18–19. The names of the three bankrupt Mennonites were never recorded.

17 For background on sixteenth-century Anabaptist marriage and ban practices, see Snyder, *Anabaptist History and Theology*, chs. 19 and 24.

the inheritor-congregation of Menno Simons's congregation at Fresenburg in Holstein. And like most Mennonite congregations in the early modern era, its leaders and members too worked to uphold the ideal of a pure community of Christian believers. Drunkenness, adultery, violent behaviour, bankruptcy and marriage to non-members were common sins earning discipline (see Apps. 4 and 8–10).[18] Only in very rare cases was doctrinal nonconformity punished.[19] Generally, all cases of discipline were dealt with in stages. First, those who were seen to have sinned were asked privately to repent and return to the moral ways of the congregation. If more pressure was required, sinners were brought before the congregational council, whose members could exclude them from communion until they repented. More contentious cases were brought to the attention of the whole congregation, where it was finally decided if the sinners should be banned from the congregation.

Besides the sometimes very brief notes in the congregation's membership book, disciplinary records from the seventeenth century are scarce. One of the earliest surviving detailed records of the process of discipline concerns the behaviour expected from couples. In 1663 Geeritt Roosen made notes about how the congregation responded to the case of a recently married couple who, it was learned, had had premarital intercourse.[20] Extra-marital sexual relations were viewed by most influential people in the congregation as grounds for expulsion. But, because the couple – Claas Dircks and Anna Beerens[21] – had intended and sought to be married in the lawful, proper and open way accepted in the congregation, their case was not so serious. Their attempts at marriage had been hampered by Claas's father, who was not happy with the match. Roosen wrote that the father's disapproval was, however, no excuse for the couple's misdeed since, in their case, they could have been married as responsible, independent adults. It was decided that their only punishment was to confess their sins publicly before the congregation.

An act of disobedience to the community of faith which was by its very nature especially difficult to punish was conversion to another church. Not counting conversions resulting from mixed marriages, at least twenty-one baptized Mennonites converted to Lutheranism in the last half of the seventeenth century, while another thirteen became Quakers.[22] There

18 Of course, comparative studies would be needed before historians could make any judgements about the uniqueness of Mennonite discipline.

19 Besides the case of the Dompelaar schism (certainly not a usual example of congregational discipline), one of the few examples concerns Riewart Dircks (see Ch. 4), who was put under enough pressure that he resigned his preaching position and left northern Germany.

20 StAHbg/MG, 248, vol. 1, 'Copia van een Broederhandeling van myn Overgrootvader Gerrit Roosen'.

21 StAHbg/MG, 147, vol. 1, pp. 35 and 41.

22 See App. 7.

were at least a further sixteen defections which resulted from mixed marriages.[23]

Mixed marriages did not always result in the loss of members. They could also bring people not of Mennonite heritage into the congregation. In 1680 or 1681 the Altona congregation member Jacob Alberts married a Lutheran woman. Margeriete, Jacob Alberts's wife, accepted baptism in 1681 at the hands of the visiting Lamist preacher Galenus Abrahamsz.[24]

Margeriete Alberts's defection was not unique. Nonetheless, only a very few one-time non-Mennonites joined Altona's Flemish congregation in the seventeenth century. Examples from the first half of the seventeenth century include Hendrick Sicks, a merchant and preacher in the 1630s, who had come from a Lutheran background; Baerent Roelifs, who had originally been a Calvinist before converting to Mennonitism in Alkmaar and later moving to Altona in 1650; and Hippolythus Denner, one of the original immersionists, who had come from a Catholic background. In the last half of the century there were, counting Margeriete, only a small handful of conversions to the Mennonite congregation.[25] In almost every one of these cases the individuals in question had only weak connections with other churches in Hamburg or Altona, and they usually were newcomers to the region who knew members or former members of Mennonite congregations. There was a good reason for this. Upon the accession of each new Danish monarch the Flemish Mennonites in Altona had their privileges renewed. Together with this grant of political, economic and religious rights came some legal limitations, including injunctions against converting local Lutherans (see Ch. 1). The conversion of new members from non-Mennonite backgrounds who had only weak ties to the local Lutheran community did not threaten the injunction.

The one act that attracted the most disciplinary attention from congregational leaders was marriage between a member and a non-member (*buitentrouwe*). During the last four decades of the seventeenth century, unapproved and mixed marriages were not a constant problem, but preachers were concerned about their sometimes great attraction.[26] Unlike other acts of discipline, which focused on maintaining a community pure in its behaviour, punishment of members who married outside was intended to keep the religious community pure not so much in its behaviour but rather in its beliefs and affiliations. Mixed marriages threatened the unity

23 See App. 4. I have counted Jürgen Weeps, Lucia Weeps, Magdaleen Mostert, Eernst Hinsbergen, Claes Jansen, Jacob van Noorden, Jacob Jacobs de Vlieger (around 1674), Maria Harmens, Harmen Harmens Elking, Maria Aeriens, Anna Marya Jacobs, Beerent Wynands, Jan Alberts, Prientge Albers, Jacob Willems Beerens and Claes Hendricks.

24 See App. 4.

25 StAHbg/MG, 147, vol. 1, pp. 7, 13, 25, 61, 121, 131 and 142.

26 See the data summarized at the beginning of App. 4.

of the community, and also potentially raised questions regarding the Mennonites' adherence to the legal prohibition in Altona against proselytizing. Historically, strict marital avoidance of unbelieving spouses had also been a characteristic setting apart the early Mennonites from several other groups of mid-sixteenth-century Anabaptists. By the mid-seventeenth century, however, many groups of Mennonites, including those in Hamburg and Altona, had started to relax the uncompromising stand of their forebears. The actions of ordinary Mennonite men and women were a major reason.

Geeritt Roosen reflected on this break with the past in a manuscript from March 1682 on mixed marriage.[27] Roosen began his long, untitled manuscript by noting that Mennonite attitudes towards mixed marriage varied greatly and that he wanted to advocate the scriptural and moderate position on this issue. Roosen cited the violent rhetoric of Deuteronomy 7: 1–3 as the biblical evidence used by strict, isolationist Mennonites (unnamed in the text) who interpreted these verses as a divine injunction against marriage with all non-believers and non-members. These more extreme co-religionists even considered it a sin punishable by expulsion from the communion of the godly to marry other Mennonites who did not hold beliefs they felt to be orthodox. Roosen, on the other hand, argued that this passage from Deuteronomy had to be placed in its historical context to grasp its meaning. The Israelites had not been forbidden to marry heathens of all descriptions but rather only those heathens whom God had specifically declared unworthy.[28] Kings David and Solomon, for example, had both had heathen wives.[29] Solomon had fallen into disfavour in the eyes of God, but this was only because he had worshipped the gods of his wives. Thus, only those who married outside the community of believers and then strayed from God's ways should be punished with expulsion; marriage outside God's chosen community itself was not grounds for divine displeasure.[30]

Although Roosen refused in his 1682 manuscript to reject all mixed marriages unconditionally, he also refused to acknowledge non-Mennonite religious beliefs and practices as fully Christian. When he was a teenager, Catholic-affiliated armies had destroyed the Mennonite settlement at Fresenburg near Oldesloe in Holstein during the Danish phase of the Thirty Years War. Although he did not refer to events of that war, his list of

27 StAHbg/MG, 248, vol. 2, '. . . over het soo genoemde buytentrouwen . . .'.

28 Ibid., fol. [5]^{v}. This point was emphasized by a later editor.

29 Roosen did not address the possibility that his example opened him up to charges of advocating polygamy. For his official statement against polygamy, written much later, see page 25 of his confession of faith included in G. Roosen, *Unschuld und Gegen-Bericht*.

30 StAHbg/MG, 248, vol. 2, '. . . over het soo genoemde buytentrouwen . . .', fols [7]^{v}–[8]^{r} and [10]^{v}.

Catholic crimes in the 1682 manuscript was long: the waging of wars, killing, raping, pillaging, mistreating Mennonites and generally acting contrary to God's will by worshipping images or dead saints, swearing oaths and baptizing infants.[31] While his attitude towards Catholics was openly hostile, his stance towards other Protestant groups was strongly ambivalent. He saw them as the heathens of the Old Testament who behaved in ungodly ways (like the Catholics) but who had not been entirely rejected by God. They were less Christian, but, unlike the godless Catholics with whom marriage was out of the question, marriages with members of other Protestant churches could be Christian marriages, provided the Mennonite partner continued to fear God and live a morally blameless life.

To illustrate the unhappy consequences of the ban too strictly applied, Roosen related a story in 1682 about a young Mennonite woman who had come to Hamburg several decades earlier (sometime around the end of the sixteenth or beginning of the seventeenth century) to escape persecution in the Netherlands.[32] She was soon employed as a servant for a non-Mennonite family, who encouraged her to find a husband. She took the advice and married a Lutheran or Calvinist but remained true to her own faith. Upon discovering that there was a Mennonite community nearby in Holstein, she visited it in order to ask to be accepted as a member. She was questioned about her lifestyle, and, when it was discovered that her husband was not a Mennonite, she was placed under the ban, which could be lifted only upon the death or conversion of her husband. Both husband and wife refused to give up their own beliefs. Because of her dilemma, the faithful Mennonite became extremely depressed. In keeping with his position, Roosen asserted that she should never have been treated this way.

In the March 1682 text, Roosen never explained the concrete reason for his interest in mixed marriages. The parallels between the young Anabaptist woman's story and the case of Jürgen Borkofsky are so striking that a connection is likely.[33] In May 1682 Borkofsky appeared before congregational leaders together with his wife and their children. He was asking to be admitted as a member of the Flemish congregation. The family had arrived from Danzig, where the couple had met and married about twenty years earlier. Borkofsky was already well known to Roosen and the other leaders of the Altona congregation; leaders and congregants may have known about his request for membership before he applied officially in May 1682. In 1656 he had been baptized in nearby Glückstadt by Jan

31 Ibid., fol. [3]^{v}.

32 The text of the story is found ibid., fols [8]^{v}–[9]^{v}.

33 For references to this and other similar cases, see App. 6.

Sievers, who later (between 1674 and his death in 1681) was a part-time preacher in the Flemish congregation. In 1658 Borkofsky moved to Königsberg in Prussia and was sent a transfer of membership (*aenwys*) by the Altona Flemish preachers in 1663 so that he could join another Mennonite congregation there. From the time of his baptism until his arrival in Prussia he remained a bachelor. Sometime during or after 1664, Joost van Steen, a one-time preacher in Altona, wrote to Altona mentioning that Borkofsky had been banned in Königsberg because he had married a Lutheran woman. When Borkofsky arrived in Altona or Hamburg he was still married to his first (Lutheran) wife, and we can reasonably assume that some people objected to his inclusion as a congregational member.

Strengthening the assumption that there was opposition in the congregation to Jürgen Borkofsky's membership, as well as more generally to the practice of mixed marriage, is evidence of the influx into the Flemish congregation of socially more conservative Mennonites from the Pieter Jansz Twisck and House Buyer congregations. These groups in Hamburg and Altona had probably never been large, and they probably lacked strong leadership in the last half of the seventeenth century. By the 1680s these two congregations were dispersing and many of their members were joining the larger Flemish congregation. The busiest period of defections from these two congregations to the Flemish congregation was between 1668 and 1675. During these years eight members of the Old Frisian congregation[34] and thirteen members of the House Buyer congregation[35] joined their Flemish neighbours. Seven of these defections took place in 1671. Equally rich in defections was the year 1682, when eight House Buyers transferred their allegiances to the Flemish.[36] This was also the same year Jürgen Borkofsky asked for membership among the Flemish and Geeritt Roosen wrote his manuscript on mixed marriage. Open and closed visions of Mennonite community were coming face to face.

The voices in favour of strict and closed boundaries did not win the day. In the last half of the seventeenth century there were at least eight newcomers (including Borkofsky) to the Flemish congregation who were granted membership or even baptized, despite their previous marriages to non-Mennonites.[37] Borkofsky was accepted as a member in April 1683, even though his wife did not convert. Two years later he returned to Prussia with a recommendation given him by Altona's Flemish preachers.

Leaders like Geeritt Roosen were not only willing to accept previously married newcomers as members, even though they had non-Mennonite

34 StAHbg/MG, 147, vol. 1, pp. 66, 67, 73, 82, 84 and 93.

35 Ibid., pp. 65, 66, 68, 70, 72, 73, 75 and 79.

36 Ibid., pp. 108, 109 and 111.

37 See App. 6.

spouses, but also were sometimes tolerant of Mennonites already baptized locally who then married non-members. In 1676 Geeritt Roosen's son Paul married Elsken Kuels in one of Hamburg's Lutheran churches. Naturally, he had not told his parents of his intentions. Despite his actions, he does not seem to have been expelled, although it is more than likely that his father or other congregational leaders confronted him privately. In any event, he remained a member of the Flemish congregation and his wife eventually accepted membership in the congregation through baptism in 1685. In other words, at the time Roosen wrote the manuscript on *buitentrouw* in 1682 one of his daughters-in-law was at least nominally a Lutheran.

Another issue around conversion and mixed marriage involved Dompelaars. For example, Elsken Roosen, the daughter of Geeritt Roosen's cousin Paul Karstens Roosen, married twice, first in 1678 to the Dompelaar widower Claes Dircksen and the second time in November 1681 to the Dompelaar Dominicus Kipping. Neither marriage was conducted by Flemish preachers (that is, they were *buitentrouwe*), but neither time was she disciplined. In early April 1682, almost exactly one month after Geeritt Roosen wrote his manuscript on mixed marriage, Kipping became a member of the Flemish congregation. Between 1662 and the beginning of the eighteenth century, a total of fifteen former Dompelaars rejoined the Flemish congregation.[38] The most active period during which Dompelaars returned to the Flemish congregation was between 1675 and 1677 when there were six transfers. By contrast, except for the initial wave of defections in 1648, the only other case in which the Flemish congregation lost a member to a competing local co-religionist congregation during the second half of the seventeenth century was Isaac Stockman's defection to the immersionists in 1661.

Following Stockman's defection, young men and women from both congregations met frequently enough that some decided to marry, despite the institutional boundary separating them. Until 1686 all marriages between a Flemish and a Dompelaar were conducted by a Dompelaar preacher. The first Flemish–Dompelaar marriage recorded by Geeritt Roosen in the congregational membership book was Hester van Eeck's union with the Dompelaar Abraham de Voß in 1668. She was allowed to remain a member of both congregations. Her case was not particularly unusual. Before mid-year 1686 there had been seven marriages involving a Flemish member which had been conducted by Dompelaar leaders.[39] The last of these took place on 5 April 1686 between Dirick Boudt and the Dompelaar Saara Coopman.

---

[38] StAHbg/MG, 147, vol. 1, pp. 53, 58, 74, 83, 88, 89, 96, 131, 136, 139 and 141.

[39] See App. 4: 1668, 1676 (twice), 1678, 1681, 1685 and 1686.

When Geeritt Roosen wrote a second manuscript on mixed marriages in June 1686,[40] he was, judging from events at the time, almost certainly preoccupied with the issue of Dompelaar–Flemish marriages. This second manuscript had the same basic message as the earlier one from 1682: marrying a non-member was not in itself a sufficient cause for expulsion from the congregation. Roosen did not, however, simply recopy his earlier manuscript. For example, he avoided the attacks on the ungodliness of other Christian churches, perhaps because he had a Lutheran daughter-in-law at the time (Elsken Kuels). If his interest in 1686 was focused on the Dompelaars, there would also have been little reason to attack the behaviour of other Christian groups.

As happened soon after Roosen's 1682 manuscript on mixed marriage with the case of Jürgen Borkofsky, a significant event in the congregation's social life took place only a short while after the composition of Roosen's June 1686 manuscript. On 26 September 1686 Abraham Coopman and Gardruydt van Werle were married in the Flemish church in Altona. Coopman was a Dompelaar and van Werle a Flemish Mennonite. This was the first marriage of its kind officially approved by the congregation, and it is probably not coincidental that it took place just a few months after Roosen had released his second manuscript on *buitentrouw*. The arrangement was easier for Flemish preachers to participate in because Abraham had explained beforehand that he was in agreement with their principles of faith. In 1689 he left the Dompelaar congregation and joined the Flemish.[41]

The van Werle–Coopman marriage was not the last of its kind.[42] There was also the 1702 marriage of Harmen Harmens Grouwel[43] and the Dompelaar Magdalena Stockman. Grouwel's relatives, like Stockman's, were also nonconformists from the point of view of the Flemish congregational council. Isaac Harmens Grouwel – probably Harmen Grouwel's father, brother or uncle – had left Altona and Hamburg soon after 1654 and settled eventually in Lübeck, where he became a Quaker.[44] He returned in 1685 to Altona, where he was married in November to a member of the Flemish congregation in an officially approved marriage.

40 StAHbg/MG, 246b, 'Bedenckinge oft teegenstellinge van het straffen der Buytengetroude door den Ban en afsonderinge.'

41 StAHbg/MG, 147, vol. 1, p. 131.

42 Roosen, *Geschichte der Mennoniten-Gemeinde*, i, p. 66, wrote that the marriage between Lücke Hingsberg and the Friedrichstadt Remonstrant Symon Nickel was the first officially approved marriage to a non-member, but this marriage was performed on 29 September 1702, many years after the 1686 marriage and even several months after the second such Flemish–Dompelaar marriage. It was also performed elsewhere, probably in Friedrichstadt. See StAHbg/MG, 147, vol. 1, p. 103; and StAHbg/MG, 6, vol. 1, p. 16.

43 StAHbg/MG, 147, vol. 1, p. 115.

44 Ibid., p. 13.

Roosen made no special mention of this union when he entered it in the membership book, which suggests either that Isaac Grouwel had convinced congregational leaders that he had broken off his connections with the Quakers, or his Quaker connections were forgotten. After the marriage, Isaac Grouwel returned with his bride to Lübeck. Like Isaac, Harmen Grouwel lived in or around Lübeck and travelled to Altona to be married. After the members of the congregation had approved of his union with Magdalena Stockman, the couple was married by one of the Flemish preachers on 25 June 1702. After the marriage, Grouwel returned to Lübeck with his new wife. Then they disappeared from the record. The Grouwel–Stockman marriage, like earlier mixed marriages not approved by Flemish preachers, was part of a long history of improving relations between members of Flemish and Dompelaar congregations. After the 1660s there were no more pamphlet wars in which the old animosities were reopened. The congregations remained separate, but, as the examples of defections and marriages show, contacts between individual Dompelaar and Flemish congregation members continued.

This leads to a major point: as much as or more than the official actions of leaders, it was the ongoing and often difficult to follow actions of ordinary members of the congregation which set the agenda with regard to marriages and community boundaries. When Geeritt Roosen wrote his manuscripts on mixed marriage, he was responding to pressure from the rank and file; their behaviour placed limits on the kinds of decisions that would have been possible to adopt. The 1680s marked a turning point in official attitudes as expressed by Geeritt Roosen, who, as the senior leader, had a great deal of moral authority useful for swaying the opinions of conservative congregants. But he was merely catching up with, not forming, a significant strand of opinion among his Mennonite peers.

Long-term trends

The kinds of social relationships that developed as a result of the behaviour of young couples had a slow but transformative effect on the congregation.[45] Instead of a closed community of homogenous believers, the Mennonite congregation was developing into an increasingly diverse and overlapping set of communities. It included citizens of Hamburg and subjects of the Danish crown; it included men and women born in the Netherlands, as well as those who knew no other world than their northern

[45] The trends discussed in this section and chapter were not unique to Mennonite communities. See David Sorkin, 'Enlightenment and Emancipation: German Jewry's Formative Age in Comparative Perspective', in Todd Endelman (ed.), *Comparing Jewish Societies* (Ann Arbor, 1997), pp. 89–112.

German birthplace; and it included merchants and artisans who worked almost exclusively with Mennonite colleagues, while others worked frequently with non-Mennonites. Given the confessionally diverse character of the urban setting in Hamburg and Altona, it was also inevitable that Mennonites would meet people of different faiths. Family life, rather than providing a guarantee of Mennonite homogeneity to counterbalance these social influences, could serve to complicate boundaries. Not only were the once clear boundaries between Dompelaars and Flemish being eroded through marriage, but the cultural gulf between Mennonites and other Protestants was also being brought into question by families that straddled the officially clear lines of division. An increasing number of families with members in the congregation were of mixed confessional affiliation. Sometimes a family's tradition of remaining part of multiple confessional communities extended over at least two generations. For example, in 1678 Jan Tomsen married a Lutheran woman, but all indications suggest that he stayed a member of the Mennonite congregation. Approximately two decades later, his son of the same name, a baptized member of the congregation, also married a Lutheran woman. Even in cases where a Mennonite converted to another Protestant church, ties with the Mennonite congregation were not necessarily broken. For example, Jacob Jacobs de Vlieger married a Calvinist and converted in the 1670s, but his son of the same name remained active in the congregation. After his baptism as a Mennonite, he married a Calvinist woman in 1691. But rather than converting as his father had done, the younger de Vlieger convinced his wife to join the Flemish congregation.[46]

In short, by at least the end of the seventeenth century the Mennonite congregation was not a closed community but rather was made up of a convergence of multiple social spheres. This reality made the ideal of a pure confessional community difficult to maintain. Geeritt Roosen's manuscripts from the 1680s were early pragmatic attempts on the part of leaders to come to terms with the challenges posed by mixed marriages.

The generation of leaders after Roosen initially tried to hold more conservatively to the old ideal of a confessionally pure community. The theme of discipline and mixed marriage was discussed several times throughout the eighteenth century. In the first half of that century, preachers continued to try to discourage congregants from marrying outsiders, but at the same time they were slowly and reluctantly diminishing their authority to punish those who married non-Mennonites.[47] As had been the case in the seventeenth century, pressure from rank-and-file congregants

---

[46] See App. 4.

[47] See entries from 1720, 1750 and 1771 in the protocol of the congregational council: StAHbg/MG, 6, vol. 1, pp. 53, 162, 256 and 268.

was channelling and forcing their decisions. In the years from 1700 to 1750 there were approximately thirty-five confessionally mixed marriages, about the same number of *buitentrouwe* as had taken place in the last half of the seventeenth century.[48]

Confessionally mixed marriages became more frequent in the last half of the eighteenth century. In 1767 Jacob Lemmerts was married in his home by the Mennonite preacher Abraham Wynands.[49] The private location for the ceremony was in itself not particularly noteworthy, for in the eighteenth century marriages regularly took place in private in Hamburg. However, in this case the ceremony may not have been allowed to take place in the Flemish church, even though the Mennonite preacher Abraham Wynands agreed to preside over the event, for the bride was a Reformed woman. In 1780 Dina Magdalena Beets, the daughter of the local Flemish preacher Gerrit Beets, married the Lutheran Jens Georg Eggert von Schoon. The Mennonites' traditional privileges from the Danish crown were no longer interpreted as an impediment against such mixed marriages. By the 1790s Eggert von Schoon had become a high-ranking official in Altona's administration.[50] At about the same time, in 1791, Gerard Peters de Voss married a Lutheran woman, Anna Margot Knaak, probably in a Lutheran church. She did not become a Mennonite. Their interconfessional marriage is significant because Gerard de Voss was twice elected as a deacon in the Flemish congregation in the early nineteenth century.[51] Just two years after Gerard and Anna Margot were married, Eliesabeth Peters Rings married a Lutheran man. It was probably the first such event to take place in public in Altona's Flemish Mennonite church. Before the marriage ceremony, the congregational council had received the approval of Altona's Lutheran officials, who already had a colleague (Eggert von Schoon) with a Mennonite wife.[52] In all these cases, the Mennonite spouse remained a member of the congregation. In short, by the end of the eighteenth century the leaders of the Mennonite congregation did little to discourage interconfessional marriages.

At the same time that official efforts to curb the frequency of confessionally mixed marriages were declining, there was a countervailing

---

48 The numbers for the first half of the eighteenth century, unlike those for the later seventeenth century, include no Dompelaar–Flemish marriages. These were no longer a factor in the eighteenth century, when the Dompelaar congregation lost its vitality. The source for the numbers is StAHbg/MG, 147, vol. 1.

49 StAHbg/MG, 147, vol. 1, p. 281.

50 Ibid., p. 332. Also see Bolten, *Historische Kirchen-Nachrichten*, i, p. 299.

51 StAHbg/MG, 147, vol. 1, p. 362.

52 Ibid., p. 342. By the late eighteenth century, the Mennonites were submitting proclamations of marriage to civic authorities in Hamburg. Around the middle of the century, they were transmitting similar records to the Danish crown in Altona. See StAHbg/MG, 149; and StAHbg/MG, 175.

trend towards extreme endogamy. A small number of wealthy eighteenth-century Mennonite families formed closed marriage circles. Some branches of the Roosen, Kramer and de Voss families were so closely interrelated that they really formed one family with three names.[53] For example, Berend I Roosen's eldest daughter Sara and his nephew Pieter de Voss were not only first cousins but also husband and wife. In turn, their son Lucas married his first cousin, Maria Kramer, the daughter of Berend's daughter Elisabeth. In other words, Lucas Pieters de Voss was Berend's heir by birth and marriage. In addition to the Roosen, Kramer and de Voss families, the van der Smissen and Linnich families formed this kind of closed family network.[54] The strategy of inbreeding helped keep prosperous family businesses in relatively central control, as well as helping to maintain the families' Mennonite character. These families were enormously wealthy and often held prominent positions in congregational government. In the eighteenth century, eleven members of the Kramer, Linnich, Roosen, van der Smissen and de Voss families held a congregational office.[55] For them, the spheres of family, business and church were intimately intertwined. These families formed a bourgeois elite which set itself apart from the Lutheran mainstream and the Mennonite rank and file. Therefore, even though these families tried to preserve the old link between kinship and confessional affiliation, they too are evidence for the growing complexity and transformation of Mennonite social life.

Conclusion

In 1711 a large procession of mourners gathered to celebrate the life of Geeritt Roosen. Roosen had died that year, just a few months short of his one-hundredth birthday. He had served his congregation since 1649, first as a deacon and then as a preacher. In that time he had not only contributed significantly to the development of Mennonite life in northern Germany, but he had also won friends from other confessional backgrounds. The funeral procession of 193 pairs[56] was almost certainly larger than Roosen's congregation, and one of the men who read a eulogy at the funeral was a Reformed preacher from Altona, Laurentius Steversloot.[57] In his will,

53 See Karla Hülsenberg, 'Untersuchungen über geschlossene Heiratskreise einiger hervorragender Hamburger Familien 1770–1840' (thesis, Pädagogische Hochschule, Göttingen, 1960), on record at StAHbg.

54 See the graphic in Münte, *Das Altonaer Handlungshaus*, between pp. 22 and 23.

55 StAHbg/MG, 147, vol. 1, pp. 182, 213, 219, 223, 229, 248, 262, 301, 308, 325, 351 and 358.

56 Ibid., p. 3.

57 The eulogies are recorded in Hermannus Schijn and Gerardus Maatschoen, *Geschiedenis der Mennoniten*, 3 vols (Amsterdam, 1743–5), iii, pp. 415–31.

Roosen granted a total of 1,000 marks *lübsch* – a significant sum – to the local Lutheran parish church, St Michaelis, its guest house, and the local plague and discipline houses.[58]

Are these examples of Mennonite assimilation? Perhaps, but the concept of assimilation should be used with caution, for it might be taken simplistically to mean that the Mennonites alone were changing and adapting. A few comments are in order. First, while it is often convenient to speak of 'the' Mennonites as though they were one cohesive group, the use of such a term should not be allowed to obscure the complexities of Mennonite life outlined in this and previous chapters. The Mennonite sphere was really a conglomeration of communities, factions and networks, and this diverse overlapping of social spheres was becoming more and more complex with time. Further examples from the eighteenth and nineteenth centuries include the involvement of Mennonites in Enlightenment and Protestant revivalist associations.[59] Secondly, not only Mennonite society but also European society generally was changing. At the same time that young Mennonites were choosing Reformed or Lutheran spouses with increasing frequency, secular as well as clerical authorities were slowly abandoning the intolerant attitudes which their predecessors had held towards earlier generations of Mennonites. Old legal limitations on Mennonite participation in public life in Hamburg were finally removed in the nineteenth century, but the transformation of attitudes had begun earlier.[60] On both sides (Mennonite and non-Mennonite) of an increasingly blurry boundary, young couples and their elders were adapting their behaviours to accommodate neighbours who in an era gone by would have been considered 'heretics'. Faced with a slow multiplication of social spheres open to congregational members in the diverse and multiconfessional setting of urban northern Germany, it became ever more difficult for congregational leaders in Hamburg and Altona to enforce standards of Mennonite identity either through discipline or education.

---

58 See StAHbg/MG, 193/14. B.C. Roosen reported (*Gerhard Roosen*, p. 55) that Geeritt Roosen had donated the crown of the church tower to St Michaelis when it was being rebuilt in the 1660s. His source was almost certainly Bolten, *Historische Kirchen-Nachrichten*, i, p. 293. I have found no independent corroboration for this information. It is probably based on a confusion of Berend Roosen (1705–88), a leading eighteenth-century Flemish deacon, with Geeritt Roosen. In 1778 Berend donated the 'Knopf und Flügel' to St Michaelis. The church had burned down in 1750 when the tower was struck by lightning. See Geffcken, *Die große St Michaeliskirche in Hamburg*, pp. 31–2 and 81.

59 See M. Driedger, 'Gerrit Karsdorp'.

60 See Whaley, *Religious Toleration and Social Change*.

Conclusion: Public Controversy and Fixed versus Flexible Standards of Confessional Identity

'When people are wont to dispute and fight/ It is of the truth that they often lose sight.'[1] When the Dompelaar preacher Jacob Denner wrote this line in the 1730s, he was expressing a common eighteenth-century objection to polemical culture. Since the Middle Ages, polemics had been a frequently practised means of attacking and chastising the perceived enemies of truth. Although these aggressive habits never disappeared in the early modern period (and are still part of academic and political culture today), they were becoming, in the opinion of a growing number of the educated class, an increasingly dysfunctional means of defending 'the truth'. One major reason for this rethinking of the value of polemics was the sixteenth-century divisions in Christendom, which saw the emergence of several powerful and interregional church blocs, each claiming the exclusive right to represent the same truth. How could 'the truth' be so fractured? To cope with this kind of problem, early modern philosophers, theologians, preachers and reformers proposed a number of alternative means of truth-seeking. On the one hand, there was the irenic spiritualism preferred by groups like the late seventeenth-century Pietists, and, on the other hand, there was the eclecticism, rationalism and empiricism preferred by eighteenth-century Enlightenment *philosophes*.[2] Denner's attitudes were very much in tune with the Pietist culture of his day.

Although some people were deeply dissatisfied with the culture of controversy, few in public life, whatever their confessional affiliation, could avoid it. In fact, the character of groups like the Pietists in early modern Lutheran Germany was shaped decisively by controversy, for their earliest years were marked by heated exchanges between moderate reformers, socio-religious radicals and defenders of the orthodox status quo. Even the Pietists' attempts to reform polemical forms of communication became a topic of controversy around the beginning of the eighteenth century.[3] And although they claimed publicly to be dissatisfied with polemical

1 Denner, *Christliche und erbauliche Betrachtungen*, p. 8: 'Durch vieles Zanken und Disputiren/ Thut man öfter die Wahrheit verlieren.'

2 Excellent recent studies of polemics, irenic reform, Pietism and the Enlightenment include Gierl, *Pietismus und Aufklärung*, and Müller, 'Irenik, eine Kommunikationsform'.

3 See Gierl, *Pietismus und Aufklärung*.

culture, leading Pietists like Johann Winckler in Hamburg did not hesitate to polemicize against non-Lutherans like the Mennonites (see Ch. 4). Jacob Denner, too, was the target of such Lutheran polemics. While he perhaps better than others avoided the temptation to become involved in heated public arguments with his enemies about 'the truth', his attitudes towards polemics were not shared by his Dompelaar predecessors, who had engaged energetically in debates with Flemish Mennonites in the 1660s (Ch. 2). Conflicts like the ones between the Flemish and Dompelaars, as well as between Mennonites and Lutherans, played key roles in the development of Mennonite identity, for the conflicts helped set 'us/them' boundaries.

In other words, Denner's claim about the truth – that controversy obscured it – does not apply to the history of collective, confessional identity. In fact, evidence supports the opposite – confessional identity was most fixed, clearest and most significant amid public controversies. However, while this is a major conclusion of my study, it is incomplete on its own. There is an equally important corollary: as controversies about group identity diminished, standards of identity became weaker or more flexible. Because people's lives could be affected greatly, more deserves to be said about the character of group identities as they fluctuated between a pole of fixed standards and a pole of flexible ones.[4]

I shall turn first to identity as it approached the pole of fixed standards. In addition to the Flemish–Dompelaar schism and Mennonite–Lutheran polemics, there are several other major examples from the preceding chapters of Mennonite identity formed and articulated in the context of debate and conflict. These include the trials of Hans Plus and the Lamist–Zonist division in the 1660s. Among the ideal-typical characteristics common to these cases are tendencies towards centralization, control, abstraction, resistance and escalation.

To understand the tendency towards centralization, the relationship between leaders and rank-and-file believers is worthy of note. Amid conflict and controversy, leaders played a central role as spokesmen or definers of identity. Usually, the men involved in defining Mennonite identity held a position in a Mennonite congregation, but others who played important roles were governmental lawyers or clergymen in non-Mennonite churches. These men acted as experts with the authority to speak on behalf of the law, the state-sanctioned church, all 'true' believers, or 'the truth'. As a consequence, ordinary Mennonites like Hans Plus in the early 1660s or Mennonites in favour of arming merchant ships in the mid-1690s were

[4] My thoughts about the varying strengths of collective identity have been shaped in their initial stages by Bruno Latour's discussion of 'hard' versus 'soft' facts in the day-to-day practice of techno-science. See Latour, *Science in Action: How to Follow Scientists and Engineers through Society* (Cambridge, Mass., 1987).

pushed to the margins of activity; they were expected to conform to official standards set for them by others.

Through inaction more than active resistance, Hans Plus and the Mennonite merchants concerned about defence refused to meet the expectations of their respective legal and congregational spokesmen. Faced with uncooperative congregants, how could leaders enforce official standards? Direct coercion was seldom an option; even governments, which had the military resources to punish 'heretics', generally avoided using these resources against Mennonites after the late sixteenth century. Within Mennonite congregations, where, at least in theory, congregants too had a voice in the governance of collective life, the prospects of successful coercion in matters of identity formation were especially difficult. At best, leaders interested in establishing a more centralized brand of control could work to persuade congregants and channel their actions and beliefs. The means they had to do this included limiting access to influential offices or resources like land and money. Another means that deserves special attention is the use of texts.

Texts played a crucial role when representatives strove to fix standards of identity. The Flemish–Dompelaar schism, the War of the Lambs, the trials of Hans Plus, Geeritt Roosen's campaigns in the 1690s to ward off Lutheran polemics and chastise lax congregants – during each of these developments Mennonite and non-Mennonite representatives alike left a substantial paper trail. Compared with oral forms of communication, textual forms carried additional authority, for they could be reproduced, studied and transported. Thus they promised to have an impact on hearts and minds that would last longer and reach a greater number of people in scattered locations. A useful hypothesis about texts which addressed issues of group identity is that they, like the ones written during the controversies described in this book, were almost invariably written in response to some crisis or controversy, even though the author may have obscured those particular circumstances. Two examples are Tieleman Jansz van Braght's *Martyrs' Mirror* (1660), written during the prelude to the Zonist–Lamist schism (Ch. 3), and Geeritt Roosen's *Unschuld und Gegen-Bericht* (1702), written in response to Lutheran polemics (Ch. 4). Both texts were influential in non-controversial circumstances after the deaths of their authors, and in neither text is there much mention of the circumstances in which they were written; therefore, the controversies which preoccupied their authors faded from memory before the texts themselves were forgotten. However, for the historian, it is important to put texts about identity back into the concrete and particular conflict-ridden contexts of their creation.

The relationship between concrete circumstances and abstract, universal claims is another significant feature of standards of collective identity which representatives tried to solidify, strengthen and control. The reason it is significant is that it is crucial for understanding how controversy encouraged clarity of group standards. When spokesmen worked to define 'the' Mennonites, they had particular goals and interests: in the case of lawyers, winning cases for their clients; in the case of Lutheran clergymen, lobbying secular officials to expel all nonconformists from their districts, as well as warning parishioners about the dangers of unbelief; and in the case of Mennonite preachers, defending against accusations and libels from confessional opponents, as well as calling for moral reform and cohesion on the part of all congregational members. Yet, although they were responding to concrete circumstances, those who claimed to define Mennonites tended to express themselves in artificially clear terms, because they wanted to transform society from the way it was to the way they felt it should be.

The desire and pressure to speak of identity in absolute terms was further encouraged by a proliferation of competing abstract standards in certain formal circumstances. For example, when pamphleteers made claims in print or when lawyers made arguments in court, they were expecting – even provoking – opposition. One clear position was juxtaposed with another clear but contrary position. The competing positions generally became more explicit and more entrenched the more their respective advocates fought with one another. As a consequence, the disagreements escalated and became ever more difficult to resolve. Because disputes forced participants to elaborate on their positions, periods of schism are always points at which it is easy for historians to find a multitude of clear statements about standards of confessional identity. This applies equally well to developments on a grand historical scale (like the Protestant–Catholic schisms of the Reformation era) and to those on a more limited scale (like the schisms between the Zonists and Lamists or Dompelaars and Flemish).

Although those times when representatives tried to formulate fixed standards provide dramatic, easy-to-find case studies of identity, they are only a part of the story of confessional identity. Following every peak of controversy there was also a broad valley of quiet. In other words, high points of public interest in group definitions did not reflect the totality of group life. Confessional controversies are easy for historians to focus on after the fact but are only part of a complete picture of past social interactions. While leaders sometimes tried to control standards of identity in a centralized way, the time, energy and material resources required to contend with opponents were often great, and for this reason representatives' activities tended to diminish with time. Group definitions were, to quote the seventeenth-century philosopher Thomas Hobbes, 'relative to a representer',[5] and representers or spokesmen were not always at work. Attempts by spokesmen, representatives, definers and categorizers to fix the significance of confessional identities once and for all were never more than attempts. They were intermittent, episodic, uneven, short-lived and fleeting. The official and public activity of defining Mennonites and Mennonitism had a dynamic and intermittent character.

In ideal-typical terms, collective identity in its flexible mode was the opposite of fixed identity. Whenever leaders weakened their attempts to control standards of identity centrally, several things happened. First, the rate of text production diminished. Secondly, representatives tended to treat others as complex individuals rather than as simple examples of abstract categories. Thirdly, participants tried to avoid rather than engage in controversies. Finally and most significantly for people's lives, group boundaries faded.

The history of the Dompelaars provides one of the best examples of group boundaries fading when central control of standards of identity weakened. Unlike his predecessors, who had built a new congregation in contradistinction to their Flemish neighbours, Denner tried to build bridges between groups rather than defend his inherited territory. He saw himself as a Christian, not an Anabaptist Christian. Right belief did matter to him, but part of his belief system included an aversion to distinct confessional boundaries; the truth, in his view, knew no human boundaries. Largely because he neglected to maintain and defend the integrity of institutions for which he was responsible, membership fell and the Dompelaars slipped into insignificance as a distinct group. Without clear boundaries, the group disappeared.

By contrast, Flemish Mennonite leaders in Hamburg and Altona paid much more attention to the maintenance of group boundaries. However, this does not mean that they never relaxed standards. During the Lamist leader Galenus Abrahamsz's 1678 visit to northern Germany, the Flemish of Hamburg and Altona decided not to delve too deeply into the issues which had led to schism in Amsterdam over a decade earlier, even though they had sided with Abrahamsz's Zonist opponents. Having met the charismatic Abrahamsz in person, it became more difficult for the Flemish to think of him in the unfriendly terms preferred by his detractors. While they never abandoned their Zonist allegiances during the early modern period, Mennonite leaders in Hamburg and Altona did moderate their attitude towards rival Mennonite factions. Whereas the divide between Zonists and Lamists had been a defining aspect of Mennonite identity in the 1660s and 1670s, these boundaries were allowed to blur with time. Formally, the two groups remained distinct, but in practice the distinctions

5 Hobbes, *Leviathan*, ch. 41.

became weaker and weaker. While the relaxation of group standards by no means had to result in the dissolution of a group, it did result in the transformation, however subtle and periodic or pronounced and long-lived, of the group's character.

At least one misunderstanding of flexible confessional identity is possible. Transformations in the direction of 'weaker' or more flexible standards of confessional identity should not be misinterpreted to mean that religion and belief were disappearing as factors in people's lives. The concept of flexible standards of identity points only to the periodically diminishing importance of strictly defined confessional religious standards. Other expressions of religious belief such as privately held convictions could continue to be central parts of people's lives at times when official partisan standards weakened.

While many of the examples above suggest how the varying intensity of representatives' interest in confessional standards could affect the lives of leaders and common believers alike, a little more is worth saying about the subject. On the one hand, the less attention spokesmen paid to defining or maintaining standards of congregational membership, the greater the freedom of public conduct available to congregation members became. On issues around which standards had been allowed to become more flexible, individuals could choose more or less for themselves whether or not to follow confessional standards in the course of their public lives. They were not forced in any particular direction. As a hypothesis, we can say that for a good part of their lives Mennonite congregational members, and other kinds of believers too, simply went about their lives without measuring themselves against strict confessional standards. Hans Plus can serve as an example. During the years of his trials he went about his business activities, travelling between Hamburg and Russia in armed merchant ships. Outside of the lawyers' and judges' offices as well as before and after his trial Plus was a 'Mennonite', but only in an inexact, informal, flexible sense. We can presume he attended sermons and other congregational events, at least during those times when he was in Altona. For the most part, however, he could interpret the meaning of his Mennonitism as he wished to suit his circumstances. Especially in the multiconfessional, mercantile, urban settings of Altona and Hamburg, it was difficult for group representatives to enforce standardized patterns of confessional behaviour. When direct monitoring diminished in intensity, the possibilities of individual flexibility increased. In turn, the freedom of action which believers enjoyed in the relative absence of regulation could have important consequences for leaders. An excellent example is the marriages of young Mennonites to members of other churches, which helped slowly to erode once clearer and more rigid boundaries separating Mennonites from their non-Mennonite host society.

Conversely, the more attention spokesmen paid to defining or maintaining standards of belief and behaviour around a particular issue, the more limited became the freedom of public conduct available to congregational members with regard to that issue. Actions or statements which might earlier have been accepted with silence could suddenly be met with open and hardened disapproval. At these times, conflicts between principle and practice were most likely, for contemporaries interpreted an individual's complex existence first and foremost in terms of abstract categories and strict expectations.

In this Conclusion and in the study as a whole I have given examples of the contingent, dynamic, emergent, situational nature of official standards of Mennonite identity. By thinking about confession in terms of the distinction between fixed and flexible standards, the historian is less likely to reduce early modern life to a constant function of confessional norms. From the point of view of the individual men and women confronted with confessional standards, confession cannot be a concept which describes an epoch unproblematically. Rather, together with familial, ethnic, professional and political affiliations, it was one of a number of possible sets of social categories and priorities which historical actors could use in the early modern period – and thereafter – to ascribe public identities to themselves and others. During the 'confessional age', individuals and groups did not always nor necessarily define themselves using categories of confessional affiliation. It is important to focus attention on the processes of entrenching institutional life and codifying moral standards – that is, times when collective identity was most pronounced and best articulated. But if we focus on these processes alone, then we risk the danger of producing an artificial and even distorted picture of the importance of confessional religion (whether Calvinist, Catholic, Jewish, Lutheran or Mennonite) in early modern Europe.[6] When studying institutional and confessional religion, we should not forget to investigate its boundaries and weak points. These boundaries and weak points become clearest when we examine the daily lives of individual believers, for whom official, confessional standards of identity did not always have the permanent, enduring, absolute significance that church leaders *sometimes* wanted them to have.

6 A recent study which emphasizes a similar point is Frank Fätkenheuer, 'Konfession im Alltag – Grenzen der Konfessionalisierungsforschung' (doctoral diss., Universität Göttingen, 2000).

Appendices

The following appendices are used most extensively in Chapter 7, but they are also referred to in Chapters 1 and 5. The data are taken from the Flemish Mennonite congregation's oldest surviving membership book (StAHbg/MG, 147, vol. 1). Unless otherwise noted, numbers in parentheses refer to pages in that source. Although entries in the membership book include notes about baptisms, marriages, offices held, discipline and deaths of individual believers, this information is organized in an unsystematic way. While references are sometimes made to events before 1655, the earliest entries in the membership book date from around the middle of the 1650s. In most cases, the lists below cover the period starting then and ending in 1700. During this period, Geeritt Roosen was the almost exclusive note-taker. After 1700 he became too old to continue the work of keeping records. His selection of information and comments gives the period until 1700 a certain continuity.

Appendix One
Flemish preachers in Hamburg and Altona

In addition to the membership book, sources for information about preachers are: StAHbg/MG, 261c; and Bolten, *Historische Kirchen-Nachrichten von der Stadt Altona*, i, pp. 291–308. Bolten's information is not always reliable. I have not included notes about visiting preachers; thus, Hendrik Teunis, whom Bolten included on his list, is not mentioned here. For a list of visiting preachers, see B.C. Roosen's notes at StAHbg/MG, 261c, 'leeraaren van doopsgesinde of Mennonitische gemeente, die als buitenleeraaren hier geweest zyn en gedient hebben'. More information about the congregation's first several preachers may exist (for example, on Hendrick Sicks, see StAHbg, Reichskammergericht, E15). Although there are no reliable dates available for their years of service, these first preachers are listed in the order in which they joined the congregation, as best as that is known. Bolten includes notes about the writings of individual preachers. For more bibliographical details, also see the *Mennonite Bibliography*.

Name	*Dates*	*Comments*
Cornelis Symons	?	Left for Groningen around 1624.
Michael Steffens	?	Ordained by Menno Simons.
Jan Barchmann	?	From Groningen. Later left for Glückstadt.
Hendrick Sicks	?	Came from a Lutheran background.
Jacob Beerens	?	According to Geeritt Roosen one of the leaders of the immersionist faction.
Jan Borchers	?	According to Geeritt Roosen another of the leaders of the immersionist faction.
Boudewyn Doom	?–1652	From Haarlem. He probably worked in Altona just before and during the disputes over baptism, communion and foot-washing. After his service in Altona he moved to Glückstadt, and from there back to Haarlem again by 1660.

Baerent Roelifs	??.09.1650–30.11.1659	From Alkmaar. Converted to Quakerism. (2)
Joost van Steen	??.05.1652–21.09.1656	From Elbing. Expelled from the congregation in 1656 for adultery. Later moved back to Prussia. (2)
Willem Wynantz	17.06.1655–21.12.1658	From Hamburg. He died unexpectedly young. (2)
Hilbrandt Harmens	20.10.1659–05.07.1665	From Campen. Returned to Campen because he could not earn a living in Altona or Hamburg.
Warner Jansen Colombier	08.04.1660–04.07.1664	Was a medical doctor. He died of plague. (46)
Geeritt Roosen	08.04.1660–20.11.1711	From Altona. Ordained on 06.07.1663 by Bastiaan van Weenigem. Last administered the sacraments in 1708. (3)
Jacob Jacobs de Vlieger	17.04.1664–21.04.1671	From Friedrichstadt. Forced to resign because of bankruptcy. He was previously a preacher in Friedrichstadt. (47, 57)
Jacob Symons de Vlieger	26.02.1665–22.05.1693	Died in office. (13)
Paul Geerling	20.09.1668–24.04.1669	From Friedrichstadt. Died in office.
Romke Gosling	31.10.1670–10.01.1694	From Friesland. Died in office. (68)
Ocke Pieters	26.12.1671–19.10.1685	From Emden. Ordained in July 1676 by Jan Sibes. Died in office. (59)
Jan de Lanoy	19.06.1681–10.03.1722	From Leiden. Ordained on 02.07.1699 by Dirck Symons Moriaans. Died in office. (97)
Pouwel Jansen Backer	19.06.1681–25.10.1694	From Amsterdam. Died in office. (100)
Pieter Verhelle	??.02.1694–29.04.1711	From Haarlem. Ordained on 02.07.1699 by Dirck Symons Moriaans. Died in office. (148)
Riewart Dircks	??.05.1697–16.08.1697	From Frisia. Left after he was charged with antitrinitarian views. (156)
Jacob Cornelis van Campen	??.08.1698–21.03.1716	From Haarlem. Ordained on 02.07.1699 by Dirck Symons Moriaans. Died in office. (158)

Appendix Two
Flemish deacons and deaconesses in Hamburg and Altona

Name	*Years of service*	*Comments*
Jan Jansen Schoemaecker	?–1657	(3)
Hendrik Pender	?–1658	(3)
Samuel Stockman	?–1661	Resigned in 1661. Changed allegiance to the Dompelaars. (3)
Jacob Symons de Vlieger	?–1665	Became a preacher in 1665. (13)
Maeycken Goverts	?–1672	One of the few women to hold a congregational office. She was very old when she died, for she had married in 1604. (19)
Harmen Goverts	?–1681	(3)
Geeritt Roosen	1649–60	(3)
Pieter Goverts	1657–74	(4, 12)
Jan Reeboom	1657–79	(3, 8)
Henderick de Jager	1670–81	(10)
Lucas Koenen	1670–88	(11)
Harmen Roosen	1670–89	In 1671 called to be a preacher, but declined to accept the position. In 1689 he resigned from his deaconship because of indebtedness. (17, 102)
Hans Harmens	1676–89	Disciplined for indebtedness in 1689. (10)
Hanss Pieters Goverts	1676–98	(56)
Eliass Janss Munster	1681–82	Died soon after arriving from Friedrichstadt. (106)
Hans Harmens Goverts	1682–97	(46)
Jan Harmens	1682–1701	(48)
Carel de Vlieger Senior	1689–95	(9)
Pieter Harmens Goverts	1689–96	(55)
Hans Geeritts Roosen	1695–1706	(69)
Carel de Vlieger Junior	1695–1710	(95)
Jan Reeboom Junior	1697–1707	(74)
Jan Elias Munster	1697–1716	(87)
Reyndert Jansen	1697–1729	(115)

Appendix Three
Approved marriages

To be counted as part of this list, a marriage must have been approved and conducted by Flemish preachers and have taken place locally. Occasionally, a visiting preacher led the ceremony. Sometimes the ceremony took place in Hamburg, for example, during wartime when the city's gates were closed and couples living there could not make the trip to Altona. Most often, however, at least during the last half of the seventeenth century, approved marriages were held in the Flemish congregation in Altona. Marriages not included are all those which occurred in another Mennonite congregation's jurisdiction, even though they may have involved members from Hamburg or Altona; and those marriages which, though conducted locally, were done without the knowledge or against the wishes of congregational members and/or leaders. For more detailed information, see Michael Driedger, 'Mennonitengemeinde von Hamburg und Altona', in Franz Schubert (ed.), *Trauregister aus den ältesten Kirchenbüchern Hamburgs: Von den Anfängen bis zum Jahre 1704* (Göttingen, 1997), pp. 85–92.

1660: 4
1661: 0
1662: 2
1663: 4
1664: 3
1665: 3
1666: 3
1667: 2
1668: 3
1669: 4
1670: 3
1671: 7
1672: 3
1673: 3
1674: 5
1675: 1
1676: 4
1677: 5
1678: 2
1679: 7
1680: 5
1681: 1
1682: 1
1683: 5
1684: 5
1685: 5
1686: 5
1687: 2
1688: 4
1689: 4
1690: 5
1691: 3
1692: 6
1693: 4
1694: 3
1695: 6
1696: 5
1697: 4
1698: 3
1699: 2
1700: 1

Appendix Four
Confessionally mixed marriages and most other unapproved marriages

With the exception of marriages between first cousins, this list includes all marriages which did not receive the approval of and were therefore not conducted by Flemish preachers. Most of these cases involved one partner who was already a baptized congregation member and another who did not belong to the congregation; in other words, they were confessionally mixed marriages (*buitentrouwe*). Names included in the first column belong to members of the Flemish congregation.

The data from Appendices 3, 4 and 5 are worth putting in some comparative statistical form. Between 1661 and 1700 the ratio of marriages which were approved and conducted locally (App. 3) to those which involved at least one congregation member and were not approved (Apps. 4 and 5) was about 3:1 (143:48). In the ten years between 1671 and 1680 forty-two couples were married locally by Mennonite preachers while there were twenty-two members who were married in nineteen unapproved ceremonies (a ratio of about 2:1). While the ratio here was lower than the overall pattern, approved marriages were still in the clear majority. Several years stand as exceptions. In 1664, 1681 and 1687 the ratio was 1:1, in 1678 it was 2:3 and in 1675 it was 1:5.

Name	*Date*	*Details*
Anna Kreecks	1663	Married a Calvinist. (33)
Jürgen Weeps	1664	Married a Lutheran. He converted to Lutheranism and was expelled. (39)
Lucia Weeps	1664	She was expelled after marrying a non-member. In 1671 she made peace with her father and the congregation. Sometime thereafter she left for Rotterdam with a recommendation from Altona's Flemish congregation. (51)
Magdaleen Mostert	1664	Expelled for marrying a non-member and for leading an extravagant lifestyle (that is, dancing and the like). (52)
Hester van Eeck	1668	Married to Abraham de Voß by the Dompelaars. She remained a member of the Flemish congregation. (34)
Eernst Hinsbergen	1671	Married a Lutheran and was excluded from communion. He became a Lutheran. (60)

Claes Jansen	1671	Married Jan de Vlieger's daughter in a Calvinist church, for which he was expelled from communion. In 1674 he was married to another person, this time in the Flemish congregation. (67 and 82)
Tryntgen Symons	1674	Married a non-member. In 1675 she left for Amsterdam. (79)
Jacob van Noorden	1674	Married a Lutheran and left the congregation. He moved to Amsterdam. (81)
Jacob Jacobs de Vlieger	after March 1674	Married a Calvinist woman in Glückstadt and converted. This was around the same time he was expelled for becoming bankrupt. (82)
Maria Harmens	1675	Married a Lutheran and converted. (69)
Harmen Harmens Elking	1675	Married a Lutheran and converted. (71)
Anna Pieters	1675	Married a Calvinist named Pieter Groot. (76)
Maria Aeriens	1675	Originally from the Pieter Jansz Twisck People. She married a soldier (*ruyter*), ran off with him and was expelled from the congregation. (67)
Magdeleena de Mols	1676	Married Jan Bruen de Wilde in the Dompelaar congregation. Jan had come from Danzig where he had been expelled from a Mennonite congregation. He later became a member. (42 and 107)
Claes Boudt	1676	Married Jacob Borcher's daughter in the Dompelaar congregation. (84)
Paul Geeritts Roosen	1676	Secretly married Elsken Kuels in a Lutheran church. Elsken was baptized as a Mennonite in April 1685. (48 and 121)
Grietgen Melcher	1677	Married without her parents' consent in a Lutheran church. She left for Friedrichstadt. (87)
Elsken Roosen	1678	Married the Dompelaar widower Claes Dircksen. Also see the entry for the year 1681. (67)
Jan Tomsen	1678	Married a Lutheran but in 1684 was buried in the Mennonite cemetery, Altona. (77)

Jan de Ruyscher and Janken Stockman	1678	Earlier in 1678, before the couple's marriage by a Lutheran pastor in Altona in November, Janken (then a widow) had run off with Konraet Koen, another congregational member. Konraet was disciplined briefly, but Jan and Janken were expelled. Janken was readmitted several years later. (62, 71 and 102)
Anna Marya Jacobs	after 1678	Married a Lutheran and was expelled. (95)
Jacob Alberts	1680 or 1681	Married a Lutheran woman. His wife Margeriete was baptized in Altona's Flemish congregation by the visiting Lamist preacher Galenus Abrahamsz in 1681. (83 and 107)
Elsken Roosen	1681	Married the Dompelaar Dominicus Kipping in November. In April 1682 Dominicus became a member of the Flemish congregation. (67 and 111)
Hinderick van Noorden	after April 1683	Married a Lutheran without knowledge of congregational leaders. He was often at sea but remained a member of the congregation 'as far as appearances are concerned'. (113)
Catrina Donders	after 1683	Married a non-member, but in 1738 she was buried in the Mennonite cemetery, Altona. (113)
Styntie Pieters de Vlieger	1684	Married a Calvinist. She must have remained a member of the congregation since she was expelled for drunkenness in 1688. (95)
Beerent Wynantz	soon after October 1684	Married a Calvinist in Amsterdam. Thereafter he was no longer considered a member. (85)
Maria Moliers	1685	Married Jan Egberts ter Borg in the Dompelaar congregation. (74)
Dirick Boudt	1686	Married the Dompelaar Saara Coopman, but he remained a member of the Flemish congregation. (82)
Jan Alberts	after 1686	Married a Lutheran and converted. (66 and 78)
Prientge Albers	1687	Married a Lutheran and converted. In 1688 she was expelled. (99)

Grietgen Mirbeeck	1687	Married Willem Jacobs, the son of a Quaker, in a Lutheran church with her parents' consent. In April 1688 Willem was baptized as a Mennonite. In March 1689 he became a soldier. (123 and 128)
Abraham Mirbeeck	1688	Married Cattelyn van Werel, a woman born to Mennonite parents who had chosen to be baptized as a Lutheran. In 1693 Cattelyn was baptized as a Mennonite after resolving a dispute with Abraham. (105 and 143)
Jacob Willems Beerens	1688 or 1689	Married secretly in another church and, when this was made public, he was expelled from communion. In 1691 he was readmitted. (128)
Claes Hendricks	1690	Married a Lutheran while engaged to the daughter of one of the congregation's members. In 1691 he was readmitted to communion. (124)
Jacob Jacobs de Vlieger	1691	Married a Calvinist. His wife Magdelena was baptized in the Flemish congregation in 1693. Jacob was probably the son of the one-time preacher Jacob Jacobs de Vlieger. (132 and 142; also see Schubert (ed.), *Trauregister*, 71)
Pietertie Geerling	1693	Married in a Lutheran church to her boyfriend Albert Jonas, who was not yet a baptized member of the congregation. The couple did not have the approval of Albert's father. (106)
Baltsar Kessel	1693	Married in the Dompelaar congregation to the Dompelaar Stintge Simons, widow of Melcher Denner. (76)
Anna Harmens Roosen	1695	Married in her father's house to her father's servant, Gabriel van Rahusen, a Waterlander Anabaptist from Leeuwarden who had been baptized by immersion and was not yet a member in Altona's Flemish congregation. (124)
Henderick Kessel	after 1695	Married a Lutheran outside of Hamburg. (149)

Jan Toomsen	1696 or 1697	Married a Lutheran but in 1715 was buried in the Mennonite cemetery, Altona. He was probably the son of Jan Tomsen (see above, 1678). (98)

Appendix Five
Unapproved marriages between first cousins

Name	*Date*	*Details*
Adriaen Noë and Sara Wynantz	1669	Married by the Old Frisian preacher Jan de Marné. They were first cousins and their marriage was not approved by Flemish leaders. They remained congregational members. (18 and 39)
Jacob Jacobs de Vlieger and Mayken Wolters	1669	Married in Friedrichstadt. Their marriage was not approved by congregational leaders, even though Jacob himself was a preacher in the Flemish congregation from 1664 to 1671. (57 and 82)
Frans Hindericks Baker and Saara Dircks Louw	1675	Married in Wandsbek. Their marriage had been approved by neither the Danish authorities nor Flemish leaders. (58 and 66)
Geert Roosen and Grietgen Kuels	1680	As Baker and Louw above. (97 and 104)
Pieter Whaling and Maria Lamber	1684	Married by the visiting preacher Foecke Floris in Maria's house. Their marriage had been approved by neither the Danish authorities nor Flemish leaders. (94 and 101)
Harmen Kessel and Anna Jacobs de Vlieger	1688	Married in Ottensen. They remained congregational members. (101 and 109)

Appendix Six
Individuals who married non-Mennonites or Dompelaars before becoming Flemish congregational members

The names in the left-hand column belong to the people accepted as members. The date in the middle column indicates the approximate date when the marriage took place.

Name	*Date*	*Details*
Jürgen Borkofsky	1663	He married a Lutheran in Königsberg before returning to Altona in May 1682 and being accepted as a member of the Flemish congregation in April 1683. He returned to Prussia in 1685. (38, 114)
Jan Teeuwsen	before 1677	He was baptized in July 1677 but his Lutheran wife did not join the congregation. (91)
Aeftien Pflips	before 1678	She married a non-Mennonite in Edam. Aeftien transferred her membership from a Mennonite congregation in Edam to Altona in 1678. She became a Lutheran in 1681, allegedly for economic reasons. (98)
Symon Backer	before 1685	He married a Lutheran in Friedrichstadt before being baptized in Altona in September 1685. (122)
Henderick Jansen Winter	between 1688 and 1692	He was married to a Dompelaar. Sometime later he transferred his membership to a Mennonite congregation in Harlingen and from there joined the Altona Flemish congregation. (141)
Hans Ketelaer	before 1691	He transferred his membership from Danzig in 1691. He had married his Calvinist wife in Copenhagen. (136, 137)

Elisabet Helling	before 1694	She arrived in Hamburg-Altona in 1694 with a Lutheran husband named Johann Zigmont Klein. She was accepted as a member and was given financial assistance. In 1696 she and her family moved to southern Germany. (153)
Otto van der Smissen	before 1697	He married a Lutheran before being baptized in 1697. (156)

Appendix Seven
Conversions to other churches not resulting from confessionally mixed marriages

Name	*Date*	*Details*
Antonie Jacobs	after 1655	He converted to Lutheranism. (8)
Pieter Hinsbergen	1659	He converted to Quakerism. (43)
Baerent Roelifs	1659	He converted to Quakerism. Moved to Alkmaar in 1660. (2)
Cornelis Beerens	1659	He converted to Quakerism, together with his father, Baerent Roelifs. Moved to Alkmaar in 1660. (16)
Eeyken Beerens	1660	She joined the Quakers in Alkmaar. (31)
Grietgen Louwert	1660	She joined the Quakers in Alkmaar. She was the daughter of Baerent Roelifs and Eeyken Beerens. (35)
Jan Beerens	1660	He joined the Quakers in Alkmaar. (39)
Neeltgen Beerens	1660	She joined the Quakers in Alkmaar. (45)
Pieter Wagenaer	1660	He was found guilty of adultery, and converted to Lutheranism. (12)
Thomas Major	1660	He converted to Quakerism and returned to England. (44)
Lucia Major	1660	She converted to Quakerism and returned to England. (44)
Poul Terlocht	after 1661	He converted to Lutheranism. (50)
Barber Alberts	after 1662	He converted to Lutheranism. (52)
Jan Boeckholt	soon after 1669	He converted to Lutheranism with his wife, Grietgen Sheers, soon after their 1669 marriage in the Flemish congregation. (62)
Grietgen Sheers	soon after 1669	She converted to Lutheranism with her husband, Jan Boeckholt, soon after their 1669 marriage in the Flemish congregation. (66)

Joseep Mostert	1671	Sometime after 1664 he and his wife Anna moved to Friedrichstadt, where it was rumoured that they had joined the Lutherans. In 1671 they became Lutherans publicly. (10)
Anna Mostert	1671	As Joseep Mostert above. (28)
Margriet Kipping	1671	She converted to Lutheranism and had her children baptized in Hamburg's St Michaelis parish. (44)
Daniel Kipping	1671	He converted to Lutheranism with his wife (Margriet) and children. (14)
Berent Claesen	after 1671	He converted to Quakerism in Friedrichstadt. (69)
Christof Beuiss	1671–2	He converted to Lutheranism. (57)
Magdeleen Beuiss	1671–2	She converted to Lutheranism. (64)
Tryntge Simons	1675	She converted to Lutheranism. (79)
Dirick Boudt	1676	He joined Antoinette Bourignon's sect. He rejoined the Flemish congregation 2–3 years later. (82)
Magdeleen Grouwel	1677	She converted to Quakerism. (34)
Claes Flores	1679	He left his wife to join Antoinette Bourignon's sect. He died the following year. (9)
Jacob Steenbreck	after 1680	He converted to Lutheranism. (56)
Abraham Roosen	after 1680	He converted to Quakerism in Amsterdam. (102)
Aeftien Pflips	1681	She converted to Lutheranism, allegedly for economic reasons. Had her children baptized. (98)
Maria Jürgens Stockman	1683	She had her child baptized by a Lutheran pastor in Altona. (99)
Pouwel Goverts	1688	He converted to Lutheranism. (55)
Jacob Hagens	1690	He converted to Quakerism. He was buried in Altona's Mennonite cemetery. (119)
Claes Boudt	1691	He converted to Lutheranism and had his children baptized in Hamburg's St Michaelis parish (see Ch. 4).
Juditha Boudt	1691	As Claes Boudt above.
Isabeel Harmens	1691	She converted to Lutheranism. (111)
Trientge van Noorden	after 1692	She converted to Lutheranism after the death of her husband. (99)

Appendix Eight
Individuals disciplined for improper financial dealings

Name	*Date*	*Details*
Jacob Jacobs de Vlieger	1671 and 1674	In 1671 he was forced to resign as preacher after he experienced financial difficulties. He remained a member of the congregation until sometime around 1674, when, after again experiencing financial problems, he left the congregation to marry a Calvinist. (82)
Jan Willems	1674	He was expelled for false financial dealings. (54)
Philip Walken	1674	His case was discussed by the congregational council, because he had built up debts. He left the region. (63)
Saara Kool and Jan Kessel	1675	It is unclear if the couple was expelled or simply chose to leave. Both had arrived originally from England. They left Altona in 1675 for Königsberg. (42, 53)
Anna Kool	1676?	She was expelled for bankruptcy and ran away. She was the wife of Philip Walken. (61)
Adriaen Fransen	1684	He became bankrupt and was disciplined. (49)
Hans Harmens	1689	He had been a deacon since 1679. After becoming bankrupt and resigning his office in 1689, he was disciplined in 1690. (10)
Harmen Roosen	1689	He had been a deacon since 1670. He was removed from office because he failed to fulfil his duties. He had probably become bankrupt. (102)

Pieter Pieters	1696	He had a dispute with Harmen Roosen over land, which led to his exclusion from communion and later his expulsion. He was readmitted, only to be expelled again in 1699 for violent behaviour. (98, 103, 163)

Appendix Nine
Individuals disciplined for violent behaviour

Name	*Date*	*Details*
Hans van Werle	1663	He was expelled for beating his servant girl and was readmitted the following year. (42)
Jürgen Stockman	1678	He was expelled for fighting with his brother. (16, 52, 105)
Hans Stockman	1678	He was expelled for fighting with his brother. After his brother's death in 1680 he was readmitted to the congregation. (16, 52, 105)
Konraet Koen	1678	He was expelled for carrying weapons and for his part in a domestic dispute. He was later readmitted. (see App. 4, 1678). (66)
Willem Koen	1678	He was expelled for threatening others with a pistol during a domestic dispute. He was later readmitted. (see App. 4, 1678). (78, 96)
Claes Boudt	1678	He began carrying weapons after declaring that he did not want to belong to the congregation (see Ch. 4). (84, 138)
Abraham Jacobs	after 1678	He became a soldier. (95)
Geeret Donder	after 1684	He became a soldier. (119)
Willem Jacobs	1689	He was expelled for participating in war. (128)
Abraham Kulper	1689	He was expelled for serving on a Swedish warship. He repented. (128)
Jürgen Harmens	after 1689	He became a soldier. (111)
Pieter Pieters	1699	He was expelled for assaulting a non-Mennonite west of Altona. (98, 103, 163; and StAHbg/MG, 6, vol. 1, pp. 7–8)
Jan Pieters	1699	He was expelled for assaulting a non-Mennonite west of Altona. (110; and StAHbg/MG, 6, vol. 1, pp. 7–8)
Dirck Jansen Schoemaker	1700	He was expelled for beating his brother. (121)

Appendix Ten
Individuals disciplined for other immoral behaviour

Name	*Date*	*Details*
Dina Olthofs	1655	She was expelled for sexual impropriety. (32)
Hans Bussenschutter	after 1655	He was not considered a full member of the congregation because of his sinful lifestyle. He had transferred his membership from Glückstadt. (16)
Jacob Jacobs	1656	Expelled for sexual impropriety. (17)
Joost van Steen	1656	He was a preacher and was expelled for an affair with Maria Olthofs. They had married outside the congregation, whose leaders did not recognize their status as husband and wife. Readmitted in 1657, he left for Prussia in 1664. (2, 44)
Maria Olthofs	1656	See entry for Joost van Steen. (32, 40)
Daniel Kipping	1657	He was expelled for drinking and dancing. He was readmitted in 1659. He later converted to Lutheranism with his wife and children in 1671. (14)
Pieter Kessel	1657	He was disciplined for drunkenness. (9)
Jan Jacobs	1659	He was expelled for drunkenness. He was readmitted in 1664. (11)
Pieter Wagenaer	1660	He was disciplined for adultery. (12)
Gardruyt Olthofs	1660	She was expelled for leading an evil life and for being unwilling to repent. She returned to the congregation in 1663. (34, 48)
Eelisabet Noë	1660	She was expelled for her role in an affair her daughter Geesken had had with Pieter Wagenaer. She was readmitted soon thereafter. (12, 19, 48)
Geesken Noë	1660	She was expelled after it was discovered that she had had a two-year affair with Pieter Wagenaer, whose child she had just had. She was readmitted in 1675. (35)
Pieter Molier	1660	He was expelled for a sinful lifestyle, but was later readmitted in 1663. (14)

Willem Olthof	1661	He was expelled for keeping an immoral household. (15)
Magdaleen Mostert	1664	She was expelled for marrying a non-member and for leading an extravagant lifestyle (that is, dancing and the like). (52)
Eelisabet Koen	1666	She was disciplined after she had an illegitimate child. (41)
François and Maria Stockman	1669	In 1665 they were married in the congregation. They were first cousins. Later it was discovered that they had had premarital sex. They were disciplined briefly and then readmitted. (46, 48)
Jan Duycker	1670	He was disciplined for drunkenness. (11)
Maria Koen	1674	She was disciplined after she had an illegitimate child. She was readmitted to another nearby Mennonite congregation in 1676. (82)
Pieter Ellen	1686	He was summoned before the congregation because of adultery. He left for Russia and was expelled. (89)
Johannes Lennich	1687	He was expelled for drunkenness. (96)
Jan Jacobs	1688	He was expelled for an evil lifestyle and for stealing. (117)
Styntie Pieters de Vlieger	1688	She was expelled for drunkenness. She had earlier married a Calvinist, which did not lead to her expulsion. (95)
Anneken Jacobs	1689	She returned from Holland with an illegitimate child and was expelled. She was readmitted in 1702. (106)
Pelgrim Harmens	1689	He was expelled for having had premarital sex. He became a father and then married the child's mother. He was readmitted in 1692. (115)
Hinderick van Sintern	1696	He was expelled for drunkenness. He later left for Pennsylvania. (92)

Bibliography

Archival Sources

Amsterdam

Gemeentearchief
  PA 565, A 941 I
  PA 1120, 1023

Universiteitsbibliotheek
  Handschriften XXVII, 567; XXVII, 578

Friedrichstadt

Stadtarchiv
  Mennonitengemeinde: 0.07; 0.31.06

Goshen, Indiana

Mennonite Historical Library
  Historical Treatises: 'A Significant Dutch Letter by Gerrit Roosen about Conditions in the Altona-Mennonite Church around 1675'

Hamburg

Staatsarchiv der Freien und Hansestadt Hamburg
  'Die Fremden in den Rechnungsbüchern der Wedde und Kämmerei von 1600–1700'
  Familienarchive: Goverts
  Genealogische Sammlungen: Roosen
  Handschriftensammlung: 130, 138, 396, 1501, 1968
  Mennonitengemeinde: 1; 1a; 2; 3; 4; 5; 6, vols 1, 3 and 5; 7; 8; 9; 16; 24; 25; 26; 27; 39; 59, vol. 1; 86, vol. 1; 145; 147, vol. 1; 148; 149; 151; 175; 176; 183; 184; 202; 203, vol. 1; 213; 214; 225; 229; 231; 231b; 242; 246b; 248, vols 1–4; 261c; 270
  Ministerium: II 5, II A1 c, III A1 I, III A1 k
  Reichshofrat: 298
  Reichskammergericht: B1b, E15, F11, H177, J2, J3, J18, M28, R25, R38, S37, S84, S172, V9

Senat: Cl. VII Lit. Ca Nr. 3 Vol. 7c (6); Cl. VII Lit. Eb Nr. 1 Vol. 1; Cl. VII Lit. Hf Nr. 1 Vol. 3g (3); Cl. VII Lit. Hf Nr. 2a Vol. 13; Cl. VII Lit. Hf Nr. 2c Vol. 1; Cl. VII Lit. Hf Nr. 4 Vol. 1a; Cl. VII Lit. Ma Nr. 3 Vol. 3f
Staatsangehörigkeitsaufsicht: A Ia 1–11

Paris

Archives Nationales
Marine, Series B^4, vol. 12

Schleswig

Schleswig-Holsteinisches Landesarchiv
Abteilung 11, Nr. 237
Abteilung 65.1, Nr. 1643, 1688, 1690, 1692, 1729a
Reichskammergericht 72

Stade

Niedersächsiches Staatsarchiv
Rep. 5a Fach 289 Nr. 19

Printed Primary Sources

NB. Some of these sources are quite rare. Those books for which there is no location listed in the *Mennonite Bibliography* are most likely to be found in the library collection of Hamburg's Staatsarchiv. The library of Hamburg's Mennonitengemeinde also has a very good collection of old printed materials. I have tried whenever possible to use the original spelling and capitalization.

Abrahamsz, G. and D. Spruyt, *Nader verklaringe Van de XIX. Artikelen* (Amsterdam, 1659)
Algemeene Belydennissen (Amsterdam, 1665).
Die alte Warheit erhöhet (n.p., n.d.)
Anabaptisticum et Enthusiasticum Pantheon Und Geistliches Rüst-Hauß Wider die Alten Quacker/ Und Neuen Frey-Geister (n.p., 1701–2)
Arents, Jan, *Eindelijke Verklaeringe Der gedoopten Christenen* (n.p., 1667)
——— *Eindelijcke Verklaringe der gedoopte Christenen*, appendix by Antoony de Grijs (2nd edn, n.p., 1668)

Arnold, Gottfried, *Unparteiischen Kirchen- und Ketzerhistorie* (Frankfurt, 1699–1700)

Benthem, Heinrich Ludolf, *Holländischer Kirch- und Schulen-Staat* (Frankfurt and Leipzig, 1698)

Besszler, M., *Einfeltiger Bericht ausz Gottes wort vom eidschweren was es sey* (Nuremberg, 1554)

Bibliotheca Reformatoria Neerlandica: Geschriften uit den tijd der hervorming in de Nederlanden, ed. Samuel Cramer and Fredrik Pijper, 10 vols (The Hague, 1903–14), vol. 7

Block, Johannes, *Muscovien-Fahrt/ Das ist: Kurzer und umbständlicher Bericht/ von der Schiffarth aus Hamburg nach Archangel* (Hamburg, 1683)

Bolten, Johann Adrian, *Historische Kirchen-Nachrichten von der Stadt Altona*, 2 vols (Altona, 1790–91)

Braght, Thieleman van, *The Bloody Theater or Martyrs Mirror of the Defenseless Christians*, trans. Joseph F. Sohm (8th edn, Scottdale, Pa., 1968)

Büsch, Johann Georg, *Versuch einer Geschichte der Hamburgischen Handlung* (Hamburg, 1797)

Confessions and Catechisms of the Reformation, ed. Mark A. Noll (Grand Rapids, Mich., 1991)

Corpus Constitutionum Imperialium (Regensburg, 1675)

Denner, Jacob, *Christliche und erbauliche Betrachtungen: Über die Sonn- und Festtags-Evangelien des ganzen Jahres* (Philadelphia, 1860)

Documents of the Christian Church, ed. Henry Bettenson (New York, 1947)

[Eschels, Jens Jacob], *Lebensbeschreibung eines Alten Seemanns* (Altona, 1835)

Glanäus, Jodocus Edzardi, *Geistliches Bad-Tuch den Newen Widertäufferschen Täuchern* (Hamburg, 1651)

——— *Nothwehr für die Kindertaufe welche die Wiedertauffer den Kindern wehren* (Hamburg, 1636 and 1637)

Götze, George Heinrich, *Catechetische Prüfung der Menninistischen Lehre, welche in Acht Catechismus-Predigten unter Göttlichen Seegen den 12. 13. 15. 16. 19. 20. 22. 23. Septembr. An. 1707 in St. Marien Kirche deutlich und erbaulich anzustellen gedenket* ([Lübeck, *c.* 1707])

Grondig Bewijs tegen den Kinder-doop uit Marc 10,14 (Amsterdam, 1693)

Grondt-steen Van Vreede en Verdraegsaemheyt, Tot Opbouwinge van den Tempel Christi Onder de Doops-Gesinde (Amsterdam, 1674)

Handelinge/ Der Ver-eenigde Vlaemse, en Duytse Doops-gesinde Gemeynten, Gehouden Tot Haerlem, A° 1649 in Junio/ Met De Dry Confessien aldaer geapprobeert/ of aengenomen (Vlissingen, 1666)

Heise, Carl Johann, *Tauf-Rede über Röm. 10, v. 10. Welche bey der Taufe Eilf in der Mennonistischen Gemeine in Hamburg gebohrner Kinder den 17den Merz des 1751sten Jahres in der Haupt-Kirche St. Petri vor dem Tauf-Stein gehalten worden, Nebst Ihrem abgelegten Glaubens-Bekenntniß* (new edn, Hamburg, 1780)

Hobbes, Thomas, *Leviathan* (1651)

Hoburg, Christian, *Drey geistreiche Tractätlein* (Hamburg and Frankfurt, 1677)

Hoburg, Philipp, *Lebens-Lauff Des seligen Christian Hoburgs* (n.p., 1698)

Karsdorp, Gerrit, *Lyk- en Gedachtenis-Reeden . . . op het hoogstsmertelyk Overlyden van Syne Koningl. Majesteit Federik de Vyfde* (Hamburg, 1766)

Katalog von der Bibliothek der Mennoniten-Gemeinde zu Hamburg und Altona (n.p., 1899)

[Klefeker, Johann (ed.)], *Sammlung der Hamburgischen Gesetze und Verfassungen in Bürger- und Kirchlichen, auch Cammer-, Handlungs- und übrigen Policey-Angelegenheiten und Geschäften samt historischen Einleitung*, 12 vols (Hamburg, 1765–1773)

Lammerenkrijgh, anders Mennonisten Kerckentwist (n.p., 1663)

Meersch, Abraham van der, '"De laatste vaderlijke lessen" (1721)', ed. P. Visser and S.B.J. Zilverberg, *Doopsgezinde Bijdragen*, 17 (1991), pp. 153–87

Mehrning, Jacob, *S. Baptismi Historia: Das ist/ Heilige Tauff-Historia* (Dortmund, 1646–7)

Moller, Johann, *Cimbria Literata, sive scriptorum ducatus utriusque Slesvicensis et Holsatici*, 3 vols (Copenhagen, 1744)

Montanus, Herman, *Nietigheydt Van den Kinder-doop* (2nd edn, Amsterdam, 1648)

Müller, Johann, *Anabaptismus. Das ist: Wiedertauffer Irrthumb* (Hamburg, 1645)

Quäcker Grewel (Hamburg, 1661)

Quäcker Quackeley (Hamburg, 1663)

Ris, Cornelis, *De Geloofsleere Der Waare Mennoniten of Doopsgezinden* (Hoorn, 1766)

——— *Glaubens-Lehre der wahren Mennoniten oder Tauf-Gesinnten* (Hamburg, 1776)

[Roosen, Geeritt], 'Geeritt Roosen und seine Geschichte der Kriegsereignisse seiner Zeit', transcription and introduction by Paul Piper, *Germania*, 1 (1899), pp. 363–74, 446–52, 527–37, 589–99, 659–68 and 725–34

——— 'Gerhard Roosen to friends in Alsace', in *Letters of the Amish Division: A Sourcebook*, ed. and trans. John D. Roth, with the assistance of Joe Springer (Goshen, Ind., 1993), pp. 67–71

——— [G.R.], *Nutzbahrer und Gründlicher Unterricht Von dem jetzo gewöhlichen Brauch und Art Der Unrahtsahmen Kachel-Ofen* (Hamburg, 1695)

——— [Gerh[ard] Roosen], *Unschuld und Gegen-Bericht der Evangelischen Tauff-gesinneten Christen* (Ratzeburg, 1702)

——— [G. Roose[n]] et al., *Schriftelick bericht over eenige aenmercklijcke puncten der Engelschen die Quaeckers genoemt worden* (Amsterdam, 1660)

Sammlung der von E. Hochedlen Rathe der Stadt Hamburg so wol zur Handhabung der Gesetze und Verfassungen als bey besonderen Eräugnissen im Bürger- und Kirchlichen, als auch Cammer-, Handlungs, und übrigen Policey-Angelegenheiten und Geschäften, ed. J.F. Blank, 6 vols (Hamburg, 1763–74)

Schijn, Hermannus, and Gerardus Maatschoen, *Geschiedenis der Mennoniten*, 3 vols (Amsterdam, 1743–5)

Schmid, Ludolph Hinrich, *Versuch einer historischen Beschreibung der an der Elbe belegenen Stadt Altona* (Hamburg, 1975 [Altona, 1747])

Schröter, Joannes, *Stammbuch Der Mennistischen Ketzerey Sambt dero Gespanschafften Lehr und Sitten* (Neyß, 1691)

Schultzen, Daniel Severin, *Wolgemeinte Warnung für der gemeinschaft des GOttesdientes der Mennonisten* (Hamburg, 1706)

Seven Brieven, Tot vervolg van twee Brieven (Rotterdam, 1665)

Simons, Menno, *The Complete Writings of Menno Simons, c. 1496–1561*, trans. Leonard Verduin and ed. John Christian Wenger (Scottdale, Pa., 1956)

Der Stadt Hamburg Statuten und Gerichts-Ordnung (Hamburg, 1771)

Stats-Anzeigen, ed. August Ludwig Schlözer, vol. 7, no. 25 (Göttingen, 1785)

Toornburg, Klaas, *Schriftuurlijcke Verhandelingh Tegens het Eed-zweeren, En voor de Wraak en Weerloose Lydsaemheyt en Volmaeckte Liefde, Die de Christenen moeten Oeffenen, aen en omtrent de Boose en Vyanden* (Alkmaar, 1688)

Twee Brieven, Een van de Dienaren, der Gemeente tot Hamborch, die haer selven de gedoopte Christenen noemen (Amsterdam, 1665)

Twisck, Pieter Jansz, *Chronijck van den Onderganc der Tijrannen* (Hoorn, 1619–20)

Verhaal Van 't gene verhandelt ende besloten is, in de By-Een-Komste Tot Leyden: door eenige Doops-gezinde leeraren en diaconen, die men Vlamingen noemt, tot dien eynde uyt verscheyde plaatzen vergadert in de maant Junii, 1660 (Amsterdam, 1661)

Weenigem, Bastiaan van, *Antidoton oft Tegengift op eenen brief geschreven uyt Hamborgh* (Rotterdam, 1669)

——— *De maniere van Doop, Voetwasschinge en Avontmael soo by de Dompelaers tot Hamborg gebruyckt wert* (Rotterdam, 1666)

Winckler, Johann, *Gründlicher Beweiß der Kinder-Tauffe aus Marc. X.v.14. . . .* (Hamburg, 1691)

——— *Der unrechtmäßig verquakerte gute Lutheraner* (Hamburg, 1693)

——— *Vertheidigung Seines Gründlichen Beweises Der Kinder-Tauffe Gegen Die Einwürffe Etlicher Holländischen Wider-Täuffer* (Hamburg, 1696)

Wynantz, Willem, *LVIII Stichtelycke Predicatien* (Amsterdam, 1660)

Zurck, Eduard van, *Codex Batavus, waer in het algemeen Kerk- publyk en Burgerlyk Recht van Holland, Zeelant, en het Ressort der Generaliteit Kortelyk Is Begrepen* (2nd edn, Delft, 1727)

Secondary Sources

Allgemeine deutsche Bibliographie (2nd edn, 56 vols, Berlin, 1967–71)

Augner, Gerd, *Die kaiserliche Kommission der Jahre 1708–1712: Hamburgs Beziehung zu Kaiser und Reich zu Anfang des 18. Jahrhunderts* (Hamburg, 1983)

Baasch, Ernst, *Hamburgs Convoyschiffahrt und Convoywesen: Ein Beitrag zur Geschichte der Schiffahrt und Schiffahrtseinrichtungen im 17. und 18. Jahrhundert* (Hamburg, 1896)

——— *Die Handelskammer zu Hamburg*, 2 vols (Hamburg, 1915)

——— *Holländische Wirtschaftsgeschichte* (Jena, 1927)

——— 'Der Verkehr mit Kriegsmaterialien aus und nach den Hansestädten vom Ende des 16. bis Mitte des 17. Jahrhunderts', *Jahrbücher für Nationalökonomie und Statistik*, 137, 3rd ser., 82 (1932), part II, pp. 538–43

Bender, Elisabeth H., 'Ernst von Wildenbruch's Drama "Der Menonit"', *Mennonite Quarterly Review*, 18 (1944), pp. 22–35

Bender, Harold S., 'The Anabaptist Vision', *Church History*, 13 (1944), pp. 3–24. Also in *Mennonite Quarterly Review*, 18 (1944), pp. 67–88

Berger, Peter L., and Thomas Luckmann, *The Social Construction of Reality: A Treatise in the Sociology of Knowledge* (Garden City, NY, 1967)

Bertram, Alfred, 'Mennoniten und Methodisten als hamburgische Körperschaften des öffentlichen Rechts', *Hanseatische Rechts-Zeitschrift*, 6 (1923), pp. 655–60

Bietenholz, Peter G., 'Philipp von Zesens Schrift *Wider den Gewissenszwang* und die Schweizer Täufer', in Michael Erbe et al. (eds), *Querdenken: Dissens und Toleranz im Wandel der Geschichte. Festschrift zum 65. Geburtstag von Hans R. Guggisberg* (Mannheim, 1996), pp. 305–17

Brecht, Martin, 'Die deutschen Spiritualisten des 17. Jahrhunderts', in

Martin Brecht (ed.), *Geschichte des Pietismus* (Göttingen, 1993), i, pp. 205–40

Brinner, Ludwig, *Die deutsche Grönlandfahrt* (Berlin, 1913)

Brock, Peter, *Freedom from Violence: Sectarian Nonresistance from the Middle Ages to the Great War* (Toronto, 1991)

Bromley, J.S., 'The North Sea in Wartime, 1688–1713', independently paginated chapter in Bromley, *Corsairs and Navies, 1660–1760* (London, 1987)

Brons, A., *Ursprung, Entwicklung und Schicksale der altevangelischen Taufgesinnten oder Mennoniten*, ed. E.M. ten Cate (3rd edn, Amsterdam, 1912)

Bruinvis, C.W., 'Oude rechtstoestand der Mennisten in Holland', *Doopsgezinde Bijdragen*, 39 (1899), pp. 181–4

Cate, S. Blaupot ten, *Geschiedenis der Doopsgezinden in Holland, Zeeland, Utrecht, en Gelderland* (Amsterdam, 1847)

Chevallier, Marjolaine, *Pierre Poiret* (Baden-Baden, 1985)

Dëmkin, A.V., '"Rospisi korablem" zapadnoevropeiskikh kuptsov, sospavlennie v Arkhangel'ske v 1658 g.', *Issledovaniia po istochnikovedeniiu istorii rossii dooktiabrskogo perioda: sbornik statei* (Moscow, 1987), pp. 89–113

Deppermann, Klaus, *Melchior Hoffman: Social Unrest and Apocalyptic Visions in the Age of Reformation*, trans. Malcolm Wren and ed. Benjamin Drewery (Edinburgh, 1987)

Dollinger, Robert, *Geschichte der Mennoniten in Schleswig-Holstein, Hamburg und Lübeck* (Neumünster, 1930)

Doornkaat Koolman, [Jan] ten, *Die Verpflichtung der Mennoniten an Eidesstatt* (Berlin, 1893)

Doornkaat Koolman, Jacobus ten, *Dirk Philips: Friend and Colleague of Menno Simons, 1504–1568*, trans. William E. Keeney, ed. C. Arnold Snyder (Kitchener, Ont., 1998)

Douwen, W. I. van, 'De afscheiding van de Huiskoopers of Oude Vlamingen (1587) en die van de Janjacobsgezinden (1599)', *Doopsgezinde Bijdragen*, 52 (1912), pp. 49–75

Driedger, Leo, *Mennonite Identity in Conflict* (Lewiston and Queenston, 1988)

——— and Donald B. Kraybill, *Mennonite Peacemaking: From Quietism to Activism* (Scottdale, Pa., and Waterloo, Ont., 1994)

Driedger, Michael, 'Crossing Max Weber's Great Divide: Comparing Early Modern European Jewish and Anabaptist Histories', in Geoffrey Dipple and Werner Packull (eds), *Radical Reformation Studies: Essays Presented to James M. Stayer* (Aldershot, 1999), pp. 157–74

——— 'The Extant Writings of Geeritt Roosen', *Mennonite Quarterly Review*, 74 (2000), pp. 159–69

——— 'Gerrit Karsdorp (1729–1811): Mennonitenprediger und Förderer der Aufklärung in Hamburg. Die Bibliothek eines Hamburger Kaufmanns', *Mennonitische Geschichtsblätter*, 56 (1999), pp. 35–53

——— 'Kanonen, Schießpulver und Wehrlosigkeit: Cord, Geeritt und B.C. Roosen in Holstein und Hamburg 1532–1905', *Mennonitische Geschichtsblätter*, 52 (1995), pp. 101–21

——— 'Mennonitengemeinde von Hamburg und Altona', in Franz Schubert (ed.), *Trauregister aus den ältesten Kirchenbüchern Hamburgs: Von den Anfängen bis zum Jahre 1704* (Göttingen, 1997), pp. 85–92

Dyck, C.J., 'The First Waterlandian Confession of Faith', *Mennonite Quarterly Review*, 36 (1962), pp. 5–13

——— 'Hans de Ries (d. 1638) and Socinianism', in Lech Szczucki (ed.), *Socinianism and its Role in the Culture of the XVI-th to XVIII-th Centuries* (Warsaw and Lodz, 1983), pp. 85–95

——— 'The Middelburg Confession of Hans de Ries', *Mennonite Quarterly Review*, 36 (1962), pp. 147–54

——— (ed.), *An Introduction to Mennonite History: A Popular History of the Anabaptists and Mennonites* (Scottdale, Pa., and Kitchener, Ont., 1967)

Dyserinck, J., *De vrijstelling van den eed voor de Doopsgezinden* (Haarlem, 1883)

Ebert-Weidenfeller, Andreas, *Hamburgisches Kaufmannsrecht im 17. und 18. Jahrhundert: Die Rechtsprechung des Rates und des Reichskammergerichtes* (Frankfurt, 1992)

Ehlers, Joachim, *Die Wehrverfassung der Stadt Hamburg im 17. und 18. Jahrhundert* (Boppard am Rhein, 1966)

Ehrenberg, Richard, 'Gewerbefreiheit und Zunftzwang in Ottensen und Altona 1543 bis 1640', independently paginated chapter in Richard Ehrenberg, *Altona unter Schauenburgischen Herrschaft* (Altona, 1893)

Fairchild, Helen Lincklaen, *Francis Adrian van der Kemp, 1752–1829: An Autobiography together with Extracts from his Correspondence* (New York and London, 1903)

Fätkenheuer, Frank, 'Konfession im Alltag – Grenzen der Konfessionalisierungsforschung' (doctoral diss., Universität Göttingen, 2000)

Feddersen, Ernst, *Kirchengeschichte Schleswig-Holsteins*, 2 vols (Kiel, 1938)

Fischer-Hübner, Martin, *Geistchristentum in der lutherischen Kirche Lauenburgs 1626–1711* (Ratzeburg, [1925])

Fix, Andrew, 'Mennonites and Collegiants in Holland, 1630–1700', *Mennonite Quarterly Review*, 64 (1990), pp. 160–77.

——— 'Mennonites and Rationalism in the Seventeenth Century', in

Hamilton, Voolstra and Visser (eds), *From Martyr to Muppy*, pp. 159–74

——— *Prophecy and Reason: The Dutch Collegiants in the Early Enlightenment* (Princeton, 1991)

Forster, Marc R., *The Counter-Reformation in the Villages: Religion and Reform in the Bishopric of Speyer, 1560–1720* (Ithaca, NY, 1992)

François, Etienne, *Die unsichtbare Grenze: Protestanten und Katholiken in Augsburg 1648–1806*, trans. Angelika Steiner-Wendt (Sigmaringen, 1991)

Friedmann, Robert, *Mennonite Piety through the Centuries: Its Genius and its Literature* (Goshen, Ind., 1949)

Friedrichs, Christopher R., *The Early Modern City, 1450–1750* (London and New York, 1995)

——— 'German Town Revolts and the Seventeenth-Century Crisis', *Renaissance and Modern Studies*, **26** (1982), pp. 27–51

——— *Urban Politics in Early Modern Europe* (London, 2000)

Froese, Wolfgang, 'Revolution, Erweckung und Entkirchlichung: Die Krefelder Mennoniten von der Zeit der französischen Revolution bis zur Gründung des Deutschen Reiches (1794–1871)' in Froese (ed.), *Sie kamen als Fremde*, pp. 105–56

——— (ed.), *Sie kamen als Fremde: Die Mennoniten in Krefeld von den Anfängen bis zur Gegenwart* (Krefeld, 1995)

Furner, Mark, 'The Repression and Survival of Anabaptism in the Emmental, 1659–1743' (Ph.D. diss., Clare College, University of Cambridge, 1998)

Geffcken, Johannes, *Die große St. Michaeliskirche in Hamburg* (Hamburg, 1862)

——— 'Hamburgische Zustände am Ende des 17ten Jahrhunderts, aus gleichzeitigen Aufzeichnungen mitgetheilt', *Zeitschrift des Vereins für Hamburgische Geschichte*, **3** (1851), pp. 597–635

——— *Johann Winckler und die Hamburgische Kirche in seiner Zeit (1684–1705)* (Hamburg, 1861)

Gierl, Martin, 'Gesicherte Polemik: Zur polemischen Natur geisteswissenschaftlicher Wahrheit und zu Anthony Graftons "Die tragischen Ursprünge der deutschen Fußnote"', *Historische Anthropologie*, **4** (1996), pp. 267–79

——— *Pietismus und Aufklärung: Theologische Polemik und die Kommunikationsreform der Wissenschaft am Ende des 17. Jahrhunderts* (Göttingen, 1997)

Goertz, Hans-Jürgen, *The Anabaptists*, trans. Trevor Johnson (New York, 1996)

——— 'Der fremde Menno Simons: Antiklerikale Argumentation im Werk eines melchioritischen Täufers', in Irwin Horst (ed.), *The Dutch*

Dissenters: A Critical Companion to their History and Ideas (Leiden, 1986), pp. 160–76

——— 'Kleruskritik, Kirchenzucht und Sozialdisziplinierung in den täuferischen Bewegungen der Frühen Neuzeit', in Heinz Schilling (ed.), *Kirchenzucht und Sozialdisziplinierung im frühneuzeitlichen Europa* (Berlin, 1994), pp. 183–98

——— 'Nationale Erhebung und religiöser Niedergang', in Hans-Jürgen Goertz (ed.), *Umstrittenes Täufertum* (2nd edn, Göttingen, 1977), pp. 259–89

——— *Religiöse Bewegungen in der Frühen Neuzeit* (Munich, 1993)

——— 'Zucht und Ordnung in nonkonformistischer Manier', in *Antiklerikalismus und Reformation: Sozialgeschichtliche Untersuchungen* (Göttingen, 1995), pp. 103–14

——— 'Zwischen Zwietracht und Eintracht: Zur Zweideutigkeit täuferischer und mennonitischer Bekenntnisse', *Mennonitische Geschichtsblätter*, **43–4** (1986–7), pp. 16–46

Goody, Jack, *The European Family: An Historico-Anthropological Essay* (Malden, Mass., and Oxford, 2000)

Gordon, Bruce, 'Conference Report: "Konfessionalisierung, Stände und Staat in Ostmitteleuropa (1550–1650)", Geisteswissenschaftliches Zentrum Geschichte und Kultur Ostmitteleuropas, Leipzig, 11–13 December 1997', *German History*, **17** (1999), pp. 90–94

Gorski, Philip S., 'Historicizing the Secularization Debate: Church, State, and Society in Late Medieval and Early Modern Europe (ca. 1300 to 1700)', *American Sociological Review*, **65** (2000), pp. 138–67

——— 'The Protestant Ethic Revisited: Disciplinary Revolution and State Formation in Holland and Prussia', *American Journal of Sociology*, **99** (1993), pp. 265–316

Goverts, Ernst F., 'Das adelige Gut Fresenburg und die Mennoniten', *Zeitschrift der Zentralstelle für Niedersächsiche Familiengeschichte (Sitz Hamburg)*, 7 (1925), pp. 41–55, 69–86 and 97–103

Gregory, Brad S., *Salvation at Stake: Christian Martyrdom in Early Modern Europe* (Cambridge, Mass., and London, 1999)

Gulik, A. van, 'Uit de geschiedenis van de overkomst der vervolgde Zwitzers in 1710 en 1711', *Doopsgezinde Bijdragen*, **48** (1908), pp. 85–105; and **49** (1909), pp. 127–55

Gutmann, Myron P., *Toward the Modern Economy: Early Industry in Europe 1500–1800* (Philadelphia, 1988)

Hamilton, Alastair, Sjouke Voolstra and Piet Visser (eds), *From Martyr to Muppy (Mennonite Urban Professionals): A Historical Introduction to Cultural Assimilation Processes of a Religious Minority in the Netherlands: The Mennonites* (Amsterdam, 1994)

Harder-Gersdorff, Elisabeth, 'Lübeck und Hamburg im internationalen

Handel mit russischem Juchtenleder in der Frühen Neuzeit (1650–1710)', *Zeitschrift des Vereins für Lübeckische Geschichte und Altertumskunde*, **67** (1987), pp. 91–141

Harrington, Joel F., and Helmut Walser Smith, 'Confessionalization, Community, and State-Building in Germany, 1555–1870', *Journal of Modern History*, **69** (1997), pp. 77–101

Haude, Sigrun, *In the Shadow of Savage Wolves: Anabaptist Muenster and the German Reformation during the 1530s* (Leiden, 2000)

Head, Randolph, 'Catholics and Protestants in Graubünden: Confessional Discipline and Confessional Identities without an Early Modern State?', *German History*, **17** (1999), pp. 321–45

Heckel, Martin, 'Die Religionsprozesse des Reichskammergerichts im konfessionell gespaltenen Reichskirchenrecht', *Zeitschrift der Savigny-Stiftung für Rechtsgeschichte, Kanonistische Abteilung*, **77** (1991), pp. 283–350.

Hershberger, Guy F. (ed.), *The Recovery of the Anabaptist Vision: A Sixtieth Anniversary Tribute to Harold S. Bender* (Scottdale, Pa., 1957)

Holenstein, André, 'Seelenheil und Untertanenpflicht: Zur gesellschaftlichen Funktion und theoretischen Begründung des Eides in der ständischen Gesellschaft', in Peter Blickle with André Holenstein (eds), *Der Fluch und der Eid: Die metaphysische Begründung gesellschaftlichen Zusammenlebens und politischer Ordnung in der ständischen Gesellschaft* (Berlin, 1993), pp. 11–63

Holzem, Andreas, 'Die Konfessionsgesellschaft: Christenleben zwischen staatlichem Bekenntniszwang und religiöser Heilshoffnung', *Zeitschrift für Kirchengeschichte*, **110** (1999), pp. 53–85

Hsia, R. Po-chia, 'Between State and Community: Religious and Ethnic Minorities in Early Modern Germany', in Andrew C. Fix and Susan C. Karant-Nunn (eds), *Germania Illustrata: Essays on Early Modern Germany Presented to Gerald Strauss* (Kirksville, Mo., 1992), pp. 169–80

——— *Social Discipline in the Reformation: Central Europe, 1550–1750* (London and New York, 1989)

Hughes, Michael, *Law and Politics in Eighteenth Century Germany: The Imperial Aulic Council in the Reign of Charles VI* (Woodbridge, 1988)

Hull, Isabel V., *Sexuality, State and Civil Society in Germany, 1700–1815* (Ithaca, NY and London, 1996)

Hull, William I., *The Rise of Quakerism in Amsterdam, 1655–1665* ([Swarthmore, Pa.], 1938)

——— *Willem Sewel of Amsterdam, 1653–1720: The First Quaker Historian of Quakerism* ([Swarthmore, Pa.], 1934)

——— *William Penn and the Dutch Quaker Migration to Pennsylvania* ([Swarthmore, Pa.], 1935)

Hülsenberg, Karla, 'Untersuchungen über geschlossene Heiratskreise einiger hervorragender Hamburger Familien 1770–1840' (thesis, Pädagogische Hochschule, Göttingen, 1960)

Hylkema, C.B., *Reformateurs: Geschiedkundige Studiën over de Godesdienstige Bewegingen uit de nadagen onzer Gouden Eeuw* (2 parts, Haarlem, 1900 and 1902)

Irwin, Joyce, 'Anna Maria van Schurman and Antoinette Bourignon: Contrasting Examples of Seventeenth-Century Pietism', *Church History*, 60 (1991), pp. 301–15

Israel, Jonathan, *European Jewry in the Age of Mercantilism, 1550–1750* (3rd edn, London and Portland, Ore., 1998)

Jecker, Hanspeter, *Ketzer, Rebellen, Heilige: Das Basler Täufertum von 1580–1700* (Liestal, 1998)

Kauffman, J. Howard, and Leo Driedger, *The Mennonite Mosaic: Identity and Modernization* (Scottdale, Pa., and Waterloo, Ont., 1991)

Keyser, Marja, 'De drukkerij van Mattheus Jacobszoon, Lübeck 1554', *Doopsgezinde Bijdragen*, new ser. 5 (1979), pp. 91–4

——— 'The Fresenburg Press: An Historical Investigation Pertaining to Menno Simons' Printing Office in Holstein, Germany, 1554–1555', in Irwin Horst (ed.), *The Dutch Dissenters: A Critical Companion to their History and Ideas* (Leiden, 1986), pp. 179–86

Klaassen, Walter, *Mennonites and War Taxes* (Newton, Kans., 1978)

Klötzer, Ralf, *Die Täuferherrschaft von Münster: Stadtreformation und Welterneuerung* (Münster, 1992)

——— 'Verfolgt, geduldet, anerkannt: Von Täufern zu Mennoniten am Niederrhein und die Geschichte der Mennoniten in Krefeld bis zum Ende der oranischen Zeit (ca. 1530–1702)', in Froese (ed.), *Sie kamen als Fremde*, pp. 13–60

Klueting, Harm, *Das konfessionelle Zeitalter 1525–1648* (Stuttgart, 1989)

Knottnerus, O.S., '"Gijlieden/ die aen alle wateren zaeyt": doperse immigranten in het Nordduitsche kustgebied (1500–1700)', *Doopsgezinde Bijdragen*, new ser. 20 (1994), pp. 11–60

Kolakowski, Leszek, 'Dutch Seventeenth-Century Anticonfessional Ideas and Rational Religion: The Mennonite, Collegiant and Spinozan Connections', trans. and intro. James Satterwhite, *Mennonite Quarterly Review*, 64 (1990), pp. 259–97 and 385–416

Koop, Karl P., 'Early Seventeenth Century Mennonite Confessions of Faith: The Development of an Anabaptist Tradition' (Ph.D. diss., Toronto School of Theology, University of St Michael's College, 1999)

Kopitzsch, Franklin, 'Altona – ein Zentrum der Aufklärung am Rande des dänischen Gesamtstaats', in Klaus Bohnen and Sven Aage Jørgensen (eds), *Der dänische Gesamtstaat* (Tübingen, 1992), pp. 91–118

Kresse, Walter, *Materialien zur Entwicklungsgeschichte der Hamburger Handelsflotte 1765–1823* (Hamburg, 1966)

Kreuder, Ursula, 'Gottfried Arnolds Sicht der Täufer', in Dietrich Blaufuß and Friedrich Niewöhner (eds), *Gottfried Arnold (1666–1714)* (Wiesbaden, 1995), pp. 165–77

Kriedte, Peter, 'Äußerer Erfolg und beginnende Identitätskrise: Die Krefelder Mennoniten im 18. Jahrhundert', in Froese (ed.), *Sie kamen als Fremde*, pp. 61–104

——— 'Taufgesinnte, Dompelaars, Erweckte: Die mennonitische Gemeinde und der Aufstieg des proto-industriellen Kapitalismus in Krefeld im 17. und 18. Jahrhundert', in Rudolf Vierhaus (ed.), *Frühe Neuzeit – Frühe Moderne? Forschungen zur Vielschichtigkeit von Übergangsprozessen* (Göttingen, 1992), pp. 245–70

Kühler, W.J., *Geschiedenis van de Doopsgezinden in Nederland (1600–1735)* (Haarlem, 1940)

——— *Het Socinianisme in Nederland* (Leeuwarden, 1980 [Leiden, 1912])

——— 'De strijd om de belijdenis in de vereenigde Vlaamsche, Friesche en Hoogduitsche gemeente te Utrecht', *Doopsgezinde Bijdragen*, **53** (1916), pp. 145–95

Lang, Peter Thaddäus, 'Konfessionsbildung als Forschungsfeld', *Historisches Jahrbuch*, **100** (1980), pp. 479–93

Latour, Bruno, *Science in Action: How to Follow Scientists and Engineers through Society* (Cambridge, Mass., 1987)

Lehe, Erich von, *Schipp op Scharhörn: Strandung eines hamburgischen Schiffes im Jahre 1755* (n.p., 1967)

Loewen, Royden, *Family, Church, and Market: A Mennonite Community in the Old and New Worlds, 1850–1930* (Urbana, Ill., 1993)

Loose, Hans-Dieter, 'Das Zeitalter der Bürgerunruhen und der großen europäischen Kriege 1618–1712', in Hans-Dieter Loose (ed.), *Hamburg: Geschichte der Stadt und ihrer Bewohner*, 2 vols (Hamburg, 1982), i, pp. 259–350

Marnef, Guido, *Antwerp in the Age of Reformation: Underground Protestantism in a Commercial Metropolis, 1550–1577*, trans. J.C. Grayson (Baltimore, 1996)

——— 'Tussen tolerantie en repressie: Protestanten en religieuze dissidenten te Antwerpen in de 16de eeuw', in Hugo Soly and Alfons K.L. Thijs (eds), *Minderheden in Westeuropese steden* (Brussels, 1995), pp. 189–213

Meihuizen, H.W., *Galenus Abrahamsz 1622–1706: Strijder voor een onbeperkte verdraagzaamheid en verdediger van het Doperse Spiritualisme* (Haarlem, 1954)

Mellink, A.F., *Amsterdam en de Wederdopers in de zestiende Eeuw* (Nijmegen, 1978)

——— 'Das münsterische Täufertum und die Niederlande', *Jahrbuch für Westfälische Kirchengeschichte*, 78 (1985), pp. 13–18

——— 'The Mutual Relations between the Münster Anabaptists and the Netherlands', *Archiv für Reformationsgeschichte*, 50 (1959), pp. 16–33

——— 'Das niederländisch-westfälische Täufertum im sechzehten Jahrhundert', in Hans-Jürgen Goertz (ed.), *Umstrittenes Täufertum* (Göttingen, 1975), pp. 206–22.

——— (ed.), *Documenta Anabaptistica Neerlandica: Amsterdam (1531–1536)* (Leiden, 1985)

Menchi, Silvana Seidel (ed.), *Ketzerverfolgung im 16. und frühen 17. Jahrhundert* (Wiesbaden, 1992)

Mennonite Bibliography, 1631–1961, 2 vols (Scottdale, Pa., and Kitchener, Ont., 1977)

Mennonite Encyclopedia, 5 vols (Hillsboro, Kans., 1955–9, 1990)

Mennonitisches Lexikon, 4 vols (Frankfurt, 1913–67)

Mohr, Rudolf, 'Bourignon, Antoinette', *Schleswig-Holsteinisches biographisches Lexikon* (Neumünster, 1979), v , pp. 48–50

Monter, William, 'Heresy Executions in Reformation Europe, 1520–1565', in Ole Peter Grell and Bob Scribner (eds), *Tolerance and Intolerance in the European Reformation* (Cambridge, 1996), pp. 48–64

Moore, R.I., *The Formation of a Persecuting Society: Power and Deviance in Western Europe, 950–1250* (Oxford and Cambridge, Mass., 1987)

Müller, Hans-Joachim, 'Irenik, eine Kommunikationsform: Das Colloquium Charitativum in Thorn 1645' (doctoral diss., Universität Göttingen, 2000)

Münte, Heinz, *Das Altonaer Handlungshaus van der Smissen 1682–1824: Ein Beitrag zur Wirtschaftsgeschichte der Stadt Altona* (Altona, 1932)

Münzing, Joachim, *Die Jagd auf den Wal: Schleswig-Holsteins und Hamburgs Grönlandfahrt* (Heide, 1978)

Neff, Christian, 'Hinrich van der Smissen', *Christlicher Gemeinde-Kalender*, 38 (1929), pp. 70–90

Neuschäfer, Hubertus, *Schlösser und Herrenhäuser in Südholstein* (Würzburg, 1985)

Nuttall, Geoffrey F., 'Early Quakerism in the Netherlands: Its Wider Context', *Bulletin of Friends Historical Association*, 44 (1955), pp. 3–18

Oesau, Wanda, Hamburgs Grönlandfahrt auf Walfischfang und Robbenschlag vom 17.-19. Jahrhundert (Glückstadt and Hamburg, [1955])

——— *Schleswig-Holsteins Grönlandfahrt auf Walfischfang und Robbenschlag vom 17. bis 19. Jahrhundert* (Glückstadt, 1937)

Oestreich, Gerhard, 'The Structure of the Absolute State', in Brigitta

Oestreich and H.G. Königsberger (eds), *Neostoicism and the Early Modern State*, trans. David McLintock (Cambridge, 1982), pp. 258–73

Oyer, John S., *Lutheran Reformers against the Anabaptists: Luther, Melanchthon and Menius and the Anabaptists of Central Germany* (The Hague, 1964)

Packull, Werner O., *Hutterite Beginnings: Communitarian Experiments during the Reformation* (Baltimore and London, 1995)

Penner, Archie, 'Pieter Jansz. Twisck – Second Generation Anabaptist/Mennonite Churchman, Writer and Polemicist (Ph.D. diss., University of Iowa, 1971)

Plett, Harvey, 'Georg Hansen and the Danzig Flemish Mennonite Church: A Study in Continuity' (Ph.D. diss., University of Manitoba, 1991)

Popkin, Richard H., 'Spinoza's Relations with the Quakers in Amsterdam', *Quaker History*, 73 (1984), pp. 14–28

Pries, Edmund, 'Anabaptist Oath Refusal: Basel, Bern and Strasbourg, 1525–1538' (Ph.D. diss., University of Waterloo, 1995)

Redekop, Calvin, *Mennonite Society* (Baltimore, 1989)

——— and Samuel Steiner (eds), *Mennonite Identity: Historical and Contemporary Perspectives* (Lanham, NY and London, 1988)

Reinhard, Wolfgang, *Ausgewählte Abhandlungen* (Berlin, 1997)

——— 'Sozialdisziplinierung – Konfessionalisierung – Modernisierung: Ein historiographischer Diskurs', in Nada Boskovska Leimgruber (ed.), *Die frühe Neuzeit in der Geschichtswissenschaft: Forschungstendenzen und Forschungserträge* (Paderborn, 1997), pp. 39–55

Reißmann, Martin, *Die hamburgische Kaufmannschaft des 17. Jahrhunderts in sozialgeschichtlicher Sicht* (Hamburg, 1975)

Roldanus, Cornelia W., *Zeventiende-eeuwsche Geestesbloei* (Amsterdam, 1938)

Roosbroeck, Robert van, 'Die Niederlassung von Flamen und Wallonen in Hamburg (1567–1605)', *Zeitschrift des Vereins für Hamburgische Geschichte*, **49–50** (1964), pp. 53–76

Roosen, Berend Carl, *Gerhard Roosen* (Hamburg, 1854)

——— *Geschichte der Mennoniten-Gemeinde zu Hamburg und Altona* (2 parts, Hamburg, 1886–7)

——— *Geschichte unseres Hauses* (n.p., 1905)

——— 'Kurze Zusammenfassung der Geschichte der Hamburg-Altonaer Mennoniten-Gemeinde, von ihrer Entstehung bis zum Altonaer Brande', *Zeitschrift des Vereins für Hamburgische Geschichte*, **3** (1851), pp. 78–108.

——— *Menno Symons* (Leipzig, 1848)

——— 'Die Mennoniten und Quäker', *Mennonitische Blätter*, **1** (1854), pp. 41–4 and 54–6

Roosen, G. Arthur, 'Die Familie Roosen und ihre Anverwandten' (privately produced manuscript, Caracas, 1952). Copies available at Staatsarchiv Hamburg, Museum für Hamburgische Geschichte and the Genealogische Gesellschaft, Sitz Hamburg

Röthel, Hans Konrad, *Bürgerliche Kultur und Bildnismalerei in Hamburg während der ersten Hälfte des 18. Jahrhunderts* (Hamburg, 1938)

Rückleben, Hermann, *Die Niederwerfung der hamburgischen Ratsgewalt: Kirchliche Bewegungen und bürgerliche Unruhen im ausgehenden 17. Jahrhundert* (Hamburg, 1970)

Samuelsson, Kurt, *Religion and Economic Action: A Critique of Max Weber*, trans. E. Geoffrey French (New York and Evanston, Ill., 1961)

Sander, Friedrich, *Der Pastor Johann Heinrich Horb* (Hamburg, 1995)

Sawatsky, Rodney James, 'History and Ideology: American Mennonite Identity Definition through History' (Ph.D. diss., Princeton University, 1977)

Schepansky, Ernst W., 'Mennoniten in Hamburg und Altona zur Zeit des Merkantilismus', *Mennonitische Geschichtsblätter*, 38, new ser. 32 (1980), pp. 54–73. Also in *Hamburger Jahrbuch für Wirtschafts- und Gesellschaftspolitik*, 24 (1979), pp. 219–34

Schilling, Heinz, 'Confessional Europe', in Thomas A. Brady, Heiko A. Oberman and James D. Tracy (eds), *Handbook of European History, 1400–1600*, 2 vols (Leiden, New York and Cologne, 1995), ii, pp. 641–81

——— 'Confessional Migration as a Distinct Type of Old European Longdistance Migration', in Simonetta Cavaciocchi (ed.), *Le migrazioni in Europa: secc. XIII–XVIII* (Florence, 1994), pp. 175–89

——— 'Innovation through Migration: The Settlements of Calvinist Netherlanders in Sixteenth- and Seventeenth-Century Central and Western Europe', *Social History – Histoire sociale* (Ottawa), 16 (1983), pp. 7–33

——— 'Die Konfessionalisierung von Kirche, Staat und Gesellschaft – Profil, Leistung, Defizite und Perspektiven eines geschichtswissenschaftlichen Paradigmas', in Wolfgang Reinhard and Heinz Schilling (eds), *Die katholische Konfessionalisierung* (Münster, 1995), pp. 1–49

——— '"Konfessionsbildung" und "Konfessionalisierung"', *Geschichte in Wissenschaft und Unterricht*, 42 (1991), pp. 447–63 and 779–94

——— *Niederländische Exulanten im 16. Jahrhundert: Ihre Stellung im Sozialgefüge und im religiösen Leben deutscher und englischer Städte* (Gütersloh, 1972)

——— 'Die niederländischen Exulanten des 16. Jahrhunderts: Ein Beitrag zum Typus der frühneuzeitlichen Konfessionsmigration', *Geschichte in Wissenschaft und Unterricht*, 43 (1992), pp. 67–78

——— *Die Stadt in der Frühen Neuzeit* (Munich, 1993)

Schindling, Anton, 'Konfessionalisierung und Grenzen von Konfessionalisierbarkeit', in Anton Schindling and Walter Ziegler (eds), *Die Territorien des Reichs im Zeitalter der Reformation und Konfessionalisierung: Land und Konfession 1500–1650*, 7 vols (Münster, 1989–1997), vii, pp. 9–44

Schlabach, Theron F., 'Mennonites and Pietism in America, 1740–1880: Some Thoughts on the Friedmann Thesis', *Mennonite Quarterly Review*, 57 (1983), pp. 222–40

Schlögl, Rudolf, *Glaube und Religion in der Säkularisierung: Die katholische Stadt – Köln, Aachen, Münster – 1700–1840* (Munich, 1995)

Schmidt, Heinrich Richard, *Dorf und Religion: Reformierte Sittenzucht in Berner Landgemeinden der Frühen Neuzeit* (Stuttgart and New York, 1995)

——— *Konfessionalisierung im 16. Jahrhundert* (Munich, 1992)

——— 'Sozialdisziplinierung? Ein Plädoyer für das Ende des Etatismus in der Konfessionalisierungsforschung', *Historische Zeitschrift*, **265** (1997), pp. 639–82

Schowalter, Otto, 'Altonaer Kaufleute des 18. Jahrhunderts auf Reisen', *Christlicher Gemeinde-Kalender*, **46** (1937), pp. 103–16

——— 'Kulturleistungen der Hamburger Mennoniten. Schiffahrt – Industrie – Welthandel', *Mennonitische Geschichtsblätter*, **3** (1938), pp. 33–48

——— 'Quer durch Altona und Hamburg auf den Spuren mennonitischer Geschichte', *Christlicher Gemeinde-Kalender*, **48** (1939), pp. 59–70

Schrader, Hans-Jürgen, 'Hoburg, Christian', in *Schleswig-Holsteinisches Biographisches Lexikon*, ed. Olaf Klose, Eva Rudolf and Ute Hayessen (Neumünster, 1979), v, pp. 133–7

Schroeder, William, *Balthasar Denner, 1685–1749: Portrait Artist* (Winnipeg, 1994)

——— and Helmut Huebert, *Mennonite Historical Atlas* (2nd edn, Winnipeg, 1996)

Schubert, Franz (ed.), *Trauregister aus den ältesten Kirchenbüchern Hamburgs: Von den Anfängen bis zum Jahre 1704* (Göttingen, 1997)

Schulze, Winfried, 'Gerhard Oestreichs Begriff "Sozialdisziplinierung in der Frühen Neuzeit"', *Zeitschrift für historische Forschung*, **14** (1987), pp. 265–302

Scott, James C., *Domination and the Arts of Resistance: Hidden Transcripts* (New Haven, 1990)

Sellert, Wolfgang, *Über die Zuständigkeitsabgrenzung von Reichshofrat und Reichskammergericht* (Aalen, 1965)

Simmel, Georg, *On Individuality and Social Forms*, ed. and intro. Donald N. Levine (Chicago and London, 1971)

——— *Soziologie: Untersuchungen über die Formen der Vergesellschaftung* (Frankfurt, 1995 [Leipzig, 1908])

Slee, J.C. van, *De Rijnsburger Collegianten* (Utrecht, 1980 [Haarlem, 1895])

Smend, Rudolf, *Das Reichskammergericht: Geschichte und Verfassung* (Aalen, 1965 [Weimar, 1911])

Smissen, Hinrich van der, *Mennostein und Mennolinde zu Fresenburg: Zur Erinnerung an den 16. September 1922* (n.p., n.d.)

Snyder, C. Arnold, *Anabaptist History and Theology: An Introduction* (Kitchener, Ont., 1995)

——— *The Life and Thought of Michael Sattler* (Scottdale, Pa., and Kitchener, Ont., 1984)

Sorkin, David, 'Enlightenment and Emancipation: German Jewry's Formative Age in Comparative Perspective', in Todd Endelman (ed.), *Comparing Jewish Societies* (Ann Arbor, 1997), pp. 89–112.

Sprunger, Mary, 'Faillissementen: Een aspect van geestelijke tucht bij de Waterlands-doopsgezinde gemeente te Amsterdam in de zeventiende eeuw', *Doopsgezinde Bijdragen*, new ser. 17 (1991), pp. 101–30

——— 'Rich Mennonites, Poor Mennonites: Economics and Theology in the Amsterdam Waterlander Congregation during the Golden Age' (Ph.D. diss., University of Illinois at Urbana-Champaign, 1993)

——— 'Waterlanders and the Dutch Golden Age: A Case Study on Mennonite Involvement in Seventeenth-Century Dutch Trade and Industry as One of the Earliest Examples of Socio-Economic Assimilation', in Hamilton, Voolstra and Visser (eds), *From Martyr to Muppy*, pp. 133–48

Stauffer, Ethelbert, 'Die Mennonitengemeinde in Hamburg-Altona', *Hamburgische Kirchenzeitung*, 4 (1928), pp. 15–18, 39–42 and 63–5

Stayer, James M., 'The Anabaptists', in Steven Ozment (ed.), *Reformation Europe: A Guide to Research* (St. Louis, Mo., 1982), pp. 135–59

——— *Anabaptists and the Sword* (Lawrence, Kans., 1972)

——— *The German Peasants' War and Anabaptist Community of Goods* (Montreal and Kingston, Ont., 1991)

——— 'Oldeklooster and Menno', *Sixteenth Century Journal*, 9 (1978), pp. 52–5

——— 'The Passing of the Radical Moment in the Radical Reformation', *Mennonite Quarterly Review*, 71 (1997), pp. 147–52

——— 'The Radical Reformation', in Thomas A. Brady, Heiko A. Oberman and James D. Tracy (eds), *Handbook of European History, 1400–1600*, 2 vols (Leiden, New York and Cologne, 1995), ii, pp. 249–82

Stein-Stegemann, Hans-Konrad, *Findbuch der Reichskammergerichtakten* (Schleswig, 1986)

Stukenbrock, Claus, 'Der Hamburger Bürgereid im 19. Jahrhundert' (internal research paper, Staatsarchiv Hamburg, 15 Oct. 1959)

Sutter, Sem, 'Die Anfänge der Mennonitengemeinde in Friedrichstadt 1621–1650', *Mennonitische Geschichtsblätter*, 37, new ser. **32** (1980), pp. 42–53.

——— 'Friedrichstadt an der Eider: An Early Experience in Religious Toleration, 1621–1727' (Ph.D. diss., University of Chicago, 1982)

——— 'Friedrichstadt: An Early German Example of Mennonite Magistrates', *Mennonite Quarterly Review*, **53** (1979), pp. 299–305

Te Brake, Wayne, *Shaping History: Ordinary People in European Politics, 1500–1700* (Berkeley, Los Angeles and London, 1998)

Thiele, Ottomar, *Salpeterwirtschaft und Salpeterpolitik: Eine volkswirtschaftliche Studie über das ehemalige europäische Salpeterwesen* (Tübingen, 1905)

Tiedemann, Claus, *Die Schiffahrt des Herzogtums Bremen zur Schwedenzeit (1645–1712)* (Stade, 1969)

Tracy, James D., *Europe's Reformations, 1450–1650* (Lanham, Md., and Oxford, 1999)

Urry, James, 'The Closed and the Open: Social and Religious Change amongst the Mennonites in Russia (1789–1889)' (D.Phil. diss., Oxford University, 1978)

Valkema Blouw, P., 'Drukkers voor Menno Simons en Dirk Philips', *Doopsgezinde Bijdragen*, new ser. **17** (1991), pp. 31–74

Veen, S. D. van, 'Foecke Floris', *Doopsgezinde Bijdragen*, **27** (1887), pp. 49–85

Veluwenkamp, J.W., '"N Huis op Archangel": De Amsterdamse koopmansfamilie Thesigh', *Jaarboek Amstelodamum*, **69** (1977), pp. 123–39

Visser, Dirk, 'A Checklist of Dutch Mennonite Confessions of Faith to 1800', *Documenta Anabaptistica Neerlandica*, bulletins **6** and **7** (1974–75)

Voolstra, Sjouke, 'The Path to Conversion: The Controversy between Hans de Ries and Nittert Obbes', in Walter Klaassen (ed.), *Anabaptism Revisited* (Scottdale, Pa., and Waterloo, Ont., 1992), pp. 98–114

Vos, Karel, 'Bastiaan van Weenigem en het eedvraagstuk', *Nederlandsch Archief voor Kerkgeschiedenis*, new ser. **6** (1909), pp. 121–38

——— *Menno Simons 1496–1561: Zijn leven en werken en zijn reformatorische denkbeelden* (Leiden, 1914)

Waite, Gary K., *David Joris and Dutch Anabaptism, 1524–1543* (Waterloo, Ont., 1990)

Westera, Bert, 'Mennonites and War in the Seventeenth and Eighteenth Centuries: The Brants Family between Pacifism and Trade in Guns', in Hamilton, Voolstra & Visser (eds), *From Martyr to Muppy*, pp. 149–55

Whaley, Joachim, 'Minorities and Tolerance in Hamburg, 16th–18th Centuries', in Hugo Soly and Alfons K.L. Thijs (eds), *Minderheden in Westeuropese steden* (Brussels, 1995), pp. 173–88

—— *Religious Toleration and Social Change in Hamburg 1529–1819* (Cambridge, 1985)

Wichmann, E.H., *Geschichte Altona's* (2nd edn, Altona, 1896)

Williams, George Huntston, *The Radical Reformation* (3rd edn, Kirksville, Mo., 1992)

Woelk, Susanne, 'Menno Simons in Oldersum und Oldesloe: "Häuptlingsreformation" und Glaubensflüchtlinge im 16. Jahrhundert', *Mennonitische Geschichtsblätter*, 53 (1996), pp. 11–33

Wuite, J., 'De scheuring tusschen het Lam en de Zon', *Doopsgezinde Bijdragen*, 40 (1900), pp. 1–37

Zeeden, Ernst Walter, *Die Entstehung der Konfessionen: Grundlagen und Formen der Konfessionsbildung im Zeitalter der Glaubenskämpfe* (Munich and Vienna, 1965)

Zijpp, N. van der, *De belijdenisgeschriften der Nederlandse Doopsgezinden* (Haarlem, 1954)

Index

NB: The appendices have been indexed only minimally.

Diploma Básico

Preparación para el Diploma Básico de Español Lengua Extranjera

Jesús ARRIBAS

Rosa Mª DE CASTRO

GRUPO DIDASCALIA, S.A.
Plaza Ciudad de Salta, 3 - 28043 MADRID - (ESPAÑA)
TEL.: (34) 914.165.511 - FAX: (34) 914.165.411

Primera edición: 1991
Segunda edición: 1993
Tercera edición: 1994
Primera reimpresión: 1995
Segunda reimpresión: 1997
Tercera reimpresión: 1997
Cuarta reimpresión: 1998
Quinta reimpresión: 1999
Sexta reimpresión: 1999
Séptima reimpresión: 2000
Octava reimpresión: 2001
Novena reimpresión: 2002

Dirección y coordinación editorial: Pilar Jiménez Gazapo
Adjunta dirección y coordinación editorial: Ana Calle Fernández
Diseño portada y fotomecánica: Departamento de Imagen Edelsa
Diseño y maquetación: Joaquín González / Luis Miguel García
Impreso en: Gráficas Rógar
Encuadernación: Perellón
ISBN: 84-7711-088-3
Depósito legal nº: M-11690-2002
Impreso en España
Printed in Spain

Prólogo

En 1988 se creó el Diploma de Español como Lengua Extranjera como único título oficial de español válido internacionalmente.

Actualmente hay tres títulos oficiales: El Certificado Inicial de Español (C.I.E.), el Diploma Básico de Español (D.B.E.) y el Diploma Superior de Español (D.S.E.). Los otorga el Ministerio de Educación y Ciencia, los organiza el Instituto Cervantes y elabora las pruebas la Universidad de Salamanca.

Este libro de actividades ha sido programado especialmente para quienes se preparan para obtener el D.B.E. , con el cual podrán acreditar un conocimiento de español suficiente en cualquier ámbito de comunicación habitual. Por ello, se adapta fielmente a los modelos oficiales de pruebas, planteando actividades de los siguientes tipos:

Comprensión y expresión oral

Textos orales con preguntas y algunas con propuestas de V / F (Verdadero / Falso).
Dibujos en viñetas, con preguntas sobre su contenido.
Propuestas de exposición oral, con sugerencias para su preparación.
(Para hacer más efectivo este bloque de actividades, acompaña a este libro una cinta grabada.)

Comprensión y expresión escrita

Textos periodísticos, con preguntas de respuesta libre, Verdadero / Falso o de selección múltiple.
Propuestas de cartas personales, con instrucciones para su redacción.
Propuestas de redacción a partir de instrucciones.

Gramática y vocabulario

Textos incompletos para rellenar huecos.
Ejercicios de selección múltiple.
Ejercicios de equivalencia léxica.
Diálogos para completar con la opción más adecuada.

Para que el estudiante pueda trabajar con el libro de forma autónoma, al final se ofrecen las claves de autocorrección, con respuestas exactas siempre que es posible y, cuando no, aproximadas. También se dan transcritos los textos orales de las grabaciones para lograr un mayor afianzamiento en la comprensión.

Hemos querido, además, que todo el conjunto de ejercicios girara en torno a diferentes aspectos de la vida cotidiana de los españoles de hoy, reflejando sus costumbres y formas de actuar y pensar más corrientes. Estos recorridos se hacen a través de diez unidades, cada una de ellas de carácter monográfico. Así el estudiante podrá establecer contacto no sólo con la lengua, sino también con la cultura en su más amplio sentido.

LOS AUTORES

Índice

Familia y costumbres. Unidad 1

A. Comprensión y expresión oral

1. Textos orales

1.1 Escuche los siguientes avisos que se dan por la megafonía de un campamento infantil. Es el día de visita de los padres. Antes de empezar a escuchar la grabación, conviene que lea usted las preguntas.

Preguntas:

1. *¿Cuál es el nombre de este campamento?*

   ....

2. *¿Qué se puede hacer en el campamento desde las diez hasta las once y media?*

   ....

3. *¿Qué deben hacer las personas que vayan a quedarse a comer en el campamento?*

   ....

4. *¿Cuándo hay que regresar al campamento?*

   ....

1.2 En un noticiario radiofónico ha oído las siguientes informaciones:

Preguntas:

1. *¿A qué se dedica el suegro de Antonio Cardeñosa?*

   ....

2. *¿Cuánto hace que don Secundino se ordenó de sacerdote?*

   ....

3. *¿Cómo ha obtenido don Agapito de la Rosa las veinte mil pesetas?*

   ....

1.3 En una emisora de radio ha oído las siguientes informaciones:

Marque V / F (Verdadero / Falso):

1. *En el zoo se pueden ver un par de focas recién nacidas.*
   V ☐ F ☐
2. *Para participar en el concurso de castillos hay que apuntarse el día anterior.*
   V ☐ F ☐
3. *La entrada al espectáculo de títeres resulta un poco cara.*
   V ☐ F ☐

2. Expresión a partir de láminas

Observe con atención la historieta. Cuando conteste a las cuestiones que le planteamos, hágalo de forma oral. Además escríbalo.

2.1 Primera lámina

Póngase en el lugar de la enfermera. ¿Qué puede estar diciéndole al padre?

....

2.2 Segunda lámina

Póngase en el lugar de la niña de la moto. ¿Qué puede estar diciéndoles a sus amigos?

....

....

2.3 Tercera lámina

Póngase en el lugar de la madre. ¿Qué puede estar diciéndole al fotógrafo?

....

3. Exposición sobre un tema general

3.1 Sobre el siguiente tema, deberá hablar durante un tiempo no superior a cinco minutos. Le sugerimos que grabe su exposición, la escuche y trate de mejorar la expresión en una segunda grabación definitiva.

Tema: EL CONFLICTO GENERACIONAL.

Sugerencias:
Padres muy estrictos.
Hijos muy rebeldes.
Hermanos mayores y hermanos pequeños.
El dinero de la semana nunca parece suficiente.
Diferente nivel de exigencia según se trate de chicos o chicas.

3.2 Sobre el siguiente tema deberá hablar durante un tiempo no superior a cinco minutos.

Tema: LOS ABUELOS EN CASA.

Sugerencias:
¿Son molestos?
Relaciones de abuelos y nietos.
Atenciones que precisan.
¿En casa o en una residencia?

B. Comprensión y expresión escrita

1. Texto periodístico informativo con preguntas sobre su contenido

Lea con atención el siguiente artículo:

En las grandes urbes se trata peor a los mayores

Los ingresos de ancianos suponen el 60% de los casos de urgencias clínicas.

Mayka Sánchez, **Madrid**

Los ancianos representan aproximadamente el 60% de las urgencias de los grandes centros hospitalarios de Madrid. La deshidratación, los problemas gastrointestinales y las complicaciones derivadas de estos procesos son, en los meses de verano, las patologías más comunes por las que esta parte de la población precisa asistencia médica. Mientras que algunos de estos ancianos regresan a sus casas al cabo 5 de unos días u horas de ser atendidos, otros permanecen ingresados durante semanas o meses.

Según señala Fernando Molina, internista del hospital La Paz, la problemática social del anciano que ingresa en un establecimien- 10 to sanitario es de dos tipos. Por un lado, está el caso del anciano con un problema médico que es traído por su familia con la intención de *aparcarlo*; y por otro, el 15 de aquel que es ingresado por un proceso agudo y que, cuando mejora, la familia se resiste a llevárselo a casa por las secuelas derivadas de ese proceso.

20 La primera situación es cada vez menos frecuente, «afortunadamente», dice Fernando Molina, que explica que suele tratarse de personas que no pueden valerse 25 por sí mismas y que sufren procesos crónicos o sus consecuencias (demencias, trombosis cerebral, fracturas de cadera e incluso cáncer).

30 Luego está el anciano que llega a urgencias por un proceso agudo que deja secuelas, como la parálisis producida por una trombosis cerebral, y, cuando es dado de 35 alta, la familia se niega a llevárselo, alegando que en casa no puede atenderlo en el nuevo estado.

En los grandes hospitales de 40 Madrid suelen ingresar al día un promedio de cuatro personas de más de 70 años con un problema social. Para Ventura Anciones, neurólogo de La Paz, 45 hasta hace unos años en los meses de verano aumentaba el número de ancianos que ingresaba por urgencias en los hospitales, «porque los familiares 50 querían dejarlo *aparcado* para irse de vacaciones».

Liberarse de molestias

«Ahora cualquier momento del año es bueno para liberarse de 55 ellos, aunque dicho así suene tremendamente duro», dice. Sin embargo, esta especie de abandono, que en la gran mayoría de los casos no es tan drástico, 60 puede ser explicable según este médico.

«Todos sabemos que en una ciudad como Madrid los pisos no son muy amplios y casi to- 65 dos los miembros de la familia están la mayor parte del tiempo fuera de casa por el trabajo, los estudios y otras obligaciones. Todo ello genera una dinámica 70 que en absoluto es favorable al anciano y que impide que se satisfagan los cuidados que precisa cuando no puede valerse por sí mismo», explica el 75 doctor Anciones.

Dos serían las posibles soluciones a esta situación, según apunta Manuel Díaz Curiel, internista y responsable del 80 servicio de urgencias de la clínica de La Concepción. «Contamos con los centros de cuidados mínimos y con la asistencia domiciliaria», aclara. «En 85 cuanto a los primeros», matiza, «no quiere decir que ofrezcan mínimas o insuficientes atenciones, sino que ofrecen todos los cuidados que precisa un an- 90 ciano que no puede valerse por sí mismo y que no puede ser atendido en casa, pero que tampoco necesita estar en el hospital», explica.

«Sin embargo, el problema que existe es que estos centros son insuficientes para la demanda que hay, y a veces se requieren largos trámites burocráticos», 100 añade. Respecto de la asistencia a domicilio, el doctor opina que «bien organizada, podría resultar barata y muy satisfactoria para una parte de esta po- 105 blación».

EL PAÍS, 3-IX-1990

Conteste a las siguientes preguntas:

1. *¿En qué tanto por ciento ingresan los ancianos en las urgencias clínicas de Madrid ?*

....

2. *¿Cuál es la estación del año en la que ingresan más ancianos en los hospitales?*

....

3. *¿Cuántos ancianos con un problema social ingresan diariamente en los hospitales?*

....

4. *¿Por qué resulta más difícil atender a los ancianos en una gran ciudad como Madrid?*

....

5. *¿Qué dos soluciones se apuntan para atender a los ancianos que necesitan cuidados?*

....

6. *¿Qué inconvenientes tienen en la actualidad los centros de cuidados mínimos?*

....

2. Texto de anuncios y convocatorias con preguntas

A continuación va a leer la convocatoria de dos tipos de ayudas para funcionarios:

PRESTACIONES POR MATRIMONIO Y NACIMIENTO DE HIJOS DEL MUTUALISTA

SUBSIDIO DE NATALIDAD.

Consiste en la entrega al mutualista de una cantidad por el nacimiento de cada hijo. Si ambos cónyuges son mutualistas, el Subsidio sólo puede reconocerse a uno de ellos.

El importe del Subsidio es de 3.000 pesetas.

SUBSIDIO DE NUPCIALIDAD.

Consiste en la entrega al mutualista de una cantidad cuando contraiga matrimonio. Si los dos contrayentes son mutualistas, ambos tienen derecho a la percepción del Subsidio.

El importe del Subsidio es de 6.000 pesetas.

PRESTACIONES POR ESTUDIOS UNIVERSITARIOS

BECA DE MATRICULA

Las Becas de matrícula se conceden por un importe máximo de 60.000 pesetas cada una, destinadas a costear tanto la matrícula propiamente dicha, como los demás gastos de inscripción en los Centros de Enseñanza donde hayan de ser cursados los estudios.

AYUDA PARA MATERIAL DE ESTUDIO

Las ayudas económicas para material de estudio, consisten en bolsas de 30.000 pesetas cada una para costear la adquisición por el beneficiario de los libros de texto y material escolar necesario para cursar aquéllos en que se haya matriculado.

BECA DE RESIDENCIA

Las becas de residencia, que en el curso 89/90 ascienden a 477.000 pesetas cada una, abonables en nueve mensualidades de 53.000 pesetas, tienen por finalidad atender los gastos de residencia del beneficiario en Colegios Mayores adscritos a la Universidad en la que se vayan a cursar los estudios.

PLAZA GRATUITA EN COLEGIO MAYOR DE MUFACE

Las Plazas gratuitas en Colegios Mayores de MUFACE cumplen el mismo objetivo que la modalidad anterior, pero al tratarse de Centros propios de MUFACE -Nuestra Señora del Pilar de Zaragoza y Juan Luis Vives de Madrid-, los gastos de residencia corren por cuenta de MUFACE.

Estas prestaciones se conceden previa convocatoria anual de la Dirección General de MUFACE, que normalmente se realiza en el mes de junio. El número de Becas y Ayudas se fija en función de las disponibilidades presupuestarias; el número de plazas gratuitas depende de las vacantes previsibles en los Colegios Mayores de MUFACE.

Los mutualistas pueden obtener Becas de Matrícula y Ayudas para Material de Estudio. Los hijos y huérfanos de mutualistas pueden concurrir a cualquiera de las modalidades, que son compatibles entre sí, salvo las Becas de Residencia y las Plazas Gratuitas.

(Revista **MUFACE**)

Conteste a las siguientes preguntas:

1. *¿Cuál es la ayuda económica para una funcionaria que haya tenido mellizos ?*

   ....

2. *¿Qué cantidad recibe como ayuda un funcionario que se casa?*

   ....

3. *¿Cuál es la cantidad mayor que se le concede a un estudiante para beca de matrícula?*

   ....

4. *¿Cuáles son los Colegios Mayores propiedad de MUFACE?*

   ....

5. *¿Para qué curso escolar es esta convocatoria de becas y ayudas?*

   ....

6. *¿Para qué se ofrecen bolsas de treinta mil pesetas ?*

   ....

7. *¿En qué fecha se convocan estas ayudas ?*

   ....

3. Artículo periodístico de opinión, con preguntas a las que deberá contestar VERDADERO/FALSO

Lea con atención el siguiente artículo:

Cuando ella gana más

Hasta hace pocos años era impensable que una mujer obtuviera un salario superior al de un hombre, salvo que se tratara de 5 alguna artista de cine o de una cantante. Y fue por entonces cuando se acuñó el término de «señor de» para referirse a los hombres que vivían del dinero 10 que ganaba su mujer.

Pero los tiempos están cambiando y aunque todavía las mujeres ganan por término medio -según el Ministerio de Ha- 15 cienda- un 22,6 por ciento menos que los hombres en el mismo puesto de trabajo, ya no resulta anecdótico encontrarse con parejas en las que ella es la 20 que aporta más dinero al hogar. Esto, en principio, no tendría por qué ser un problema, pero la realidad cotidiana nos demuestra que sí lo es. Según las estadís- 25 ticas, el 20 por ciento de los conflictos conyugales surgen a causa del dinero y muchos de ellos se deben a las peleas sobre quién debe manejarlo y aportar- 30 lo. En los casos más graves, el hombre se niega incluso a que su mujer trabaje fuera de casa porque se siente herido en su virilidad. Le han educado para ser el 35 proveedor de alimento para su familia y si no lo consigue, piensa que ha fracasado.

A medida que el nivel cultural es más alto, el hombre no suele 40 oponerse a que su esposa tenga un trabajo remunerado; pero de eso, a admitir tranquilamente que su compañera gane más que él, va un mundo... En ocasiones, el 45 rechazo se produce a consecuencia de los comentarios malintencionados de amigos y familiares: «Menudo chollo has encontrado» (risitas irónicas), «O 50 sea que la que manda en *tu* casa es ella» (sonrisas conmiserativas). Y lo peor de todo es que muchos de estos hombres son incluso modernos y liberales en otros 55 aspectos de su vida y no se atreven a expresar clara y abiertamente su preocupación. En los casos más graves se han llegado 60 a detectar problemas físicos originados por la angustia, como estrés, depresión y, sobre todo, falta de deseo sexual, impotencia o eyaculación precoz.

65 Los cimientos se hunden.

Hay que reconocer en su favor que mientras las mujeres viven una época de conquistas, los hombres pasan por una situa- 70 ción de crisis. A su alrededor se derrumban los principios fundamentales que les enseñaron cuando eran pequeños; la superioridad del varón, el mito del 75 sexo fuerte, la norma tradicional de mujer en casa y el hombre a conseguir el sustento, etc... Se encuentran perdidos y desconcertados, no saben cuál es su

80 papel y, lo que es peor, viven cada logro femenino como una pérdida de prerrogativas masculinas.
85 La situación puede llegar a hacerse insostenible cuando ambos tienen una profesión similar, y es ella la triunfadora, la admirada y la conocida. Los celos
90 profesionales les hacen sentir que han fracasado y, en ocasiones, viven el triunfo de sus compañeras como una agresión.
Incluso llegan a sentir miedo y a
95 dudar del amor de su pareja, al suponer -por aquello del *tanto tienes, tanto vales*- que al tener menor categoría y sueldo, ella no podrá admirarlo y de ahí, a dejar
100 de quererlo y respetarlo, sólo hay un paso.
Pero todas estas elucubraciones, normalmente nada tienen que ver con los sentimientos y la
105 forma de actuar de las mujeres, salvo por el hecho de que ellas también lo pasan mal. Aguantan estoicamente determinados
110 reproches, aún a sabiendas de que el verdadero problema es otro, o tratan de engañarse pensando que los malos modos de su marido son pasajeros y que se
115 deben a problemas laborales.
En estos casos, la única solución es hablar claramente y a pecho descubierto sobre el asunto. Tratar de hacer entender al hombre
120 que su virilidad no puede medirse por unos cuantos miles de pesetas más o menos y que la teoría del macho protector y proveedor de alimentos se re-
125 monta a la prehistoria cuando ésa era la única forma de que sobrevivieran la madre y las crías. Si es necesario, se debe llegar incluso a pactar soluciones tem-
130 porales, si la crisis es muy grave. Por ejemplo, lo que hicieron Sonia (ejecutiva de publicidad) y Francisco (delineante): Apor-
135 tar el mismo dinero para el mantenimiento de la casa e ingresar el resto del salario de ella en una cartilla a su nombre y al de sus dos hijos. Pasado un tiempo él
140 comprendió que era una tontería que todos vivieran peor por un orgullo mal entendido.

Esperanza Rodríguez. Revista SER PADRES HOY, nº190, Septiembre 1990.

Lea las siguientes frases. Señale V (verdadero) o F (falso) en relación con el contenido del artículo. A continuación, busque la parte del texto en la que se ha basado para escribir V/F y escríbala en las líneas de puntos.

1. *Las mujeres siempre han tenido salarios superiores a los de los hombres.*

V□ F□ ....

2. *Todos los maridos que tienen salarios menores que sus mujeres sufren de impotencia.*

V□ F□ ....

3. *En ocasiones, el hombre no soporta el triunfo profesional de su mujer.*

V□ F□ ....

4. *Las mujeres están viviendo un buen momento en el acceso al mundo profesional.*

V□ F□ ....

5. *Los hombres están encantados con los logros profesionales de las mujeres.*

V□ F□ ....

6. *Los conflictos conyugales, en un veinte por ciento, se deben a causas económicas.*

V□ F□ ....

7. *A nivel cultural más alto, menor oposición del hombre a que la mujer trabaje.*

V□ F□ ....

4.Redacción de una carta a partir de instrucciones

Rosa y Félix, amigos suyos, van a casarse y le han enviado a usted una invitación para que asista a su boda. Como no puede asistir, se lo va a comunicar en una carta. La carta deberá contener al menos lo siguiente:

1. Encabezamiento y despedida.
2. Felicitación.
3. Motivo por el que no puede asistir.
4. Adelánteles que les envía un regalo.

C. Gramática y vocabulario

1. Texto incompleto con 10 huecos

El siguiente texto está incompleto. Deberá rellenar cada uno de los huecos con la palabra más apropiada.

¿Cuándo se le debe decir a un niño que es adoptado? Hacia los tres años parece la edad más oportuna para empezar a informarle. A algunos padres adoptivos les asusta .....: momento en que han de hablar con el niño, ... piensan que la verdad les va a hacer daño. Sin .... , no hay razón para preocuparse, porque el niño seguramente ..... a aceptarlo con toda naturalidad, siempre que se haga a una .... temprana.

A los tres años los niños lo preguntan .... y una de las cosas que más les interesa .... saber de dónde vienen. Por eso esta edad es la .... para comunicarles lo que tanto parece preocupar a los padres. .... que dejarle muy claro que él ha sido un .... elegido y deseado.

2. Ejercicios de selección múltiple. Gramática

En cada una de las siguientes frases hay un hueco que deberá rellenar con una de las cuatro expresiones, eligiendo la que sea más correcta.

1. Los padres y los hijos .... respetar mutuamente.
   a) deberse b) se deben c) se tienen d) deben
2. La vió por la calle y ....
   a) la enamoró a ella. b) se quiso con ella. c) se enamoraba de ella. d) se enamoró de ella.
3. .... muy tristes porque no nos escribes.
   a) Yo y papá estamos b) Papá y mamá estamos c) Papá y yo estamos d) Papás estamos
4. A mi abuela no .... el dinero de la pensión.
   a) se la llega b) se le llega c) le llega d) la llega
5. ¿................................ la familia está en crisis?
   a) Es verdad que b) Es de verdad c) Es la verdad d) La verdad es que

6. Cuando nació su hermano, se .... desplazado.
   a) ha sentido b) hubo sentido c) sintió d) sintiera

7. Mi hermana .... un violinista de la orquesta.
   a) va a casar b) va a casar con c) se va a casar con d) se va a casar

8. *Inés, ¿quieres a Alvaro .... esposo?*
   a) por b) de c) para d) a manera de

9. *Mi sobrina está .... de un momento a otro.*
   a) para que dé a luz b) para dar a luz c) para que diese a luz d) para que diera a luz

10. Tu hija está ....
   a) más y más alta. b) alta cada vez más. c) cada vez más alta. d) alta más cada vez.

11. .... la reprendían, se encerraba en su habitación.
   a) Toda vez que b) Siempre c) Siempre cuando d) Siempre que

12. Nuestra nueva casa es .... anterior.
   a) comodísima que la b) la más cómoda que la c) más cómoda de la d) más cómoda que la

13. ¿Te gustaría .... unos días con los abuelos?
   a) de pasar b) pasando c) que pases d) pasar

14. .... te trate la vida, no te deprimas.
   a) Aunque mal b) No obstante mal c) Por muy mal que d) Por que

15. Por mi cumpleaños, ... una moto.
   a) regalaron b) a mí regalaron c) me han regalado d) han regalado

16. Te .... si vieras lo joven que está la bisabuela.
   a) sorprende b) sorprendía c) sorprendiera d) sorprendería

17. Hijo, no hagas caso .... te hable.
   a) el primero que te b) primero el que c) a el primero que d) al primero que

18. .... tengo aquí, son los encargos de mamá.
   a) Éstos que b) Unos que c) Aquéllos que d) De que

19. No .... el divorcio sea la mejor solución para tu caso.
   a) creo de que b) creo el que c) creo que d) creo

20. ¡Ay, ... es mi niño!
   a) cuánto guapo b) cómo de guapo c) qué guapo d) guapo

3. Ejercicio de selección múltiple. Vocabulario

En cada una de las siguientes frases hay un hueco que deberá rellenar con una de las cuatro palabras, eligiendo la más apropiada.

1. *¿Quién no ha sentido alguna vez deseos de .... a su jefe contra la pared?*
   a) atropellar b) asesinar c) estrujar d) estrellar
2. Cuando cumplió el año y medio, ... en comer sola.
   a) decidió b) quiso c) se empeñó d) deseó
3. Ya solo .... dos hermanos en casa.
   a) vivimos b) habitamos c) cohabitamos d) alojamos
4. Los abuelos dan siempre buenos consejos a sus ....
   a) sobrinos b) primos c) yernos d) nietos
5. La hija de mi hermano es mi ....
   a) sobrina b) prima c) tía d) nuera
6. Nacieron los dos el mismo día. Son ....
   a) iguales. b) mellizos. c) un par. d) un dúo.
7. ¿Pero es que no sabes hacer otra .... que oír música?
   a) actividad b) faena c) tarea d) cosa
8. No hay .... de que mis padres me comprendan.
   a) fórmula b) razón c) manera d) modales
9. Voy a pedir .... para llegar más tarde a casa esta noche.
   a) licencia b) pase c) libertad d) permiso
10. *Papá, que ya eres .... para hacer deporte.*
    a) grande b) más grande c) muy grande d) mayor

4.Vocabulario. Equivalencia

Cada una de las siguientes frases va seguida de tres expresiones (A,B y C), con una de las cuales puede construir un significado equivalente. Señale cuál de ellas es.

1. No se deben pagar con los hijos los conflictos personales.
   a) los problemas propios. b) los conflictos de una persona. c) los problemas de la persona.
2. Mi hijo va a terminar ya los estudios secundarios.
   a) ha terminado ya b) ya está a punto de terminar c) está por terminar ya
3. El día que nació fue explorado minuciosamente por el pediatra.
   a) Al nacer el día b) Cuando nació c) Al día de nacer
4. Mamá, danos un bocadillo de chorizo.
   a) colócanos b) métenos c) prepáranos
5. Lola, después de divorciarse, vivió momentos muy malos.
   a) pelearse b) separarse c) alejarse
6. A mi marido lo han destinado a Guinea.
   a) han retirado b) han enviado c) han movido
7. Pero niño, ¿por qué vienes tan sucio?
   a) tanto b) así de c) así
8. Por navidad, tenemos la costumbre de reunirnos todos.
   a) poseemos la costumbre de b) solemos de c) acostumbramos a
9. Cuando empieza el colegio, mi hijo siempre hace propósito de estudiar mucho.
   a) el tiempo del curso b) el tiempo de clase c) el curso
10. A mí en casa sólo me dan seis euros semanales.
    a) por semana. b) esta semana. c) en la semana.
11. Estos asuntos sólo deben tratarse en el seno del hogar.
    a) en el dormitorio. b) en familia. c) en el centro de la casa.

5. Completar diálogos con la opción más adecuada

1. - ¿A qué hora debo estar en casa .... tarde?
   - A las ocho y media.
   a) la   b) esa   c) esta   d) aquella
2. - ¿Cuándo es .... cumpleaños de la abuela?
   - El 14 de julio.
   a) el   b) los   c) un   d) este
3. - Vamos a quedar .... jueves para ir al cine.
   - No puedo porque tengo que ir al dentista.
   a) en   b) de   c) para   d) el
4. - ¿Has visto .... notas que ha traído tu hija?
   - Pues no son tan malas.
   a) las   b) unas   c) aquellas   d) algunas
5. - ¡Hay que ver .... alto que está el niño!
   - Es verdad. Parece mentira que sólo tenga ocho años.
   a) el   b) lo   c) lo de   d) cómo de
6. - No debes beber .... agua tan fría - le aconsejó la madre.
   - Es que ya no me duele la garganta.
   a) una   b) la   c) el   d) lo
7. - ¿Podría usted decirme de qué cuantía es ....beca?
   - Es la mínima: trescientos sesenta euros.
   a) tu   b) vuestra   c) mía   d) su
8. - A mí me gustan mucho las fiestas. Lo paso muy bien.
   - Yo también disfruto si están .... amigos.
   a) míos   b) mis   c) los mis   d) los míos
9. - ¿Con cuál de las dos camisas te quedas?
   - Con ....
   a) ambas   b) dos   c) sendas   d) algunas
10. - El .... día de la semana que puedo ir es el lunes.
    - ¡Vaya! Precisamente es el día que yo no puedo.
    a) primero   b) uno   c) principal   d) primer

Turismo.

Unidad **2**

A. Comprensión y expresión oral

1. Textos orales

1.1 Escuche los siguientes avisos que se dan por la megafonía de un aeropuerto y a continuación elija la opción correcta: V / F (Verdadero / Falso). Antes de empezar a escuchar la grabación, conviene que lea usted las frases.

1. *El vuelo 601 tiene como destino Lisboa.*

   V ☐ F ☐

2. *Están avisando a una señora para que acuda a información.*

   V ☐ F ☐

3. *Los pasajeros con tarjetas verde y naranja embarcarán antes que los demás.*

   V ☐ F ☐

1.2 En un noticiario radiofónico ha oído las siguientes informaciones:

Preguntas:

1. *¿Adónde debe usted ir si quiere ver una corrida de toros?*

   ....

2. *¿Qué espectáculo puede ver en San Lorenzo del Escorial?*

   ....

3. *¿Cuándo actúa Pavarotti?*

   ....

1.3 El guía de una excursión se dirige a los viajeros por la megafonía del autocar y les comunica lo siguiente:

Preguntas:

1. *¿A qué hora han llegado los turistas a Toledo?*

   ....

2. *¿Dónde van a dejar el autocar?*

   ....

3. *¿Cuándo van a conocer los turistas el programa de visitas de la tarde?*

   ....

2. Expresión a partir de láminas

Observe con atención la historieta. Cuando conteste a las cuestiones que le planteamos, hágalo de forma oral. Además escríbalo.

2.1 Primera lámina

Póngase en el lugar del caballero de la última viñeta. ¿Qué diría usted?

....

....

2.2 Segunda lámina

Póngase en el lugar de esta chica en la última viñeta. ¿Qué diría usted?

....

2.3 Tercera lámina

Póngase en el lugar del conductor. ¿Qué diría usted?

....

3. Exposición sobre un tema general

3.1 Sobre el siguiente tema, deberá hablar durante un tiempo no superior a cinco minutos. Le sugerimos que grabe su exposición, la escuche y trate de mejorar la expresión en una segunda grabación definitiva.

Tema: VACACIONES EN LA PLAYA O EN LA MONTAÑA.

Sugerencias:
Juegos en la playa.
Tomar el sol unos días es muy agradable, pero a veces...
Hay mucha gente en las playas.
En la montaña se pueden hacer excursiones.
Debemos llevar ropa algo especial.

3.2 Sobre el siguiente tema deberá hablar durante un tiempo no superior a cinco minutos.

Tema: LOS VALORES SOCIALES DEL TURISMO.

Sugerencias:
Conocemos nuevas gentes.
Los extranjeros no son tan raros, ¿o sí?
Nuevas amistades.
Los transportes actuales ponen las cosas más fáciles.

B. Comprensión y expresión escrita

1. Texto periodístico informativo con preguntas sobre su contenido

Lea con atención el siguiente artículo:

Las vacaciones insatisfechas

Aviones sin ruedas y comerciantes que acosan, entre las últimas reclamaciones de los viajeros

RAFAEL RUIZ

Ha terminado otro período de vacaciones, el navideño, y entre felicitaciones y deseos de bienestar se han colado quejas de viajeros no del todo satisfechos. La República Dominicana, la India, el Sáhara y Túnez, como destinos-estrella del otoño, y Marraquech, como meta predilecta de las rutas de fin de año, ponen el escenario. Para algunos, aviones antiguos han convertido los viajes más cómodos en imprevisibles aventuras; para otros, ciertos vehículos todo terreno dieron un toque demasiado pesado a la aventura.

Santos Robles cuenta tantas maravillas de Santo Domingo como desventuras de su itinerario. Firma en representación de un grupo de 52 personas. «Contratamos el viaje con la mayorista Travelplan, que utilizaba los servicios de Antillana de Navegación. Como esta compañía aérea no tiene permiso de Aviación Civil para operar desde España, hemos sufrido retrasos continuos y demoras de hasta un día sin ningún tipo de explicación. La solución que daban los operadores consistía en traslados a Lisboa, Caracas, etcétera, para hacer trasbordos. Así, el viaje, que tiene duración de ocho horas, se alargó hasta casi 24.»

Santos Robles detalla las condiciones del avión: «Antillana ha llegado a despegar de Lisboa con los pasajeros aún de pie», «aquello parecía una sauna, sin aire acondicionado», «no es extraño que en el despegue se desprendiera la cubierta de plástico de la salida de emergencia». El mayor problema parece ser que se presentó a la hora de volver a España: «El día de la salida nos informaron que el avión de Antillana no podía despegar y que se retrasaba el viaje 24 horas. La gente empezó a ponerse nerviosa al correr el rumor, que confirmó después el gerente de la compañía aérea, gracias a la mediación de Carlos Fragío, cónsul de la Embajada de España, de que el avión no tenía ruedas. Se las había prestado a una compañía canadiense que había reventado las suyas en el aterrizaje».

EL PAÍS, 21-I-1990

Conteste a las siguientes preguntas:

1. *¿En qué meses han preferido los turistas viajar a Sáhara y Túnez?*

   ....

2. *¿Cuál ha sido el destino preferido por los turistas durante el mes de diciembre?*

   ....

3. *¿A quién se deben las opiniones que en este artículo vienen entrecomilladas?*

   ....

4. *¿Con qué compañía aérea realizaron el viaje estos turistas?*

   ....

5. *¿Por qué hacía tanto calor en el avión?*

   ....

6. *¿Por qué no pudo despegar el avión para volver a España el día previsto?*

   ....

2. Texto de anuncios y convocatorias con preguntas

A continuación va a leer tres bloques de sugerencias en torno a algunas actividades turísticas:

Excursiones pedestres. El grupo Ademón, con base en Málaga, ha preparado las siguientes actividades de montañismo para febrero: excursión al paraje natural del Torcal de Antequera (4 de febrero), por 1.800 pesetas para los socios de la Sociedad Excursionista de Málaga, 2.800 los no socios; curso de iniciación de escalada en roca (6, 10, 11, 13, 17 y 18 de febrero), desde 8.850 pesetas los socios federados hasta 13.000 los no socios. Los precios incluyen viaje, monitores, guías y alojamiento. Información e inscripciones en la Sociedad Excursionista de Málaga, República Argentina, 9 , Málaga (de 8 a 10 de la noche), o llamando a Ademón : 952/ 28 82 73.

Circuito por Túnez. Viajes Turkana sale todos los lunes desde Madrid en avión con destino a Túnez, para visitar en ocho días sus playas y pueblos más típicos, desde la isla de Yerba hasta Hammamet. Por 70.000 pesetas, media pensión. Reservas en: Santa María, 20. Madrid. (91/ 420 14 670).

Tertulias. La librería de viajes Años Luz sigue con su ciclo de tertulias abiertas al público. Los jueves, a partir de las siete y media de la tarde. Para este primer trimestre los temas a tratar son: La fotografía en los viajes (25 enero), el todo terreno (1 febrero), Zimbabue y Zanzíbar (15 febrero), Berlín, la capital alternativa (1 marzo), Ecuador (15 Marzo), la bicicleta de montaña (22 marzo) y Namibia (29 marzo). En Francisco de Ricci, 8. Madrid. (91 / 243 01 92).

EL PAÍS, 21-I-1990

Conteste a las siguientes preguntas:

1. *Una vez en El Torcal de Antequera, ¿qué medio de transporte se va a utilizar para realizar la excursión?*

   ....

2. *¿Por qué la excursión a El Torcal de Antequera tiene dos precios distintos?*

   ....

3. *¿Cuántos días dura el curso de iniciación de escalada en roca?*

   ....

4. *¿Cuánto dura el viaje del Circuito por Túnez?*

   ....

5. *¿En qué dirección puede hacer su reserva para el Circuito por Túnez?*

   ....

6. *¿Qué ofrece la librería Años Luz en el anuncio?*

   ....

2

3. Artículo periodístico de opinión, con preguntas a las que deberá contestar VERDADERO/FALSO

Lea con atención el siguiente artículo:

LA REVOLUCIÓN DEL SOL

El sol no forma parte de nuestro ocio, en un sentido pleno, hasta bien entrado el siglo. Porque incluso cuando la civilización occidental descubrió playas y montañas como lugares de ocio, el astro solar seguía siendo rehuido: «estar moreno» no se llevaba, no era la moda. «Ligar bronce»* se ha convertido en una auténtica obsesión colectiva, en un valor socialmente prestigioso y también en una gran industria que mueve mucho dinero: hay cremas para proteger la piel antes, durante y después del baño, y las hay en graduación y clase casi ilimitadas y existen también para potenciar el bronceado y hacerlo más duradero. Nada hay que objetar a este fenómeno industrial. Sólo que no se puede confiar a ciegas en cremas y lociones para neutralizar los efectos de la acción solar. Los médicos llevan mucho tiempo insistiendo en lo nocivo de las largas exposiciones al sol, en el riesgo que para la salud tiene ese crecimiento desmesurado de la melanina. No desconocen, naturalmente, sus secuelas positivas: suministra al organismo, por ejemplo, calcio y vitamina C. Pero tampoco ignoran las contrapartidas si el sol se toma de modo abusivo: además de las lesiones de la piel, que pueden ser gravísimas, está demostrada la etiología solar de muchos cánceres dermatológicos, y asimismo el influjo del sol en los procesos de envejecimiento. Y no deja de resultar paradójico que una civilización tan «juvenilizada» como la nuestra practique, a veces de modo tan desaforado, un culto solar que redunda en la aceleración de esa vejez que tanto se teme. Pero estas contradicciones forman parte también de nuestros valores. Aceptar sin más estas paradojas parece poco inteligente. Tomar el sol es un derecho y debe ser una fuente de placer, no de innecesarias y, a veces, muy graves patologías.

*«Ligar bronce» : ponerse moreno.

ABC, 19-VIII-1990

Lea las siguientes frases. Señale V (verdadero) o F (falso) en relación con el contenido del artículo. A continuación, busque la parte del texto en la que se ha basado para escribir V/F y escríbala en las líneas de puntos.

1. *Tomar el sol es una costumbre relativamente reciente.*

   V ☐ F ☐ ....

2. *Entre las muchas cremas solares, hay una para quitar instantáneamente el bronceado de la piel.*

   V ☐ F ☐ ....

3. *Cualquier crema que se venda en las farmacias sirve para combatir los efectos nocivos del sol.*

   V ☐ F ☐ ....

4. *Los médicos aconsejan no tomar el sol en exceso.*

   V ☐ F ☐ ....

5. *El sol es beneficioso para las personas que carecen de calcio y vitamina C.*

   V ☐ F ☐ ....

6. *Tomando el sol de forma abusiva se evita el cáncer de piel.*

   V ☐ F ☐ ....

7. *La sociedad actual busca siempre parecer joven.*

   V ☐ F ☐ ....

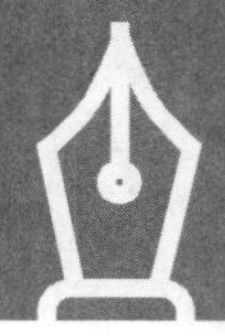

4. Redacción de una carta a partir de instrucciones

En el folleto de una agencia de viajes ha visto usted el siguiente anuncio:

TARIFAS ESPECIALES PARA JÓVENES			
MADRID-PARIS	13.650 PTS.	BARCELONA-MULHOUSE	12.700 PTS.
MADRID-NIZA	11.700 PTS.	BARCELONA-TOULOUSE	5.800 PTS.
MADRID-BURDEOS	7.700 PTS.	BARCELONA-NIZA	7.700 PTS.
MADRID-TOULOUSE	7.700 PTS.	BARCELONA-LYON	10.650 PTS.
MADRID-LYON	12.650 PTS.	PALMA-PARIS	11.700 PTS.
MADRID-MARSELLA	11.700 PTS.	ALICANTE-PARIS	13.650 PTS.
MADRID-ESTRASBURGO	20.850 PTS.	VALENCIA-PARIS	12.650 PTS.
BARCELONA-BURDEOS	10.500 PTS.	MALAGA-PARIS	16.550 PTS.
BARCELONA-PARIS	10.650 PTS.	SEVILLA-PARIS	16.550 PTS.
BARCELONA-MARSELLA	7.700 PTS.		

Información sobre Francia:
MAISON DE LA FRANCE. Alcalá, 63. Tel. 276 31 44. MADRID.
Gran Vía de las Corts Catalanes, 656. Tel 318 01 91. BARCELONA.

Escriba una carta a la dirección que se indica en el anuncio, solicitando más información sobre un viaje que usted habrá elegido previamente. La carta deberá contener al menos lo siguiente:

1. Encabezamiento y despedida.
2. Alusión al folleto en que ha visto el anuncio.
3. Fecha y duración de su posible viaje.

5. Componer una redacción a partir de instrucciones

Componga una redacción de 150 a 200 palabras (15 ó 20 líneas) sobre el tema:

EL ÚLTIMO VIAJE QUE USTED HA REALIZADO

1. *Motivo del viaje.* 2. *Lugares que visitó.* 3. *Duración.* 4. *Alojamiento.*

C. Gramática y vocabulario

1. Texto incompleto con 10 huecos

El siguiente texto está incompleto. Deberá rellenar cada uno de los huecos con la palabra más apropiada.

Ávila es la capital de la provincia del mismo nombre. Es la ciudad más alta de España (1.130 m). La parte antigua de la ciudad está rodeada por unas murallas que fueron construidas en la Edad Media y que .... las mejor conservadas de España. Se puede acceder a la ciudad por .... de sus nueve puertas y pasear por sus calles en las que .... palacios del siglo XVI y muchas iglesias. La catedral es de transición entre los .... románico y gótico y fue levantada sobre el lugar .... alto de la ciudad.

Después de una visita por sus principales monumentos, puede usted .... en alguno de los restaurantes los platos .... de la región, como las judías del Barco, el cochinillo asado y .... ternera de Ávila. Como punto final de la comida, puede .... de postre yemas de Santa Teresa. Desde el mirador del Rastro se .... un extenso valle regado por el río Adaja.

2. Ejercicios de selección múltiple. Gramática

En cada una de las siguientes frases, hay un hueco que deberá rellenar con una de las cuatro expresiones, eligiendo la que sea más correcta.

1. El viaje en avión es .... rápido que en tren.
   a) más b) muy más c) mucho d) menos
2. Cuando.................. del hotel, no olvides dejar la llave de la habitación en recepción.
   a) sales b) salgas c) salieras d) hayas salido
3. .... la playa se pueden dar largos paseos.
   a) Dentro de b) Sobre c) Encima de d) Por
4. Mañana .... en un restaurante de cuatro tenedores.
   a) comimos b) comeremos c) habremos comido d) estaremos comiendo

5. Hemos estado en el museo contemplando .... murales de arte contemporáneo.
   a) espléndidos b) espléndidas c) espléndido d) espléndida

6. .... nos gusta comer al aire libre.
   a) Nosotros b) A ti y a mí c) A mí y a ti d) Tú y yo

7. ¿Con este pase .... me han dado tengo acceso a todas las salas del Museo del Prado?
   a) el cual b) de que c) el que d) que

8. .... una cerveza bien fría, por favor.
   a) Me traiga b) A mí traes c) Tráigame d) Traes

9. ¿Cuánto cuesta la habitación .... pensión completa?
   a) a b) con c) de d) en

10. La catedral de Sevilla es .... que la de Burgos.
   a) mayor b) más mayor c) grande, más d) muy grande

11. ¿A .... está el cambio del dólar?
   a) qué b) cuanto c) como d) cuánto

12. Vamos a comprar .... recuerdo para los amigos.
   a) alguno b) algún c) cualquiera d) ningún

13. Mañana habrá una excursión .... hace buen tiempo.
   a) a menos que b) a condición de que c) siempre que d) si

14. No se .... las tiendas hasta las nueve y media.
   a) abre b) abren c) tienen abiertas d) abrirá

15. .... corramos, no llegaremos a tiempo a la estación.
   a) Por mucho que b) Por que c) Sin embargo d) De que

16. Se divierten .... dormir a los demás huéspedes del hotel.
   a) no dejar b) no dejando c) sin que dejen d) no dejan

17. Trabaja .... en un restaurante chino.
   a) siendo camarero b) como un camarero c) como camarero d) camarero

18. .... por la escalera porque el ascensor está estropeado.
   a) Suban b) Se suban c) Subirse d) Súbanse

19. .... el pasaporte a Elena.
   a) Dala b) Déla c) Dale d) Le dé

20. Para llamar a cobro revertido, ¿ ....?
   a) cómo hacer b) cómo se hace c) qué hace d) cómo hace

3.Ejercicio de selección múltiple. Vocabulario

En cada una de las siguientes frases hay un hueco que deberá rellenar con una de las cuatro palabras, eligiendo la más apropiada.

1. El acueducto de Segovia fue .... por los romanos.
   a) izado b) erecto c) construido d) fabricado
2. ¿A qué .... se sirve el desayuno?
   a) tiempo b) hora c) horas d) momento
3. Santander tiene algunas de las .... más limpias de Europa.
   a) playas b) puertos c) arenas d) acantilados
4. La Exposición Universal de Sevilla se .... en 1992.
   a) conmemorará b) va a dar c) festejará d) celebrará
5. Este año .... al festival de cine de San Sebastián.
   a) vamos a ir b) marcharemos c) visitaremos d) viajaremos
6. En España casi todas las autopistas son ....
   a) de pago. b) de peaje. c) de pagar. d) de paga.
7. Santo Domingo de Silos es un .... monasterio de Burgos.
   a) anciano b) anticuado c) antiguo d) añejo
8. ¿Le .... a usted visitar la sala capitular?
   a) gusta b) conviene c) viene d) interesa
9. Merece especial .... el sepulcro de los Reyes Católicos.
   a) curiosidad b) atención c) aviso d) contemplación
10. Se suele servir la cerveza con una ....
   a) aperitivo b) canapé c) tapadera d) tapa

4.Vocabulario. Equivalencia

Cada una de las siguientes frases va seguida de tres expresiones (A,B y C), con una de las cuales se puede construir un significado equivalente. Señale cuál de ellas es.

1. Visité España por primera vez a los quince años.
   a) cuando tenía quince años b) hace quince años c) durante quince años.
2. Al año que viene voy a realizar un curso en la Universidad Internacional Menéndez Pelayo de Santander.
   a) estoy para realizar b) me matricularé en c) me enrolaré en.
3. Andorra es un buen sitio para ir de compras.
   a) ir a la compra b) comprar c) la compraventa.
4. Por las noches la gente de Madrid se reúne en las terrazas del Paseo de la Castellana.
   a) en las azoteas b) en los balcones c) en los bares al aire libre.
5. ¿Está usted enfermo del riñón? La solución es el balneario de Babilafuente.
   a) La solución es un baño en b) La solución es tomar baños en c) Acuda con la bañera a.
6. La red de paradores nacionales garantiza estancias muy gratas.
   a) La red de parados de la nación b) Alguno de los paradores nacionales c) El conjunto de paradores nacionales.
7. Toledo celebra sus fiestas en el Corpus Christi.
   a) festeja b) celebra su santo en c) va de fiesta en.
8. Debíamos alquilar un coche para recorrer la comarca.
   a) comprar a plazos un coche b) tomar un coche en alquiler c) arrendar un coche.
9. Desde la torre se divisa gran parte de la ciudad.
   a) ve casi toda b) vigila casi toda c) nos ve en toda.
10. Por favor, ¿por dónde se va a la oficina de correos?
    a) por dónde anda b) cómo puedo llegar a c) dónde aparece.

5. Completar diálogos con la opción más adecuada

1. - ¿Con .... agencia vamos a viajar este año?
   - Yo creo que no debemos cambiar de agencia.

   a) qué *b) cual* *c) cuya* *d) de qué*

2. - ¿Dónde se sacan las entradas para visitar este monumento?
   - En esa ....

   a) ventanita *b) ventanilla* *c) ventanuca* *d) ventana*

3. - Mira, éste es el hotel con vistas al mar del .... nos hablaron.
   - ¿Nos quedamos o buscamos otro?

   a) qué *b) cuál* *c) cual* *d) el cual*

4. - No seas .... y déjame el asiento.
   - Sí, mujer, siéntate donde quieras.

   a) comodazo *b) muy cómodo* *c) comodón* *d) el más cómodo*

5. - ¿Queréis que esta tarde .... lleve a visitar el Madrid de los Austrias?
   - Y ¿por qué no vamos mejor a tomar unas tapas?

   a) vos *b) a vosotros* *c) vuestros* *d) os*

6. - Parece que tarda el tren.
   - ¿No .... han comunicado a ustedes que viene con retraso?

   a) los *b) les* *c) las* *d) le*

7. - Consulta en el plano dónde está la Plaza Porticada.
   - No hace falta. Entre las dos calles .... aceras están levantadas.

   a) cuyas *b) que las* *c) cuya* *d) de que las*

8. - Tengan .... cuidado con los carteristas si van al Rastro.
   - ¿Y por qué hay que tener cuidado?

   a) vosotros *b) vosotras* *c) vos* *d) ustedes*

9. - He traído una crema protectora para .... tengan la piel delicada.
   - ¿Nos podemos bañar después de habérnosla dado?

   a) que *b) quienes* *c) quiénes* *d) aquéllos*

10. - ¿Qué cuadros vamos a ver ahora?
    - Pasen .... a la sala de Velázquez.

    a) con mi *b) conmigo* *c) contigo* *d) a mí*

Economía y trabajo. Unidad 3

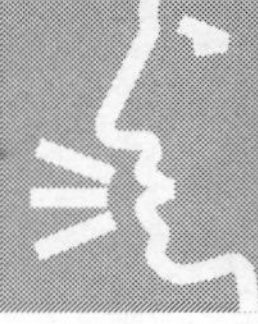

A. Comprensión y expresión oral

1. Textos orales

1.1 Escuche los siguientes avisos que se dan por megafonía a un numeroso grupo de aspirantes a ocupar un puesto de trabajo. Antes de empezar a escuchar la grabación, conviene que lea usted las preguntas.

Preguntas:

1. *¿A cuántas pruebas deberán someterse los aspirantes?*

   ....

2. *¿Cuál es la primera prueba que debe realizar una candidata que se llama Mari Carmen García?*

   ....

3. *¿Cuándo va a ser el reconocimiento médico?*

   ....

1.2 En un noticiario radiofónico ha oído las siguientes informaciones:
Señale V(verdadero) o F(falso):

1. *Si todavía no ha cumplido usted los veinticinco años, ¿puede usted acceder a alguno de estos puestos?*

   V ☐ F ☐ ....

2. *¿Hay más de treinta plazas para los alumnos de Turismo?*

   V ☐ F ☐ ....

3. *¿Puede solicitar alguien estos puestos en su nombre?*

   V ☐ F ☐ ....

1.3 Un breve noticiario económico que oye por la radio le da la siguiente información:

Preguntas:

1. *¿Qué moneda ha experimentado baja esta semana con respecto a la peseta?*

   ....

2. *¿Qué bolsa se ha recuperado más esta semana?*

   ....

3. *¿Qué día está dando la radio este noticiario?*

   ....

2.Expresión a partir de láminas

Observe con atención la historieta. Cuando conteste a las cuestiones que le planteamos, hágalo de forma oral. Además escríbalo.

2.1 Primera lámina

Póngase en el lugar del jefe. ¿Qué le ha podido decir a quien ha entrado a solicitar empleo?

....

2.2 Segunda lámina

¿Qué dirá uno de los pescadores en la cuarta viñeta?

....

....

2.3 Tercera lámina

Póngase en el lugar del albañil que habla con los demás. ¿Qué les puede estar diciendo?

....

3.Exposición sobre un tema general

3.1 Sobre el siguiente tema, deberá hablar durante un tiempo no superior a cinco minutos. Le sugerimos que grabe su exposición, la escuche y trate de mejorar la expresión en una segunda grabación definitiva.

Tema: TRABAJO BIEN REMUNERADO PERO POCO SATISFACTORIO.

Sugerencias:
¿Qué es más importante: la remuneración o la satisfacción?
No se trabaja bien si no se está satisfecho profesionalmente.
Tampoco se trabaja bien si el sueldo es bajo.
El trabajo voluntario.

3.2 Sobre el siguiente tema deberá hablar durante un tiempo no superior a cinco minutos.

Tema: TRABAJO FÍSICO O TRABAJO INTELECTUAL.

Sugerencias:
Ventajas del trabajo físico.
Ventajas del trabajo intelectual.
Inconvenientes del trabajo físico.
Inconvenientes del trabajo intelectual.
Algunos trabajos pueden desarrollar los dos factores.

B. Comprensión y expresión escrita

1. Texto periodístico informativo con preguntas sobre su contenido

Lea con atención el siguiente artículo:

Los controladores aéreos aplazan la convocatoria de huelga

S.G.C., Madrid

La asociación de controladores aéreos ha aplazado la convocatoria de una huelga en el sector hasta que se reúnan con el director general de Aviación Civil. 5 Este cambio de posturas se debe a la carta que recibieron de la Administración en la que les ofrecían la posibilidad de dialogar en una reunión de la mesa de 10 concertación, cuya fecha no se ha fijado todavía pero que, según el presidente de la asociación de controladores aéreos, 15 Juan María García Gil, se puede celebrar a lo largo de esta semana.

García Gil calificó de positivo 20 el tono de la carta en la que se ofrecen a negociar el problema de los controladores de Zaragoza, aunque señala que la misiva «dice cosas diferentes a lo que 25 estipula el plan de transición». Ese plan significaría que los controladores de Zaragoza deberían dar instrucciones a los 30 militares y pedir un traslado voluntario «forzosamente», según el presidente que añadió que han recibido amenazas de altos cargos en caso de que no 35 se cumplieran los destinos.

EL PAÍS, 5-IX-1990

Conteste a las siguientes preguntas:

1. *¿Hasta cuándo han aplazado los controladores la convocatoria de huelga?*

   ....

2. *¿Quién es Juan María García Gil?*

   ....

3. *¿Quién ha amenazado a los controladores en el caso de que los destinos no se cumplan?*

   ....

4. *¿Para qué fecha se ha fijado la reunión de la mesa de concertación?*

   ....

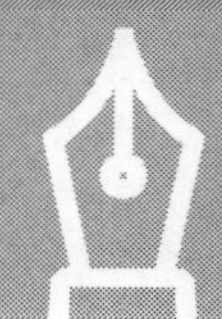

2. Texto de anuncios y convocatorias con preguntas

En un periódico ha visto usted estos anuncios:

EMPRESA DE HOSTELERÍA

NECESITA CAMAREROS

- Veinte a treinta años.
- Experiencia mínima de un año.

Teléfono 597 47 75

De doce a dos y de cinco a siete. Sr.Roldán

GRAN JOYERÍA

PARA PRÓXIMA APERTURA

NECESITA:

DEPENDIENTES/AS

PEDIMOS: Edad 20/35 años.
FORMACIÓN: Bachiller superior-BUP
Facilidades para las relaciones con el público. Seriedad e integridad.
OFRECEMOS: Sueldo fijo. Seguridad Social del Régimen General desde el primer día. Posibilidad de promoción. Ambiente de trabajo agradable.
Interesados, dirigirse con curriculum y fotografía reciente al Apartado de Correos número 38099 - Madrid 28080

Conteste a las siguientes preguntas:

Anuncio primero

1. *¿Qué puesto de trabajo se ofrece?*

   ....

2. *¿Qué edad deben tener los candidatos?*

   ....

3. *¿Cuánto tiempo deben haber trabajado antes en un puesto similar?*

   ....

Anuncio segundo

1. *¿Qué empleados se solicitan en el anuncio?*

   ....

2. *¿Qué nivel de estudios se exige?*

   ....

3. *¿Qué tipo de salario se ofrece: cobrar una cantidad fija o una comisión por ventas?*

   ....

4. *¿Qué debe enviar si está interesado en esta oferta?*

   ....

3

3. Artículo periodístico de opinión, con preguntas a las que deberá contestar VERDADERO/FALSO

Lea con atención el siguiente artículo:

Minero, 26 años

El cuerpo de Antonio Suárez Mella, ayudante minero de 26 años, el tercero de los tres trabajadores atrapados el pasado jueves por un desprendimiento en el pozo Polio, de la empresa Hunosa, fue encontrado sin vida la madrugada del lunes. Con los siniestros mineros ocurre como con los accidentes de tráfico: la opinión pública sólo se conmueve cuando un suceso produce simultáneamente un gran número de víctimas, como hace unos días en Yugoslavia, pero apenas registra el goteo regular de noticias que dan cuenta de una nueva víctima a añadir a la estadística. Y, sin embargo, un millar de mineros han perdido la vida en España en los últimos 10 años. Es seguro que si todas esas víctimas se hubieran producido en un mismo día, la opinión pública se habría manifestado con indignación pidiendo medidas drásticas, más seguridad, la urgente intervención de las autoridades.

Según un estudio de UGT, el índice de siniestralidad de la minería española supera en un 120% a la media de los países de la Comunidad Europea (y es cuatro veces mayor que en el Reino Unido, por ejemplo). Es cierto que las especiales condiciones geológicas de la cuenca asturiana favorecen esa siniestralidad, en particular por derrabe del carbón. Pero ello habría de traducirse en unas más severas medidas preventivas, cuando lo cierto es que la inversión en seguridad sigue estando en España muy por debajo de la de otros países: en 1987, la quinta parte que en el conjunto de Europa.

Con todo, algunos accidentes típicamente mineros como las explosiones de gas grisú y los desprendimientos en derrabe, son ahora menos frecuentes que hace 15 ó 20 años merced a las medidas de seguridad adoptadas. Hunosa -que da empleo a 19.000 de los 27.000 trabajadores del sector en Asturias- destinó el pasado año 2.500 millones de pesetas a medidas de seguridad y prevención, incluyendo programas de formación profesional de los jóvenes mineros. Pero la experiencia indica que ello no basta. Entre otras cosas, porque la mecanización de los sistemas de trabajo ha dado ocasión a accidentes de nuevo tipo, como el incendio, el pasado mes de diciembre, de una cinta transportadora en el pozo Mosquitera, con el balance de cuatro trabajadores muertos. En total, 26 mineros perdieron la vida en el Principado a lo largo de 1989, elevando así un índice de siniestralidad que había venido descendiendo desde 1985.

A su vez, lo que ocurre en las minas es un reflejo de la situación en la mayoría de los sectores productivos. España sigue siendo, según datos aportados en marzo pasado por CC OO, el país del Occidente industrializado con mayor porcentaje de accidentes laborales: el 13% de los asalariados, el doble que en 1983, sufrieron a lo largo de 1989 algún accidente en el trabajo. El número de muertos por tales accidentes se elevó ese año a 1.981, lo que supuso un incremento del 14% respecto a 1988. En el último cuarto de siglo, un total de 60.000 trabajadores perdieron la vida en accidentes laborales en España, y cientos de miles más quedaron inválidos. Cifras demasiado escandalosas como para tomarlas a beneficio de inventario.

EL PAÍS, 5-IX-1990

Lea las siguientes frases. Señale V (verdadero) o F (falso) en relación con el contenido del artículo. A continuación, busque la parte del texto en la que se ha basado para escribir V/F y escríbala en las líneas de puntos.

1. *Todavía falta por encontrar a tres de los seis mineros atrapados en el pozo Polio.*

   V □ F □ ....

2. *Mil mineros han perdido la vida en España desde 1980.*

   V □ F □ ....

3. *En España hay aproximadamente los mismos accidentes de minería que en el Reino Unido.*

   V □ F □ ....

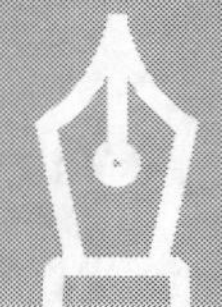

4. *La empresa Hunosa tiene empleados a todos los trabajadores de la minería en Asturias.*

V ☐ F ☐ ....

5. *En 1989 hubo en el Principado de Asturias más accidentes mineros que en años anteriores.*

V ☐ F ☐ ....

6. *La geología de Asturias es la única causa de que haya tantos accidentes en la minería.*

V ☐ F ☐ ....

7. *La explosión de gas grisú provoca menos accidentes en la actualidad que hace 16 años.*

V ☐ F ☐ ....

4.Redacción de una carta a partir de instrucciones

En un periódico ha visto usted la siguiente oferta de empleo:

COMPAÑÍA INTERNACIONAL
solicita para su Departamento Financiero

LICENCIADO EN EMPRESARIALES

BUEN NIVEL DE FRANCÉS HABLADO.
NO SE PRECISA EXPERIENCIA.

Se ofrece: Incorporación a una sólida empresa. Remuneración del orden de los 2.000.000 de pesetas brutas, negociables. Seguridad Social. Incorporación inmediata. Formación a cargo de la empresa. Ventajas sociales.
Interesados envíen *curriculum vitae* con dirección y teléfono de contacto al apartado de correos de Madrid número 21.023. Distrito postal número 28080. Referencia Licenciado Empresariales.

Escriba una carta interesándose por esta oferta de empleo. Se supone que también envía el curriculum. La carta deberá contener al menos lo siguiente:

1. Encabezamiento y despedida.
2. Pida usted más aclaraciones sobre las ventajas sociales que se ofrecen.
3. Pida que le aclaren también si se trata de un puesto exclusivamente para hombres.
4. Solicite también que le expliquen en qué consiste la formación que le van a dar en la empresa.
5. Como el anuncio ofrece incorporación inmediata, pregunte en qué fecha empezaría usted a trabajar.
6. Acláreles que usted ya está trabajando en un puesto parecido.

C. Gramática y vocabulario

1. Texto incompleto con 10 huecos

El siguiente texto está incompleto. Deberá rellenar cada uno de los huecos con la palabra más apropiada.

A Juan Alvaro no le importa madrugar. Cuando se levanta, aún es de noche y los únicos ruidos que se oyen en la casa son sus pisadas, yendo de acá para allá, del cuarto de baño a la cocina, de la cocina .... dormitorio. ¿Cómo le va a importar madrugar todos los días, ... de haber estado tres años en el paro, andando de .... en despacho, siempre con el curriculum a punto, ... conseguir nada. Ahora, todas las mañanas se .... hacia la parada del autobús a las siete y cuarto en .... Media hora más tarde está llegando al edificio .... trabaja. Ya sentado delante de su mesa lo primero que .... es abrir la correspondencia, después la clasifica según su asunto y por .... contesta las cartas que requieren respuesta. Parece poca cosa, pero este trabajo le lleva .... la mañana.

2. Ejercicios de selección múltiple. Gramática

En cada una de las siguientes frases, hay un hueco que deberá rellenar con una de las cuatro expresiones, eligiendo la que sea más correcta.

1. No pienso .... más por hoy.
   a) trabajar b) que trabaje c) de trabajar d) a trabajar
2. No han vuelto a despedir a .... más.
   a) alguno b) alguien c) ninguno d) ningún
3. El capataz se llevaba muy bien con .... trabajadores.
   a) las b) unas c) ningunos d) sus
4. Este mes .... una paga extraordinaria para toda la plantilla.
   a) ha habido b) hubo c) tuvo d) ha estado
5. El jefe no se atrevía .... del despacho.
   a) salir b) a salir c) de salir d) para salir

6. Le despidieron .... siempre tarde al trabajo.
   a) porque llegó b) como llegaba C) porque llegaba d) aunque llegaba
7. Le ordenaron que lo .... todo.
   a) empaquete b) empaquetara c) empaquetar d) empaquetaría
8. Y me preguntó .... experiencia.
   a) si tenía b) que tenía c) tener d) si tendré
9. Oiga, ..., ¿retiramos ya la grúa?
   a) el jefe b) jefe usted c) tú, jefe d) jefe
10. Me ofrecían buen sueldo .... aceptar las otras condiciones.
   a) pero no pude b) sino que pude c) no obstante poder d) pero pude
11. .... cuarenta años cuando le ascendieron a subdirector.
   a) Ya había tenido b) Tendría c) Tiene d) Tuvo
12. Los pescadores, ... en alta mar, tienen pocas oportunidades de divertirse.
   a) estando b) al estar c) habiendo estado d) para estar
13. Disgustos, fatigas, malos sueldos: .... lo olvidó al jubilarse.
   a) todas b) todo c) el todo d) todos
14. Le ruego .... descuente del sueldo.
   a) a mí no me lo b) no me lo c) que no me lo d) no a mí lo
15. Ya .... marcharnos a casa.
   a) hora es de b) es hora c) es la hora d) es la hora de
16. Se pasan la vida ....
   a) hablando de las vacaciones b) en hablar de las vacaciones c) con hablar de las vacaciones d) para hablar de las vacaciones
17. .... es un trabajo duro.
   a) Conducir tren b) El conducir tren c) El conducir de un tren d) Conducir el tren
18. .... de las huelgas, la producción ha disminuido.
   a) Por motivo b) Motivado c) A motivo d) Como motivo
19. .... trabaja usted, ... deja trabajar a los demás.
   a) Ni (...), no b) Ni (...), ni c) No (...), no d) Y no (...), y no
20. No tenemos una base económica .... montar nuestro negocio.
   a) sobre cual b) sobre el que c) sobre la cual d) sobre cuya

3.Ejercicio de selección múltiple. Vocabulario

En cada una de las siguientes frases hay un hueco que deberá rellenar con una de las cuatro palabras, eligiendo la más apropiada.

1. .... de esta factoría está cualificado.
   a) El gentío b) El personal c) El grupo d) El estamento
2. Llama a un .... para que nos arregle el desagüe.
   a) fontanero b) aguador c) forjador d) soldador
3. Pasaremos mañana por su casa para .... la factura.
   a) recobrar b) cobrar c) obtener d) sacar
4. No soy partidario de una inversión tan ....
   a) valiente b) valerosa c) brava d) arriesgada
5. Nunca .... había trabajado como profesor.
   a) de antes b) primeramente c) antes d) entonces
6. La gobernanta siempre nos trata de .... manera.
   a) fea b) mala c) malvada d) antipática
7. Ha subido el petróleo .... ha bajado el dólar.
   a) además b) también c) y además d) así como
8. Este empleo ofrece pocas posibilidades de ....
   a) movimiento b) ascensión c) promoción d) escalada
9. ¿Tiene usted .... en contabilidad?
   a) experimento b) experimentación c) expectativa d) experiencia
10. La subida de los precios ha hecho que la inflación ....
    a) incremente b) engorde c) aumente d) se hinche

4. Vocabulario. Equivalencia

Cada una de las siguientes frases va seguida de tres expresiones (A,B y C), con una de las cuales se puede construir un significado equivalente. Señale cuál de ellas es.

1. Se precisa un delineante para empresa constructora.
   a) Es necesidad b) Se necesita c) Hay necesidad
2. El índice de desempleo ha descendido en el último trimestre del año.
   a) durante los meses de octubre, noviembre y diciembre
   b) desde primeros de octubre a primeros de diciembre
   c) este año en el final del trimestre
3. El secretario debe hacerse cargo de atender las llamadas.
   a) hacerse el cargo de b) encargarse de c) encargar de
4. Este trabajo está muy bien pagado.
   a) retribuido b) asalariado c) gratificado
5. Seguro que la comunidad internacional puede soportar una subida del precio del petróleo.
   a) Quizá b) Probablemente c) Es verdad que
6. Se necesitan vendedores dispuestos a viajar.
   a) a realizar viajes b) a preparar viajes c) a realizar un viaje
7. Está ya todo preparado para la apertura de nuestras oficinas en Barcelona.
   a) iniciar b) comenzar c) inaugurar
8. Apenas quedan ya pedidos sin atender.
   a) Casi no hay b) No quedan c) No hay
9. Cuando vaya a una entrevista, debe usted ir bien aseado.
   a) bien peinado b) al aseo c) muy limpio
10. Para ocupar este puesto de trabajo es requisito imprescindible ser español.
    a) es indispensable b) es conveniente c) es muy aconsejable

5. Completar diálogos con la opción más adecuada

1. - Me ha preguntado el jefe si .... el fax a nuestra filial de Lisboa.
   - Dile que acabo de enviarlo.

   a) enviaras b) mandaras c) has enviado d) hayas enviado

2. - ¿Cuándo .... el horario de verano? No me gusta la jornada partida.
   - A mí no me importa demasiado venir por las tardes.

   a) comienza b) comenzó c) empezara d) empiece

3. - Ya tengo montado casi todo el motor.
   - Creo que mañana antes del mediodía lo ....

   a) terminábamos b) termináramos c) acabemos d) habremos terminado

4. - De buena gana me .... un descanso de dos días.
   - ¿Por qué no pides un permiso sin sueldo?

   a) tomara b) tomaría c) tome d) tomase

5. - ¿A cuántos trabajadores .... el mes pasado?
   - Al diez por ciento de la plantilla.

   a) despidieron b) echan c) echarán d) despiden

6. - Cuando .... a luz, avísanos para ir a verte.
   - Yo os agradecería que no fuerais al hospital. Prefiero veros en casa.

   a) das b) darás c) has dado d) hayas dado

7. - A Fernando le han ascendido. Ahora es jefe de taller.
   - Se lo .... porque llevaba muchos años esperándolo.

   a) mereció b) merecerá c) mereciera d) merecía

8. - Todos ustedes, como aspirantes al puesto, deben pasar por una entrevista.
   - ¿Nos .... la fecha de la entrevista por carta?

   a) comunicaron b) comunicarían c) avisen d) comunicarán

9. - Con la paga extraordinaria voy a comprarte unos gemelos de oro.
   - Esa frase me suena. .... el tercer año que la dices.

   a) Sería b) Fue c) Era d) Es

10. - En este trabajo de secretario no se .... nunca a qué hora se sale.
    - No te quejes, que por lo menos tienes un mes de vacaciones.

    a) sabe b) sabes c) sabrá d) supo

Gastronomía.

Unidad **4**

A. Comprensión y expresión oral

1. Textos orales

1.1 Escuche la siguiente receta que una experta gastrónoma da por la radio y a continuación elija la opción correcta: V / F (Verdadero / Falso). Antes de empezar a escuchar la grabación, conviene que lea usted las frases.

1. *Una pieza de cordero que pese un kilo debe estar en el horno tres horas.*
   V ☐ F ☐
2. *Si se corta la carne en crudo, será más fácil después partirla.*
   V ☐ F ☐
3. *Es conveniente untar la pieza con mantequilla.*
   V ☐ F ☐
4. *Cuando ya esté dorado, hay que añadir vino blanco.*
   V ☐ F ☐

1.2 En un noticiario radiofónico ha oído la siguiente información:
Preguntas:

1. *¿En qué local se van a celebrar las reuniones gastronómicas?*

   ....

2. *¿Cuándo va a tener lugar este encuentro?*

   ....

3. *¿Cómo va a terminar cada una de las reuniones?*

   ....

4. *¿Van a venir cocineros galos?*

   ....

1.3 El «maitre» de un pequeño restaurante tiene la costumbre de sugerir a sus comensales los platos de la carta, dirigiéndose a ellos de viva voz:
Preguntas:

1. *¿Qué plato de carne les recomienda?*

   ....

2. *¿Qué les sugiere para los postres?*

   ....

3. *¿Para quién recomienda las hamburguesas?*

   ....

4. *¿Por qué quiere llevarse el abrigo de la señora?*

   ....

2. Expresión a partir de láminas

Observe con atención la historieta. Cuando conteste a las cuestiones que le planteamos, hágalo de forma oral. Además escríbalo.

2.1 Primera lámina

Póngase en el lugar del caballero de la última viñeta. ¿Qué diría usted?

....

2.2 Segunda lámina

Póngase en el lugar de la madre de la última viñeta. ¿Qué le diría a la niña?

....

2.3 Tercera lámina

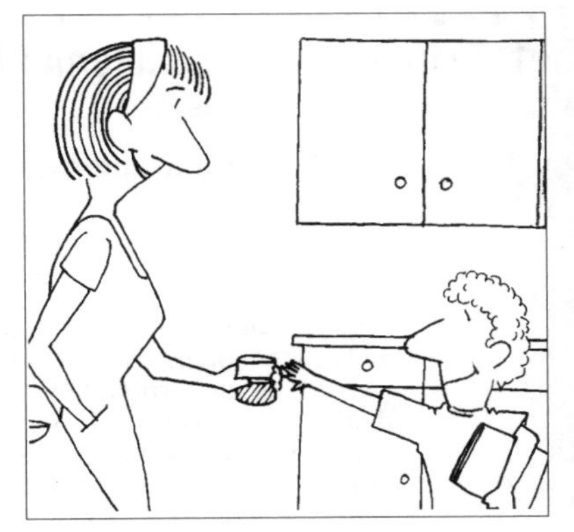

Póngase en el lugar de la persona que le ofrece el zumo al niño. ¿Qué le diría?

....

3. Exposición sobre un tema general

3.1 Sobre el siguiente tema, deberá hablar durante un tiempo no superior a cinco minutos. Le sugerimos que grabe su exposición, la escuche y trate de mejorar la expresión en una segunda grabación definitiva.

Tema: ¿CUÁLES SON SUS PLATOS PREFERIDOS?

Sugerencias:
Distinga entre primeros platos y segundos platos.
Postres.
Un plato especial que le prepararon un día.
Un plato que usted sabe preparar.

3.2 Sobre el siguiente tema deberá hablar durante un tiempo no superior a cinco minutos.

Tema: LOS PLATOS Y LAS BEBIDAS DE MI REGIÓN.

Sugerencias:
Cada región tiene sus platos típicos.
Qué comemos normalmente.
Qué comemos como plato extraordinario.
Los quesos.
Los postres.
Los dulces.

4

B. Comprensión y expresión escrita

1. Texto periodístico informativo con preguntas sobre su contenido

Lea con atención el siguiente artículo:

El restaurante Betelu

El restaurante Betelu se halla en la calle Florencio Llorente de Madrid, en un barrio que no se distingue precisamente por la 5 abundancia de buenos restaurantes. Su comedor, pequeño pero acogedor, es regentado por un matrimonio que se esfuerza por atender a sus clientes con 10 toda amabilidad. La carta está compuesta de una sabia mezcla de platos de cocina gallega y navarra, entre los que destacan los sabrosos pimientos rellenos 15 de bacalao, la ensaladilla de salmón fresco, el besugo a la espalda, el cogote de merluza y las chuletas de cordero lechal.

Si decide comer en Betelu, no 20 olvide pedir de postre leche frita o la tarta de manzana casera. No dude en aceptar el vino clarete de la Rioja navarra que le sugerirán para acompañar la 25 comida.

Después de los postres le obsequiarán con una copita de aguardiente de hierbas, licor de manzana o pacharán, que le 30 ayudarán a una buena digestión.

El precio está entre 2.000 y 2.500 pesetas. Si no ha reservado mesa con anterioridad, pue- 35 de encontrarse con el comedor lleno.

Conteste a las siguientes preguntas:

1. *¿En qué lugar de Madrid está el restaurante Betelu?*

   ....

2. *¿Qué plato de carne se recomienda?*

   ....

3. *¿Cuál de los postres pediría usted?*

   ....

4. *¿Qué tipo de bebida le van a recomendar?*

   ....

5. *¿Cuánto puede costarle el cubierto?*

   ....

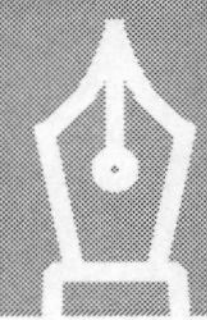

2. Texto de anuncios y convocatorias con preguntas

A continuación va a leer una información extraída de la Guía CAMPSA 1990.

PANES (ASTURIAS)

Distancias: Oviedo, 138 Km. Madrid, 427 Km.
Altitud: 50 m. - Habitantes: 566. Tlf.: 985.
Oficina de Información: Mayor, s/n.

***VISITAR**: Iglesia de **San Juan** y **Santa María**, románicas. **Palacio de los Mier**. **Abadía de Cimiano**.*
***ALREDEDORES**: Desfiladero de la HERMIDA: panorámicas. **Colegiata de Santa María de Lebeña**.*

RESTAURANTES

CASA JULIÁN
(En NISERÍAS - PEÑAMELLERA ALTA). (C-6312). Ctra. Panes-Cangas de Onís. Tlf.:41 41 79. Con habitaciones. Conjunto hotelero con restaurante, hotel y tienda, en este tranquilo paraje asturiano. Cocina sencilla y sabrosos guisos caseros. Patatas rellenas, fabes con almejas, salmón del Cares, reo al horno, merluza de pincho, brazo de gitano y arroz con leche. 2.500 ptas.

COVADONGA
Plaza de la Iglesia. Tlf.:41 41 62. Sopa de mariscos, fabada asturiana, entrecot al cabrales, salmón del Cares, arroz con leche. 2.500 ptas.

LOS MONTAÑEROS
(En CARIÑENA DE CABRALES, a 27 Km.) Servando Ruiz Gómez, s/n. Tlf.: 84 52 11. Fabada, Habas con jabalí, menestra de verduras, chuletón al Cabrales, arroz con leche. 2.500 ptas.

Conteste a las siguientes preguntas:

1. *¿Cuál de los tres restaurantes es el más caro?*

   ....

2. *¿Hay algún postre común en los tres restaurantes? Diga cuál.*

   ....

3. *¿En qué lugar exacto está el restaurante «Covadonga»?*

   ....

4. *¿En cuál de estos establecimientos puede además pasar la noche?*

   ....

3. Artículo periodístico de opinión, con preguntas a las que deberá contestar VERDADERO/FALSO

Lea con atención el siguiente artículo:

Valor nutritivo del queso

El queso es, ciertamente, un producto alimenticio muy valioso. Procede de la leche coagulada y tiene en su composición proteínas de alta calidad, grasas, calcio y vitaminas liposolubles.
5 Pese a su alto valor nutritivo, se consume en bajas cantidades en España, tanto en relación con el consumo de leche (322 g./persona y día, mientras que el de queso es sólo de 15g./persona y día) como también al comparar con otras poblaciones euro-
10 peas. En Italia y Francia se consumen 33 y 39 g./persona y día, respectivamente.
La razón de la diferencia de consumo puede estar en la tradición que existe en la Europa comunitaria de consumir el queso como postre, que en España
15 choca con la costumbre de tomar frutas, dado que son más abundantes en nuestro clima que en el centro de Europa. En efecto, la tradición de consumo de queso en España lo sitúa antes como objeto
20 de aperitivo, plato frío o recurso de bocadillo que como plato fuerte, en forma de tablas de queso o como postre, tan habituales en naciones como Francia.

BLANCO Y NEGRO, 26-VIII-1990

Lea las siguientes frases. Señale V (verdadero) o F (falso) en relación con el contenido del artículo. A continuación, busque la parte del texto en la que se ha basado para escribir V/F y escríbala en las líneas de puntos.

1. *El queso apenas tiene valor nutritivo.*
   V ☐ F ☐ ....
2. *En España se prefiere el queso como aperitivo.*
   V ☐ F ☐ ....
3. *El queso es rico en proteínas.*
   V ☐ F ☐ ....
4. *En el queso abundan los hidratos de carbono.*
   V ☐ F ☐ ....
5. *En España se consume más queso que en Francia e Italia.*
   V ☐ F ☐ ....
6. *Las tablas de queso son un plato habitual en España.*
   V ☐ F ☐ ....
7. *Los españoles suelen preferir de postre la fruta.*
   V ☐ F ☐ ....

4. Redacción de una carta a partir de instrucciones

En sus últimas vacaciones en el Levante español, sus amigos le invitaron a comer en su casa un plato denominado paella, del que le ha quedado un recuerdo imborrable.
Escriba una carta a estos amigos pidiéndoles la receta lo más detallada posible.
La carta deberá contener al menos lo siguiente:

1. Encabezamiento y despedida.
2. Alusión al recuerdo de sus vacaciones.
3. Agradecimiento por la invitación.
4. Ofrézcales, si lo desean, enviar a cambio alguna receta típica de la cocina de su país.

5. Componer una redacción a partir de instrucciones

Componga una redacción de 150 a 200 palabras (15 ó 20 líneas) sobre el tema:

COMER EN CASA O COMER EN EL RESTAURANTE.

1. *Ventajas de comer en casa.*
2. *Mi restaurante favorito.*
3. *Comentario sobre los precios.*
4. *La propina.*

C. Gramática y vocabulario

1. Texto incompleto con 10 huecos

El siguiente texto está incompleto. Deberá rellenar cada uno de los huecos con la palabra más apropiada.

Desde hace unos años se viene diciendo que los alimentos fritos son tóxicos y aumentan el nivel de colesterol en la sangre. Sin embargo, la cocina andaluza ha demostrado tradicionalmente que los pescados fritos no sólo no son tóxicos .... que además son muy digeribles. Como se suele freír con .... de oliva en la zona de Andalucía, hay que recordar que .... aceite impregna de grasa los alimentos en menor cantidad que .... grasas. Esto se pone de manifiesto en los populares envoltorios .... papel en los que se sirven pescaditos como los salmonetes y los chanquetes, ... no dejan nunca huella en el papel que .... envuelve.

Los pescados fritos en aceite de oliva quedan .... una capa protectora que les hace conservar su .... marino y sus propiedades. El complemento perfecto para un plato de pescadito frito es un buen .... de Jerez.

2. Ejercicios de selección múltiple. Gramática

En cada una de las siguientes frases, hay un hueco que deberá rellenar con una de las cuatro expresiones, eligiendo la que sea más correcta.

1. La tarta causó impresión. Los comensales .... con entusiasmo.
   a) la han recibido b) lo recibieron c) lo han recibido
   d) la recibieron
2. ¡Qué hermosa noche .... para cenar en la terraza!
   a) es b) hace c) hay d) existe
3. ¡Cuánto .... haber probado el pulpo a la gallega!
   a) me divierte el b) gusto c) me alegro de d) gusto de
4. Cuando .... la harina, déjelo reposar durante diez minutos.
   a) haya sido añadida b) hubo sido añadida c) se habrá añadido d) hubiera sido añadida

5. .... probar el cocido madrileño antes de irme.
   a) Debo de b) Tengo de c) Tengo que d) Tengo

6. Boquerones en vinagre. .... lo que más me gusta.
   a) Aquello es b) Eso es c) Ello es d) Esos es

7. Ya está la mesa preparada. ....
   a) Sentarse b) Se sienten c) Sentaos d) A sentarse

8. La cuenta .... lo más pronto posible, por favor.
   a) me lo traiga b) tráigamela c) traigala a mí d) traiga

9. El vino tinto se debe servir .... temperatura ambiente.
   a) a b) con c) de d) dentro de

10. ¿No .... mejor pedir pescado en la cena?
   a) era b) sería c) fuera d) sea

11. .... convenga reservar una mesa en el restaurante.
   a) A lo mejor b) Es probable c) Quizá d) Así pues

12. Tienes que ponerle .... azúcar al flan.
   a) más b) poco más c) un poco de más d) un poco más

13. ¿Es esta servilleta ....?
   a) de ti b) suya c) la de ti d) suya de usted

14. Pasen ustedes al bar. No esperen ustedes ....
   a) de pie b) a pie c) por pie d) sobre pie

15. Te advierto que no tengo .... gana de comer.
   a) alguna b) una c) la d) ninguna

16. ¿No .... para cenar otra vez huevos fritos con patatas?
   a) hubiste puesto b) habrás puesto c) hayas puesto
   d) hubieras puesto

17. Así vestido pareces un jefe .... cocina.
   a) para b) en c) de d) a

18. No .... la sopa, que está muy caliente.
   a) empezar b) empezaréis c) empecéis d) empezasteis

19. No invitéis .... a cenar, que es un glotón.
   a) ése b) a ése c) aquél d) a ésos

20. ¿ .... es este tenedor que estaba en el suelo?
   a) Cuyo b) Quién c) De quién d) De cuyo

3.Ejercicio de selección múltiple. Vocabulario

En cada una de las siguientes frases hay un hueco que deberá rellenar con una de las cuatro palabras, eligiendo la más apropiada.

1. El sabor picante no .... a todas las comidas.
   a) sienta *b) conviene* *c) adapta*
2. Para .... el pescado se necesita harina y huevos.
   a) envolver *b) rebozar* *c) cubrir*
3. Vamos a acompañar los espárragos con .... mayonesa.
   a) caldo *b) guarnición* *c) salsa*
4. En una ensaladera .... el atún desmenuzado.
   a) se vierte *b) se tira* *c) se pone*
5. La gelatina que .... se deja en sitio fresco.
   a) resta *b) permanece* *c) queda*
6. Hoy he traído merluza porque parecía muy ....
   a) fría *b) fresca* *c) reciente*
7. El arroz está ya ....
   a) en punto *b) puntual* *c) en su punto*
8. Hay que lavar las verduras para que queden .... limpias.
   a) bien *b) mucho* *c) muchísimo*
9. No le .... tanta sal al tomate.
   a) arrojes *b) eches* *c) tires*
10. En una sartén se .... la mantequilla.
    a) hace líquida *b) derrite* *c) desintegra*

4. Vocabulario. Equivalencia

Cada una de las siguientes frases va seguida de tres expresiones (A,B y C), con una de las cuales se puede construir un significado equivalente. Señale cuál de ellas es.

1. En una cacerola se pone el aceite a calentar.
   a) para que se caliente *b) caliente* *c) por calentar*
2. La única forma de adelgazar es comer menos.
   a) comer muy poco *b) no comer* *c) no comer demasiado*
3. La comida principal de los españoles suele ser la del mediodía.
   a) primera *b) más importante* *c) que importa*
4. Espero que este menú sea de su agrado.
   a) esta comida *b) este alimento* *c) este plato*
5. ¡Qué ricos están los calamares fritos!
   a) buenos *b) óptimos* *c) bellos*
6. De primer plato os voy a servir una sopa de marisco.
   a) principio *b) primero* *c) aperitivo*
7. Los tenedores indican la categoría de los restaurantes.
   a) el índice *b) el grado* *c) la clasificación*
8. El buen vino debe llevar su etiqueta de origen en la botella.
   a) procedencia *b) nacimiento* *c) nación*
9. En España se cena alrededor de las diez.
   a) casi a *b) un poco más tarde de* *c) sobre*
10. No nos traiga vino. Preferimos agua mineral.
    a) agua medicinal *b) agua embotellada* *c) agua en botella*

5. Completar diálogos con la opción más adecuada

1. - Ese asado que están sirviendo .... muy apetitoso.
   - Sí, pero ya sabes que yo soy vegetariano.

   a) viene estando b) está siendo c) debe de estar d) ha estado

2. - Camarero, ¿tardará mucho la paella?
   - Diez minutos. ¿Por qué no .... el vino? Les traeré un aperitivo.

   a) van probándose b) tienen probado c) han de probar d) van probando

3. - ¿Qué les pongo de postre? Tenemos albaricoques y paraguayas.
   - Prefiero un helado. Estas frutas tempranas no .... nunca.

   a) terminan de madurar b) deben madurar c) van madurandos d) maduraron

4. - Hoy de aperitivo .... unos calamares a la romana y caracoles.
   - ¿Ves cómo no piensas más que en comer?

   a) vengo pidiendo b) vamos a pedir c) acabamos por pedir d) pedirnos

5. - ¿Qué negocio van a poner ustedes aquí?
   - .... un restaurante con autoservicio.

   a) Debemos poner b) Estamos montando c) Poníamos d) Habríamos montado

6. - ¿Les quedan a ustedes torteles?
   - No. .... la masa ahora.

   a) Habíamos hecho b) Venimos haciendo c) Vamos a hacer d) Hacer

7. - Este queso está demasiado curado.
   - Es verdad. No lo .... con este cuchillo.

   a) puedo partir b) partía c) habré partido d) debo de partir

8. - ¿Qué os traigo hoy del mercado?
   - Hoy .... marisco para hacer una paella.

   a) debes de traer b) debes c) trajiste d) debes traer

9. - ¿Tienes judías verdes de esas tan tiernas?
   - No, pero .... recibirlas.

   a) vamos a ir b) se puede c) es posible que d) estamos a punto de

10. - ¿Me compras un helado en ese puesto?
    - No te lo voy a comprar porque ya .... frío.

    a) empieza a hacer b) comienza haciendo c) iba haciendo d) hizo

Arte.

Unidad **5**

A. Comprensión y expresión oral

1. Textos orales

1.1 Escuche la siguiente información y a continuación elija la opción correcta: V / F (Verdadero / Falso). Antes de empezar a escuchar la información, conviene que lea usted las frases.

1. *Está permitido fotografiar los cuadros.*

   V ☐ F ☐

2. *En la sala hay un cuadro mitológico de Rubens.*

   V ☐ F ☐

3. *Hay un retrato en el que aparece el hijo del Greco.*

   V ☐ F ☐

1.2 Escuche la siguiente información y a continuación conteste a las preguntas que le formulamos. Antes de empezar a escuchar la grabación, conviene que lea usted las preguntas.

Preguntas:

1. *¿Dónde se ha celebrado esta exposición?*

   ....

2. *¿Qué fotógrafos son mencionados en esta información?*

   ....

3. *¿Cuál es el motivo de las fotografías de Ricardo Esteban?*

   ....

1.3 Escuche el siguiente aviso y a continuación conteste a las preguntas que le formulamos. Antes de empezar a escuchar la grabación, conviene que lea usted las preguntas.

Preguntas:

1. *¿Qué es lo primero que va a visitar el tercer grupo?*

   ....

2. *¿Por qué no pueden ir todos juntos?*

   ....

3. *¿En qué ciudad se encuentran estos turistas?*

   ....

2. Expresión a partir de láminas

Observe con atención la historieta. Cuando conteste a las cuestiones que le planteamos, hágalo de forma oral. Además escríbalo.

2.1 Primera lámina

Póngase en la situación de la mujer de la última viñeta. ¿Qué le estará diciendo a él?.

....

2.2 Segunda lámina

Póngase en la situación del escultor en la segunda viñeta. ¿Qué puede estar diciendo? ¿Qué dice en la tercera viñeta?

....

....

2.3 Tercera lámina

Póngase en la situación del pintor de la tercera viñeta. ¿Qué les dice a las personas que están mirando?

....

3. Exposición sobre un tema general

3.1 Sobre el siguiente tema, deberá hablar durante un tiempo no superior a cinco minutos. Le sugerimos que grabe su exposición, la escuche y trate de mejorar la expresión en una segunda grabación definitiva.

Tema: ¿CUÁL DE LAS BELLAS ARTES ES SU PREFERIDA?

Sugerencias:
Artes para contemplar.
Artes para ejercitar.
Las visitas a los museos.
Las exposiciones.
Los catálogos.

3.2 Sobre el siguiente tema deberá hablar durante un tiempo no superior a cinco minutos.

Tema: DESCRIBA UN CUADRO QUE CONOZCA.

Sugerencias:
Tema del cuadro.
En qué lugar lo ha visto.
Qué sabe del pintor.
Otras obras del mismo pintor.
Por qué le gusta.

B. Comprensión y expresión escrita

1. Texto periodístico informativo con preguntas sobre su contenido

Lea con atención el siguiente artículo:

Largas colas el primer día de la exposición 'Velázquez' en el Museo del Prado

Cerca de 7.500 personas visitaron ayer la muestra, que reúne 80 obras del pintor sevillano.

FIETTA JARQUE

Las colas de gente que deseaba visitar la exposición *Velázquez*, que ayer se abrió al público en el Museo del Prado, llegaron a prolongarse en la calle hasta la cuesta de Moyano, a unos 400 metros de la puerta de entrada. Dentro, la cola seguía por las escaleras y un largo pasillo. Al cierre del museo, a las siete de la tarde, habían visitado la muestra alrededor de 7.500 personas. La exposición, que reúne 80 de las 90 obras que se conservan del pintor sevillano, estará abierta al público hasta el 30 de marzo, desde las nueve de la mañana hasta las siete de la tarde.

El visitante resopló incrédulo, mientras movía la cabeza ante el espectáculo que descubría. Alargó el cuello un poco más para ver el detalle de la pintura y repitió el gesto, que terminó esta vez con una sonrisa. *Retrato de un hombre joven*, una de las obras de Velázquez que se exponen actualmente en el Museo del Prado y que procede del Museo de Múnich, fue una de las recompensas o de los hallazgos de este visitante que había pasado cerca de dos horas de espera para visitarla.

Fuera, las colas de gente llegaron a medir, ayer, hasta 400 metros de longitud. Recorrían la fachada principal, el paseo a lo largo del jardín Botánico y llegaban hasta la cuesta de Moyano. Sin embargo, según comentaron algunos resignados visitantes, la cola era ordenada y avanzaba rápidamente. Dentro, las salas no estaban abarrotadas, se podían ver tranquilamente las pinturas y muchas personas, con el catálogo en la mano, se detenían casi ante cada cuadro.

Pero no todos tuvieron la misma experiencia. La señora Madison, una turista inglesa, contemplaba sin prisas un cuadro de Botticelli en el pasillo, al lado del largo último tramo de la cola. «No, no he venido al Prado a apreciar los fondos de este museo», se apresuró a explicar. «Yo también vine a la exposición de Velázquez, pero no he podido entrar».

«Vine ayer porque los carteles decían que se inauguraba el 23, y me dijeron que vuelva al día siguiente. Vine temprano hoy, pagué mi entrada, y, como no hablo español, nadie me supo explicar qué cola debía formar. Me metí en una durante una hora, al llegar me dijeron que ésa no era. Luego fui a otra y al final me dijeron que me había equivocado. A la tercera renuncié y aquí estoy, viendo los otros cuadros», afirmó.

Confusión

Es fácil que los turistas extranjeros se sientan desorientados, porque las señales que indican el camino a la exposición son muy bonitas, pero no muy explícitas. Un personaje de *La fragua de Vulcano*, el joven Apolo, indica con lánguido gesto de su dedo índice la dirección a seguir. «Se ha querido organizar todo tan bien, que es todo una confusión», comenta uno de los vigilantes del museo. «Pero eso es porque se trata del primer día, luego ya todo irá mejor».

A la entrada de la exposición se han instalado unas mesas donde se venden catálogos y carteles de la exposición. Se ha hecho una edición de 15.000 ejemplares del catálogo, que se vende a un precio de 3.500 pesetas. Ayer, cuatro horas después de haber sido abierta al público la muestra, se habían vendido cerca de 3.000 ejemplares. Por el momento, el museo no ha editado ninguna otra guía de la exposición, ni un folleto de mano. Como única ayuda se encuentran los habituales expositores con hojas explicativas generales sobre la vida y principales obras del pintor sevillano pertenecientes a la colección del Prado.

El horario de visita es el habitual del museo, pero, si la afluencia de público es excesiva, se ha considerado ampliarlo a mayor número de horas.

EL PAÍS, 25-I-1990

Conteste a las siguientes preguntas:

1. *¿Dónde se pueden adquirir catálogos y carteles de la exposición?*

....

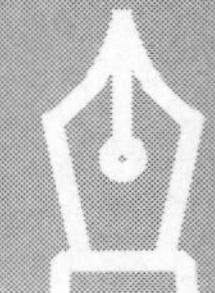

2. *¿Durante cuántas horas al día se puede visitar la exposición?*

....

3. *¿Cuándo se clausurará la exposición?*

....

4. *¿Dónde se celebra la exposición?*

....

5. *¿Qué día asistieron menos de 7.500 personas?*

....

6. *Mencione en una frase algún problema que haya podido encontrarse un turista en la exposición.*

....

7. *¿En qué caso está previsto que se amplíe el horario de visita?*

....

2. Artículo periodístico de opinión, con preguntas a las que deberá contestar VERDADERO/FALSO

Lea con atención el siguiente artículo:

Un juego de espejos

(FRAGMENTO)

CARLOS SAURA

Los cuadros con espejos siempre me han fascinado. Desde siempre me he sentido atraído por aquellas pinturas en donde además de ser ventana, espacio imaginativo o recreación de una realidad, aparece un espejo. Y así como el espejo de la realidad invierte la imagen y se desplaza con nosotros, el espejo en el cuadro es un cuadro dentro del cuadro, un cuadro enmarcado ya, que señala con discreción aquello que el pintor desea acentuar añadiéndole un misterio que emana del espejo.

Mi recuerdo de *Las meninas* -y de alguna manera mi descubrimiento de la pintura- está íntimamente unido a cómo estaba puesto el cuadro en el antiguo Museo del Prado.

Para mí, *Las meninas* no es el cuadro brillante y luminoso que hoy se contempla -hermosísimo, sin duda- sino ese otro cuadro austero, de sobrios colores, que se encontraba en su inmensidad enfrentado a un espejo -inmenso también- que lo reflejaba. Esa puesta en escena espectacular, teatral y extraordinaria supuso para mí el reencuentro con el tiempo en cada una de sus misteriosas dimensiones. Allí, en ese instante, se generaba el presente, el pasado y el futuro. Allí estaba yo, reflejado en el espejo, como un presente invertido, como invertido estaba delante de mí, detrás de mí, *Las meninas*, de Velázquez.

Si uno rotaba lentamente delante del espejo que reflejaba *Las meninas*, terminaba por darse de sopetón con el cuadro original. Allí el cuadro desprovisto del aura mágica de los espejos, tenía otra entidad y otro interés, me parecía como sin vida, como una gigantesca estampa que no participaba de la vida, de mi vida al menos.

Quienes, entonces, daban la espalda a *Las meninas* y se miraban en el espejo quedaban deslumbrados al verse integrados en tan extraordinario telón de fondo. A mí me impiden ver el cuadro en su totalidad pero agachándome ligeramente, un poquito a la izquierda, consigo encontrar un hueco que me permite adentrarme en el misterio: la puerta entreabierta por donde aquel señor de negro se recorta, a medio camino entre uno y otro escalón; el espejo-cuadro donde se refleja la realeza bajo el rojo del cortinaje, pintado con la sabiduría de la pincelada rápida, exacta, lo que denota una autoridad, seguridad y displicencia que se desprende de todos los cuadros del Velázquez maduro.

Ese narcisismo inevitable de verse dentro del cuadro a través del espejo que lo refleja queda muy velazqueño: a Velázquez le hubiera gustado que sus buenos amigos se integraran en su obra. Creo que debería haber un espejo frente a cada cuadro valioso para duplicar su imagen y darnos así la posibilidad de que pudiéramos intervenir, aunque fuera fugazmente, de puntillas y con pudor, en las obras que admiramos.

EL PAÍS, 23-I-1990

Lea las siguientes frases. Señale V (verdadero) o F (falso) en relación con el contenido del artículo. A continuación, busque la parte del texto en la que se ha basado para escribir V/F y escríbala en las líneas de puntos.

1. *Al autor del artículo los cuadros con espejos siempre le han fastidiado.*

   V □ F □ ....

2. *Antes el cuadro de* Las meninas *estaba colocado frente a un gran espejo.*

   V □ F □ ....

3. *Cada cuadro importante debería tener un espejo delante.*

   V □ F □ ....

4. *El personaje que aparece por una puerta a medio abrir va vestido de un color indefinido.*

   V □ F □ ....

5. *El autor del artículo prefiere el recuerdo de* Las meninas *como estaban colocadas antes.*

   V □ F □ ....

6. *La puesta en escena de* Las meninas *le transporta al autor del artículo solamente al pasado.*

   V □ F □ ....

3.Texto de anuncios y convocatorias con preguntas

En la sección denominada AGENDA, el diario EL PAÍS publica las siguientes convocatorias. Léalas.

Centro cultural de la Villa.

Tlf.:275 60 80 / Plaza de Colón, s/n. / Metro Colón y Serrano / Director: Antonio Guirau.

- Venta anticipada con cinco días para todos los espectáculos. Horario de taquilla: de 11 a 13.30 y de 17 a 20 horas. Lunes, descanso.

- **Sala II**. Sábado, a las 19.30 horas, ciclo *Los Cuartetos de Beethoven*. Cuarteto Margand, de París. *Cuartetos Opus 18, número 1, en fa mayor; opus 59, número 1, en fa mayor y en la menor.* Butaca: 500 ptas.

20.00 horas.

- **Conferencia**. *Aquello que los Gobiernos ocultan sobre los OVNIS*. Colegio Mayor Chaminade. Paseo de Juan XXIII, 9. Ciudad Universitaria.

- **Teatro**. *Vade Retro*, por el Grupo Taormina. Centro Cívico Pozo del Tío Raimundo. Avenida de las Glorietas, 19.

- **Conferencia - concierto** de música cósmica. Centro cultural Neo-humanismo. Olmo,10.

- **Conferencia**. *El renacimiento de la religión*, por Kamar Fazal. Junta Municipal de Moncloa. Plaza de la Moncloa, 1.

- **Conferencia**. El mensaje de la naturaleza, por Octavio Guerra. Hastinapura. Gran vía, 54.

- **Conferencia**. *La vida del toro en el campo colmenareño.* Dentro del IV Curso de Tauromaquia. Universidad Popular. Huerta del convento, 1. Colmenar Viejo.

Teatro español. Ayuntamiento de Madrid / Tlf.: 429 62 97 / Príncipe, 25 / Metro Sevilla / Director: Gustavo Pérez Puig.
- **El príncipe constante**. Compañía invitada Teatro de Hoy presenta *El príncipe constante*, de Pedro Calderón de la Barca; versión, José María Rodríguez Méndez y Alberto González Vergel; con Juan Carlos Naya, María Kosty, Andrés Resino, Toni Fuentes y la colaboración de Carlos Mendy. Escenografía y figurines: José Hernández. Música: Gustavo Ros. Coreografía: Jaime Montoya. Luminotecnia: José L. Rodríguez. Director: Alberto González Vergel. Martes, miércoles y jueves, a las 19 horas; viernes y sábado, a las 19 y 22.30 horas; domingo, a las 17 y a las 20 horas. Localidades a la venta con 5 días de anticipación. Horario de taquilla, de 11.30 a 13.30 y de 17.00 a 20.00 horas. Lunes, cerrado.

Conteste a las siguientes preguntas:

1. *¿Dónde debe usted ir si está interesado en escuchar música clásica?*

....

2. *¿A qué hora hay representación los jueves en el Teatro Español?*

....

3. *¿Cómo se titula la conferencia de Octavio Guerra?*

....

4. *¿En qué lugar se puede asistir a alguna otra representación teatral aparte de la del Teatro Español?*

....

5. *¿En qué horario puede sacar entradas para el Centro Cultural de la Villa?*

....

6. *¿En qué localidad tiene lugar una conferencia sobre tema taurino?*

....

4.Redacción de una carta a partir de instrucciones

Ha recibido en herencia una escultura con la firma de Pablo Gargallo. Aunque siempre le han dicho que era auténtica, usted duda y, por ello, decide escribir a un especialista de Barcelona. La carta deberá contener al menos lo siguiente:

1. Encabezamiento y despedida.
2. Debe decir que adjunta una fotografía.
3. Aludir al material y al tamaño de la pieza.
4. Pedir al especialista que le envíe una factura por sus servicios.

C. Gramática y vocabulario

1. Texto incompleto con 10 huecos

El siguiente texto está incompleto. Deberá rellenar cada uno de los huecos con la palabra más apropiada.

LA ESCULTURA

La escultura es la más universal y antigua de las artes. Desde los orígenes de la Humanidad, el hombre ha esculpido sobre la piedra, ha tallado la madera o el marfil y ha buscado la forma a partir de los materiales que encontraba en su entorno. Al .... tuvo una finalidad religiosa y más tarde, estética.

.... primeros nombres de escultores que han llegado .... nosotros son los de la Grecia clásica, de los .... no quedan apenas obras originales. La escultura griega floreció entre los .... V y III a.C. Los romanos heredaron la tradición de la escultura griega .... sobresalieron en el retrato. Los temas de la escultura fueron casi exclusivamente religiosos en la .... Media. En España, desde el siglo XVII, las cofradías encargaron para las procesiones de la Semana Santa .... de Jesús y de la Virgen en madera policromada. La escultura del siglo XX busca nuevos .... como el acero, los plásticos y el metacrilato. El escultor actual hace lo .... que el escultor primitivo: utiliza los materiales que tiene a su alcance.

2. Ejercicios de selección múltiple. Gramática

En cada una de las siguientes frases, hay un hueco que deberá rellenar con una de las cuatro expresiones, eligiendo la que sea más correcta.

1. Vamos a ir a Córdoba para .... la Mezquita.
   a) que visitemos b) visitar c) el visitar de d) la visita de
2. .... los frescos de Goya en la ermita de San Antonio de la Florida.
   a) Están para restaurar b) Están restaurando c) Son de restaurar d) Acaban por restaurar

3. No podremos visitar .... cuevas de Altamira si no hemos pedido antes autorización.
a) las b) unas c) esas d) ningunas

4. El teatro romano .... es el de Mérida.
a) mayormente conservado b) más bien conservado c) mejor conservado d) el mejor conservado

5. No te olvides .... mañana visitaremos la Alhambra de Granada.
a) que b) de que c) el que d) en que

6. ¿.............................. a qué hora abren la basílica de San Juan de Baños?
a) Ustedes sabéis b) Vosotros saben c) Usted sabes d) Ustedes saben

7. Nos dijeron .... a la torre para ver la ciudad.
a) subir b) que subiéramos c) que subimos d) que hay de subir

8. Hoy ya hemos recorrido .... monumentos.
a) bastante de b) suficientes de c) bastantes d) los bastantes

9. ¿La pintura abstracta no .... comprendo.
a) lo b) le c) la d) me la

10. En el Camino de Santiago abundan los monasterios .... iglesias medievales.
a) e b) y c) así como d) además

11. ¿ .... podemos encontrar un buen guía?
a) Adonde b) Adónde c) Dónde d) En dónde

12. Esta escultura de Pablo Serrano, ... la miro, más me gusta.
a) contra más b) a medida que c) a más d) cuanto más

13. Este es el .... día de nuestra estancia en Sigüenza.
a) doceavo b) doce c) duodécimo d) décimo y segundo

14. Nos hemos quedado .... en la sala de conciertos.
a) sin entrar b) sin que entremos c) por entrar d) porque entremos

15. Ese edificio que ves .... es el Palacio Real.
a) ahí b) ay c) hay d) de ahí

16. .... tengo tiempo, volveré otro día.
a) De que no b) Porque no c) Ya que no d) Como no

17. ¿Has visto .... son estos tapices?
a) cuanto modernos b) qué de modernos c) lo modernos que d) que modernos

18. Hay varios monumentos de interés en Olivenza, ... la portada de la Biblioteca.
a) entre los que destaca b) destacando c) y se destaca d) al destacar

19. El Barrio Gótico de Barcelona ocupa la parte de la ciudad .... estaba dentro de las viejas murallas.
    a) la cual b) que c) donde d) cuya
20. Es muy probable que el origen de Santa María la Nueva .... al siglo VII.
    a) se remonta b) es de remontarse c) es remontado d) se remonte

3.Ejercicio de selección múltiple. Vocabulario

En cada una de las siguientes frases hay un hueco que deberá rellenar con una de las cuatro palabras, eligiendo la más apropiada.

1. La bóveda de la catedral de Plasencia tiene .... de estrella.
   a) silueta b) forma c) aspecto d) contorno
2. Una puerta románica .... a la biblioteca.
   a) entra b) abre c) conduce d) viene
3. Granadilla .... dentro de una muralla sin torres.
   a) yace b) está ubicada c) está colocada d) está puesta
4. El Ayuntamiento de Tudela fue construido en el siglo XVIII .... la catedral.
   a) junto b) orilla de c) próximo d) cerca de
5. A la izquierda del pórtico de San Pablo se abre un nicho de .... fondo
   a) grande b) gordo c) amplio d) grueso
6. La iglesia del Monasterio de Uclés consta de .... de espaciosas proporciones.
   a) una nave b) un corredor c) un ámbito d) un pasillo
7. Jorge Manuel Teotocópuli .... un pincel en su mano derecha.
   a) agarra b) atrapa c) sostiene d) prende
8. En Tarragona no todo son playas. Hay también .... romanos.
   a) baldosines b) azulejos c) ladrillos d) mosaicos
9. El Museo Picasso de Barcelona cuenta con un .... fondo de obras del pintor.
   a) riquísimo b) acaudalado c) grueso d) abultado
10. *La Biblioteca del Escorial posee libros con .... de estilo flamenco.*
    a) menudencias b) pequeñeces c) miniaturas d) tatuajes

4. Vocabulario. Equivalencia

Cada una de las siguientes frases va seguida de tres expresiones (A, B y C), con una de las cuales se puede construir un significado equivalente. Señale cuál de ellas es.

1. Las fuentes de La Granja constituyen uno de los mayores atractivos del Real Sitio.

   a) el mayor   b) uno de los más grandes   c) uno entre los muchos

2. La colegiata de San Patricio es la única iglesia consagrada a este santo irlandés.

   a) dedicada   b) puesta   c) propuesta

3. Sobre las puertas de algunas casas nobiliarias hay escudos.

   a) ennoblecidas   b) nobles   c) ricas

4. La pintura al óleo seca más despacio que la acuarela.

   a) El óleo   b) El aceite   c) La pintura al aceite

5. Las imágenes góticas de la Virgen siempre sonríen.

   a) muestran una sonrisa   b) se ríen   c) ríen

6. Se precisa especialista para restaurar una pintura.

   a) Se necesita   b) Es necesario   c) Falta

7. El balcón de esta fachada parece de estilo italiano.

   a) debe de ser   b) debe ser   c) es parecido

8. Intervinieron en la construcción unos 10.000 obreros.

   a) los   b) aproximadamente   c) más de

9. La copia de la Gioconda tiene un marco de caoba.

   a) está enmarcada en   b) tiene un marco en   c) marca en

10. Esta iglesia data del siglo XIII.

   a) tiene fecha del   b) fecha en el   c) es del

5. Completar diálogos con la opción más adecuada

1. - ¿Dónde han puesto la exposición de esculturas de Botero?
   - Para .... la exposición hay que ir al Paseo de Recoletos.

   a) ver b) que viéramos c) verla d) que veamos

2. - ¿Cómo han roto en la fuente el brazo de La Cibeles?
   - Lo rompieron .... la victoria de su equipo.

   a) celebrar b) habiendo celebrado c) celebrado d) celebrando

3. - ¿Qué vamos a hacer esta tarde?
   - Una vez .... Salamanca, saldremos para Zamora.

   a) visitamos b) visitada c) visitando d) visitar

4. - No llevamos ningún recuerdo de este viaje.
   - Con .... unas fotos ya tenemos bastante.

   a) que sacas b) sacar c) sacando d) sacado

5. - ¿Por dónde se entra en la Cámara Santa?
   - Vete hasta el final y .... por aquella escalera.

   a) bajando b) bajar c) baja d) a bajar

6. - Aquí expone Antonio López. .... a ver la exposición.
   - Sí. Y compraremos una reproducción de uno de sus cuadros.

   a) Entrar b) Entrando c) Entrad d) Haber entrado

7. - ¡Qué gran concertista era Andrés Segovia!
   - Sobre todo .... el concierto de Aranjuez.

   a) interpretando b) interpretar c) interpretado d) interpreta

8. - ¿Qué hacen tantos pintores en el Parque de Berlín?
   - .... en un concurso de pintura al aire libre.

   a) Haber participado b) Participado c) Participaron d) Participar

9. - ¿A qué hora se puede visitar la Catedral de Burgos?
   - Vayan allí y .... cuál es el horario de visita.

   a) preguntar b) pregunten c) preguntamos d) haber preguntado

10. - ¿Qué es lo más interesante de la ciudad?
    - No se vaya sin .... el Museo de Tapices.

    a) que visite b) visitando c) haber visitado d) visiten

A. Comprensión y expresión oral

1. Textos orales

1.1 Escuche los siguientes avisos que se dan por la megafonía de un hospital y a continuación conteste a las preguntas que le formulamos. Antes de empezar a escuchar la grabación, conviene que lea usted las preguntas.

Preguntas:

1. *¿Adónde tiene que ir el doctor Gaytán?*

   ....

2. *¿En qué zona del hospital se puede fumar?*

   ....

3. *¿Qué recibirán a cambio las personas que den sangre?*

   ....

1.2 En un noticiario radiofónico ha oído los siguientes consejos emitidos por un médico:

Marque V / F (Verdadero / Falso).

1. *Todas las verduras hay que tomarlas hervidas.*

   V ☐ F ☐

2. *Los helados caseros siempre ofrecen más garantías.*

   V ☐ F ☐

3. *Se puede beber agua de manantiales si está limpia.*

   V ☐ F ☐

4. *En caso de duda, es preferible consumir agua mineral.*

   V ☐ F ☐

1.3 En una charla sobre los cuidados del bebé, el pediatra da los siguientes datos sobre dentición infantil:

Marque V / F (Verdadero / Falso).

1. *Los primeros dientes le salen al bebé a las veinte semanas justas.*

   V ☐ F ☐

2. *Las muelas salen después de los colmillos.*

   V ☐ F ☐

3. *Los dientes de leche se empiezan a perder a los seis años.*

   V ☐ F ☐

2.Expresión a partir de láminas

Observe con atención la historieta. Cuando conteste a las cuestiones que le planteamos, hágalo de forma oral. Además escríbalo.

2.1 Primera lámina

Póngase en el lugar de la madre de esta niña. ¿Qué puede decirle al dentista?

....

2.2 Segunda lámina

Póngase en el lugar del médico. Invente una frase que pueda decirle el médico al padre del niño.

....

....

2.3 Tercera lámina

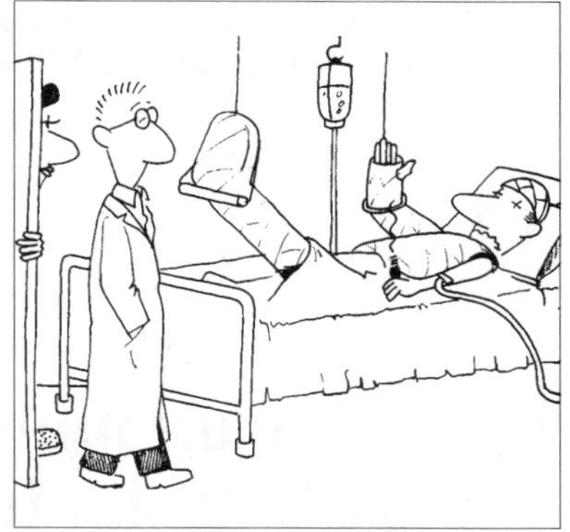

¿Qué puede decirle la enfermera al paciente?

....

3. Exposición sobre un tema general

3.1 Sobre el siguiente tema, deberá hablar durante un tiempo no superior a cinco minutos. Le sugerimos que grabe su exposición, la escuche y trate de mejorar la expresión en una segunda grabación definitiva.

Tema: LOS TRASPLANTES DE ÓRGANOS.

Sugerencias:
La donación voluntaria.
¿Sería usted donante?
Para que haya trasplantes tiene que haber donantes.
¿Trasplantes de cualquier órgano?
El mercado de órganos. Trasplantes desinteresados.
Trasplantes de órganos de animales a humanos.

3.2 Sobre el siguiente tema deberá hablar durante un tiempo no superior a cinco minutos.

Tema: FUMAR, ¿SÍ o NO?

Sugerencias:
Los perjuicios que acarrea el consumo de tabaco.
Fumadores y no fumadores. Sus derechos.
Fumadores pasivos.
La venta de tabaco a los menores.
Lugares donde fumar está o debería estar prohibido.

B. Comprensión y expresión escrita

1. Texto periodístico informativo con preguntas sobre su contenido

Lea con atención el siguiente artículo:

SANIDAD

Gran eficacia de un nuevo fármaco para trasplantes

PITTSBURGH (EE.UU.).(Efe)- Un fármaco experimental llamado FK-506 ha resultado ser altamente positivo contra el rechazo de los órganos trasplantados a los seres humanos, informaron ayer científicos de la Universidad norteamericana de Pittsburgh (Pensilvania). El doctor Thomas Starzl, director del programa de trasplantes del mencionado centro de estudios, afirmó que el FK-506 tiene efectos superiores a la ciclosporina, un fármaco que produce hipertensión y reacciones negativas en el hígado.

Starzl ofreció detalles de las investigaciones durante el congreso internacional de la Sociedad de Trasplantes, en San Francisco. Asimismo, los expertos destacaron que en los trasplantes de corazón sólo el 20 por ciento de los pacientes que recibieron el FK-506 sufrieron rechazos de los órganos, en tanto que en los tratamientos con ciclosporina hay un 40 por ciento de rechazos.

Sólo el 18 por ciento de los pacientes tratados con la nueva droga experimentaron hipertensión, comparado con el 60 por ciento de los que reciben ciclosporina, señalaron los médicos. Además, Robert Corry, directivo de la Unión de Organos para Compartir, indicó que este medicamento «es muy efectivo para los trasplantes de hígado».

Los investigadores de la Universidad de Pittsburgh manifestaron que 42 pacientes jóvenes que participaron en el estudio, y a los que les fueron implantados diversos órganos, no necesitaron altas dosis de esteroides.

Según los médicos, el nuevo medicamento, que es derivado de un hongo que se cultiva en Japón, también ayuda a los pacientes jóvenes en los casos avanzados de rechazo de los órganos implantados. El fármaco FK-506 producido por «Fujisawa Pharmaceutical» de Osaka, Japón, ha recibido la autorización estadounidense para ser utilizado de forma experimental.

LA VANGUARDIA, 27-VIII-1990

Conteste a las siguientes preguntas:

1. *¿Para qué es útil el FK-506?*

   ....

2. *¿Cuáles son los inconvenientes de la ciclosporina?*

   ....

3. *¿Dónde ha presentado el doctor Starzl su comunicación sobre el FK-506?*

   ....

4. *¿De dónde se obtiene el FK-506?*

   ....

5. *¿Para qué es especialmente eficaz el FK-506?*

   ....

2. Texto de anuncios y convocatorias con preguntas

A continuación va a leer el texto de una convocatoria:

34/90

BALEARES

HOSPITAL "SON DURETA"
DE PALMA DE MALLORCA

Programa de montaje de lavandería

PRESUPUESTO: 99.771.034 PTAS.

La consulta y entrega de la correspondiente documentación, así como la presentación de proposiciones, se efectuará en los lugares y plazos que se indican en el anuncio publicado en el *Boletín Oficial del Estado* número 207, de 29 de agosto de 1990.

MINISTERIO DE SANIDAD Y CONSUMO
INSTITUTO NACIONAL DE LA SALUD

Conteste a las siguientes preguntas:

1. *¿Qué ministerio realiza la presente convocatoria?*

   ....

2. *¿En qué fecha ha sido publicada la convocatoria oficial?*

   ....

3. *¿Para qué es esta convocatoria?*

   ....

4. *¿En qué lugar hay que presentar los documentos requeridos?*

   ....

3. Artículo periodístico de opinión, con preguntas a las que deberá contestar VERDADERO/FALSO

Lea con atención el siguiente artículo:

Abejas y avispas

(FRAGMENTO)

Síntomas

La picadura por avispa puede quedar establecida en tres grados: leve, moderado y grave. En las formas moderadas puede haber lipotimia en el momento de la picadura, enrojecimientos, placas de urticaria y picor generalizados. En las graves puede desarrollarse un cuadro de extrema urgencia que se denomina «shock» anafiláctico con espasmo de los bronquios. Asociadamente puede haber ansiedad, fiebre, debilidad muscular, sudoración profusa, dificultad respiratoria con edema de laringe y ronquera, náuseas, vómitos, diarrea, dolor de cabeza, vértigo, estado confusional, tensión baja y pulso rápido, etcétera. En los casos extremos y mortales se produce rápido «shock» anafiláctico con parada cardiorrespiratoria.

En la picadura de abeja los casos más graves suelen producirse más por picaduras múltiples que por fenómenos alérgicos. En los puntos de inoculación hay hinchazón, enrojecimiento y picor. Las manifestaciones generales vienen determinadas por alteraciones de la sangre (hemólisis), edema generalizado y graves lesiones del sistema nervioso central y del corazón.

En ocasiones pueden desarrollarse reacciones tardías, pasadas horas o incluso días tras la picadura o accidente. De la misma forma, pueden ser locales o generalizadas y a su vez de diferente intensidad o gravedad. Las alteraciones locales tardías pueden consistir en dolor con hinchazón y enrojecimiento persistentes. A veces puede haber urticaria y picor más o menos generalizado. Las reacciones tardías generales son semejantes en grado y en sintomatología a las descritas en los procesos alérgicos agudos. En general, si aparecen después de setenta y dos horas tras la picadura suelen ser de escasa consideración.

Tratamiento

Se debe extraer el aguijón de las abejas y lavar la herida poniendo compresas frías. Las formas generalizadas serán tratadas según su intensidad y a criterio del médico. En los casos leves o moderados se administrarán antihistamínicos, corticoides, pomadas locales y tratamiento sintomático. En las formas graves con «shock» anafiláctico y parada cardiorrespiratoria se prestará la ayuda urgente de reanimación cardiopulmonar hasta trasladar al enfermo a lugar adecuado de asistencia especializada.

Las personas alérgicas deben llevar consigo siempre un pequeño estuche con medicinas de urgencia, tipo adrenalina para inyección subcutánea o aquellas otras que el médico les recomiende. También deben ser tratadas (desensibilizadas) mediante extractos de himenópteros, produciendo una especie de vacunación.

Doctor Eduardo Sanz
y doctor Delfín González

BLANCO Y NEGRO, 26-VIII-1990

Lea las siguientes frases. Señale V (verdadero) o F (falso) en relación con el contenido del artículo. A continuación, busque la parte del texto en la que se ha basado para escribir V/F y escríbala en las líneas de puntos.

1. *La picadura de avispa nunca tiene importancia.*

   V □ F □ ....

2. *Una picadura de avispa puede causar la muerte.*

   V □ F □ ....

3. *La picadura de abeja suele producir cortes de digestión.*

   V □ F □ ....

4. *Los efectos de las picaduras de abeja pueden notarse varios días después de haberse producido aquéllas.*

   V □ F □ ....

5. *Cuando le pique una abeja no se le ocurra sacar el aguijón.*
V ☐ F ☐ ....

6. *Las personas alérgicas deben ponerse a diario una inyección por si les pica alguna abeja.*
V ☐ F ☐ ....

4.Redacción de una carta a partir de instrucciones

En la revista «Salud Perfecta» hay un consultorio abierto para los lectores. Escriba una carta realizando una breve consulta relacionada con la salud. La carta deberá contener al menos lo siguiente:

1. Algunos datos personales del consultante.
2. Breve exposición del asunto que quiere consultar.
3. Pida que le contesten personalmente en vez de a través de la revista, para lo cual debe incluir un sobre franqueado con su dirección.

5. Componer una redacción a partir de instrucciones

Componga una redacción de 150 a 200 palabras (15 ó 20 líneas) sobre el tema:

ACTIVIDADES PARA MANTENERSE CON BUENA SALUD.

1. *Alimentación.*
2. *Ejercicio y deporte.*
3. *Hábitos perjudiciales para la salud.*
4. *La visita periódica al médico.*

C. Gramática y vocabulario

1. Texto incompleto con 10 huecos

El siguiente texto está incompleto. Deberá rellenar cada uno de los huecos con la palabra más apropiada.

Los medicamentos no deben tomarse nunca sin que los prescriba el médico. Tampoco deben tomarse sin tenerse en cuenta las dosis recomendadas. La dosis media es la .... produce un efecto determinado al 50% de las .... a las que se administra. Por lo cual, siempre se .... tener en cuenta que cada individuo necesita una .... distinta de medicamento, dependiendo de su edad, su peso y los .... factores relacionados con el funcionamiento de su organismo. .... dosis usuales para el adulto de 20 a 60 .... y con un peso aproximado de 70 kilos deben reducirse a .... de los 60 años en una cuarta parte. En los niños, la dosis debe ser .... a su peso corporal. También en la mujer la dosis debe .... en una cuarta parte porque su peso suele ser menor que el del varón.

2. Ejercicios de selección múltiple. Gramática

En cada una de las siguientes frases, hay un hueco que deberá rellenar con una de las cuatro expresiones, eligiendo la que sea más correcta.

1. ¡Ay, cómo .... los oídos!
   a) duelen mis b) me duelen c) duelen d) me duelan
2. No voy a tener más remedio .... al médico.
   a) que ir b) ir c) de ir d) a ir
3. Este plan de adelgazamiento me .... por el especialista.
   a) ha recomendado b) es recomendado c) ha estado recomendado d) ha sido recomendado
4. No conviene que .... la herida.
   a) tocar b) toquéis c) tocas d) tocaseis

5. La salud es .... importa.
   a) el que b) lo que c) que d) lo cual
6. ¡ .... daño me ha hecho el dentista!
   a) El b) Cuán c) Cuánto de d) Qué
7. Ya .... haber llamado al médico.
   a) deberías de b) habías debido de c) debías d) habrías debido de
8. Ponle el termómetro, ... tiene fiebre.
   a) a ver si b) si c) en caso de que d) a menos que
9. La familia está muy satisfecha de que ....
   a) ha mejorado. b) haya mejorado. c) había mejorado. d) mejoró.
10. Hasta el próximo miércoles no .... el alta.
   a) la dan b) dan a ella c) le dan d) la dan a ella
11. El cirujano ha dicho que .... en cama una semana más.
   a) le tenemos b) le tendríamos c) le tengamos d) tenerle
12. A mi hijo .... la cabeza con bastante frecuencia.
   a) duele a menudo b) suele doler c) generalmente duele d) suele dolerle
13. No sé .... debo dirigirme para consultar esto.
   a) quién b) al quién c) a quién d) a el que
14. Parece que ya no le duele tanto, ¿.........................?
   a) es verdad b) de verdad c) no es verdad d) no es de verdad
15. .... las seis cuando le llevaron al quirófano.
   a) Son b) Fueron c) Serían d) Serán
16. La convalecencia ha sido muy buena. Ya no se resiente ....
   a) de nada b) por nada c) en nada d) con nada
17. Como la madre estuvo enferma, el niño crece ....
   a) en raquítico. b) de raquítico. c) por raquítico. d) raquítico.
18. ¿No sería .... que lo consultaras con tu ginecólogo?
   a) más bueno b) más bien c) más mejor d) mejor
19. No se acostumbra .... tan fácilmente a las lentillas.
   a) uno b) todos c) alguno d) ninguno
20. Estaría enfermo, ... tenía una cara radiante.
   a) a pesar de que b) ni c) acaso d) pero

3. Ejercicio de selección múltiple. Vocabulario.

En cada una de las siguientes frases hay un hueco que deberá rellenar con una de las cuatro palabras, eligiendo la más apropiada.

1. El 42% de los tumores son ....
   a) malos b) muy malos c) malísimos d) malignos
2. Cuando se sospecha que hay .... de la columna vertebral, no se debe mover al accidentado.
   a) fractura b) rompedura c) herida d) fracción
3. Hay que tomar precauciones para no .... el sida.
   a) coger b) tomar c) contraer d) pillar
4. La alimentación durante la .... es muy importante.
   a) lactancia b) época de la leche c) leche d) láctea
5. La picadura de los insectos a veces hace que .... la piel.
   a) aumente b) crezca c) se infle d) se inflame
6. Esta tarde le ha subido .... a cuarenta.
   a) el calor b) la calentura c) la fiebre d) la calor
7. El dolor de .... se denomina tortícolis.
   a) pescuezo b) cogote c) collar d) cuello
8. ¿Qué se debe hacer en caso de .... doméstico?
   a) incidente b) acontecimiento c) suceso d) accidente
9. La aspirina es un remedio eficaz para cuando se ....
   a) tiene frío. b) está frío. c) es frígido. d) está resfriado.
10. Hay que diagnosticar la enfermedad lo más .... posible.
   a) antes b) precozmente c) rápida d) anteriormente

4. Vocabulario. Equivalencia

Cada una de las siguientes frases va seguida de tres expresiones (A,B y C), con una de las cuales se puede construir un significado equivalente. Señale cuál de ellas es.

1. Nada como una buena crema para cuidar su piel.
   a) Lo mejor es una buena crema   b) Nada buena es una crema   c) Cualquier crema es buena
2. Las amígdalas son con frecuencia la causa de afecciones del corazón.
   a) muchas veces   b) siempre   c) algunas veces
3. El consumo excesivo de grasas nos hace engordar.
   a) engrosa.   b) engorda.   c) hace gordos.
4. Hay que tomar precauciones para evitar que los niños se lleven a la boca cuanto encuentren.
   a) procurar   b) tener cuidado   c) impedir
5. Los colirios sirven para corregir algunos trastornos de los ojos.
   a) ojerosos.   b) ojales .   c) oculares.
6. Tratándose de un bebé prematuro, todas las precauciones son pocas.
   a) Cuando se trata   b) Cuando se dice   c) Cuando se refiere
7. El ciclismo exige un buen estado físico.
   a) El deporte cíclico   b) El motociclismo   c) La bicicleta
8. El adolescente experimenta cambios importantes en su anatomía.
   a) padece   b) sufre   c) duele
9. Mi abuela está llena de achaques.
   a) dolencias.   b) fiebres.   c) sarpullidos.
10. Hay que quitarle ya el chupete a este niño.
    a) arrebatarle   b) robarle   c) retirarle

5. Completar diálogos con la opción más adecuada

1. - ¿En este hospital .... pasan consulta?
   - Antes no, pero ahora sí la pasamos.

   a) claro b) ciertamente c) también d) cierto

2. - ¿Esta vacuna contra la gripe es eficaz?
   - No nos ha fallado .... cuando la hemos aplicado en la fecha adecuada.

   a) tampoco b) algunas veces c) nunca d) rara vez

3. - ¿Hay alguna farmacia en este barrio?
   - Tienen una muy ...., dos calles más arriba.

   a) adelante b) aquí c) dentro d) cerca

4. - ¡Cuánta fiebre tiene el niño!
   - Con estos comprimidos se le pasará ....

   a) primero b) pronto c) temprano d) todavía

5. - Doctor, siento un dolor en el pecho.
   - A ver, respire .... varias veces.

   a) bajo b) medio c) casi d) despacio

6. - Creo que tengo un cálculo en el riñón.
   - Pues procure guardar cama y .... beba mucha agua.

   a) más b) además c) tampoco d) incluso

7. - No sé qué hacer para adelgazar.
   - Comiendo menos es .... lo conseguirás mejor.

   a) como b) que c) igual d) cuanto

8. - Yo cada día me encuentro menos ágil.
   - Te sentirías mejor .... si hicieras algo de ejercicio.

   a) sin embargo b) de alguna manera c) tal vez d) tampoco

9. - Tengo un dolor de cabeza insoportable.
   - Con una aspirina se te pasará ....

   a) bien b) mejor c) rápidamente d) buenamente

10. - ¿Qué se puede hacer para mantenerse en forma?
    - Andar un .... todos los días.

    a) tanto b) tanto más c) poco más d) poco más o menos

A. Comprensión y expresión oral

1. Textos orales

1.1 Escuche los siguientes avisos que se dan por la megafonía de una estación y a continuación conteste a las preguntas que le formulamos. Antes de empezar a escuchar la grabación, conviene que lea usted las preguntas.

Preguntas:

1. *¿De dónde viene el tren que va a Valladolid y León?*

....

2. *¿En qué estaciones se va a detener dicho tren?*

....

3. *¿A qué hora va a llegar el Talgo que viene de París?*

....

4. *¿Para quién se ha preparado un tren especial?*

....

1.2 En un noticiario local ha oído las siguientes informaciones.
Marque V / F (Verdadero / Falso):

1. *Va a haber mucho tráfico en el paseo de la Castellana a partir de las ocho de la tarde.*
   V ☐ F ☐
2. *En la avenida de la Reina Victoria están arreglando las aceras.*
   V ☐ F ☐
3. *El conductor del Seat Málaga vive en Gerona.*
   V ☐ F ☐
4. *A Luis Salazar le envían un aviso para que se dirija a Huelva.*
   V ☐ F ☐

1.3 En un programa de radio escucha usted las siguientes sugerencias sobre algunos cruceros que puede realizar:

Preguntas:

1. *¿Con qué frecuencia sale el «Costa Marina»?*

....

2. *¿Cuánto cuesta el crucero que dura una semana?*

....

3. *¿Cómo se llama el barco que sale de Génova?*

....

4. *Si usted desea pisar tierra griega, ¿qué crucero de los dos debe realizar?*

....

2.Expresión a partir de láminas

Observe con atención la historieta. Cuando conteste a las cuestiones que le planteamos, hágalo de forma oral. Además escríbalo.

2.1 Primera lámina

Póngase en el lugar del policía de la última viñeta. ¿Qué puede estar diciéndole al conductor?

....

2.2 Segunda lámina

Póngase en el lugar del niño. ¿Qué puede estar diciéndole al marinero?

....

2.3 Tercera lámina

Póngase en el lugar de este señor. ¿Qué le dice a la secretaria?

....

3. Exposición sobre un tema general

3.1 Sobre el siguiente tema, deberá hablar durante un tiempo no superior a cinco minutos. Le sugerimos que grabe su exposición, la escuche y trate de mejorar la expresión en una segunda grabación definitiva.

Tema: TRANSPORTE PÚBLICO O TRANSPORTE PRIVADO.

Sugerencias:
El transporte en las grandes ciudades.
El transporte interurbano.
¿Transporte público gratuito?
La calidad del transporte público.

3.2 Sobre el siguiente tema deberá hablar durante un tiempo no superior a cinco minutos.

Tema:
LA RADIO ES EL MEDIO DE COMUNICACIÓN DE MASAS MÁS DIRECTO.

Sugerencias:
La noticia en prensa, televisión y radio.
¿Para qué casos urgentes puede servir especialmente la radio?
Algún ejemplo concreto de empleo de la radio en un acontecimiento importante.
La radio se puede oír en cualquier parte.

B. Comprensión y expresión escrita

1. Texto periodístico informativo con preguntas sobre su contenido

Lea con atención el siguiente artículo:

Una tromba de agua aisla por tierra Madrid con el sur de España

EL PAÍS, **Madrid**

La fuerte tromba de agua que cayó ayer tarde en la zona sureste de la región cortó las comunicaciones terrestres entre la Comunidad de Madrid y el sur de España. La carretera nacional IV estuvo cerrada durante al menos tres horas, según la Dirección General de Tráfico (DGT), mientras que Renfe tuvo que suspender todos sus viajes entre la capital y las zonas sur y sureste de España. Aranjuez sufrió una fuerte riada debido al desbordamiento del Mar de Ontígola. Carabaña sigue desde la noche del sábado sin comunicaciones por tierra.

La carretera de Andalucía, donde hubo retenciones de más de 20 kilómetros, fue abierta de forma intermitente desde las diez de la noche, después de que los bomberos achicaran el agua acumulada en el punto kilométrico 48, según la DGT.

No obstante, la circulación fue lenta una vez abierta la vía debido al barro y los materiales acumulados.

Renfe no pudo hacer circular trenes entre Andalucía y Murcia debido a que dos de sus principales líneas pasan por Aranjuez, donde una riada recorrió las calles. Miles de pasajeros se vieron afectados por este corte.

EL PAÍS, 10-IX-1990

Conteste a las siguientes preguntas:

1. *¿Por qué quedaron cortadas las comunicaciones entre Madrid y el sur de España?*

   ....

2. *¿Cuánto tiempo estuvo cortada la nacional IV?*

   ....

3. *¿En qué lugar se acumuló especialmente el agua?*

   ....

4. *¿A qué población afectó el desbordamiento del Mar de Ontígola?*

   ....

5. *¿A qué organismo corresponden las siglas DGT?*

   ....

6. *¿Por qué no pudieron circular trenes entre Andalucía y Murcia?*

   ....

2. Texto de anuncios y convocatorias con preguntas

A continuación va a leer unos avisos sobre el tráfico en Madrid:

Carreras hípicas

Las carreras nocturnas que se celebrarán en el Hipódromo ocasionarán previsiblemente problemas de tráfico. Se recomienda que, si se tiene que utilizar la carretera de La Coruña, se acceda a ella a través de las salidas de Cristo Rey o Arco de la Victoria, y se evite hacerlo por la carretera de El Pardo y la de Castilla, donde se efectúan las obras.

Calles con obras. La plaza de Castilla, por la construcción de un túnel; el paseo de la Castellana, entre Cuzco y la plaza de Lima, tiene obras en el carril-bus; la avenida de Pablo Iglesias y el paseo de Rosales, por la realización de sendos aparcamientos para residentes; la carretera de Castilla, la de El Pardo y el puente de los Franceses. Continúan los problemas de tráfico ocasionados por las obras que se están llevando a cabo en la M-30 a la altura del puente de Vallecas.

Calles cortadas. El acceso a la M-30 por la calle de Embajadores.

EL PAÍS, 30-VIII-1990

Conteste a las siguientes preguntas:

1. *¿Adónde se puede salir por Cristo Rey?*

   ....

2. *¿Por qué es mejor no ir por la carretera de El Pardo?*

   ....

3. *¿Dónde están construyendo un túnel?*

   ....

4. *¿Qué obra se está realizando en el paseo de Rosales?*

   ....

5. *¿En qué avenida están construyendo un aparcamiento?*

   ....

6. *¿Por dónde no se puede llegar de ninguna manera a la M-30?*

   ....

3. Artículo periodístico de opinión, con preguntas a las que deberá contestar VERDADERO/FALSO

Lea con atención el siguiente artículo:

Lejanías

La política ferroviaria de cercanías en los grandes núcleos urbanos, y muy particularmente en Madrid y Barcelona, se ha revelado, más allá de las buenas intenciones de sus planificadores y ejecutores, como un ejemplo flagrante de imprevisión y de falta de capacidad para evaluar las necesidades reales de los usuarios. El resultado es la prestación deficiente, llena de incertidumbre y cada vez más alejada de la demanda, de un servicio público al que los insuperables problemas del tráfico han convertido en el medio de transporte casi único y más seguro de que disponen los centenares de miles de ciudadanos que viven en los barrios extremos, en las ciudades-dormitorio y en el conglomerado de urbanizaciones que rodean los centros administrativos y comerciales de las grandes capitales.

Los graves sucesos que vienen ocurriendo en algunas líneas de la periferia de Madrid son la reacción lógica y humanamente comprensible - por más que sus derivaciones violentas y destructivas sean absolutamente condenables- de quienes todos los días se encuentran sometidos al calvario de un servicio ferroviario deficiente y a la lucha desigual contra el reloj para tratar de llegar puntualmente a sus trabajos. Y lo que es lamentable es que los responsables del Ministerio de Transportes hayan tenido que esperar a que la situación devenga en graves alteraciones del orden público para intentar resolver las carencias más llamativas de este servicio: el incumplimiento de los horarios y la escasez de unidades en las horas punta.

Dentro de las distintas parcelas de actuación de Renfe, la de cercanías es considerada como la de más futuro e, incluso económicamente, más rentable que otras, dadas las posibilidades de aumento de una demanda estimulada por la cada vez mayor inviabilidad del transporte privado en el acceso por carretera a las grandes concentraciones urbanas. Cuando el monstruo del tráfico amenaza con asfixiar Madrid, Barcelona y otras grandes capitales, es absolutamente incomprensible que la red ferroviaria de penetración en sus núcleos urbanos siga revelándose asmática, insuficiente e ineficaz.

Esta situación pone al descubierto, una vez más, los efectos parciales del saneamiento financiero como única política, porque conlleva de forma paralela el deterioro del servicio prestado. Es decir, lo mismo que ha sucedido en Telefónica en los últimos años, con el resultado de poner bajo mínimos la calidad del servicio. Una política que, en el caso de Renfe, ha contribuido a que el fuerte crecimiento de la demanda experimentado últimamente en el servicio ferroviario de cercanías haya dejado viejas las previsiones para 1991. Ello constituye además un dato revelador de la preocupante descoordinación con que las distintas administraciones- estatal, autonómica y local- abordan un problema que como el del tráfico en las grandes ciudades exige una apuesta política planificada. Cuando uno de los ejes de esta política se basa en el transporte público asombra que la improvisación y las imprevisiones sean las armas con las que se pretende convencer a los ciudadanos sobre las ventajas del tren frente al coche particular.

EL PAÍS, 21-I-1990

Lea las siguientes frases. Señale V (verdadero) o F (falso) en relación con el contenido del artículo. A continuación, busque la parte del texto en la que se ha basado para escribir V/F y escríbala en las líneas de puntos.

1. *Los trenes de cercanías funcionan muy bien en Madrid y Barcelona.*

   V ☐ F ☐ ....

2. *Debido a los problemas de tráfico, los trenes de cercanías son casi el único medio para llegar al centro de la ciudad desde las ciudades-dormitorio y las urbanizaciones.*

   V ☐ F ☐ ....

3. *Los dos defectos más importantes de los trenes de cercanías son la impuntualidad y los pocos trenes que hay de servicio en las horas de mayor demanda.*

   V ☐ F ☐ ....

4. *El Ministerio de Transportes llevaba dos años empeñado en solucionar el problema.*
V ☐ F ☐ ....
5. *En Telefónica no ha ocurrido lo mismo que en Renfe, porque sus servicios funcionan perfectamente.*
V ☐ F ☐ ....
6. *El aumento en el número de viajeros ha superado las previsiones que Renfe había hecho para 1991.*
V ☐ F ☐ ....
7. *Resulta asombroso que pretendan convencernos de que es mejor utilizar el coche particular que el tren.*
V ☐ F ☐ ....

4. Redacción de una carta a partir de instrucciones

Hace ya tres meses que solicitó a la Compañía Telefónica Nacional de España (CTNE) la instalación de una línea en su domicilio. Escriba una carta a dicha compañía recordándoles su petición. La carta deberá contener al menos lo siguiente:

1. Encabezamiento y despedida.
2. Fecha en que solicitó la línea.
3. Pregunte cuándo se la van a instalar.
4. Invente una causa por la que a usted le es urgente la instalación.

5. Componer una redacción a partir de instrucciones

Componga una redacción de 150 a 200 palabras (15 ó 20 líneas) sobre el tema:

LOS MEDIOS DE TRANSPORTE URBANOS.

1. *Los transportes de su lugar de residencia.*
2. *Rapidez y seguridad.*
3. *Los precios.*
4. *¿Podrían mejorar?*

C. Gramática y vocabulario

1. Texto incompleto con 10 huecos

El siguiente texto está incompleto. Deberá rellenar cada uno de los huecos con la palabra más apropiada.

¿Qué haríamos sin el teléfono? Si un día, sin previo aviso, nos cortaran la línea telefónica a todos, nos parecería que vivíamos en otro mundo. Ya no .... llamar a casa para decir que íbamos a llegar .... tarde, sino que tendríamos que ir a decirlo .... mismos; con lo cual, ya no nos interesaría volver a salir, ... entre tanto ir y venir se nos habría hecho .... para llegar adonde íbamos. Tampoco podríamos felicitar a nuestros amigos .... navidad; así que tendríamos que aprender de nuevo a .... cartas y felicitaciones, tarea que ya tenemos casi olvidada a fuerza .... no hacerlo. Miles de mensajeros llenarían las calles, llevando en .... vehículos a toda velocidad nuestros recados y avisos. Por ...., no nos corten el teléfono, porque ya no sabemos vivir sin él.

2. Ejercicios de selección múltiple. Gramática

En cada una de las siguientes frases, hay un hueco que deberá rellenar con una de las cuatro expresiones, eligiendo la más correcta.

1. Los controladores aéreos han amenazado .... ir a la huelga.
   a) con b) de c) por d) para
2. Los permisos de conducir .... a la norma europea.
   a) se ha adaptado b) se han adaptado c) ha sido adaptado d) han adaptado
3. Para hablar con Bilbao, ... usted el prefijo 94.
   a) marcas b) marcarse c) marque d) marca
4. Van a desviar toda la circulación .... de Ocaña.
   a) que procediera b) que hubiera procedido c) la cual proceda d) que proceda
5. Un crucero por el Mediterráneo es .... regalo que puedes hacerme, querido.
   a) mejor b) el más bueno c) el más buen d) el mejor

6. Este tren tiene parada en ....
   a) las estaciones todas. b) todas las estaciones. c) las todas estaciones. d) todas estaciones.
7. ¿ .... parece bien que le llame mañana?
   a) A usted b) La c) Le d) A usted la
8. Me preguntó si .... billete de ida y vuelta.
   a) llevaba b) llevo c) llevara d) he llevado
9. Viaja mucho: tan pronto está en Sevilla .... en Zaragoza.
   a) que b) cuanto c) o d) como
10. Al director le llegó la noticia de .... por telegrama.
    a) la su dimisión b) la dimisión suya c) su dimisión d) dimisión suya
11. .¿ .... sale el tren Talgo Madrid-París?
    a) Cuál es la hora que b) Qué hora c) A cual hora d) A qué hora
12. Pasado mañana .... desde Segovia a cobro revertido.
    a) me han de llamar b) me habrán de llamar c) me van a llamar d) habrán de llamarme
13. Retransmitirán .... satélite la final de la Copa del Mundo.
    a) con b) a c) por d) desde
14. Desde que se ha inventado el fax la comunicación por escrito .... más rápidamente.
    a) se hizo b) se hacía c) se hará d) se hace
15. No pudo enviar a tiempo la crónica a su periódico porque el télex .... estropeado.
    a) estuvo b) estaba c) estuviera d) está
16. ¿ .... tardará en llegarle el dinero si se lo envío por giro postal?
    a) Qué b) De cuánto c) Cuánto d) A cuánto
17. Los telegramas de felicitación que llegaron fueron ....
    a) más de millar b) mil y más c) mucho más de mil d) más de mil
18. .... cruzar el estrecho en trasbordador porque me mareo.
    a) Ni me se ocurre b) Ni ocúrreseme c) Ni me ocurre d) Ni se me ocurre
19. No nos vamos a mover de aquí .... el helicóptero.
    a) hasta que llega b) hasta que llegara c) hasta que llegue d) hasta llegar
20. .... en autocar y papá que vaya en el tren con el equipaje.
    a) Yo, tú y mamá vamos b) Mamá, tú y yo vamos c) Mamá, tú y yo van d) Tú, yo y mamá vamos

3.Ejercicio de selección múltiple. Vocabulario.

En cada una de las siguientes frases hay un hueco que deberá rellenar con una de las cuatro palabras, eligiendo la más apropiada.

1. El vuelo 605 .... un retraso de dos horas.

   a) padece b) sufre c) sale d) soporta

2. En el kilómetro 206 de la carretera nacional IV hay un ....

   a) variable. b) atajo. c) variante. d) desvío.

3. La policía de .... está para algo más que poner multas.

   a) tránsito b) tráfico c) autopista d) carreras

4. Esta carta puede ir con .... de veinte pesetas.

   a) franquicia b) una estampa c) un sello d) una marca

5. Enviar este telegrama le .... trescientas pesetas.

   a) costará b) cobrará c) costeará d) hará pagar

6. Las carreteras han quedado .... a causa de la nieve.

   a) estorbadas b) bloqueadas c) tapadas d) taponadas

7. El satélite no comienza a enviar .... hasta el domingo que viene.

   a) señas b) señalización c) signo d) señal

8. Te estoy llamando desde .... de teléfono.

   a) una cabina b) un gabinete c) un cubículo d) una caja

9. Durante los meses de verano, miles de trabajadores marroquíes .... la Península.

   a) traspasan b) pasan c) cruzan d) transitan

10. Me .... una multa por exceso de velocidad.

    a) han dado b) han puesto c) han colocado d) han metido

4.Vocabulario. Equivalencia

Cada una de las siguientes frases va seguida de tres expresiones (A,B y C), con una de las cuales se puede construir un significado equivalente. Señale cuál de ellas es.

1. Los controladores franceses son la raíz del problema del tráfico aéreo en media Europa.
   a) la causa principal   b) lo principal   c) la mayor parte
2. Se están construyendo nuevas vías de acceso a la ciudad de Valencia.
   a) sendas   b) carreteras   c) calles
3. Las autoridades marítimas están preocupadas por el aumento del tráfico de drogas.
   a) de marina   b) del mar   c) de la marítima
4. Rogamos a todo el pasaje que lean las instrucciones que encontrarán delante de su asiento.
   a) todos los viajantes   b) todos los viajeros   c) toda la tripulación
5. Me han perdido el equipaje. Al parecer, lo han enviado a Roma.
   a) el equipamiento   b) la valija   c) las maletas
6. A veces el billete sencillo cuesta lo mismo que el de ida y vuelta.
   a) individual   b) de ida   c) simple
7. ¿Cuánto falta para llegar a Manila?
   a) queda   b) resta   c) hay
8. Lo siento, señor. El telefonillo está averiado.
   a) destrozado.   b) inservible.   c) estropeado.
9. ¿A qué hora sale el primer tren para La Coruña?
   a) parte   b) discurre   c) va
10. Vamos a regresar por Lisboa.
   a) retroceder   b) volver   c) tornar

5. Completar diálogos con la opción más adecuada

1. - No sé si es éste el autobús.
   - El autobús que va .... la estación se toma en la otra calle.

   a) de b) a c) junto a d) con

2. - ¿A qué hora sale el tren para Valencia?
   - El tren .... Valencia sale a las 13:15 horas.

   a) por b) hasta c) de d) entre

3. - ¿Cómo te van a enviar los discos que has pedido?
   - Seguramente los enviarán .... reembolso.

   a) de b) por c) contra d) ante

4. - ¿Cómo te has enterado de la noticia?
   - Me la han comunicado por fax .... Barcelona.

   a) por b) desde c) entre d) durante

5. - ¿Esta línea de metro llega a la estación de Chamartín?
   - No llega .... la estación.

   a) contra b) entre c) hacia d) hasta

6. - ¿Por qué te has empeñado en venir en tren?
   - Ya sabes que es .... miedo al avión.

   a) para b) por c) bajo d) excepto

7. - Apenas se puede caminar con tanto tráfico.
   - Claro, porque dejan los coches .... la acera.

   a) encima de b) encima c) hacia d) debajo de

8. - ¿A qué hora van a repartir mañana estos paquetes?
   - Tienen que estar repartidos .... las once.

   a) antes de b) antes c) delante de d) ante

9. - ¿No ha llegado todavía el mensajero?
   - No, ya advirtieron que llegaría .... las dos.

   a) después b) alrededor de c) próximo a d) cerca

10. - ¿Dónde hay una cabina de teléfono?
    - Hay una justo .... la iglesia.

    a) frente b) enfrente de c) contra d) delante

A. Comprensión y expresión oral

1. Textos orales

1.1 Escuche los siguientes avisos que se dan por la megafonía de un centro educativo el primer día de clase y, a continuación, elija la opción correcta: V / F (Verdadero / Falso). Antes de empezar a escuchar la grabación, conviene que lea usted las frases.

1. *Estos avisos se están dando a las nueve.*
   V ☐ F ☐
2. *En este colegio hay alumnos de cuatro cursos diferentes.*
   V ☐ F ☐
3. *Los alumnos de Segundo deben ir a la biblioteca.*
   V ☐ F ☐
4. *Los alumnos que lleguen tarde al colegio no podrán entrar.*
   V ☐ F ☐

1.2 En un noticiario radiofónico ha oído la siguiente información:
Preguntas:

1. *¿Qué nombre reciben las bromas entre soldados en los cuarteles?*
   ....
2. *¿Qué institución ha denunciado los hechos a los que se alude en la información?*
   ....
3. *¿Ha habido algún herido por esta causa?*
   Sí ☐ No ☐
4. *¿Por qué no prohíbe el Ejército esta clase de bromas?*
   ....

1.3 En un informe de televisión ha oído lo siguiente:
Preguntas:

1. *¿A qué años se refieren estos datos?*
   ....
2. *¿Ha habido más divorcios que separaciones?*
   Sí ☐ No ☐
3. *¿Por qué prefieren los matrimonios separarse a divorciarse?*
   ....

2.Expresión a partir de láminas

Observe con atención la historieta. Cuando conteste a las cuestiones que le planteamos, hágalo de forma oral. Además escríbalo.

2.1 Primera lámina

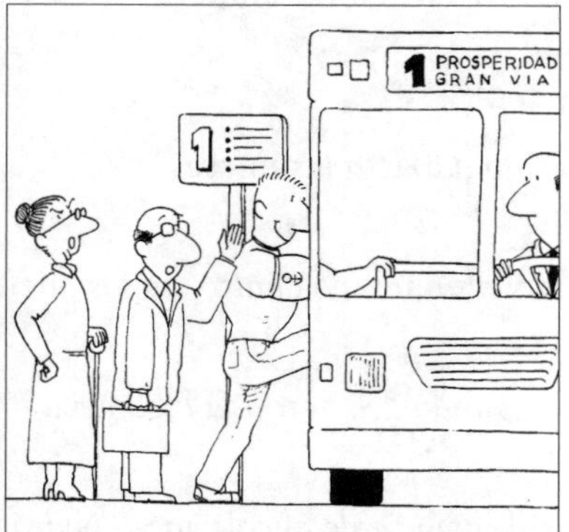

Póngase en el lugar de la señora. ¿Qué le diría al hombre que se ha saltado la cola?

....

2.2 Segunda lámina

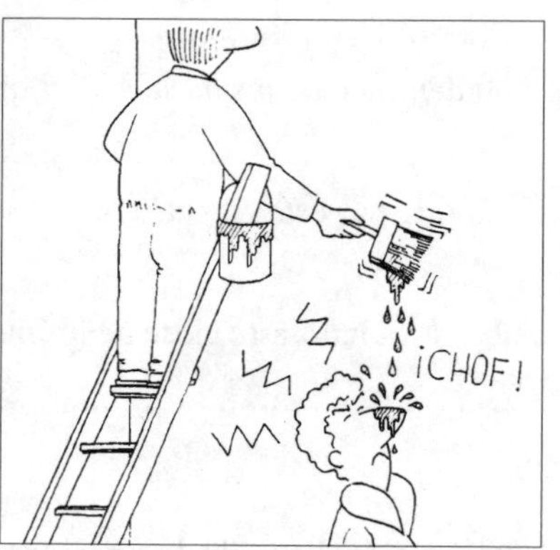

Póngase en el lugar del pintor en la última viñeta. ¿Qué le dice a la señora?

....

2.3 Tercera lámina

Póngase en el lugar de la señora en la última viñeta. ¿Qué le dice al conductor del otro automóvil?

....

3. Exposición sobre un tema general

3.1 Sobre el siguiente tema, deberá hablar durante un tiempo no superior a cinco minutos. Le sugerimos que grabe su exposición, la escuche y trate de mejorar la expresión en una segunda grabación definitiva.

Tema: LOS HORARIOS Y LAS COSTUMBRES EN TORNO A LA COMIDA EN MI PAÍS.

Sugerencias:

¿Cuántas comidas?
Horarios.
Alimentos más comunes.
Los postres.
La comida principal.

3.2 Sobre el siguiente tema deberá hablar durante un tiempo no superior a cinco minutos.

Tema: LAS COSTUMBRES FAMILIARES EN NAVIDAD.

Sugerencias:

Días festivos.
Vacaciones escolares.
Los regalos.
Las reuniones familiares.
Las tradiciones.

B. Comprensión y expresión escrita

1. Texto periodístico informativo con preguntas sobre su contenido

Lea con atención el siguiente artículo:

Los varones españoles se sienten discriminados frente a las mujeres.

SANTIAGO REGO

Santander. La mayoría de los recursos de amparo que llegan al Tribunal Constitucional por discriminación sexual en el trabajo son presentados por hombres, al contrario de lo ocurrido en los primeros años de funcionamiento de dicho tribunal, según reveló ayer Luis López Guerra, magistrado del Constitucional.

Luis López Guerra dirige el seminario «Derechos fundamentales y recurso de amparo» en la Universidad Internacional Menéndez Pelayo (U I M P), en Santander. Ante la sorpresa de los periodistas, señaló que, tras los recursos presentados por supuestas vulneraciones cometidas por los jueces - que son los más frecuentes-figuran los relativos a la igualdad de derechos, y entre ellos los de discriminación sexual en el trabajo en favor de las mujeres, principalmente en aspectos como los turnos y horarios nocturnos, permisos de maternidad, etcétera.

Oposición de los hombres

Según López Guerra, no hay datos estadísticos concretos, pero aseguró que los magistrados del Tribunal Constitucional han visto con sorpresa en los últimos cinco años cómo crece la oposición de los hombres españoles a las medidas laborales tradicionales, que protegen a la mujer en el trabajo.

López Guerra también se refirió al caso de la mujer de Mataró, que quiere que su futuro vástago sea una niña. Subrayó que, tarde o temprano, el Tribunal Constitucional tendrá que pronunciarse con respecto a tan polémica sentencia, así como con respecto a la manipulación genética.

EL INDEPENDIENTE, 5-IX-1990

Conteste a las siguientes preguntas:

1. *¿Quiénes presentan más recursos de amparo por discriminación sexual: los hombres o las mujeres?*

   ....

2. *¿Cuál es la profesión del Sr. López Guerra?*

   ....

3. *Sobre otro asunto, distinto al de la discriminación sexual, hay también muchos recursos presentados en el Tribunal Constitucional. ¿De qué asunto se trata?*

   ....

4. *Cite usted un caso concreto de derecho de las mujeres en el trabajo que moleste a los hombres.*

   ....

5. *Al final del artículo se cita el caso de una mujer. ¿Qué desea esta mujer?*

   ....

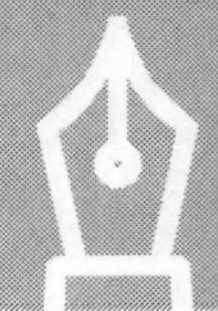

2. Texto de anuncios y convocatorias con preguntas

A continuación va a leer el texto de una convocatoria:

> **Escuelas de otoño**
> Los días 12, 13 y 14 de octubre, el Seminario Permanente de Educación para la Paz de la Asociación Pro Derechos Humanos organiza un encuentro para: «reflexionar y debatir sobre el juego, los juguetes y las campañas navideñas»; presentar la carpeta *Aprende a vivir, aprende a jugar*, organizar y coordinar las diferentes campañas que a raíz de este encuentro y esta carpeta surjan. Preinscripciones: cheque nominativo de 1.000 pesetas a Asociación Pro Derechos Humanos, calle de José Ortega y Gasset, 77, 2º A, 28006 Madrid. Información en el teléfono (91) 402 23 12.

Conteste a las siguientes preguntas:

1. *¿En qué fechas se celebra esta actividad?*

   ....

2. *¿Cuál es el motivo fundamental en torno al cual giran las actividades que en la convocatoria se proponen?*

   ....

3. *¿Cómo se paga el importe de la inscripción?*

   ....

4. *¿Qué se debe hacer si se desea tener más información?*

   ....

3. Artículo periodístico de opinión, con preguntas a las que deberá contestar VERDADERO/FALSO

Lea con atención el siguiente artículo:

El tabaco es bueno para la amistad

(Fragmento)

Por ANTONIO BURGOS

Tantas campañas se hacen en contra del tabaco, que algunos debemos estar públicamente a favor, al menos para contrarres-tar esa presión social que con-vierte al fumador virtualmente en un delincuente. Fuimos educados en el exquisito culto al tabaco, ceremonia social de la que también va a cumplirse en 1992 su Quinto Centenario par-ticular sin que nadie lo pondere. Y por una cuestión de fidelidad a los principios que recibimos, so-mos algunos los que seguimos defendiendo el tabaco contra viento y marea, entre otras cosas por un criterio de libertad: cada cual puede irse matando de la forma que tenga más por conve-niente, y somos muchos los que, por ejemplo, echamos en falta una auténtica presión social contra el alcohol, en este tiem-po de jóvenes «litronas»* y de culto al güisqui. Cada vez que me subo a un avión pienso lo absurdo que es este mundo en que vivimos, que se mueve por modas, y donde la salud tampo-co escapa a las modas. Se sube usted al avión y, si es fumador, recibe todas en el mismo lado. Ya he comentado en esta página que le condenan a viajar en los últi-mos asientos, eso si encuentra plaza libre de fumador, lo cual no siempre ocurre. Pero en cuanto el avión ha despegado, ese mismo sistema que por los altavoces le anuncia que no pue-de fumar si no se encuentra entre los ciudadanos apestados del fondo, y que tampoco puede ha-cerlo en los pasillos, ni en los lavabos; ese mismo sistema -decía-, al instante le ofrece toda suerte de bebidas alcohólicas, que trae la azafata en el carrito y que le son ofrecidas gratuita-mente en determinados trayec-tos y en determinadas clases de tarifas.

Y mi pregunta es muy simple: ¿por qué no ponen en los aviones zonas de «no bebedores»? Si a usted, señora, le molesta tanto el olor del cigarrillo que me estoy tirando «a pecho», como decía-mos de muchachos, también a mí me molesta el vaho a alcohol que echa ese lingotazo de coñac que se está usted metiendo para el chaleco. Quien haya padeci-do, como servidor ha sufrido, en un vuelo transatlántico desde

Nueva York las incomodidades de un grupo de estudiantes americanos que descubren la libertad del alcohol para los menores de veintiún años, vomitona incluida, me dará toda la razón en pedir también las zonas de «no bebedores» en los aviones. Y se planteará, como me planteo, lo absurdo de esta lucha social contra el tabaco, fuente de inspiración, compañía de los solitarios, alivio para los nervios y excusas para trabar conversación.

BLANCO Y NEGRO, 20-V-1990

(*)Litronas: botellas de cerveza de un litro.

Lea las siguientes frases. Señale V (verdadero) o F (falso) en relación con el contenido del artículo. A continuación, busque la parte del texto en la que se ha basado para escribir V/F y escríbala en las líneas de puntos.

1. *El autor de este artículo está a favor de las campañas contra el tabaco.*

   V □ F □ ....

2. *En los aviones a los fumadores siempre se les reservan los mejores asientos.*

   V □ F □ ....

3. *El título del artículo afirma que fumar fomenta las buenas relaciones con las demás personas.*

   V □ F □ ....

4. *En los aviones hay también zonas reservadas para personas que no beben.*

   V □ F □ ....

5. *En el artículo se citan expresamente tres bebidas alcohólicas: cerveza, güisqui y coñac.*

   V □ F □ ....

6. *En América los menores de edad no pueden consumir bebidas alcohólicas.*

   V □ F □ ....

7. *El autor del artículo alude a un grupo de estudiantes sudamericanos.*

   V □ F □ ....

4. Redacción de una carta a partir de instrucciones

Usted va a venir a España para vivir en una familia durante cierto tiempo con el compromiso de cuidar a los niños.

Escriba una carta en la que deberá pedir algunas informaciones. La carta deberá contener al menos lo siguiente:

1. Encabezamiento y despedida.
2. Horarios de las comidas.
3. Obligaciones.
4. Tiempo libre.
5. Quiénes componen la familia.
6. Algunos datos sobre su llegada.

C. Gramática y vocabulario

1. Texto incompleto con 10 huecos

El siguiente texto está incompleto. Deberá rellenar cada uno de los huecos con la palabra más apropiada.

NORMAS PARA ECHARSE LA SIESTA.

La siesta es una de las aportaciones más importantes de España a la cultura universal. Aunque la vida moderna no facilita precisamente esta sana costumbre, los españoles se las arreglan, ... pueden, para seguir practicándola. No importa que sea sólo un .... de hora después de la comida, aletargados ante el televisor. .... suficientes quince minutos para levantarse con nuevos ánimos, dispuestos .... afrontar la segunda parte de la jornada. No hace falta .... desnudarse. Basta con aflojarse un poco el nudo de la .... o el cinturón, estirar hacia delante las dos .... y, a ser posible, colocar los pies en alto. La cabeza debe .... reclinada hacia atrás para facilitar que se .... ligeramente la boca. Esta postura no es precisamente la .... estética que podemos ofrecer los españoles; pero se debe tener en cuenta que la siesta es una ceremonia que se celebra en la intimidad.

2. Ejercicios de selección múltiple. Gramática

En cada una de las siguientes frases, hay un hueco que deberá rellenar con una de las cuatro expresiones, eligiendo la que sea más correcta.

1. Si acaso .... que no llego a tiempo, es que no voy a comer.
   a) vieras b) veas c) verás d) veías
2. En esta casa se cena ....
   a) nueve y media b) en las nueve y media c) por las nueve y media d) a las nueve y media
3. Está muy mal educado: .... termina de comer, eructa.
   a) en cuanto b) a la vez que c) como d) al
4. La costumbre es dar la mano cuando te presentan ....
   a) alguien b) a alguien c) alguno d) algunos

5. No olvides que debes limpiarte con la servilleta ....

a) antes que bebas b) antes que bebieras c) antes que beber d) antes de beber

6. .... ceder el asiento en los transportes públicos a los ancianos.

a) Se debe de b) Debe de c) Se debe d) Deberse

7. Los españoles tienen la costumbre de desayunar ....

a) pequeño b) el poco c) muy poco d) en poco

8. No .... tomar un aperitivo antes de la comida.

a) apetece a mí b) a mí me apetece c) me apetece d) apetecerme

9. En verano la gente sale mucho .... la noche.

a) en b) con c) a d) por

10. En este restaurante .... mesas reservadas para no fumadores.

a) son b) están c) han d) hay

11. ¿Es que aquí .... los pasos de peatones?

a) no respeta nadie b) no respeta alguien c) respeta nadie d) nadie no respeta

12. .... las doce campanadas el último día del año, hay que tomar doce uvas para tener buena suerte.

a) Sonando b) Cuando suena c) Cuando suenan d) Cuando suene

13. Cuando nace un niño, ... de primer apellido el del padre y de segundo el de la madre.

a) se le pone b) se le ponga c) se ponga d) se pone

14. Los nombres de persona llevan don .... doña delante.

a) y b) e c) o d) también

15. Si no se tiene .... con una persona, se debe utilizar el usted.

a) mucho de confianza b) en mucha confianza c) mucha confianza d) confianza en mucho

16. Si le invitan a comer, no olvide .... llevar algún obsequio.

a) que es costumbre b) es costumbre c) ser costumbre d) se acostumbra

17. «Buenos días» .... el saludo común por las mañanas.

a) son b) esos son c) eso es d) es

18. Hasta mañana, ... bien.

a) duermas b) que duermas c) duermes d) dormir

19. Las tiendas pequeñas .... cerradas de dos a cuatro y media.

a) suelen ser b) acostumbran estar c) suelen estar d) acostumbran ser

20. Mi marido y yo dormimos ....

a) separando camas. b) con camas separadas. c) en camas separadas . d) sobre camas separadas.

3.Ejercicio de selección múltiple. Vocabulario.

En cada una de las siguientes frases hay un hueco que deberá rellenar con una de las cuatro palabras, eligiendo la más apropiada.

1. ¿Qué horas son éstas de llegar ....?

   a) al domicilio b) a la casa c) a casa d) al hogar

2. Le .... el marido a la mujer.

   a) inquirió b) cuestionó c) interrogó d) preguntó

3. Te he dicho mil veces que no te metas en mi ....

   a) vivencia. b) vida. c) biografía. d) vitalidad.

4. Es que nunca está la cena ....

   a) preparada. b) confeccionada. c) guisada. d) cocinada.

5. Yo no puedo estar en dos .... a la vez.

   a) localidades b) espacios c) plazas d) sitios

6. Tú siempre tienes .... para salirte con la tuya.

   a) un argumento b) una discusión c) una excusa d) una culpa

7. Si no estás .... en esta casa, ya sabes dónde está la puerta.

   a) con gusto b) a gusto c) al gusto d) gustoso

8. Bueno, mujer, no .... Yo hago la cena

   a) disgustes. b) te contradigas. c) alteres. d) te enfades.

9. No es eso. Es que todas las noches me .... igual.

   a) acoges b) recoges c) recibes d) tomas

10. *¡Ay!, si no fuera porque te quiero ....*

    a) tanto. b) todo. c) cuanto. d) tanto más.

4. Vocabulario. Equivalencia

Cada una de las siguientes frases va seguida de tres expresiones (A,B y C), con una de las cuales se puede construir un significado equivalente. Señale cuál de ellas es.

1. Se ha enamorado de una mujer mucho más joven que él.
   a) de bastante menos edad b) más pequeña c) menos madura
2. Se necesita secretaria de dirección bilingüe.
   a) con un par de lenguas b) bilingual c) que hable dos idiomas
3. En esta década ha vuelto a ponerse de moda el rock.
   a) En estos diez años b) Desde los diez años c) De diez años en adelante
4. Mi abuela sigue preparando unas natillas exquisitas.
   a) elegantes b) lujosas c) estupendas
5. Aquí solemos tomar el café muy concentrado.
   a) beber b) digerir c) comer
6. No se debe dar la espalda a la persona con la que estás hablando.
   a) volver la cara b) estar de cara c) estar frente
7. Le gusta pasar desapercibido en las reuniones.
   a) Le apetece b) Le conviene c) Prefiere
8. Este hombre siempre va hecho un desastre.
   a) con traje de sastre b) vestido con ropa deportiva c) mal arreglado
9. Mi hermana es muy simpática con todo el mundo.
   a) caritativa b) placentera c) amable
10. ¿Cuándo vas a ser un poco más sensato?
   a) sensible b) prudencial c) prudente

5. Completar diálogos con la opción más adecuada

1. - Ya viene Rosalía. Vamos a escondernos.
 - A Rosalía no le gustan las bromas, ... dejadla en paz.
 a) ya que b) así que c) porque d) aunque
2. - ¿Por qué no eres más amable con mis amigas?
 - .... estoy harto de verte siempre con ellas.
 a) A causa de b) Por c) Porque d) Por miedo a que
3. - ¿Te dejan llegar tarde a casa?
 - No me dejan .... me acompañe alguno de mis hermanos.
 a) excepto b) salvo que c) no obstante d) incluso
4. - Vamos a comprarle unas flores.
 - Te advierto que le gustan los libros .... las flores.
 a) más que b) que c) mejor d) tanto que
5. - No iré a la fiesta .... me lo pida.
 - No entiendo por qué. Es muy simpático.
 a) si b) si no c) a pesar de d) aunque
6. - Habría ido al funeral .... lo hubiera sabido.
 - Pues yo, aunque lo hubiera sabido, no habría ido.
 a) a menos que b) si c) a condición de d) con tal de
7. - ¿Qué vamos a poner de cena?
 - Tenemos pescado; .... no pongas cuchillos de carne.
 a) por lo tanto b) más bien c) con todo d) sino
8. - ¿Dejan fumar en este restaurante?
 - Hemos dispuesto las mesas .... los fumadores no molesten.
 a) que b) como c) para d) de tal manera que
9. - ¡Qué antipática es Concha!
 - No es capaz de sonreír ni .... le agradan las cosas.
 a) a condición de que b) por si c) aun cuando d) pero
10. - ¿Por fin vamos a celebrar el aniversario de nuestra graduación?
 - Va a ser difícil, ... resulta imposible reunir a todos.
 a) aun cuando b) por tanto c) en vista de que d) así pues

9 Unidad — Ecología.

A. Comprensión y expresión oral

1. Textos orales

1.1 Escuche los siguientes avisos que se dan por la megafonía de un zoológico y, a continuación, elija la opción correcta: V / F (Verdadero / Falso). Antes de empezar a escuchar la grabación, conviene que lea usted las frases.

1. *Los visitantes pueden dar de comer a los animales.*
   V ☐ F ☐
2. *No se paga por entrar en el delfinario.*
   V ☐ F ☐
3. *Los leones comen al mediodía.*
   V ☐ F ☐
4. *La exhibición de papagayos está provisionalmente cerrada.*
   V ☐ F ☐

1.2 En un noticiario radiofónico ha oído la siguiente información:

Preguntas:

1. *¿Es lo mismo desertización que desertificación?*
   Sí ☐ *No* ☐
2. *¿Qué parte de España es la más afectada por la desertificación?*
   ....
3. *¿Qué se puede hacer para solucionar el problema de la desertización?*
   ....
4. *¿Por qué la inversión de 8.000 millones al año no es suficiente?*
   ....

1.3 En la guía radiofónica de una emisora de Barcelona ha escuchado usted la siguiente información:

Preguntas:

1. *¿Dónde puede contemplar la exposición «Natura misteriosa»?*
   ....
2. *¿De dónde proceden las especies exhibidas?*
   ....
3. *¿Cuál es el horario de visita durante el mes de noviembre?*
   ....

2. Expresión a partir de láminas

Observe con atención la historieta. Cuando conteste a las cuestiones que le planteamos, hágalo de forma oral. Además escríbalo.

2.1 Primera lámina

Póngase en el lugar de quien habla por teléfono. ¿Qué estará diciendo?

....

....

2.2 Segunda lámina

Póngase en el lugar del personaje que protesta. ¿Qué estará diciendo?

....

2.3 Tercera lámina

Póngase en el lugar del trabajador de la excavadora. ¿Qué les dirá a los manifestantes?

....

3. Exposición sobre un tema general

3.1 Sobre el siguiente tema, deberá hablar durante un tiempo no superior a cinco minutos. Le sugerimos que grabe su exposición, la escuche y trate de mejorar la expresión en una segunda grabación definitiva.

Tema: LA CONTAMINACIÓN EN LAS GRANDES CIUDADES.

Sugerencias:

Las zonas industriales.
El tráfico.
Las calefacciones.
Fórmulas para hacer que disminuya la contaminación.
La contaminación acústica.

3.2 Sobre el siguiente tema deberá hablar durante un tiempo no superior a cinco minutos.

Tema: LA CONSERVACIÓN DE LA NATURALEZA ES RESPONSABILIDAD DE TODOS.

Sugerencias:

La educación en la familia y en la escuela.
Nuestro comportamiento puede afectar al medio ambiente.
La responsabilidad de los gobiernos.
La responsabilidad de las grandes industrias.
A veces los intereses económicos prevalecen sobre los intereses ecológicos.

B. Comprensión y expresión escrita

1. Texto periodístico informativo con preguntas sobre su contenido

Lea con atención el siguiente artículo:

MAREA NEGRA

Greenpeace acusa al «Aragón» de provocar la mancha en Madeira

MADRID

El petrolero de bandera española «Aragón» podría ser el causante de la marea negra que afecta al archipiélago portugués de 5 Madeira, según declaró ayer en Madrid la organización ecologista Greenpeace, informa Efe.

Según los técnicos consultados por esta organización, los pri- 10 meros análisis parecen confirmar las sospechas iniciales sobre el origen de la mancha, de siete kilómetros de extensión, que ha aparecido en las costas de 15 Madeira.

Otras fuentes técnicas, ajenas a la citada organización ecologista, han manifestado también que, a pesar de lo raro del caso, 20 «podría tratarse de un escape procedente del «Aragón», dadas las especiales características del crudo maya», petróleo mexicano que transportaba el 25 buque siniestrado.

Durante estos días se ha especulado con la posibilidad de que la marea tuviera su origen en una avería de un tercer bar- 30 co, o en los petroleros que surcan la zona.

Sin embargo, las dos hipótesis han quedado descartadas.

El «Aragón» sufrió un accidente 35 el pasado 29 de diciembre frente a la costa de Madeira en el que perdió alrededor de 25.000 toneladas de crudo.

EL MUNDO, 24-1-1990

Conteste a las siguientes preguntas:

1. *¿A qué área geográfica ha afectado el derrame de petróleo del «Aragón»?*

   ....

2. *¿Qué dimensión tiene la mancha que ha aparecido en las costas de Madeira?*

   ....

3. *¿De dónde procedía el petróleo que transportaba el «Aragón»?*

   ....

4. *Mencione otra hipótesis distinta para el vertido de petróleo en las proximidades de Madeira.*

   ....

5. *¿Cuánto petróleo se vertió al mar?*

   ....

6. *¿En qué mes del año ocurrió este accidente?*

   ....

2. Texto de anuncios y convocatorias con preguntas

A continuación va a leer la convocatoria de un premio:

PREMIOS FORD PARA LA CONSERVACIÓN DE LA NATURALEZA

Por primera vez en España, la Fundación para la Conservación de la Naturaleza y del Patrimonio Histórico-Artístico y la compañía Ford convocan los Premios Internacionales para la Conservación de la Naturaleza y el Patrimonio. Los ganadores de las diversas categorías recibirán un premio en metálico de 2.000 libras esterlinas, y el ganador absoluto un cheque por valor de 5.000 libras. Todos los interesados de cualquier nacionalidad que deseen participar en este concurso pueden dirigirse, para mayor información, a C.B. & A.; calle Núñez de Balboa 30, 5º B. 28001 Madrid. Tels. (91) 4354885 y 4354812. El plazo de presentación de los trabajos a estos Premios finalizará el próximo día 15 de noviembre.

Conteste a las siguientes preguntas:

1. *¿Qué empresa privada convoca este premio?*

   ....

2. *¿Qué otra institución convoca el premio?*

   ....

3. *¿Quién puede recibir 2.000 libras esterlinas de premio?*

   ....

4. *¿En qué moneda recibirá el premio el ganador?*

   ....

5. *¿En qué dirección puede usted pedir más información sobre estos premios?*

   ....

6. *¿Cuándo acaba el plazo para poder participar?*

   ....

3. Artículo periodístico de opinión, con preguntas a las que deberá contestar VERDADERO/FALSO

Lea con atención el siguiente artículo:

La España quemada

(Fragmento)

De las numerosas causas de desertización del suelo de España, la más directa, rápida, abundante y grave es la de los incendios forestales. La sospecha de que una gran parte está siendo ocasionada por manos deliberadas es firme, y se cree en la existencia de organizaciones criminales que dirigen, preparan y realizan estos actos en lugares determinados por su conveniencia. A España se le está yendo el suelo fértil por los cambios climatológicos desfavorables y todavía no previstos; por la industrialización, que no tiene normas suficientes de protección o no las cumple; por una polución humana que, al paso de la demografía y de la elevación de nivel de vida, se come la tierra; por el tornado de las vacaciones de acampada de los sin sensibilidad, que pisan, ensucian y queman. Y por este azote de los incendios de verano, que este año, como algunos anteriores, se ha cebado especialmente en Galicia, aprovechándose de sequías excepcionales en esa región, pero también de intereses y negocios diversos.

Autoridades gallegas han dicho que estos centenares de incendios que se producen cada mes se deben no sólo a manos directamente criminales, sino a organizaciones; a mafias, como término genérico. No las nombran. Pueden ser los interesados en recoger los restos de madera a precios insignificantes y con posibilidades de comercialización inmediata a precios altos; los que quieren que se cambien las plantaciones de árboles por otros utilizables con más rapidez; quienes desean unos terrenos limpios para construir urbanizaciones, industrias o viviendas, o por intereses menores de convertir en siembras zonas forestales.

La Guardia Civil ha detenido a casi 2.000 personas, y las ha tenido que soltar por razones diversas: o son tontos de pueblo o pirómanos de psiquiátrico, o, simplemente, no hay pruebas contra ellos. Puede ser que si las denuncias genéricas de las autoridades se hicieran más precisas, la investigación llegaría a encontrar a los verdaderos culpables y a evitar que continuasen con sus prácticas criminales.

La incultura con respecto al árbol es antigua en España. Hubo una viajera francesa del siglo XVII, la condesa D'Aulnoy, que escribió que en España una ardilla podría viajar desde los Pirineos al extremo sur sin bajarse nunca de las copas de los árboles. Aun aceptando la exageración literaria, hay datos suficientes para probar que la deforestación es acelerada en nuestro país, y que no se corresponde con la de otras zonas climatológicas semejantes o próximas en Europa, aunque el fenómeno de la desertización sea general en la Tierra. Aquí se achaca especialmente a la sequía; pero también se puede culpar a la disminución constante de la masa forestal el que haya menos lluvias. Ninguna política hidráulica ha sido tan amplia y tan eficaz a lo largo de los tiempos como para paliar estos efectos en la flora. Y por consiguiente, en la fauna, que ecológicamente corresponde a los territorios hoy devastados y que está desapareciendo simultáneamente.

Los incendios multiplican las causas naturales no atajadas y las artificiales, que son crecientes y que se están permitiendo, aunque sólo sea *por falta de pruebas*, y las medidas para cortarlos tampoco son suficientes, aun con la participación de aviones y helicópteros, de pueblos enteros, de fuerzas de orden público y de la colaboración del ejército. Habrá que aumentar la escalada de la represión de culpables, y al mismo tiempo, la de prevención y lucha; los plazos de la gran desertización van aumentando, y un poco más tarde ya no habrá remedio para la pobreza.

EL PAÍS, 27-VIII-1990

Lea las siguientes frases. Señale V (verdadero) o F (falso) en relación con el contenido del artículo. A continuación, busque la parte del texto en la que se ha basado para escribir V/F y escríbala en las líneas de puntos.

1. *Se cree que la mayoría de los incendios forestales son provocados.*

   V □ F □ ....

2. *A pesar de los cambios climatológicos y de la industrialización, España no ha perdido suelo fértil.*

   V □ F □ ....

3. *La madera procedente de los incendios no tiene ningún valor.*
   V □ F □ ....

4. *La Guardia Civil ha detenido a muchas personas relacionadas con los incendios.*
   V □ F □ ....

5. *Según una escritora del siglo XVII, toda España, de norte a sur, estaba cubierta de árboles.*
   V □ F □ ....

6. *España es el único país del mundo que está afectado por la desertización.*
   V □ F □ ....

7. *Una causa de que haya menos lluvia es que cada vez hay menos árboles.*
   V □ F □ ....

4. Redacción de una carta a partir de instrucciones

Escriba una carta al alcalde de su pueblo o de su ciudad protestando por el alto nivel de ruidos de su barrio. La carta deberá contener al menos lo siguiente:

1. Encabezamiento y despedida.
2. Señale cuál es su barrio.
3. Especifique la procedencia de los ruidos.
4. Apunte posibles soluciones.
5. No es la primera vez que se queja usted.

5. Componer una redacción a partir de instrucciones

Componga una redacción de 150 a 200 palabras (15 ó 20 líneas) sobre el tema:

PROTEGER LA NATURALEZA.

1. *La contaminación ambiental. Sus causas.*
2. *La contaminación acústica.*
3. *Comportamientos poco ecológicos.*
4. *El futuro de la Humanidad.*

C. Gramática y vocabulario

1. Texto incompleto con 10 huecos

El siguiente texto está incompleto. Deberá rellenar cada uno de los huecos con la palabra más apropiada.

Para 1993 todos los automóviles del ámbito de la Comunidad Económica Europea deberán utilizar un catalizador para eliminar el plomo de las gasolinas. El plomo es un componente .... se utiliza para aumentar la potencia y para mejorar las prestaciones .... motor; pero el plomo es también un metal que contamina .... el aire sino también los ríos y como consecuencia, más tarde, el agua del ....
La gasolina sin plomo o gasolina verde cada vez .... mayor demanda. Mientras que en España son muy .... las gasolineras en las que se expende, en otros países como Francia .... Italia, cada vez es mayor la respuesta a esta demanda. .... caso que puede servir de ejemplo a España es el del .... Unido, país que hace sólo dos años se encontraba en la .... situación que nuestro país. Pero si se quiere que el empleo de gasolinas menos contaminantes se extienda, habrá que mantenerlas en unos precios más bajos.

2. Ejercicios de selección múltiple. Gramática

En cada una de las siguientes frases, hay un hueco que deberá rellenar con una de las cuatro expresiones, eligiendo la que sea más correcta.

1. ¿ .... es la causa de la mayoría de los incendios?
   a) Qué b) Quién c) Cuál d) De qué
2. Se ha comprobado que el plomo .... un metal nocivo.
   a) sea b) es c) era d) ha sido
3. El plan de conservación del Mediterráneo .... en el plazo más breve posible.
   a) ha de desarrollarse b) ha de desarrollar c) ha desarrollado d) se desarrollase
4. La mancha de petróleo impedía faenar .... los pesqueros.
   a) hasta b) incluso c) a d) hacia
5. Los plásticos han degradado el paisaje .... las ciudades.
   a) torno a b) en derredor de c) en torno a d) alrededor

6. Los vertidos industriales dejan .... indefensos frente a las infecciones.

   a) los delfines b) a delfines c) a los delfines d) delfines

7. Las prácticas de tiro están .... prohibidas durante los meses de julio y agosto.

   a) totalmente b) todo c) en total d) total

8. .... se sabe es que los delfines tienen su sistema inmunológico afectado.

   a) Lo único que b) Único c) Único que d) Los únicos que

9. El parque de Doñana .... en las marismas del Guadalquivir.

   a) es b) es situado c) está situado d) se sitúa

10. Los síntomas indicaban .... de una epidemia en toda regla.

    a) se trataba b) que se trataba c) tratar d) tratarse

11. ¿ .... importa el bosque?

    a) A qué b) A quién c) Quién le d) A quién le

12. La forma de evitar .... es tenerlos limpios.

    a) que ardan los bosques b) arder los bosques c) que arden los bosques d) ardiendo los bosques

13. La cigüeña está encontrando dificultades .... en los lugares tradicionales.

    a) por anidar b) a anidar c) para anidar d) en anidar

14. .... el agujero en la capa de ozono, de seguir agrandándose, puede acabar con la vida en la tierra.

    a) Es dicho que b) Es dicho c) Se dice d) Se dice que

15. Los daños .... sobre la masa forestal son irreparables.

    a) los cuales la lluvia ácida causa b) los que causa la lluvia ácida c) que causa la lluvia ácida d) los que la lluvia ácida causa

16. .... los venenos para matar animales salvajes.

    a) Se prohibe b) Está prohibido c) Están prohibidos d) Es prohibido

17. .... la entrada de vehículos en La Pedriza para que no se deteriore el medio natural.

    a) Ha habido que limitar b) Ha habido de limitar c) Ha tenido limitado d) Ha habido para limitar

18. La contaminación acústica no sólo influye en el estado físico de las personas .... en su estado psicológico.

    a) pero b) además c) pero además d) sino también

19. ¿Por qué .... las hojas a los árboles este año tan pronto?

    a) se le caen b) se las caen c) se les cae d) se les caen

20. Los olmos están desapareciendo del paisaje en .... Europa.

    a) casi toda b) casi todo c) casi el todo de d) casi la totalidad

3. Ejercicio de selección múltiple. Vocabulario.

En cada una de las siguientes frases hay un hueco que deberá rellenar con una de las cuatro palabras, eligiendo la más apropiada.

1. El urogallo es una de nuestras especies más ....
   a) irritadas. b) amenazadas. c) acuciadas. d) agobiadas.

2. .... de las aguas fue la causa de la muerte de miles de animales.
   a) El creciente b) El crecimiento c) El acrecentamiento d) La crecida

3. ¿Por qué .... nuestros bosques?
   a) tallan b) acortan c) recortan d) talan

4. El buitre leonado es .... en peligro de extinción.
   a) un género b) una clase c) una especia d) una especie

5. Las hormigas .... mensajes por medio de olores.
   a) radian b) echan c) remiten d) transmiten

6. Al salir de la curva, aparecieron las majestuosas .... de Gredos.
   a) cumbres b) picos c) sierra d) valles

7. Las plagas son .... más resistentes a los pesticidas.
   a) por veces b) de vez en cuando c) cada vez d) a veces

8. Grandes .... del sur de Europa se están desertizando.
   a) fragmentos b) trozos c) pedazos d) zonas

9. .... de jóvenes se ha encargado de limpiar los alrededores de la laguna de Peñalara.
   a) Una banda b) Un enjambre c) Un grupo d) Un agrupamiento

10. Las migraciones son para las aves el mejor seguro de ....
    a) vivencia. b) vida. c) supervivencia. d) convivencia.

4. Vocabulario. Equivalencia

Cada una de las siguientes frases va seguida de tres expresiones (A,B y C), con una de las cuales se puede construir un significado equivalente. Señale cuál de ellas es.

1. La comadreja es el más pequeño de nuestros carnívoros.
   a) el menor b) el inferior c) el mínimo
2. Muchos árboles presentan unas bolitas con apariencia de frutos: son las agallas.
   a) semejantes a b) que parecen c) similares
3. Los furtivos conocen perfectamente las costumbres de los animales.
   a) muy bien b) buenamente c) por excelencia
4. El suelo está muy erosionado por causa de los incendios.
   a) de las hogueras. b) de los rescoldos. c) del fuego.
5. Es probable que todos los delfines listados del Mediterráneo actualmente estén contaminados.
   a) hoy en día b) en el acto c) habitualmente
6. La concha de peregrino además de su sorprendente memoria, posee un sentido interno del tiempo.
   a) a pesar de b) aparte de c) a la vez que
7. Aquí habita una tribu cuyos antepasados eran cazadores de cabezas.
   a) vive b) reside c) se aloja
8. La conservación del medio ambiente es una aspiración de todos.
   a) totalitaria. b) universal. c) total.
9. Muy poco se sabe sobre la vida en las zonas abisales del océano.
   a) Escaso b) Casi nada c) Nada
10. Hay especies que han sufrido grandes mutaciones en el transcurso de los últimos mil años.
    a) transformaciones b) modificaciones c) mudanzas

5. Completar diálogos con la opción más adecuada

1. - ¿Todavía no han apagado el incendio?
   - Dice el jefe de bomberos .... hasta mañana.
   a) que no se apagará b) no se apagará c) no apagar d) que no apagar
2. - ¿Qué está escrito en ese cartel?
   - Que .... mantener limpio el río.
   a) necesita b) es de necesidad c) es necesario d) necesario
3. - ¿Por qué me dices que apague la radio?
   - Porque estoy harto .... música todo el día.
   a) de oír b) que oiga c) oída d) en oír
4. - ¿De dónde sale tanto humo?
   - De aquella chimenea .... allá lejos.
   a) está b) estando c) que hay d) habiendo
5. - ¿Qué tema habéis tratado hoy en clase?
   - Hemos estado hablando .... el medio ambiente.
   a) a proteger b) que proteger c) proteger d) de proteger
6. - La mejor protección del mar consiste .... vertidos industriales.
   - Y también en procurar que no se derrame petróleo.
   a) no hacer b) en no hacer c) no haciendo d) no hagan
7. - ¿Cómo ha podido llegar a ser tan seca esta región?
   - He oído .... desde hace tres años.
   a) que no llueve b) no llover c) no llueve d) no llovería
8. - ¿Qué nombre tienen esos peces .... a estribor?
   - No son peces. Son los delfines.
   a) saltando b) los que saltan c) que salta d) que saltan
9. - En esta ciudad cada día hay más tráfico.
   - Es verdad. No sé .... a tiempo.
   a) que llegaremos b) llegaremos c) si llegar d) si llegaremos
10. - ¿Qué estás viendo en la televisión con tanto interés?
    - Están hablando .... huelga de recogida de basuras.
    a) que hay b) de que hay c) de haber d) que haber

10 Unidad Deportes y espectáculos.

A. Comprensión y expresión oral

1. Textos orales

1.1 Escuche las siguientes informaciones y, a continuación, elija la opción correcta: V / F (Verdadero / Falso). Antes de empezar a escuchar la grabación, conviene que lea usted las frases.

1. *El locutor ha anunciado los próximos partidos de rugby.*

   V ☐ F ☐

2. *El partido de fútbol podrá verse por televisión.*

   V ☐ F ☐

3. *No se ha anunciado ningún acontecimiento deportivo para el domingo.*

   V ☐ F ☐

1.2 Escuche la siguiente información y a continuación conteste a las preguntas que le formulamos. Antes de empezar a escuchar la grabación, conviene que lea usted las preguntas.

Preguntas:

1. *¿En qué hipódromo ha ganado el caballo Carbonado?*

   ....

2. *¿Cuál es la distancia que ha recorrido en su carrera?*

   ....

3. *¿Cómo estaba la pista?*

   ....

1.3 Escuche el siguiente aviso y a continuación conteste a las preguntas que le formulamos. Antes de empezar a escuchar la grabación conviene que lea usted las preguntas.

Preguntas:

1. *¿Qué ha sido suspendido?*

   ....

2. *¿Cuándo se pueden devolver las entradas?*

   ....

3. *¿Por qué se ha suspendido el acto?*

   ....

2. Expresión a partir de láminas

Observe con atención la historieta. Cuando conteste a las cuestiones que le planteamos, hágalo de forma oral. Además escríbalo.

2.1 Primera lámina

Póngase en la situación del jinete nº 7 y exprese su reacción.

....

....

¿Cuál es el comentario que haría en la viñeta tercera uno de los espectadores que apostó por el nº 7?

....

¿Y en la cuarta viñeta?

....

2.2 Segunda lámina

Exprese lo que puede estar pensando la mujer en cada una de las tres viñetas. Después, escríbalo en los globos correspondientes.

2.3 Tercera lámina

Póngase en la situación del mago en la viñeta 3º. ¿Qué estará diciendo?

....

....

¿Y en la viñeta 4º?

....

....

¿Qué podría estar diciendo el conejo desde el trapecio?

....

....

3. Exposición sobre un tema general

3.1 Sobre el siguiente tema, deberá hablar durante un tiempo no superior a cinco minutos. Le sugerimos que grabe su exposición, la escuche y trate de mejorar la expresión en una segunda grabación definitiva.

Tema: LA VIOLENCIA EN EL DEPORTE.

Sugerencias:
Los deportes de masas generan más violencia.
El deporte le sirve a mucha gente como escape de sus frustraciones.
Los deportes en los que hay choque entre los participantes (fútbol, rugby, baloncesto) frente a otros en los que no hay choque (tenis, voleibol, atletismo)
La competencia entre ciudades, regiones o naciones se refleja en el deporte.

3.2 Sobre el siguiente tema deberá hablar durante un tiempo no superior a 5 minutos.

Tema: UNA PELÍCULA QUE HE VISTO HACE POCO.

Sugerencias:
Resuma en qué circunstancias la vio (día y hora, vídeo o sala de cine, etc.)
La interpretación de los actores.
Resumen del argumento.
Puede relacionar el tema con el de otras películas.

B. Comprensión y expresión escrita

1. Texto periodístico informativo con preguntas sobre su contenido

Lea con atención el siguiente artículo:

Se apagaron los bellos ojos tristes de Silvana Mangano

Un cáncer acabó ayer con la vida de la gran actriz italiana

Madrid.
Silvana Mangano -la actriz inolvidable de «Arroz amargo», «Muerte en Venecia», «Teorema» y «Ojos negros»- fallecía ayer de madrugada en la clínica madrileña de La Luz. Un cáncer la había ido matando lentamente. El 4 de diciembre había sido operada y, pocos días después, entraba en un coma profundo del que ya no ha despertado.
Sus últimos días fueron de una infinita soledad, tras separarse de Dino de Laurentis y perder a su hijo en accidente aéreo. Desde 1986 vivía en Madrid, donde reside su hija menor, Francesca, casada con José Antonio Escrivá, hijo del actor y realizador español Vicente Escrivá.
Nacida en Roma el 21 de abril de 1930, Silvana Mangano fue descubierta para el cine por Giusseppe de Santis, periodista, crítico cinematográfico, ayudante de Visconti y guionista, realizador de «Caccia Trágica» (1947), que la incluyó en su película «Arroz amargo». Aquella película la consagraría como la mujer símbolo del neorrealismo italiano, junto a Ana Magnani.
La actriz contrajo matrimonio con el productor Dino de Laurentis en 1949. Tuvo tres hijas y un hijo, Federico, que desapareció en 1981, a los 26 años, en un accidente aéreo en Alaska. El matrimonio se separó en 1983.
La consagración de Silvana Mangano como gran actriz llegó de la mano de directores geniales: Lucino Visconti y Pier Paolo Pasolini. Con el primero hizo «Muerte en Venecia» (1970), «Luis II de Baviera» (1972) y «Retrato de familia en un interior» (titulada en castellano «Confidencias») (1974). Con Pasolini actuó en «Edipo Rey» (1976), «Teorema» (1968) y «El Decamerón» (1971). Su último gran papel lo hizo, junto a Marcello Mastroiani, en «Ojos negros», dirigida por el sovietico Mijalkov. Su mirada penetrante, altiva y desencantada sigue inquietando nuestra memoria.

Adaptación de la crónica de J.Bermejo en EL INDEPENDIENTE, 17-XII-1989

Conteste a las siguientes preguntas:

1. *¿Con quién estuvo casada la actriz Silvana Mangano?*

....

2. *¿Cómo y cuándo perdió a su hijo?*

....

3. *¿Donde falleció Silvana Mangano?*

....

4. *¿De qué fue símbolo la actriz?*

....

5. *¿Cuántos años tenía cuando murió?*

....

6. *¿Cuántos años llevaba separada de su marido?*

....

7. *¿Con qué directores importantes trabajó?*

....

2. Texto de anuncios y convocatorias con preguntas

El diario EL INDEPENDIENTE publica todos los domingos un suplemento titulado JÓVENES con información, artículos de opinión y recomendaciones para la juventud. Una de las secciones del suplemento está dedicada a la televisión.

1.- **Asterix.-** El espacio «Apaga y vámonos» está dedicado esta semana a Asterix, el personaje de historietas que el pasado 29 de octubre celebró su 30 Aniversario. Junto a su biografía de viñetas se ofrece un reportaje del Parque Asterix de Paris y una entrevista con su dibujante.
-Martes. TVE-1, 18.50 h.

2.- **Duros de roer.-** El programa divulgativo «Ustedes mismos» está dedicado a algo tan complicado como nuestro esqueleto y los huesos que lo forman.
-Viernes. TVE-1, 19.20 h.

3.- **Gremlins.-** «Sábado cine» ofrece esta película, dirigida por Joe Dante en 1984. Cuenta la historia de unas pequeñas criaturas cubiertas de pelo cuyo simpático aspecto hace que se conviertan en atractivas mascotas, sobre todo para los niños. Sin embargo, una parte de ellos se comporta de manera perversa y goza con fastidiar al género humano.
-Sábado. TVE-1, 22.00 h.

4.- **Carlitos.-** Las aventuras de Carlitos, su perro Snoopy, Lino y demás amigos son hoy los protagonistas del espacio «Largometraje juvenil»; una divertida película de dibujos animados.
-Domingo. TVE-2, 10.30 h.

5.- **Secuencias.-** Con el título de «Trucos de caracterización», Christopher Tucker, uno de los más destacados creadores de maquillaje y efectos especiales, explica sus secretos en películas como «El hombre elefante», «Los niños de Brasil» o las series «Einstein» y «Yo, Claudio».
-Miércoles, TVE-2, 17.30 h.

6.- **Jean Michel Jarre.-** El espacio «Fuera de serie» emite la grabación del último concierto de Jean Michel Jarre en el puerto de Londres. Como todos los organizados por este intérprete y compositor, supuso un gran espectáculo musical y visual.
-Sábado. TVE-2, 22.00 h.

7.- **Kim de la India.-** Una película basada en una de las obras más conocidas del escritor Rudyard Kipling. Ambientada en la India colonial de 1880, está protagonizada por Errol Flynn.
-TM3, 18.00 h.

8.- **Música, Música.-** Este programa emite el último concierto de Tom Jones en el londinense «Hammersmith Odeon». Se ofrecen también imágenes de la vida del cantante, que ha regresado a los escenarios tras varios años inactivo.
-Sábado. TM3, 22.30 h.

9.- **Komikia.-** Historia del comic desde sus comienzos, incluyendo entrevistas a los principales dibujantes del género.
-Martes. ETB-1, 21.55 h.

10.- **El Padrino.-** Basado en la novela de Mario Puzo, muestra las vicisitudes de los «capos» de la mafia y de sus familias. Película mítica interpretada por Marlon Brando, Al Pacino y James Caan.
-Lunes. ETB-2, 22.10 h.

11.- **Bruce Springsteen.-** El programa «Pop Pop» estará hoy con el cantante norteamericano Bruce Springsteen, uno de los mitos de los años ochenta.
-Domingo. CS, 17.00 h.

12.- **Gallipoli.-** Este filme narra la historia de dos amigos, corredores autralianos y su final sangriento en la batalla de Gallipoli, doloroso episodio de la historia de Australia.
-Sábado. ETB-1 y 2, 23.50 h.

EL INDEPENDIENTE *Jóvenes.*
17-XII-1989

Conteste a las siguientes preguntas:

1. *¿Qué canales de TV aparecen en estas recomendaciones?*

....

2. *Clasifique los programas según un criterio que usted mismo debe adoptar.*

....

3. *¿Cuál de estos programas es el que se emitirá más tarde?*

....

4. *¿Cuál de estos programas es el que se emitirá más temprano?*

....

5. *¿Para qué día de la semana se recomiendan más programas?*

....

6. *¿Para qué día de la semana se recomiendan menos programas?*

....

7. *Ordene los programas del sábado según su horario.*

....

3. Artículo periodístico de opinión, con preguntas de selección múltiple

Lea con atención el siguiente artículo:

¡Átame!

(Fragmento)

Dirección y guión: Pedro Almodóvar. Fotografía: J. L. Alcaine. Música: Ennio Morricone. España, 1989. Intérpretes: Victoria Abril, Antonio Banderas, Loles León, Julieta Serrano, María Barranco, Rossy de Palma y Francisco Rabal. Estreno en Madrid: *Fuencarral y Madrid.*

Pedro Almodóvar, cineasta de enorme singularidad, pues todo cuanto hace no se parece en absoluto a lo que hace ningún otro, llegó por ahora a su punto más alto en *La ley del deseo.*

Le fue probablemente difícil a Almodóvar afrontar una nueva película después de la formidable fuerza que puso en aquélla. Pero, hombre de imaginación fertilísima, salió airoso del atolladero con *Mujeres al borde de un ataque de nervios*, película sostenida por un guión equilibrado, pero más brillante que honda.

El resultado se titula *¡Átame!* y ha despertado gran expectación. *¡Átame!* tiene ambiciones narrativas, dramáticas y poéticas similares a las de *La ley del deseo.*

Como de costumbre, Almodóvar entrelaza en ¡Átame! dos hilos conductores del relato. Uno de estos hilos, predominante, cuenta una hermosa y originalísima historia de amor. El otro, en contrapunto, cuenta una historia de desamor, de impotencia. Dos lados de una moneda que nunca llegan a ser tal moneda, pues el engarce recíproco entre esos sus dos lados es endeble, lo que crea en el relato un desdoblamiento que hace del filme una especie de mayonesa cortada: no hay plena interrelación entre sus dos componentes esenciales. Hay sólo interrelación mecánica, más obra de cálculo que de genuino aliento fabulador.

Allí donde discurre el amor entre Victoria Abril y Antonio Banderas -pese al esquematismo de los personajes y la artificiosidad de algunos diálogos, que los intérpretes remontan con mucho talento y fuerza de convicción- todo funciona. Hay entre ellos escenas memorables e inventos visuales magníficos: cuando ambos fingen dormir, el cambio de casa, la paliza callejera, la llamada a la madre, entre otras.

Pero el mundo que les envuelve, y del que es eje Francisco Rabal que carga con un personaje engolado, está construido con materiales de muy inferior fuste, pues se trata de una rosario de escenas planas, rutinarias e incluso a veces pura y simplemente malas. La nada campea allí, jalonada por algún chiste visual y, sobre todo, por una serie de dilaciones cuya única virtud es que el espectador añore la otra historia, situada muy por encima de ésta, y agradezca cuando se produce la vuelta a la pantalla de Victoria Abril y Antonio Banderas. Si estas escenas son involuntariamente malas, mal asunto: error. Pero si son así aposta, peor asunto: marrullería, trampa.

EL PAÍS, 27-VIII-1990

Lea las siguientes frases. Señale V (verdadero) o F (falso) en relación con el contenido del artículo. A continuación, busque la parte del texto en la que se ha basado para escribir V/F y escríbala en las líneas de puntos.

1. *Pedro Almodóvar es un director de cine que realiza películas muy originales.*

   V☐ F☐ ....

2. *«Átame» es la segunda película de Pedro Almodóvar.*

   V☐ F☐ ....

3. *Pedro Almodóvar está preparando una película que se titulará «Mujeres al borde de un ataque de nervios».*

   V☐ F☐ ....

4. *La película «Átame» sólo cuenta una bella y original historia de amor.*

   V☐ F☐ ....

5. *De las dos historias que hay en la película «Átame», la predominante es la que cuenta una historia de odio.*

   V☐ F☐ ....

6. *Dos historias, una de amor y otra de odio, componen el argumento de la película «Átame».*

   V☐ F☐ ....

7. *Los protagonistas de la historia de amor son Victoria Abril y Francisco Rabal.*

   V☐ F☐ ....

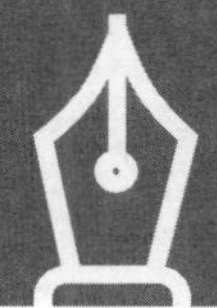

4. Redacción de una carta a partir de instrucciones

Se dispone usted a pasar las Navidades en Madrid. En un periódico ha estado examinando cuáles son los espectáculos a los que podría asistir durante esos días y ha elegido éste:

Una obra Intocable que justifica la vigencia de nuestros Clásicos

El Alcalde de Zalamea

Calderón de la Barca

Director: Rafael Pérez Sierra
Intérpretes:
(Por orden de diálogo)
Enrique Navarro
Carlos Alberto Abad
José M. Gambín
Resu Morales
Juan Gea
Félix Casales
Joaquín Climent
César Diéguez
Adriana Ozores
Blanca Apilánez
Jesús Puente
Antonio Carrasco
Miguel Palenzuela
Angel García Suárez
Vicente Gisbert
Adaptación del texto:
Francisco Brines
Tratamiento Musical y Efectos Sonoros:
Manuel Balboa
Iluminación:
Juan Gómez Cornejo
Escenografía y Vestuario:
Pedro Moreno
Dirección Escénica:
José Luis Alonso

FUNCIÓN ÚNICA 8 TARDE. **TEATRO DE LA COMEDIA**. DEL 14 DE DICIEMBRE AL 14 DE ENERO

Escriba una carta a Sara y Luis, sus amigos de Madrid, encargándoles que saquen entradas para una fecha determinada.
La carta deberá contener al menos lo siguiente:

1. Saludar y despedirse.
2. Invitar a Sara y Luis a que asistan con usted.
3. Fijar la fecha.
4. Aludir a la obra y al teatro.
5. Manifestar por qué tiene tanto interés en ver la obra.
6. Ruégueles también que le envíen, si es posible, una edición de la obra en español para poder leerla antes de verla.

5. Componer una redacción a partir de instrucciones

Componga una redacción de 150 a 200 palabras (15 ó 20 líneas) sobre el tema:

MIS DEPORTES FAVORITOS.

1. Deportes para ver. 2. Deportes para practicar 3. Las instalaciones deportivas 4. Los deportes en televisión.

C. Gramática y vocabulario

1. Texto incompleto con 10 huecos

El siguiente texto está incompleto. Deberá rellenar cada uno de los huecos con la palabra más apropiada.

La Universidad Autónoma de Madrid, dentro de su programa actual de conciertos, ha ofrecido al público el titulado «Música para Vicente Aleixandre». En él se han vuelto a estrenar las canciones escritas por siete autores españoles .... versos del poeta Aleixandre, interpretadas el pasado .... de julio por primera vez en España.

En la primera .... del concierto, escuchamos varias canciones de compositores españoles. Entre .... , una escrita por Esplá sobre un texto de Clemencia Miró, ... lleva por título «Campo de cruces». La influencia de Rodrigo ..... notó en las canciones de José Peris, organizador de estos .... y músico de reconocida fama.

El público, predominantemente universitario, ... durante más de tres minutos al finalizar los .... compases. Tanto la soprano Atsuko-Kudo .... el pianista Antón Cardó dejaron una buena muestra de sus excelentes cualidades y tuvieron que saludar varias veces.

2. Ejercicios de selección múltiple. Gramática

En cada una de las siguientes frases, hay un hueco que deberá rellenar con una de las cuatro expresiones, eligiendo la que sea más correcta.

1. .... que el equipo llegará a la final.
   a) Supongo b) Supuse c) He supuesto d) Supondré
2. No podemos ir al cine .... no tenemos tiempo.
   a) por que b) porque c) porqué d) por qué
3. .... la obra antes de ir a verla.
   a) Debemos de leer b) Tenemos leída c) Tenemos por leer d) Tenemos que leer.
4. El partido fue muy emocionante .... el árbitro pitó el final.
   a) a la vez que b) después que c) mientras d) hasta que.
5. Elefantes y focas .... la máxima atracción de aquella tarde de circo.
   a) fueran b) fue c) fuimos d) fueron

6. Se ha suspendido la corrida ....

a)porque ha llovido mucho b) aunque llueve c) para que llueva d) cuando lloviera mucho

7. .... actores secundarios para el rodaje.

a) Es necesario b) Se necesitan c) Se necesita d) Son necesitados.

8. La carrera duró 1 minuto 45 segundos .... la yegua Alparo.

a) y quedó ganador b)al quedar ganadora c) resultando ganadora d)y resultó ganadora.

9. .... en 10 segundos es ya una buena marca.

a) Correr los 100 metros b) Corriendo los 100 metros c) Corridos los 100 metros d) Haberse corrido los 100 metros.

10. El sonido del violonchelo es .... el del violín.

a) de grave que b) más grave como c) más grave que d) tan grave que.

11. El último disco de Mecano .... mucho a mis amigas.

a) las ha gustado b) le han gustado c) a ellas ha gustado d) les ha gustado.

12. No sé .... han aplazado el partido de dobles.

a) a qué b) de qué c) la causa de que d) por qué.

13. .... los aficionados llenaron las gradas.

a) De temprano b) Desde muy temprano c) De que fue temprano d) Al temprano.

14. ¿Si ganara Karpov la partida, ya .... campeón?

a) estaría b) sería c) fuera d)será

15. No .... muchos toreros que hayan perdido la vida en el ruedo.

a) ha habido b) han habido c) habría d) habrían.

16. ¿Perdices y faisanes .... prefiere el cazador.

a) es la pieza que b) son las piezas que c) son de las piezas de que d) son piezas las que.

17. El rally París-Dakar es una prueba .... todos los años.

a) a celebrarse b) que se celebra c) celebrándose d) que se habrá celebrado.

18. No se oía bien la orquesta .... ruido de la calle.

a) ya que era b) por haber c) habiendo d) por culpa del

19. La obra .... desde las primeras filas.

a) se ve muy mejor b)se ve más bien c) se ve mucho bien d) se ve mejor.

20. Si .... buen tiempo, navegaríamos hasta Formentera.

a) hiciera b) haría c) hacía d) hizo.

3. Ejercicio de selección múltiple. Vocabulario.

En cada una de las siguientes frases hay un hueco que deberá rellenar con una de las cuatro palabras, eligiendo la más apropiada.

1. La película .... exactamente una hora y cuarenta y cinco minutos.
   a) dura b) tarda c) consiste d) blanda
2. No te olvides de comprar con antelación las .... para el concierto.
   a) entradas b) billetes c) reservas d) invitaciones
3. Anoche se .... la obra con gran éxito de público y crítica.
   a) empezó b) estrenó c) inauguró d) abrió
4. ¿Quién te acompañará a la .... de la exposición?
   a) inauguración b) cláusula c) abertura d) iniciación
5. El equipo español .... al francés en las semifinales del torneo de tenis.
   a) consiguió b) derrotó c) perdió d) ganaron
6. Si fuera presidente del gobierno, prohibiría los .... de boxeo.
   a) partidos b) combates c) juegos d) deportes
7. ¿Qué .... se necesita para practicar el judo?
   a) túnica b) juego c) vestidura d) equipo
8. La ciudad de Barcelona será la .... de los Juegos Olímpicos.
   a) final b) plaza c) sede d) lugar
9. El equipo del Estudiantes de baloncesto perdió en su .... frente al Barcelona.
   a) campo b) terreno c) pista d) cancha
10. Cuando vaya a España, quiero asistir a una .... de toros.
    a) carrera b)corredura c) corrida d) cacería

4. Vocabulario. Equivalencia

Cada una de las siguientes frases va seguida de tres expresiones (A,B y C), con una de las cuales se puede construir un significado equivalente. Señale cuál de ellas es.

1. No estoy muy seguro de si tendremos entradas para el fútbol.
   a) Dudo si b) Estoy casi seguro de que c) No tengo ninguna duda de que
2. La película no duró más que hora y media.
   a) duró más que b) no duró ni c) sólo duró
3. Hay noticias a las ocho y media por el canal 1 de TV.
   a) Dan b) Son c) Ocurren
4. Arancha Sánchez Vicario derrotó a Steffi Graf en el torneo de Roland Garros.
   a) combatió b) venció c) humilló
5. Con el disco que ha grabado, va a ser seguramente el número uno en ventas.
   a) probablemente será b) va a ser con toda seguridad c) es seguro que va a ser
6. De todos los bailarines, quien se llevó los aplausos más entusiastas del público fue Antonio Gades.
   a) el menos aplaudido b) el más aplaudido c) el que más aplaudió
7. Madonna le ha pedido a Pedro Almodóvar ser la protagonista de una de sus películas.
   a) que sea el protagonista b) el protagonismo c) el papel principal
8. Perico Delgado va a correr este año en la Vuelta a España y en el Tour de Francia.
   a) participar b) estar c) aparecer
9. En los Juegos Olímpicos de 1992, se espera la más alta participación de los cinco continentes.
   a) la mayor b) gran c) mayor
10. Angel Cristo no corre peligro en la jaula de los leones porque es un excelente domador.
    a) no está peligroso b) no siente peligro c) no peligra

5. Completar diálogos con la opción más adecuada

1. - ¿Cuándo vamos a ir al cine?
   - Iremos .... la película que ha obtenido el Oscar.

   a) cuando estrenan   b) estrenando   c) a estrenar   d) cuando estrenen

2. - No hay plaza de toros .... nosotros.
   - Pues será una ciudad muy pequeña.

   a) adonde vivimos   b) de donde vivimos   c) que vivimos   d) donde vivimos

3. - Este ciclista nunca disputa los finales de etapa.
   - Porque corre .... su director de equipo.

   a) como le ordena   b) cómo le ordena   c) que le ordena   d) que ordena

4. - Desde aquí no se oye bien a los músicos.
   - No se oye .... buenas condiciones acústicas la sala.

   a) como no tiene   b) para que no tenga   c) no tiene   d) porque no tiene

5. - Papá, me gustaría ser actriz.
   - Hija, ... actriz hay que estudiar mucho.

   a) a ser   b) para ser   c) que seas   d) al ser

6. - El desfile de modelos de hoy es a beneficio de UNICEF.
   - Pues .... así yo no pienso ir.

   a) aunque sea   b) aunque fue   c) habiendo sido   d) para que sea

7. - ¿Os gustó la función de teatro?
   - Sí. Aplaudimos tanto .... las manos.

   a) nos dolían   b) para que nos dolieran   c) que nos dolían   d) dolían

8. - ¿Por qué te gusta tanto este tenista?
   - Porque .... ningún otro.

   a) saca mejor   b) saca mejor que   c) saca más bien   d) saca más bien que

9. - No vamos a seguir bien el concierto .... el programa.
   - Sí, mejor es que no lo olvidemos.

   a) si no llevamos   b) a no llevar   c) no llevando   d) si no lleváramos

10. - Nos hemos quedado sin entradas para el ballet.
    - Si hubieras ido cuando te dije, las ....

    a) tenemos   b) tendremos   c) tuviéramos   d) tendríamos

Clave de Textos orales.

Unidad 1. Familia y costumbres.

Texto 1.1

Buenos días a todos. Bienvenidos al campamento «Los Ciervos». Hoy vamos a tener un horario especial, debido a que celebramos el día de visita de las familias. Son ahora las diez. Hasta las once y media, los padres podrán visitar las instalaciones, acompañados de sus hijos. A partir de esa hora, tendrán tiempo libre para ausentarse del campamento si lo desean. Las familias que prefieran quedarse por aquí podrán utilizar la piscina y los campos de deportes. A las dos en punto, serviremos la comida, a la que están invitados todos los familiares; pero les rogamos que nos comuniquen si van a comer con nosotros o no, para organizar la cocina y el comedor. Les advertimos que, en cualquier caso, todos los niños deberán estar de vuelta en el campamento a las ocho y media. Muchas gracias por su atención.

Texto 1.2

Aquí «Radio La Vega, Emisora Comarcal». Noticias de sociedad. Como todos los días a esta hora, vamos a informarles de los ecos de sociedad de nuestra comarca. El pasado sábado, en la parroquia de Gemúñez, contrajeron matrimonio la señorita Pepita Esteban, hija del conocido farmacéutico de la localidad, y don Antonio Cardeñosa, profesor del instituto del vecino municipio de Piedrahonda. A partir del próximo domingo, todos los pueblos de nuestra comarca comenzarán a celebrar las primeras comuniones. Especial relevancia va a tener la celebración en Garcinuño, en donde su párroco, nuestro querido don Secundino, cumple ese día las bodas de oro de su ministerio sacerdotal. El conocido poeta de nuestra región, don Agapito de la Rosa, ha recibido la flor natural y el premio de veinte mil pesetas, destinado al vencedor de los Juegos Florales celebrados en la capital la semana pasada.

Texto 1.3

Y ahora vamos a darles a ustedes unas sugerencias sobre lo que pueden hacer este fin de semana para entretener a sus hijos, y al mismo tiempo pasarlo bien ustedes. En el zoológico de La Magdalena, los pequeños pueden disfrutar contemplando las dos pequeñas crías de foca que han nacido hace pocos días.

En la playa del Sardinero, como todos los años por estas fechas, mañana domingo a las doce tendrá lugar el tradicional concurso de castillos de arena. Los que deseen participar deben inscribirse allí mismo, en la playa, una hora antes del concurso. La compañía de títeres «Gorgorito» presentará hoy sábado, a las seis de la tarde, su espectáculo «Esta bruja no dibuja» en la Plaza Porticada. Todos los niños sabéis que la entrada es gratuita. No faltéis, porque habrá globos y numerosas sorpresas para todos.

Unidad 2. Turismo.

Texto 1.1

Atención. Se ruega a los señores pasajeros del vuelo de Iberia seis cero uno con destino Londres, que se dirijan a la puerta número nueve para proceder al embarque. Señor Atienza, señor Atienza, diríjase al mostrador de información. Se ruega a los señores pasajeros con tarjetas color naranja y verde exclusivamente embarquen en primer lugar.

Texto 1.2

Durante los meses de agosto y septiembre, muchos pueblos de España celebran sus fiestas patronales. En la capital, se celebran las fiestas de San Cayetano, San Lorenzo y la Paloma con verbenas populares. En San Sebastián de los Reyes hay encierros y corridas de toros. En San Lorenzo del Escorial, el próximo día 16 habrá un concierto a cargo de la Orquesta de Cámara de Madrid. Y el 1 de septiembre, el tenor Pavarotti cantará en el Palacio de los Deportes de Madrid.

Texto 1.3

Señoras y señores, estamos llegando a la imperial ciudad de Toledo. Son ahora las diez menos cuarto de la mañana. Dejaremos aparcado nuestro autocar en las proximidades del Alcázar y desde allí nos dirigiremos a las visitas que tenemos programadas para esta mañana: la Catedral, la Casa de El Greco, y San Juan de los Reyes. Si alguno de ustedes, por cualquier circunstancia, se separara del grupo, le recordamos que a las dos en punto el autocar se dirigirá al Parador Nacional, donde tenemos reservadas las mesas para la comida. Después de los postres, les comunicaré cuál va a ser el programa de la tarde. Muchas gracias y feliz estancia en Toledo.

Unidad 3. Economía y Trabajo.

Texto 1.1

Buenos días. Soy la Sra. Jiménez. Así es como deben llamarme desde ahora. Les voy a explicar en qué van a consistir las pruebas de admisión. En primer lugar, todos van a contestar a un cuestionario con cincuenta preguntas en torno a su vida personal y a sus trabajos anteriores. Cuando hayan terminado esta prueba, pasarán en grupos a las siguientes de esta manera: desde el apellido A hasta la G inclusive, harán las pruebas psicotécnicas en la primera planta; desde la H hasta la M inclusive, tendrán la entrevista personal en este despacho que está a la izquierda; y, por último, desde la N a la Z van a realizar las pruebas de mecanografía e informática. Esta tarde expondremos la lista de los admitidos, que deberán pasar el reconocimiento médico mañana por la mañana, a las ocho en punto, en este mismo lugar. Ya saben que es obligatorio realizar todas las pruebas. Buena suerte.

Texto 1.2

Con vistas a la campaña de verano, el Ayuntamiento de Madrid ofrece puestos de trabajo para los jóvenes menores de veinticinco años: Sesenta plazas de monitores de tiempo libre para acompañar a grupos de niños que van a pasar quince días en las playas del litoral cantábrico. Hay también una interesante oferta de treinta plazas para puntos de Información Turística en la capital. Esta oferta está dirigida a los alumnos de las escuelas de Turismo. Para asistir a los ancianos que no pueden acompañar a sus familiares durante las vacaciones, se ha organizado un servicio de ayuda domiciliaria para el que se van a precisar por lo menos ciento cincuenta jóvenes. Para más información, los interesados deben dirigirse en persona al Ayuntamiento, Area de Servicios Sociales, Plaza de la Villa, número 5.

Texto 1.3

Durante la presente semana, el dólar se ha recuperado algo con respecto a la peseta. Hoy viernes se cotiza a 97,350. Sin embargo, la libra esterlina ha descendido ligeramente y ha quedado a 185,070. La semana bursátil ha resultado bastante más tranquila que las inmediatamente precedentes, destacando las recuperaciones registradas en Tokio (7,5%), Francfort (5,31%) y Londres (4,75%).

Unidad 4. Gastronomía.

Texto 1.1

Hoy les vamos a dar una receta muy sencilla con la que podrán ofrecer a sus amigos un plato estupendo: Cordero lechal asado. Conviene que compre usted cordero que de verdad sea lechal, es decir muy tierno. Pida usted al carnicero que le dé algunos cortes a la pieza para que después pueda trincharlo más fácilmente. Se le pone un poco de ajo. Se unta ligeramente con manteca de cerdo y se le echa sal. Debe estar en el horno a temperatura media durante treinta minutos por cada medio kilo de peso. De vez en cuando rocíelo con su propio jugo. Cuando esté casi dorado añádale un poquito de vino blanco y déjelo otro cuarto de hora en el horno. Debe servirlo bien caliente, acompañado de una buena ensalada.

Texto 1.2

Los próximos días 6, 7 y 8 de septiembre, tendrá lugar en San Sebastián un encuentro de los más famosos cocineros del País Vasco.

El objetivo del encuentro es doble: por una parte, intercambiar información sobre la denominada «nueva cocina vasca» de la que tanto se habla durante los últimos años; y por otra, potenciar los platos tradicionales que están en todos los recetarios de las abuelas de la región. Esta mezcla inteligente de lo nuevo y lo viejo está poniendo a la cocina del norte a la cabeza de las de nuestra nación. Las reuniones tendrán lugar en el Club Náutico de la capital donostiarra. Cada día, dos cocineros rematarán sus intervenciones con la presentación de dos platos por ellos elegidos, que los asistentes al congreso podrán degustar. Han prometido su asistencia cocineros franceses que se muestran cada vez más interesados por las artes culinarias de sus vecinos del sur.

Texto 1.3

Buenas noches, señores. ¿Qué tal están ustedes? Hoy les voy a recomendar para cenar algunos platos muy especiales. Pueden pedir para comenzar un revuelto de setas con gambas. Las setas son de cardo y nos las han traído hoy mismo de unos pinares que hay aquí, muy próximos. Les van a encantar. También les puedo servir un pudin de pescado en su punto o, si prefieren las sopas, les puedo recomendar una de champiñón. De segundo, tenemos un besugo al horno que siempre acompañamos con patatas. La carne también está muy bien, especialmente la ternera asada con salsa. A los niños, podemos ponerles una buena hamburguesa con patatas fritas. ¿Qué les parece? Luego ya me dirán si quieren algún postre. Tenemos unas tartas caseras deliciosas. Si me deja usted su abrigo, señora, se lo llevo al guardarropa. Así no le molestará.

■ Unidad 5. Arte

Texto 1.1

Ahora vamos a entrar en la sala del museo especialmente dedicada a pintura española. Procuren no alejarse demasiado. Les recuedo que en este museo está prohibido sacar fotografías. Aquel cuadro que tenemos enfrente es una de las muchas versiones de *La Inmaculada* que pintó Murillo. A su derecha pueden ustedes admirar una pintura mitológica de un discípulo de Rubens. A su izquierda, el *Retrato de un caballero desconocido*, de El Greco. También es de El Greco este otro cuadro que representa a su hijo ante una vista de la ciudad de Toledo. También cuenta esta sala con una pintura de Goya: la tienen a su espalda. Es un retrato de la Condesa de Chinchón. A la salida podrán ustedes encontrar tarjetas postales con la reproducción de todos estos cuadros.

Texto 1.2

Ayer se clausuró la exposición de fotografía que ha estado abierta en el Palacio de Cristal del Retiro desde el pasado día 15 de mayo. Aunque se trataba de obras de autores de hoy, ha llamado la atención especialmente la sala dedicada al famoso fotógrafo Ortiz Echagüe. Sus juegos de luces y sombras siguen siendo una lección para los fotógrafos actuales que, con equipos mucho más complejos, no siempre son capaces de igualar su maestría. De las cerca de mil fotografías expuestas, hay que resaltar sobre todo la serie titulada «Árboles Secos», que es un homenaje a los olmos que están desapareciendo del paisaje de nuestra España. Su autor, Ricardo Esteban, es un joven de diecinueve años que lleva practicando el arte de la fotografía desde los catorce.

Texto 1.3

Atiendan un momento, por favor. Cuando bajemos del autocar, vamos a visitar la Universidad de Salamanca. Como el grupo es demasiado numeroso, lo vamos a dividir en tres grupos pequeños. Procuren ustedes seguir las indicaciones de sus respectivos guías. El primer grupo va a visitar con su guía el edificio de las Escuelas Menores; el segundo verá conmigo la fachada de la Universidad y su interior; y el tercero, acompañado por la señorita Alejandra, visitará la casa rectoral donde vivió Unamuno. Los grupos irán rotando para terminar la visita hacia las doce del mediodía.

■ Unidad 6. Salud.

Texto 1.1

Doctor Gaytán, doctor Gaytán acuda al quirófano con urgencia. Se recuerda a todos los visitantes de este hospital que está prohibido fumar en todas la dependencias. Les recordamos a todos los visitantes que este hospital tiene un servicio de donación de sangre en la planta baja. Les agradecemos de antemano su donación desinteresada.

Texto 1.2

Ahora que llegan los meses de verano, son más frecuentes las afecciones intestinales. Por eso, les vamos a dar algunos consejos prácticos para evitar estos problemas: Lave siempre las frutas y verduras, incluso añadiéndole al agua dos gotas de lejía cuando se trate de verduras con las que va preparar sus ensaladas. No consuma helados que no sean de fabricación industrial. No beba agua de arroyos, pozos o manantiales por muy limpia que le parezca. Si no consume el agua habitual, es preferible que la pida siembre embotellada, pero procure que la abran en su presencia.

Texto 1.3

Los primeros dientes le salen al bebé entre los 6 y 8 meses, pero no se preocupen si ocurre más tarde. El resto de los dientes le van a salir entre los ocho y los doce meses. Las primeras muelas o molares aparecen en torno al año; y los últimos dientes que aparecen son los colmillos, también llamados caninos, que salen a partir del año y medio aproximadamente. A partir de los seis años, empezarán a caerse estos dientes de leche, que irán desapareciendo progresivamente hasta los trece años.

■ Unidad 7. Transportes y Comunicaciones.

Texto 1.1

Tren procedente de Atocha con destino Valladolid y León. Va a efectuar su entrada por vía 3. Este tren tiene paradas hasta Avila, en Villalba y El Escorial. Se ruega a los señores viajeros que no crucen las vías. Utilicen los pasos subterráneos. Tren Talgo Puerta del Sol procedente de París, que tenía prevista su llegada a las 9.30 horas, circula con un retraso de 20 minutos. Atención. Aviso para los trabajadores que se dirigen a la vendimia francesa en el tren especial. Este tren está situado en vía 12 y va a efectuar su salida dentro de breves minutos.

Texto 1.2

Y ahora vamos a informarles del estado del tráfico en las próximas horas.

El Partido de fútbol que tendrá lugar a las 9 de la noche en el estadio Santiago Bernabeu, puede provocar retenciones en el paseo de La Castellana y alrededores; así que es aconsejable que utilicen los transportes públicos desde una hora antes del partido hasta su finalización. Recuerden también que siguen las obras de asfaltado en la avenida de la Reina Victoria por lo que se recomienda utilizar la calle San Francisco de Sales para dirigirse a la Ciudad Universitaria. Nos llega en estos momentos un aviso de socorro. Se ruega a Luis Salazar, que viaja hacia Huelva en un Seat Málaga color blanco, que se ponga en contacto con su domicilio en Gerona por causa familiar grave.

Texto 1.3

Los cruceros italianos, con salida desde Barcelona, Génova o Venecia, son este verano los que tienen una mayor demanda. Hoy le vamos a sugerir dos posibles viajes: el «Costa Marina» es una modernísima nave que sale todos los lunes de Barcelona para un crucero de siete días, en el que toca los puertos de Palma de Mallorca, Ibiza, Palermo, Nápoles y Génova. El precio está alrededor de las 132.000 pesetas. Si prefiere usted acercarse a las puertas del misterioso oriente en un barco con historia, al «Achille Lauro», que parte de Génova, le llevará a Nápoles, Alejandría, Estambul, Atenas y Capri, en una travesía de 14 días, que le costará no menos de 288.000 pesetas.

Unidad 8. Comportamiento social.

Texto 1.1

Por favor, presten atención todos los alumnos y alumnas del centro. Los cursos de primero y segundo van a permanecer en el patio de recreo hasta dentro de media hora; es decir, hasta las nueve y media. Y los alumnos de tercero y del Curso de Orientación Universitaria pasarán ahora al salón de actos, donde van a conocer a los profesores que serán sus tutores este año. Ya sabéis que no se puede abandonar el recinto del colegio sin un permiso firmado del Jefe de Estudios. Recordad también que está prohibido fumar incluso en los patios. Las puertas del colegio, como en años anteriores, se cerrarán diez minutos después de la entrada. El alumno que llegue tarde deberá entrar en el colegio por la puerta de secretaría. Que tengáis todos un curso muy provechoso.

Texto 1.2

La Oficina de Información al Soldado ha vuelto a insistir una vez más en un tema ya muy antiguo, que sigue siendo motivo frecuente de noticias en todos los medios de comunicación: las «novatadas». Cuando un soldado llega al cuartel, es frecuente que tenga que hacer frente a bromas pesadas que en ocasiones acaban en tragedia. A veces se trata sólo de revolverle la cama para que, al acostarse, no pueda meterse en ella fácilmente: es lo que se conoce con el nombre de «petaca». Otros prefieren mandar al novato a visitar al capitán para pedirle la funda del mástil o cualquier otra fantasía. Pero no todas las novatadas son tan inocentes. Durante el pasado año, diez soldados tuvieron que ser atendidos en centros hospitalarios por diversas lesiones: quemaduras, contusiones, etc. Incluso, alguno tuvo que recibir asistencia psiquiátrica. ¿Cuándo se va a hacer de verdad efectiva la prohibición de recibir a los soldados en los cuarteles con esta clase de bromas? El Ejército hace ya mucho que las prohibió; pero lo cierto es que los soldados las siguen sufriendo cada año.

Texto 1.3

El número de matrimonios que se han separado el pasado año 1989 fue de 34.692. Esta cifra puede parecernos grande o pequeña, pero adquiere su dimensión real si la relacionamos con la de 1985, en el que hubo 25.046 separaciones. Es decir, que en los últimos cinco años, las separaciones matrimoniales han aumentado un 38,5%. En el mismo periodo, los divorcios aumentaron en un 26,09%. Aunque separaciones y divorcios han aumentado progresivamente durante los últimos cinco años, parece confirmarse la tendencia a preferir la fórmula de la separación, tal vez porque a las parejas esta opción les resulta económicamente menos gravosa.

Unidad 9. Ecología.

Texto 1.1

Rogamos a todos los visitantes que se abstengan de echar comida a los animales. Dentro de quince minutos, dará comienzo la exhibición de nuestros simpáticos delfines. La entrada al delfinario no está incluida en el pase al parque zoológico. Deberán sacar su entrada en las taquillas del mismo delfinario. Atención, por favor, a las doce en punto los cuidadores darán de comer a los leones. No deje de visitar con sus niños la instalación de papagayos que les divertirán con sus juegos. La entrada es gratuita.

Texto 1.2.

El director del proyecto «Lucha contra la Desertización en el Mediterráneo», José Ángel Carrera, ha afirmado que el 16% de la superficie de España está en grave peligro de desertificación, es decir, de desertización por la acción del hombre sobre el medio. Las áreas geográficas en las que el proceso es más evidente están en Granada, Almería y Murcia. Aseguró también que hay soluciones técnicas para frenar este proceso, la más importante de las cuales es la reforestación o plantación de especies autóctonas. Aunque el Estado aporta anualmente 8.000 millones de pesetas para luchar contra la desertificación, el esfuerzo no es suficiente, ya que la acción de los incendios contrarresta todos los años gran parte de dicho esfuerzo.

Texto 1.3

La exposición «Natura misteriosa» va a continuar abierta en Barcelona durante todo el año. En ella podrá contemplar reptiles, insectos y anfibios de los cinco continentes. Hasta el día de hoy ha sido visitada por 150.000 personas desde que se inauguró a finales de diciembre de 1989. Las especies más admiradas son las crías de la araña viuda negra y las de la araña de plata. Hay también dos camaleones africanos, dos especies de ranas sudamericanas de colores y crías del lagarto pakistaní, de vistosos colores marrón y amarillo. Los horarios de visita de esta exposición que se halla en el parque zoológico de Barcelona, en el paseo de Picasso, son de 9.30 a 19.30 en agosto; de 10.00 a 19.00 en septiembre y de 10.00 a 17.00 desde octubre a diciembre. No se pierda esta oportunidad.

Unidad 10. Deporte y Espectáculos

Texto 1.1

Tomen nota de los principales acontecimientos deportivos que van a celebrarse en los próximos cinco días: El martes, día 12, baloncesto; el Real Madrid se enfrentará en Belgrado al Partizan. El miércoles, día 13, y transmitido por TV 2, a las 20 horas, el encuentro internacional de fútbol España-Suiza, que se jugará en Tenerife. El jueves, día 14, en Stuttgart, partidos de la final de la Copa de Davis entre la República Federal de Alemania y Suecia. El viernes, día 15, en Sierra Nevada, desde las 12 del mediodía, descenso masculino de la Copa del Mundo. El sábado, día 16, y transmitido por TV 2, a las 17.30 h., encuentro de balonmano entre el Atlético de Madrid y el Michelín-Valladolid.

Texto 1.2

La temporada de otoño en el hipódromo de La Zarzuela finalizó ayer con la disputa, como ya viene siendo tradicional, del Premio Francisco Cadenas, una de las carreras más largas de cuantas componen el calendario de pruebas. La victoria fue para «Carbonado», de la cuadra Torrejón, que cubrió los 3.200 metros del recorrido en cabeza. El estado de la pista, muy embarrada por la lluvia caída durante los últimos días, influyó decisivamente en el resultado de esta competición y, por supuesto, de todas las demás.

Texto 1.3

Atención, por favor. El Auditorio Nacional nos ruega que emitamos el siguiente aviso relacionado con el XII Ciclo de Cámara y Polifonía: Por prescripción facultativa, la cantante Teresa Berganza comunica la suspensión definitiva del recital programado para el miércoles 22 de noviembre.

Con el fin de cubrir esta notable ausencia, la Orquesta y Coro Nacionales de España, responsables de la organización del Ciclo, ha conseguido la contratación del insigne barítono americano Thomas Hampson, una de las actuales figuras del bel canto.

Los espectadores que lo deseen pueden devolver las entradas en el Auditorio Nacional de Música, en el horario habitual de taquillas, hasta el miércoles día 22 inclusive y hasta una hora antes de la celebración de dicho concierto.

Clave de Ejercicios

Unidad 1. Familia y Costumbres.

A. Comprensión y Expresión oral

1.1 (Texto: Buenos días a todos...) 1. «Los Ciervos».-2.Visitar las instalaciones.-3.Comunicarlo con antelación.-4. A las ocho y media.-**1.2** (Texto: Aquí Radio La Vega...) 1. Es farmacéutico.- 2. Cincuenta años.- 3. Siendo el vencedor de los juegos florales **1.3** (Texto: Y ahora vamos a darles a ustedes...) 1. V.- 2. F.- 3. F.- **2.1** Enhorabuena. Ha tenido usted mellizos.- **2.2** Mirad qué moto me ha regalado mi padre por tener buenas notas.- **2.3** Ahora ya estamos todos. Ya puede usted sacar la foto.

B. Comprensión y Expresión escrita

1 1.En un sesenta por ciento.-2.Hasta hace unos años, ingresaban más ancianos en verano; pero ahora, en cualquier época del año.-3.Un promedio de cuatro personas.- 4. Porque los pisos son pequeños y los familiares casi nunca están en casa.-5.Los centros de cuidados mínimos y la asistencia domiciliaria.-6.Son insuficientes.- **2** 1.Seis mil pesetas.- Seis mil pesetas.- 3.Sesenta mil pesetas.-4. Nuestra Señora del Pilar en Zaragoza y Juan Luis Vives en Madrid.-5. Para el curso 1989-1990.-6.Para material de estudio.-7.En el mes de junio.-**3** 1.Falso: « ... las mujeres ganan por término medio un 22,6 por ciento menos que los hombres ...».2.Falso: « En los casos más graves se han llegado a detectar problemas físicos ... como ... impotencia ...».3. Verdadero: « ... pero de eso, a admitir tranquilamente que su compañera gane más que él, va un mundo ...».4. Verdadero: «Hay que reconocer en su favor que mientras las mujeres viven una época de conquistas ...».5. Falso: « ... y, en ocasiones, viven el triunfo de sus compañeras como una agresión».6. Verdadero:« ... el 20 por ciento de los conflictos conyugales surgen a causa del dinero ...».7. Verdadero: «A medida que el nivel cultural es más alto, el hombre no suele oponerse a que su esposa tenga un trabajo remunerado». **4** (Ejemplo): León, 16 de abril de 1991.- Queridos Rosa y Félix: He recibido la invitación de vuestra boda y os podéis imaginar la alegría que me ha producido. No sabéis lo que siento tener que deciros que no puedo asistir. Precisamente en esas fechas estaré realizando los exámenes para obtener el Diploma Básico de Español y ya sabéis lo importante que es para mí sacarlo pronto. Como quiero que tengáis un recuerdo mío siempre presente en vuestra casa, os enviaré en los próximos días un regalo. Espero que os guste. Os deseo toda la felicidad del mundo en vuestro matrimonio y os mando un fuerte abrazo. Karen.

C. Gramática y Vocabulario

1 •el •porque •embargo •va •edad •todo •es •mejor •Hay •niño. **2** 1.b) se deben-2.d) se enamoró de ella-3.c) Papá y yo estamos.-4.c)le llega-5.a) Es verdad-6.c) sintió-7.c) se va a casar con-8.a) por-9.b)para dar a luz-10.c) cada vez más alta-11.d) Siempre que-12.d) más cómoda que la-13.d) pasar- 14.c) Por muy mal que-15.c) me han regalado-16.d) sorprendería-17.d) al primero que-18.a) Éstos que-19.c) creo que-20.c) qué guapo. **3** 1.d) estrellar.-2.c) se empeñó.-3.a) vivimos.-4.d) nietos.-5.a) sobrina.-6.b) mellizos.-7.d) cosa.-8.c) manera.-9.d) permiso.-10.d) mayor. **4** 1.a) los problemas propios.-2.b) ya está a punto de terminar.-3.b) Cuando nació.-4.c) prepáranos.- 5.b) separarse.-6.b) han enviado.-7.b) así de.-8.c) acostumbramos a.-9.c) el curso.- 10.a) por semana.-11.b) en familia. **5** 1.c) esta.-2.a) el.-3.d) el.-4.a) las.-5.b) lo.-6.c) el.-7.d) su.-8.b) mis.-9.a) ambas.-10.d) primer.

Unidad 2. Turismo.

A Comprensión y Expresión oral

1.1 (Texto: Atención. Se ruega a ...) 1.F.-2.F.-3.V.- **1.2** (Texto: Durante los meses ...) 1. A San Sebastián de los Reyes.-2. Un concierto.-3.El uno de septiembre. **1.3** (Texto: Señoras y ...) 1. A las diez menos cuarto.-2. En las proximidades del Alcázar.-3-Después de comer.-**2.1** Estos zapatos no son los míos. **2.2** ¡Qué mala suerte! Está lloviendo. **2.3** Es que me he distraído.

B. Comprensión y Expresión escrita

1. (Texto: Las vacaciones ...) 1. En los meses de otoño.-2. Marraquech.-3. A Santos Robles.-4. Antillana de Navegación.-5. Porque no había aire acondicionado.-6. Porque el avión no tenía ruedas. 2 (Texto: Excursiones pedestres ...)1. Van a ir a pie.-2. Porque uno de ellos es para los socios federados y el otro para los no socios.-3. Seis días.-4. Ocho días.-5. En Madrid, calle Santa María 20.-6. Un ciclo de tertulias. 3(Texto: La revolución del sol) 1. Verdadero: «El sol no forma parte de nuestro ocio ... hasta bien entrado el siglo». 2. Falso: « ... hay cremas para proteger la piel ... y hacerlo más duradero». 3. Falso: « ... no se puede confiar a ciegas en cremas y lociones ...». 4. Verdadero: «Los médicos llevan mucho tiempo insistiendo en lo nocivo de las largas exposiciones al sol». 5. Verdadero ... suministra al organismo calcio y vitamina C». 6. Falso: « ...está demostrada la etiología solar de muchos cánceres dermatológicos ...». 7. Verdadero: « ... que una sociedad tan «juvenilizada» ... practique ... un culto solar ...».

C. Gramática y Vocabulario

1 (Texto: Ávila) •son •una/alguna •hay •estilos •más •comer •típicos •la •pedir/tomar •ve/contempla. **2** 1.a)más.-2.b)salgas.-3.d)Por.-4.b)comeremos.-5.a)espléndidos.-6.b)A ti y a mí.-7.d)que.-8.c)Tráigame.-9.b)con.-10.a)mayor.-11.d)cuánto.-12.b)algún.-13.d)si.-14.b)abren.-15.a)Por mucho que.-16.b)no dejando.-17.c)como camarero.-18.a)Suban.-19.c)Dale.-20.b)cómo se hace. **3** 1.c)construido.- 2.b)hora.- 3.a)playas.-4.d)celebrará.-5.a)vamos a ir.-6.b)de peaje.-7.c)antiguo.-8.d)interesa.-9.b)atención.-10.d)tapa. **4** 1.a)cuando tenía quince años.-2.b)me matricularé en.- 3.b)comprar.- 4.c)en los bares al aire libre.-5.b)La solución es tomar baños en.-6.c)el conjunto de paradores nacionales.-7.a)festeja.-8.b)tomar un coche en alquiler.-9.a)ve casi toda.-10.b)cómo pudo llegar a. **5** 1.a)qué.-2.b)ventanilla.-3.c)cual.-4.c)comodón.-5.d)os.-6.b)les.-7.a)cuyas.-8.d)ustedes.-9.b)quienes.-10.b)conmigo.

Unidad 3. Economía y Trabajo.

A Comprensión y Expresión oral

1.1 (Texto: Buenos días. Soy la Sra. Jiménez ...) 1. A seis.-2. un cuestionario con cincuenta preguntas.-3. A las ocho de la mañana del día siguiente.- **1.2** (Texto: Con vistas a la campaña ...)1. V.- 2. F.- 3. F.- **1.3** (Texto: Durante la presente semana ...) 1. La libra esterlina.- 2.La de Tokio.- 3.El viernes.- **2.1** Vuelva usted cuando esté más presentable.- **2.2** Ya hemos puesto el tejado. Ha quedado perfecto.- **2.3** Esta vez sí que hemos tenido suerte.

B. Comprensión y Expresión escrita

1 1. Hasta reunirse con el director general de Aviación Civil.- 2.El presidente de la asociación de controladores aéreos.-3.Algunos altos cargos.- 4.Un día aún no fijado de esta semana.- **2**. Anuncio primero:1.El de camarero.-2.Entre veinte y treinta años.- 3.Al menos un año.-Anuncio segundo:1.Dependientes de joyería de ambos sexos.- 2. Bachillerato.-3. Sueldo fijo.- 4.Un currículum y una fotografía reciente.-**3** 1. Falso:« ... es cuatro veces mayor que en el Reino Unido ... ».4. Falso:« ... da empleo a 19.000 de los 27.000 trabajadores ...».5. Verdadero:« ... 26 mineros perdieron la vida ... elevando así un índice de siniestralidad ...».6. Falso:« ... lo cierto es que la inversión en seguridad sigue estando en España muy por debajo de la de otros países ...».7. Verdadero:« ... las explosiones de gas grisú ... son ahora menos frecuentes que hace 15 ó 20 años ...».

C. Gramática y Vocabulario

1 •al •después •despacho •sin •dirige/encamina •punto •donde •hace •último/fin •toda. **2** 1.a) trabajar.-2.c) ninguno.-3.d) sus.-4.a) ha habido.-5.b) a salir.-6.c) porque llegaba.-7.b) empaquetara.-8.a) si tenía.-9.d) jefe.-10.a) pero no pude.-11.b) Tendría.-12.a) estando.-13.b) todo.-14.c) que no me lo.-15.d) es la hora de.-16.a) hablando de las vacaciones.-17.d) Conducir el tren.-18.a) Por motivo.- 19.b) Ni (...), ni.-20.c) sobre la cual.- **3** 1.b) El personal.-2.a) fontanero.-3.b) cobrar.-4.d) arriesgada.-5.c) antes.-6.b) mala.- 7.c) y además.-8.c) promoción.-9.d) experiencia.-10.c) aumente. **4** 1.b) Se necesita.-2.a) durante los meses de octubre, noviembre y diciembre.-3.b) encargarse de.-4.a) retribuido.-5.c) Es verdad que.-6.a) a realizar viajes.-7.c) inaugurar.-8.a) Casi no hay.-9.c) muy limpio.-10.a) es indispensable. **5** 1.c) has enviado.-2.a) comienza.-3.d) habremos terminado.-4.b) tomaría.-5.a) despidieron.- 6.d) hayas dado.-7.d) merecía.-8.d) comunicarán.-9.d) Es.- 10.a) sabe.

Unidad 4. Gastronomía.

A. Comprensión y Expresión oral

1.1 (Texto: Hoy les vamos a dar una receta ...) 1.F.-2. V.-3. F.-4 V.- **1.2** (Texto: Los próximos días 6, 7 y 8 de septiembre ...) 1. En el Club Náutico.-2.Los días 6, 7 y 8 de septiembre.- 3.Con la degustación de dos platos.- 4.Sí.- **1.3** (Texto: Buenas noches señores ...) 1.Ternera asada con salsa.-2.Tartas caseras.-3.Para los niños.-4.Porque así no le molestará.-**2.1** Pero, ¿cómo ha subido tanto la cuenta?.- **2.2** Vamos a guisar las setas para comerlas hoy.- **2.3** ¿Te apetece un zumo de naranja?.

B. Comprensión y Expresión escrita

1 1.En la calle Florencio Llorente.-2.Chuletas de cordero lechal.-3.Leche frita o tarta de manzana casera.-4.Un clarete de la Rioja navarra.-5.entre 2.000 y 2.500 pesetas. **2** 1. Los tres restaurantes tienen los mismos precios.-Sí; arroz con leche.-3.En la Plaza de la Iglesia.-4.En Casa Julián.- **3** 1. Falso:«Pese a su alto valor nutritivo ...».2.Verdadero: « ... la tradición de consumo de queso en España lo sitúa antes como objeto de aperitivo».3.Verdadero:« ... tiene en su composición proteínas de alta calidad.» 4.Falso:« ... tiene en su composición proteínas ..., grasas, calcio y vitaminas».5.Falso« ... se consume en bajas cantidades en España ... al comparar con otras poblaciones europeas ...».6.Falso:« ... la tradición de consumo de queso en España lo sitúa antes ... que como plato fuerte, en forma de tablas de queso...».7.Verdadero: « ... que en España choca con la costumbre de tomar frutas».

C. Gramática y Vocabulario

1 •sino •aceite •este/el •otras •de •que •los •con •sabor •vino. **2** 1.d) la recibieron.-2.b) hace.-3.c) me alegro de.-4.a) haya sido añadida.-5.c) Tengo que.-6.b) Eso es.-7.d) A sentarse.-8.b) tráigamela.-9.a) a.-10.b) sería.-11.c) Quizá.-12.a) más.-13.b) suya.-14.a) de pie.-15.d) ninguna.-16.b) habrás puesto.-17.c) de.-18.c) empecéis.-19.b) a ése.-20.c) De quién. **3** 1.b) conviene.-2.b) rebozar.-3.c) salsa.-4.c) se pone.-5.c) queda.-6.b) fresca.-7.c) en su punto.-8.a) bien.-9.b) eches.-10.b) derrite. **4** 1.a) para que se caliente.-2.c) no comer demasiado.-3.b) más importante.-4.a) esta comida.-5.a) buenos.-6.b) primero.-7.c) la clasificación.-8.a) procedencia.-9.c) sobre.-10.b) agua embotellada. **5** 1.c) debe de estar.-2.d) van probando.-3.a) terminan de madurar.-4.b) vamos a pedir.-5.b) Estamos montando-6.c) Vamos a hacer.-7.a) puedo partir.-8.d) debes traer.-9.d) estamos a punto de.-10.a) empieza a hacer.

Unidad 5. Arte.

A. Comprensión y Expresión oral

1.1 (Texto: Ahora vamos a entrar en la sala del museo ...)1. F.-2. F.-3.V. **1.2** (Ayer se clausuró la exposición ...) 1. En el Palacio de Cristal del Retiro.- 2. Ortiz Echagüe y Ricardo Esteban.-3. Los árboles secos.- **1.3** (Texto: Atiendan un momento, por favor. Cuando bajemos ...) 1. La casa rectoral donde vivió Unamuno.-2. Porque el grupo es demasiado numeroso.-3. En Salamanca.- **2.1** El cuadro ha quedado torcido.- **2.2** ¡Qué desastre! Cuando ya casi estaba terminado... .- **2.3** ¿Podrían retirarse un poco, por favor?

B. Comprensión y Expresión escrita

1 1. A la entrada de la exposición.-2. Durante diez horas.-3. El 30 de marzo.-4. En el Museo del Prado.-5. El primer día de la exposición.-6. Las señales indicativas no eran muy claras.-7. Si hubiera demasiado público. **2** 1. Falso:«Los cuadros con espejos siempre me han fascinado.».-2. Verdadero: « ... que se encontraba en su inmensidad enfrentado a un espejo ...».-3. Verdadero:«Creo que debería haber un espejo frente a cada cuadro valioso.».-4. Falso« ... la puerta entreabierta por donde aquel señor de negro se recorta ...».-5. Verdadero:«Mi recuerdo de Las Meninas está intimamente unido a cómo estaba puesto el cuadro ...».-6. Falso:«Esa puesta en escena ... supuso para mí el reencuentro con el tiempo en cada una de sus misteriosas dimensiones.»**3** 1. A la sala II del Centro Cultural de la Villa.-2. A las siete de la tarde.-3.El mensaje de la naturaleza.-4. En el Centro Cívico Pozo del Tío Raimundo.-5. De once a una y media y de cinco a ocho.-6. En Colmenar Viejo.

C. Gramática y Vocabulario

1 •principio/comienzo •Los •hasta •cuales/que •siglos •y •Edad •imágenes/tallas •materias •mismo. **2** 1.b) visitar.-2.b) están restaurando.-3. a) las.-4. c) mejor conservado.-5.b de que.-6. d) Ustedes saben.-7. b) que subiéramos.-8.c) bastantes.-9.c) la.-10.b) y.-11.d) Dónde.-12.d) cuanto más.-13.c) duodécimo.-14.a) sin entrar.-15.a) ahí.-16.d) Como no.-17.c) lo modernos que.-18.a) entre los que destaca.-19.b) que.-20.d) se remonte. **3** 1.b) forma.-2.c) conduce.-3.b) está ubicada.-4.d) cerca de.-5.c) amplio.-6.a) una nave.-7.c) sostiene.-8.d) mosaicos.-9.a) riquísimo.-10.c) miniaturas. **4** 1.b) uno de los más grandes.-2.a) dedicada.-3.b) nobles.-4.a) El óleo.-5.a) muestran una sonrisa.-6.a) se necesita.-7.a) debe de ser.-8.b) aproximadamente.-9.a) está enmarcada en.-10.c) es del. **5** 1.a) ver.-2.d) celebrando.-3.b) visitada.-4.b) sacar.-5.c) baja.-6.c) Entrad.-7.a) interpretando.-8.d) Participar.-9.b) pregunten.-10.c) haber visitado.

Unidad 6. Salud.

A. Compresión y Expresión oral

1.1 (Texto: Doctor Gaytán, Doctor Gaytán acuda ...)1. Al quirófano.-2. en ninguna.-3. Nada. La donación es desinteresada. **1.2** (Texto: Ahora que llegan los meses de verano ...) 1. F.-2. F.-3. F.-4. V. **1.3** (Texto: Los primeros dientes ...) 1. F.-2. F.-3.V. **2.1** Doctor, mi hija tiene dolor de muelas.- **2.2** El niño está muy bien de salud.- **2.3** ¡Por Dios! ¿Cómo se le ocurre fumar en la cama?

B. Comprensión y Expresión escrita

1 1.Para evitar el rechazo de los órganos trasplantados.-2. Produce hipertensión y reacciones negativas en el hígado.-3. En el congreso internacional de la Sociedad de Trasplantes, en San Francisco.-4. De un hongo que se cultiva en Japón.-5. Para los trasplantes de hígado. **2** 1.El Ministerio de Sanidad y Consumo.-2. El 29 de agosto de 1990.-3. Para montar una lavandería.-

4. En los lugares que se indican en el Boletín Oficial del Estado. **3** 1. Falso:«La picadura por avispa puede quedar establecida en tres grados: leve, moderada y grave.»2. Verdadero: «En los casos extremos y mortales ...».-3. Falso: «En la picadura de abeja los casos más graves ... y graves lesiones del sistema nervioso central y del corazón».-4. Verdadero: « ... pasadas horas o incluso días tras la picadura o accidente ...».-5. Falso: «Se debe extraer el aguijón de las abejas ...».-6. Falso: «Las personas alérgicas deben llevar consigo un pequeño estuche con medicinas de urgencia...».

C. Gramática y Vocabulario

1 •que •personas •debe •dosis •otros/demás •las •años •partir •proporcional •reducirse **2** 1.b) me duelen.-2. a) que ir.-3.d) ha sido recomendado.-4.b) toquéis.-5.b) lo que.-6.d) Qué.-7.c) debías.-8.a) a ver si.-9.b) haya mejorado.-10.c) le dan.-11.c) le tengamos.-12.d) suele dolerle.-13.c) a quién.-14.c) no es verdad.-15.c) serían.-16.a) de nada.-17.d) raquítico.-18.d) mejor.-19.a) uno.-20.d) pero. **3** 1.d) malignos.-2.a) fractura.-3.c) contraer.-4.a) lactancia.-5.d) se inflame.-6.c) la fiebre.-7.d) cuello.-8.d) accidente.-9.d) está resfriado.-10.b) precozmente. **4** 1.a) Lo mejor es una buena crema.-2.a) muchas veces.-3.b) engorda.-4.a) procurar.-5.c) oculares.-6.a) Cuando se trata.-7.c) La bicicleta.-8.b) sufre.-9.a) dolencias.-10.c) retirarle. **5** 1.c) también.-2.c) nunca.-3.d) cerca.-4.b) pronto.-5.d) despacio.-6.a) además.-7.a) como.-8.c) tal vez.-9.c) rápidamente.-10.c) poco más.

Unidad 7. Transportes y Comunicaciones.

A. Comprensión y Expresión oral

1.1 (Texto: Tren procedente ...) 1.Viene de Atocha.-2. En Villalba, El Escorial y Ávila.-3. A las diez menos diez de la mañana.-4. Para los vendimiadores que van a trabajar a Francia.- **1.2** (Texto: Y ahora vamos a ...)1. V.-2. F.-3. V.-4 F. **1.3** (Texto: Los cruceros italianos ...) 1. Todos los lunes.-2. Aproximadamente, 132.000 pesetas.-3. Achille Lauro.-4. El segundo, que dura 14 días. **2.1** ¿Me enseña su documentación, por favor? **2.2** Oiga, acaba de hundirse un barco. **2.3** Haga el favor de echar esta carta al Correo.

B. Comprensión y Expresión escrita

1 1.Porque llovió torrencialmente.-2. Unas tres horas.-3. En el Km. 48 de la carretera de Andalucía.-4. A Aranjuez.-5. A la Dirección General de Tráfico.-6. Porque tenían que pasar por Aranjuez. **2** 1. A la carretera de La Coruña.- 2.Porque está en obras.-3.En la Plaza de Castilla.-4.Un aparcamiento.-5.En la Avenida de Pablo Iglesias.-6.Por la calle de Embajadores. **3** 1. Falso:«El resultado es la prestación deficiente ...».-2. Verdadero:« ... un servicio público al que los insuperables problemas de tráfico han convertido en el medio de transporte casi único ...».-3. Verdadero:« ... carencias más llamativas ... el incumplimiento de los horarios y la escasez de unidades en las horas punta».-4. Falso:« los responsables del Ministerio de Transportes hayan tenido que esperar a que la situación devenga en graves alteraciones del orden público».-5. Falso:« ... lo mismo que ha sucedido en Telefónica los últimos años ...».-6. Verdadero: «El fuerte crecimiento de la demanda ... haya dejado viejas las previsiones para 1991».-7. Falso: « ... con las que se pretende convencer ... sobre las ventajas del tren frente al coche particular.»

C. Gramática y Vocabulario

1 •podríamos •más •nosotros •porque •tarde •por •escribir •de •sus •favor. **2** 1.a) con.-2.b) se han adaptado.-3.c) marque.-4.d) que proceda.-5.d) el mejor.-6.b) todas las estaciones.-7.c) Le.-8.a) llevaba.-9.d) como.-10.c) su dimisión.-11.d) A qué hora.-12.c) me van a llamar.-13.c) por.-14.d) se hace.-15.b) estaba.-16.c) Cuánto.-17.d) más de mil.-18.d) Ni se me ocurre.-19.c) hasta que llegue.-20.b) Mamá, tú y yo vamos. **3** 1.b) sufre.-2.b) desvío.-3.b) tráfico.-4.c) un sello.-5. a) costará.-6.b) bloqueadas.-7.d) señal.-8.a) una cabina.-9.c) cruzan.-10.b) han puesto. **4** 1.a) La causa principal.-2.b) carreras.-3.a) de marina.-4.b) todos los viajeros.-5.c) las maletas.-6.b) de ida.-7.a) queda.-8.d) estropeado.-9.a) parte.-10.b) volver.-**5** 1.b) a.-2.c) de.-3.c) contra.-4.b) desde.-5.d) hasta.-6.b) por.-7.a) encima de.-8.a) antes de.-9.b) alrededor de.-10.b) enfrente de.

Unidad 8. Comportamiento social.

A. Comprensión y Expresión oral

1.1 (Texto:Por favor, presten atención ...) 1. V.-2. V.- 3. F.-4. F.- **1.2** (Texto: La oficina de información al soldado ...) 1. Novatadas.-2. La Oficina de Información al Soldado.-3. Sí.-4. Ya las prohibió hace mucho. **1.3** (Texto: El número de matrimonios que se han separado ...) 1. Al periodo entre 1985 y 1989.-2. No.-3. Porque les resulta más barato.- **2.1** Oiga usted, haga el favor de no saltarse la cola.- **2.2** No sabe cuánto lo siento. Déjeme limpiarle las manchas.- **2.3** ¿Podría usted ayudarme a cambiar la rueda, por favor?

B. Comprensión y expresión escrita

1 1.Los hombres.-2. Juez del Tribunal Constitucional.-3. Las vulneraciones de los jueces.-4. Los turnos y horarios nocturnos; y los permisos de maternidad.-5. Poder elegir el sexo de su futuro hijo.- **2** 1. los días 12, 13 y 14 de octubre.-2. El juego, los juguetes y las campañas navideñas.-3. Enviando un cheque nominativo de 1.000 pesetas.-4. Llamar al teléfono (91) 4022312.- **3** 1. Falso:« ... algunos debemos estar públicamente a favor, al menos para contrarrestar esa presión social ...».-2. Falso:« ... le condenan a viajar en los últimos asientos ...».- 3. Verdadero:«El tabaco es bueno para la amistad».-4. Falso:« ... ¿por qué no ponen en los aviones zonas de no bebedores?».-5. Verdadero:« ... litronas y el culto al güisqui.».-Y más adelante ... ese lingotazo de coñac ...».-6. Verdadero:« ... un grupo de estudiantes americanos que descubren la libertad del alcohol para los menores de ventiún años».-7. Falso:« ... desde Nueva York ... un grupo de estudiantes americanos ...».

C. Gramática y Vocabulario

1 •cuando •cuarto •Son •a •ni •corbata •piernas •estar/quedar •abra •más. **2** 1.a) vieras.-2.d) a las 9 y media.-3.a) en cuanto.-4.b) a alguien.-5.b) antes de beber.-6.c) Se debe.-7.c) muy poco.-8.c) me apetece.-9.d) por.-10.d) hay.-11.a) no respeta nadie.-12.c) Cuando suenan.-13.a) se le pone.-14.c) o.-15.c) mucha confianza.-16.a) que es costumbre.-17.d) es.-18.b) que duermas.-19.c) suelen estar.-20.c) en camas separadas. **3** 1.c) a casa.-2.d) preguntó.-3.b) vida.-4.a) preparada.-5.d) sitios.-6.c) una excusa.-7.b) a gusto.-8.d) te enfades.-9.c) recibes.-10.a) tanto. **4** 1.a) de bastante menos edad.-2.c) que hable dos idiomas.-3.a) En estos 10 años.-4.c) estupendas.-5.a) beber.-6.a) volver la cara.-7.a) Le apetece.-8.c) mal arreglado.-9.c) amable.-10.c) prudente.-**5** 1.b) así que.-2.c) Porque.-3.b) salvo que.-4.a) más que.-5.d) aunque.-6.b) si.-7.a) por lo tanto.-8.d) de tal manera que.-9.c) aun cuando.-10.c) en vista de que

Unidad 9. Ecología.

A. Comprensión y Expresión oral

1.1 (Texto: Rogamos ...)1. F.-2. F.-3. V.-4. F.- **1.2**(Texto: El director del proyecto "Lucha contra" ...)1.No.-2. Granada, Almería y Murcia.-3. Plantar especies autóctonas.-4. Por causa de los incendios. **1.3** (Texto: La exposición "Natura misteriosa" ...)

1.En el zoo de Barcelona.-2. De todo el mundo.-3. De 10 de la mañana a 5 de la tarde. **2.1** ¡Por favor, vengan pronto. Se ha incendiado el monte!.- **2.2** Esto es por culpa de la contaminación. **2.3** Por favor, retírense. Yo sólo cumplo con mi trabajo.

B. Comprensión y Expresión escrita

1 1.Al archipiélago de Madeira.-2. Siete kilómetros.-3. De Méjico.-4. La avería de algún otro barco.-5. Aproximadamente 25.000 toneladas.-6. En diciembre. **2** 1. La Ford.-2. La Fundación para la Conservación de la Naturaleza y del Patrimonio Histórico-Artístico.-3. El ganador de cualquier categoría.-4. En libras esterlinas.-5. En la calle Núñez de Balboa 30, 5ºB, Madrid.-6. El día 15 de noviembre.- **3** 1. Verdadero:« ... La sospecha de que una gran parte está siendo ocasionada por manos deliberadas es firme ...».-2. Falso:« A España se le está yendo el suelo fértil por los cambios climatológicos desfavorables ...».-3. Falso:« ... con posibilidades de comercialización a precios altos ...».-4. Verdadero:« ... a casi 2.000 personas ...».-5. Verdadero:« ... la condesa D'Aulnoy, que escribió ... sin bajarse nunca de las copas de los árboles».-6. Falso:« ... aunque el fenómeno de desertización sea general en la Tierra».-7. Verdadero:« ... también se puede culpar a la disminución constante de la masa forestal el que haya menos lluvias».

C. Gramática y Vocabulario

1 •que •del •no •sólo •mar •tiene •pocas/escasas •e •un •Reino •misma **2** 1.c) Cuál.-2.b)es.-3.a) ha de desarrollarse.-4.c) a.-5.c) en torno a.-6.c) a los delfines.-7.a) totalmente.-8.a) Lo único que.-9.c) está situado.-10.b) que se trataba.-11.d) A quién le.-12.a) que ardan los bosques.-13.c) para anidar.-14.d) Se dice que.-15.c) que causa la lluvia ácida.-16.c) Están prohibidos.-17.a) Ha habido que limitar.-18.d) sino también.-19.d) se les caen.-20.a) casi toda.- **3** 1.b) amenazadas.-2.b) El crecimiento.-3.d) talan.-4.d) una especie.-5.d) transmiten.-6.a) cumbres.-7.c) cada vez.-8.d) zonas.-9.c) Un grupo.-10.c) supervivencia **4** 1.a) el menor.-2.b) que parecen.-3.a) muy bien.-4. c) del fuego.-5.a) hoy en día.-6.b) aparte de.-7.a) vive.-8.b) universal.-9.b) Casi nada.-10.a) transformaciones. **5** 1.a) que no se apagará.-2.c) es necesario.-3.a) de oír.-4.c) que hay.-5.d) de proteger.-6.b) en no hacer.-7.a) que no llueve.-8.d) que saltan.-9.d) si llegaremos.-10.b) de que hay.

Unidad 10. Deportes y Espectáculos.

A Comprensión y Expresión oral

1.1 (Texto: Tomen nota ...) 1. F.-2. V.-3. V.- **1.2** (Texto: La temporada de otoño ...) 1. En el de la Zarzuela.-2. 3.200 metros.-3. Con barro por la lluvia que había caído.- **1.3** (Texto:Atención por favor ...) 1. El recital de Teresa Berganza.-2. Hasta el día 22.-3. Porque Teresa Berganza está enferma.-**2.1** ¡Qué pena! He estado a punto de ganar. **2.2** 1ª viñeta: Cuánta gente tengo delante. 2ª viñeta: Ya estoy más cerca de la taquilla. 3ª viñeta: ¡Vaya, qué contrariedad! Con la ilusión que tenía por ver esta película. **2.3** 3ª viñeta: ¡Conejo maldito! Me estás estropeando la función. 4ª viñeta: Yo no bajo. Estoy harto de estar siempre debajo de tu chistera.

B. Comprensión y Expresión escrita

1 1. Con Dino de Laurentis.-2. En un accidente aéreo, en 1981.-3. En la Clínica de La Luz, de Madrid.-4.Del neorrealismo italiano.-5. Cincuenta y nueve.-6. Seis.-7. Con Luchino Visconti, Passolini y Mijalkov. **2** 1. TVE-1,TVE-2, TM3, ETB-1, ETB-2 y CS.-2. Puede usted haberlos clasificado según su tema: cine, musicales, programas divulgativos ...; según el público a que van dirigidos: infantil, juvenil, adulto; según el horario de emisión; etc.-3. La película « Gallipoli».-4. La película de dibujos animados «Carlitos».-5. Para el sábado.-6. Para el jueves.-7. Sábado Cine:«Gremlins»; Fuera de serie: Concierto de Jean-Michel Jarre; Música, Música: Concierto de Tom Jones; «Gallipoli». **3** 1. Verdadero:« ... todo lo que hace no se parece en absoluto a lo que hace ningún otro ...».-2. Falso:(Se citan al menos dos películas más: "La ley del deseo" y "Mujeres al borde de un ataque de nervios").-3. Falso:« ... salió airoso del atolladero ...».-4. Falso:« ... Almodóvar entrelaza en "Átame" dos hilos conductores del relato.».-5. Falso:« ...cuenta una hermosa y originalísima historia de amor».-6. Verdadero:« ... dos hilos conductores del relato.».-7. Falso:« ... Victoria Abril y Antonio Banderas ...».

C. Gramática y Vocabulario

1 •con •mes •parte •ellas •que •se •conciertos •aplaudió •últimos •como. **2** 1.a) Supongo.-2.b) porque.-3.d) Tenemos que leer.-4. c) hasta que.-5.d) fueron.-6.a) porque ha llovido mucho.-7.b) Se necesitan.-8.d) y resultó ganadora.-9.a) Correr los 100 metros.-10.c) más grave que.-11.d) les ha gustado.-12.d) por qué.-13.b) Desde muy temprano.-14.b) sería.-15.a) ha habido.-16.b) son las piezas que.-17.b) que se celebra.-18.d) por culpa del.-19.d) se ve mejor.-20.a) hiciera. **3** 1.a) dura.-2.a) entradas.-3.b) estrenó.-4.a) inauguración.-5.b) derrotó.-6.b) combates.-7.d) equipo.-8.c) sede.-9.d) cancha.-10.d) corrida.- **4** 1.a) Dudo si.-2.c) sólo duró.-3.a) Dan.-4.b) venció.-5.a) probablemente será.-6.b) el más aplaudido.-7.c) el papel principal.-8.a) participar.-9.a) la mayor.-10.c) no peligra.-**5** 1.d) cuando estrenen.-2.d) donde vivimos.-3.a) como le ordena.-4.d) porque no tiene.-5.b) para ser.-6.a) aunque sea.-7.c) que nos dolían.-8.b) saca mejor que.-9.a) si no llevamos.-10.d) tendríamos.